Kingdoms of Memory
•
Empires of Ink

Cezary Galewicz

Kingdoms of Memory • Empires of Ink

The Veda and the Regional Print Cultures of Colonial India

Jagiellonian University Press

Reviewer
Prof. dr hab. Lidia Sudyka

Cover designer
Paweł Sepielak

With the financial support of the Centre for Comparative Studies in Civilisations at the Jagiellonian University in Kraków

This book draws from research supported by National Science Centre Poland, grants No 2012/05/B/HS2/04103 and No 2018/31/B/HS2/02328

First edition, Kraków 2020

ISBN 978-83-233-4391-2
ISBN 978-83-233-9769-4 (e-book)

JAGIELLONIAN
UNIVERSITY
PRESS

www.wuj.pl

Jagiellonian University Press
Editorial Offices: ul. Michałowskiego 9/2, 31-126 Krakow
Phone: +48 12 663 23 80, Fax: +48 12 663 23 83
Distribution: Phone: +48 12 631 01 97, Fax: +48 12 631 01 98
Cell Phone: +48 506 006 674, e-mail: sprzedaz@wuj.pl
Bank: PEKAO SA, IBAN PL80 1240 4722 1111 0000 4856 3325

Table of Contents

Preface 7

Introduction 11

I. Objects, spaces and practices 27

I.1. The book as an object circulating in space 29

I.2. The rebel book of the Veda 31

II. The Veda before print 33

II.1. The beginnings: the travelling Veda 33

II.2. The living libraries: the memorized Veda 37

II.2.1. The basic level 39

II.2.2. The advanced level 42

II.3. Performance and spectacle: the ritual Veda 56

II.4. Scribes and scripture: the handwritten Veda 57

II.5. The Veda commented upon 90

II.5.1. The imperial commentary 92

II.6. The Veda in the empire of writing 100

III. The coming of print to Indian subcontinent 103

III.1. The missionary, the government and the commercial printers 103

III.2. Preachers, printers and pundits 104

III.2.1. The Jesuit printers of the western coast 105

III.2.2. German Danish evangelists on the Coromandel coast 110

III.2.3. The media revolution of Serampore 1800–1837 134

III.2.4. Later missionary print cultures 138

III.3. The Empire in print and the ethnographic state 146
III.3.1. The infernal machine 150
III.3.2. The Government Press and imperial typography ... 152
III.3.3. Print, catalogues and native knowledge 162
III.3.4. The ethnographic state in print 168
III.4. Indian commercial printing after 1835 (new beginnings) ... 171

IV. The Printed Veda 177
IV.1. The lost and the imagined Veda 178
IV.2. The recovered and the philological Veda 185
IV.2.1. *Les Maîtres de la philologie védique* 191
IV.3. The imperial Veda 193
IV.3.1. The 'Report on the Vedas' 193
IV.3.2. Max Müller and his patrons 198
IV.4. The printed Veda for *paṇḍitas* and pundits 201
IV.5. The Veda printed by Indians in India 204
IV.5.1. The polluting ink 211
IV.5.2. Whose is the printed Veda? 214
IV.5.3. The codex and the *pothī* 228

V. Towards social history of print cultures in colonial India 237
V.1. Printing revolution and social change 238
V.2. Publishing Indian religions in print 241
V.2.1. Printing and appropriation of the past 244
V.3. Regional print cultures and the Veda 250
V.4. Towards a new understanding of reading cultures 253

Abbreviations 257

References 259

Appendix 283

General Index 295

I have long wished to obtain a copy of the Veda; and am now in hopes I shall be able to procure all that are extant. A Brahman this morning offered to get them for me for the sake of money. If I succeed, I shall be strongly tempted to publish them with a translation, pro bono publico.

William Carey, Calcutta 1802

Preface

The Veda may not seem to be the best candidate for a study concerned with the history of print and print culture. Unlike the Bible in Europe, the Veda was not the first book to be printed in India, but rather the last.[1] And, also unlike the Bible, it has never—as had happened to Luther's Bible in the hands of 16th century German Protestants—aspired to become the agent of mass reformation through its literal translation into the vernacular. Even the project of the late Bengal reformer, Ram Mohan Roy, which had envisaged such a conception of the Veda, stemmed from radically different circumstances and attempted social reform through rationalizing Hinduism, using the philosophy of the Veda. Others aimed at the rebirth of an imagined nation rather than a religion, though a redefined form of the latter was believed to have become a vehicle for the former. A case apart here may be found in Dayānanda Sarasvatī's interpretation of the Veda in the second half of 19th century, which even earned him the nickname of 'the Luther of India'. His basic approach to Vedic textuality, however, appears to have been altogether different from that of the early German Protestants. Dayānanda preferred his readers to accept the message of the

1 It is only partially true that the earliest printed editions of the Veda appeared in Europe. A lithographed edition of a part of the *Ṛgvedasaṃhita* edited by Rev. J. Stevenson appeared in 1833 in Bombay (Stevenson 1833). The earliest edition by on indigenous Indian printer appears to be the text of *Śukla Yajurveda Vājasaneyi Saṃhitā*, printed in *pothī* form in Calcutta in 1844. Among the earliest editions to appear in Europe are Rosen 1838, Stevenson 1842, and Müller 1849.

Veda as explained by him rather than allowing the Veda speak by itself. However, neither the Veda as a whole, nor any specific Vedic text, ever aspired to be the object of mass reading consumption when the first native modern editors took it to print. What were the motifs behind the indigenous (native) Indian printer-publishers choosing to edit the Veda in print? And what were the consequences: can they be looked at in isolation from the opinions, ideas, and images of the Veda formed by others? These are some of the questions that remain at the background of the present study.

A history of the early printed Veda, as attempted in the present study, remains, by necessity, part of the history of the book in India and should be seen against its background. Writing a history of the printed Veda, to some extent, becomes part of writing a history of the book. And one history of the book, for the whole of India, would probably amount to as big a challenge as weaving one narrative for the history of the book in Europe or a history of India in general, be it political, economic, social, or cultural history. This study draws rather from a limited number of selected regional case studies, while admitting cautious generalizations under given presuppositions. One such presupposition is that regional history is the maximum level for which a history of the book for India can be sketched. Another is that 'the book' should be understood here in a very broad sense, not only that suggesting bound printed matter in the form of a codex. Its core idea is meant to stem from functionally parallel objects to those understood broadly as 'the book'. While the main focus remains with early print in one selected core area, the historical background of regional manuscript cultures cannot be avoided to put the meanings in the proper context.

As the title of this study suggests, I suppose a link—a relationship between the type and character of civilizational organization of space (and time) and the type of dominating medium(s) operating and organizing this space. What informs this basic supposition is an old idea of Harold Innis, a Canadian pioneer of media and communication studies, which I have attempted to retrieve and take as an inspiration and one of my guidelines here. The simple supposition, that each and every polity in the past had to somehow communicate its credentials and mission to its subjects, enemies and allies, as well as retain potential for social and symbolic mobilization through some manner of communication, requires the identification of means and networks for this communication, i.e. the media. An important dimension of the (meaning of) the media hinted at here is that envisioned vaguely by a follower of Harold Innis, Marshall McLuhan, and refreshed much later on by Bruno Latour. In looking for the ways to articulate the new cultural meanings produced by indigenous printers and publishers who attempted to bring the Veda in print to the new reading constituencies—whether produced by their respective choice, calculation, expectation, or imagination—I shall try to include the background made of the relationship between the printer-publisher, his community of origin, the emerging new public sphere, and the colonial state. However, this relationship is not going to be seen as having been dominated by the concept of colonial oppression or exploitation, but rather as having been stimulated by complex interactive transactions, in which both sides brought their own agendas even if, not only on the surface, it might appear that the balance favoured one side unequally.[2]

Many people, colleagues, and friends were of great help at different stages of this book and the research that preceded it. I owe them more than I think I can express in words. Some deserve special mention: Christian Jacob for early inspiration, colonel Vijay Gaekwad for hospitality and links to the Maratha world. Bhagyalatha Pataskar, Saraju Rath, Gerhard Oberhammer, Irina Glushkova, Kulbhushan Birnale, Vinayak Pachalag, Dušan Deak for his expert help in Marathi, Lidia Sudyka for reading the initial stages of the book, Herman Tieken for his help with Dutch sources, Chemprol Raja, Vinod Bhattatiripad for his enthusiasic help and knowledge. C. Rajendran, Venu Panicker, Agnieszka, Agata & Zdzichu, Maryla & Fabrizo for hosting me, Marcin for inspiration, Elena for reading and encouragement, Zoja & Marcel for patience, and Manoor Jatavedan Nambudiri, Naras Ravindran Nambudiri and all Tirunavaya and Trichur Nambudiris who shared their knowledge and passion with me.

The method followed while organizing the material for this book was for the most part eclectic. The book stems as much from archive work—both physical and electronic, private collection search, and ethnographic field study—as it does from close reading of primary textual sources, predominantly those in Sanskrit. In the preparation and writing of this book, I benefitted from grants from the National Science Centre, which made possible both manuscript and other rare sources search as well as field study in India.

---

2 For an adaptation of Bachtinian category of dialogue to the analysis of cultural production of meaning in 18th and 19th century South India, see Irschick 1994: 10–14.

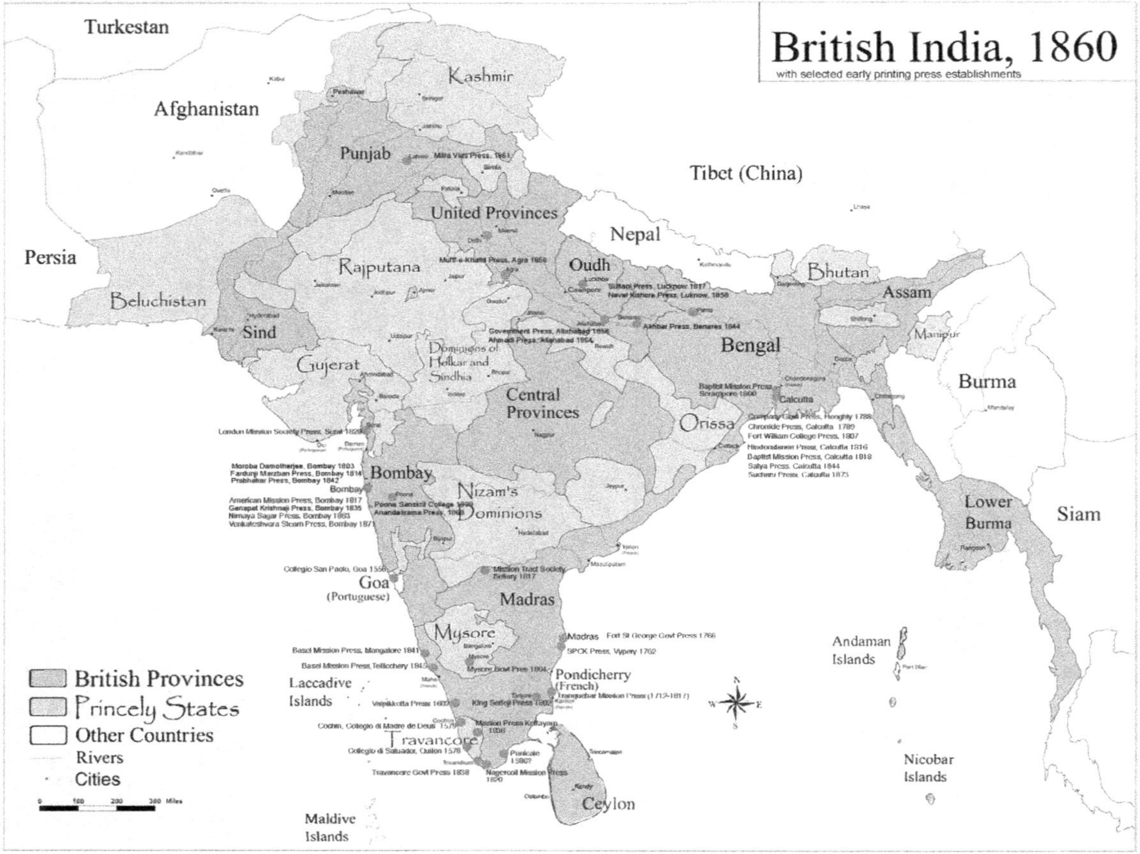

Map 1. Early printing press establishments in India featuring in the [present study Author upon https://commons.wikimedia.org/wiki/MAP 1_Printing_British_india_1860 copy.pdf lub jpg. accessed: accessed October 20, 2018].

Fig. 1. Memorizing the Ṛgveda. Brahmaswam Maṭham, Trichur, Kerala, 2006 [photo CG]

Fig. 2. Anyōnyam: competition in Ṛgveda recitation. Kaṭavallūr, Kerala, 2002 [photo CG]

Fig.3. A night session of Trisandhā: *anusvara mudra*, Tirunāvaya school, Kerala, 2004 [photo CG]

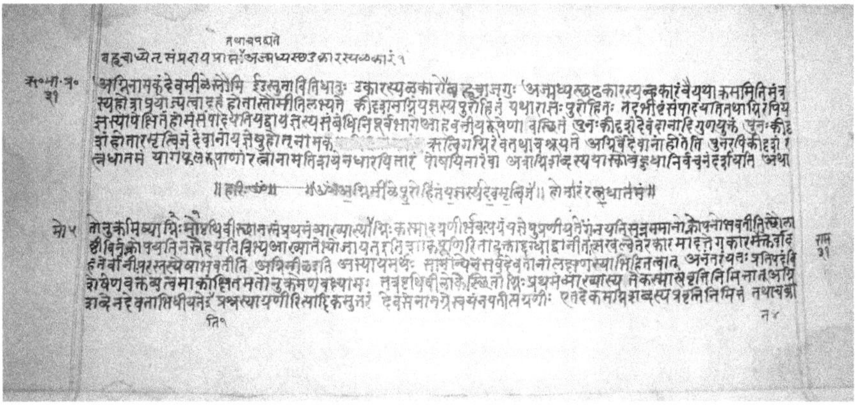

Fig.4. Ṛgveda 1.1.1 (center) 'framed' by Sāyaṇa's commentary, BORI, Pune, MS No. 3, Viśrāmbhāg Collection I (DCMDC, p. 15), folio 31v, prob. early 19th century [photo CG]

Fig.5. Bartholomaeus Ziegenbalg leaving Tranquebar, *London Chronicle* 1890

L'EZOUR-VEDAM

OU

ANCIEN COMMENTAIRE

DU

VEDAM,

Contenant l'exposition des opinions religieuses & philosophiques des Indiens.

Traduit du *SAMSCRETAN* par un Brame.

Revu & publié avec des observations préliminaires, des notes & des éclaircissements.

TOME I.

YVERDON,

Dans l'Imprimerie de M. De Felice.

M. DCC. LXXVIII.

Fig.6. *L'Ezour Vedam* (title page), Yverdon 1788

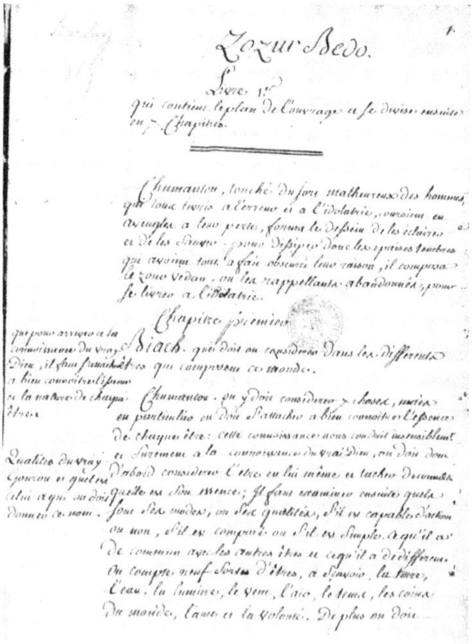

Zozur Bedo.

Livre 1er

qui contient le plan de l'ouvrage et se divise ensuite en 7 chapitres.

Chumantou, touché du sort malheureux des hommes, qui tous livrés à l'erreur et à l'idolatrie, couroient en aveugles a leur perte, forma le dessein de les éclairer et de les sauver. pour dissiper donc les epaisses tenebres qui avoient tout a fait obscurci leur raison, il composa le zour vedam, où les rappellant abandonnés, pour se livrer a l'idolatrie.

Chapitre premier

que pour arriver a la connoissance du vray Dieu, il faut s'attacher a bien connoitre l'essence et la nature de chaque être.

Biach. que doit on considerer dans les differents êtres qui composent ce monde.

Chumantou. on y doit considerer 7 choses, mais en particulier on doit s'attacher a bien connoitre l'essence de chaque être: cette connoissance nous conduit infailliblement et surement a la connoissance du vrai Dieu, on doit donc d'abord considerer l'etre en lui même et tacher de connoitre quelle est son essence; il faut examiner ensuite quels sont ses modes, ou ses qualités, s'il est capable d'action ou non, s'il est composé ou s'il est simple, ce qu'il a de commun avec les autres êtres et ce qu'il a de different. On compte neuf sortes d'êtres, a sçavoir, la terre, l'eau, la lumiere, le vent, l'air, le tems, les coins du monde, l'ame et la volonté. De plus on doit

Qualités du vray Gourou et quel est celui a qui on doit donner ce nom.

Fig. 7. « Zozur Bedo » ; traduction française du YADJOUR VEDA, 4e livre des Védas. XVIIe–XVIIIe siècle [description by BNF]

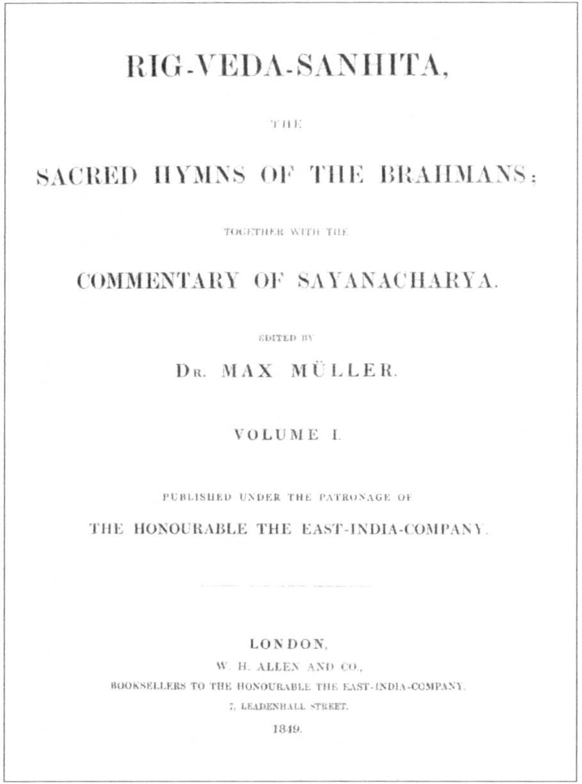

RIG-VEDA-SANHITA,

THE

SACRED HYMNS OF THE BRAHMANS;

TOGETHER WITH THE

COMMENTARY OF SAYANACHARYA.

EDITED BY

Dr. MAX MÜLLER.

VOLUME I.

PUBLISHED UNDER THE PATRONAGE OF

THE HONOURABLE THE EAST-INDIA-COMPANY.

LONDON,

W. H. ALLEN AND CO.,

BOOKSELLERS TO THE HONOURABLE THE EAST-INDIA-COMPANY.

7, LEADENHALL STREET.

1849.

Fig. 8a. *Ṛgveda saṃhitā*, vol. I., ed. by Max Müller, first edition of 1849, title page, recto

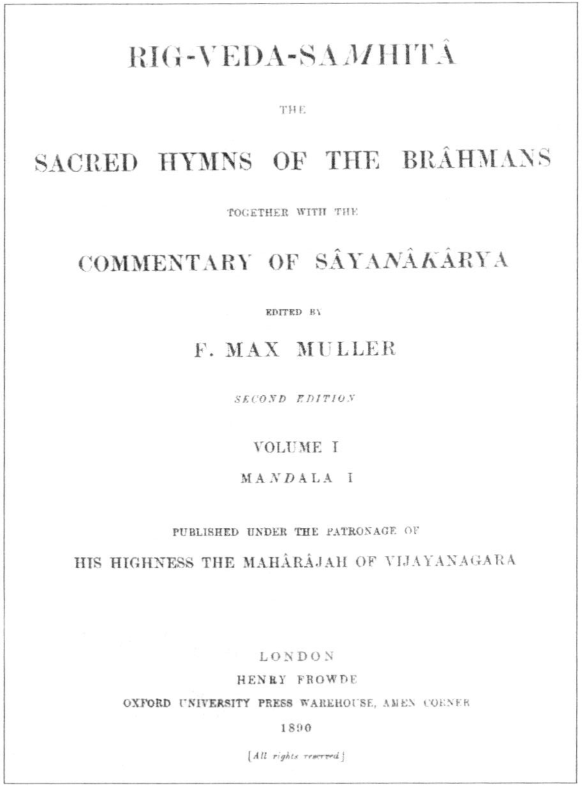

RIG-VEDA-SAMHITÂ

THE

SACRED HYMNS OF THE BRÂHMANS

TOGETHER WITH THE

COMMENTARY OF SÂYANÂKÂRYA

EDITED BY

F. MAX MULLER

SECOND EDITION

VOLUME I

MANDALA I

PUBLISHED UNDER THE PATRONAGE OF

HIS HIGHNESS THE MAHÂRÂJAH OF VIJAYANAGARA

LONDON

HENRY FROWDE

OXFORD UNIVERSITY PRESS WAREHOUSE, AMEN CORNER

1890

[*All rights reserved*]

Fig. 8b. *Ṛgveda saṃhitā*, vol. I., ed. by Max Müller, second edition of 1890, title page, recto

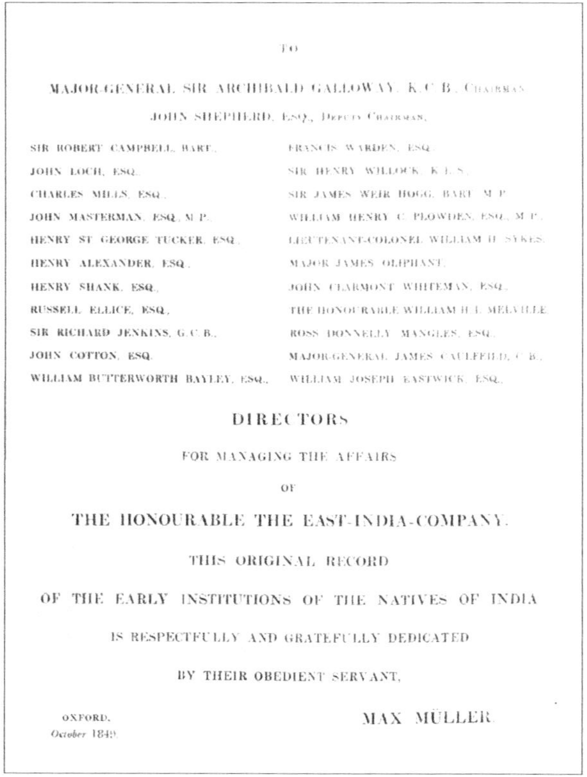
TO

MAJOR-GENERAL SIR ARCHIBALD GALLOWAY, K.C.B., CHAIRMAN

JOHN SHEPHERD, ESQ., DEPUTY CHAIRMAN,

SIR ROBERT CAMPBELL, BART.,	FRANCIS WARDEN, ESQ.,
JOHN LOCH, ESQ.,	SIR HENRY WILLOCK, K.L.S.,
CHARLES MILLS, ESQ.,	SIR JAMES WEIR HOGG, BART., M.P.,
JOHN MASTERMAN, ESQ., M.P.,	WILLIAM HENRY C. PLOWDEN, ESQ., M.P.,
HENRY ST GEORGE TUCKER, ESQ.,	LIEUTENANT-COLONEL WILLIAM H. SYKES,
HENRY ALEXANDER, ESQ.,	MAJOR JAMES OLIPHANT,
HENRY SHANK, ESQ.,	JOHN CLARMONT WHITEMAN, ESQ.,
RUSSELL ELLICE, ESQ.,	THE HONOURABLE WILLIAM H.L. MELVILLE,
SIR RICHARD JENKINS, G.C.B.,	ROSS DONNELLY MANGLES, ESQ.,
JOHN COTTON, ESQ.,	MAJOR-GENERAL JAMES CAULFEILD, C.B.,
WILLIAM BUTTERWORTH BAYLEY, ESQ.,	WILLIAM JOSEPH EASTWICK, ESQ.,

DIRECTORS

FOR MANAGING THE AFFAIRS

OF

THE HONOURABLE THE EAST-INDIA-COMPANY,

THIS ORIGINAL RECORD

OF THE EARLY INSTITUTIONS OF THE NATIVES OF INDIA

IS RESPECTFULLY AND GRATEFULLY DEDICATED

BY THEIR OBEDIENT SERVANT,

OXFORD,
October 1849.

MAX MÜLLER.

Fig. 9a. *Ṛgveda saṃhitā*, vol. I., ed. by Max Müller, first edition of 1849, title page, verso

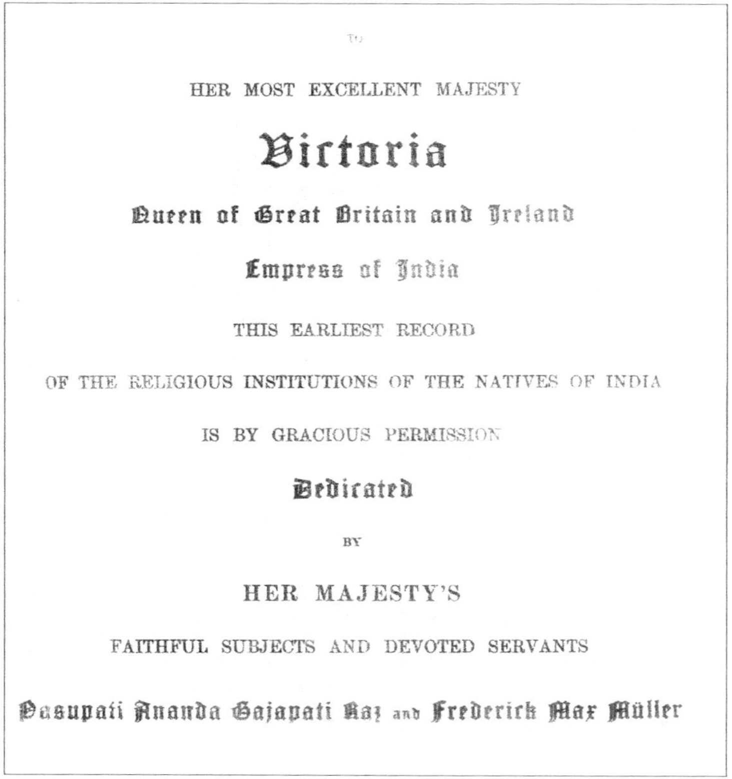
TO

HER MOST EXCELLENT MAJESTY

Victoria

Queen of Great Britain and Ireland

Empress of India

THIS EARLIEST RECORD

OF THE RELIGIOUS INSTITUTIONS OF THE NATIVES OF INDIA

IS BY GRACIOUS PERMISSION

Dedicated

BY

HER MAJESTY'S

FAITHFUL SUBJECTS AND DEVOTED SERVANTS

Pasupati Ananda Gajapati Raz and Frederick Max Müller

Fig. 9b. *Ṛgveda saṃhitā*, vol. I., ed. by Max Müller, second edition of 1890, title page, verso

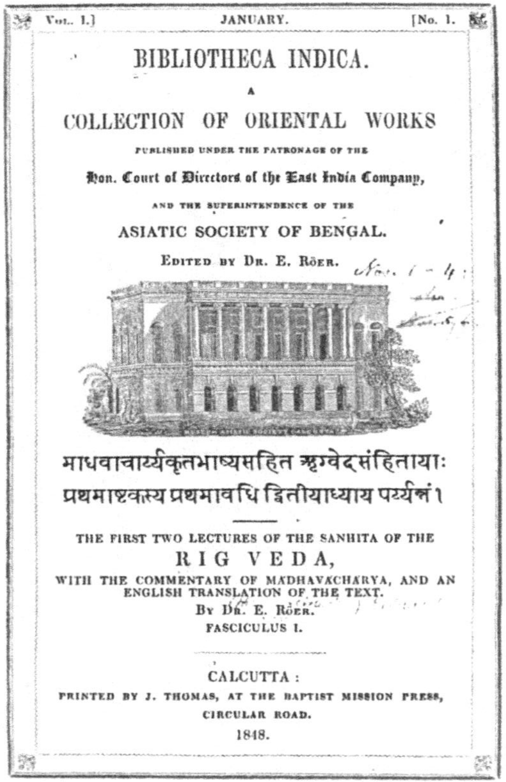
Vol. I.] JANUARY. [No. 1.

BIBLIOTHECA INDICA.

A

COLLECTION OF ORIENTAL WORKS

PUBLISHED UNDER THE PATRONAGE OF THE

Hon. Court of Directors of the East India Company,

AND THE SUPERINTENDENCE OF THE

ASIATIC SOCIETY OF BENGAL.

EDITED BY DR. E. RÖER.

माधवाचार्य्यकृतभाष्यसहित ऋग्वेदसंहितायाः
प्रथमाष्टकस्य प्रथमावधि द्वितीयाध्याय पर्य्यन्तं।

THE FIRST TWO LECTURES OF THE SANHITA OF THE

RIG VEDA,

WITH THE COMMENTARY OF MADHAVACHARYA, AND AN ENGLISH TRANSLATION OF THE TEXT.

BY DR. E. RÖER.

FASCICULUS I.

CALCUTTA:

PRINTED BY J. THOMAS, AT THE BAPTIST MISSION PRESS, CIRCULAR ROAD.

1848.

Fig.10. *Ṛgveda saṃhitā* (First two lectures), ed. E. Röer, Calcutta, Baptist Missionary Press 1848

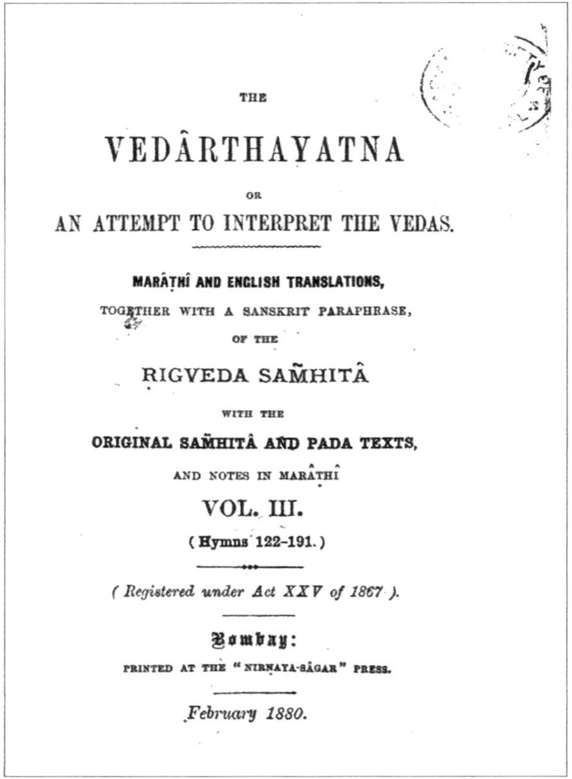
THE

VEDÂRTHAYATNA

OR

AN ATTEMPT TO INTERPRET THE VEDAS.

MARÂṬHÎ AND ENGLISH TRANSLATIONS,

TOGETHER WITH A SANSKRIT PARAPHRASE,

OF THE

RIGVEDA SAM̃HITÂ

WITH THE

ORIGINAL SAM̃HITÂ AND PADA TEXTS,

AND NOTES IN MARÂṬHÎ

VOL. III.

(Hymns 122–191.)

(*Registered under Act XXV of 1867*).

Bombay:

PRINTED AT THE "NIRṆAYA-SÂGAR" PRESS.

February 1880.

Fig. 11. *Vedārthayatna*, vol. III, Bombay: Nirṇaya Sāgara Press 1880, title page

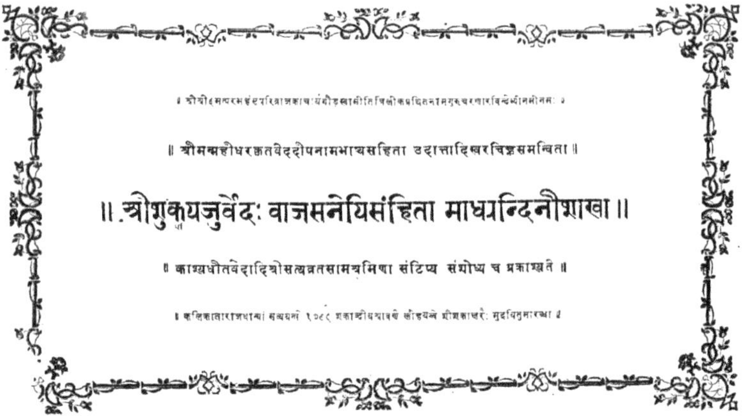

Fig.12. *Śukla Yajurveda Vājasaneyisaṃhitā*, Calcutta, Satya Press 1844

Fig.13. *Sasvāhākaraprayoganirṇayā samantrakośā ca ṛksaṃhitā*, ed. Wāsudev Laxman Śāstrī Paṇśīkar, Bombay: Nirṇaya Sāgara Press, Śake 1832, AD 1910 (1911), title page

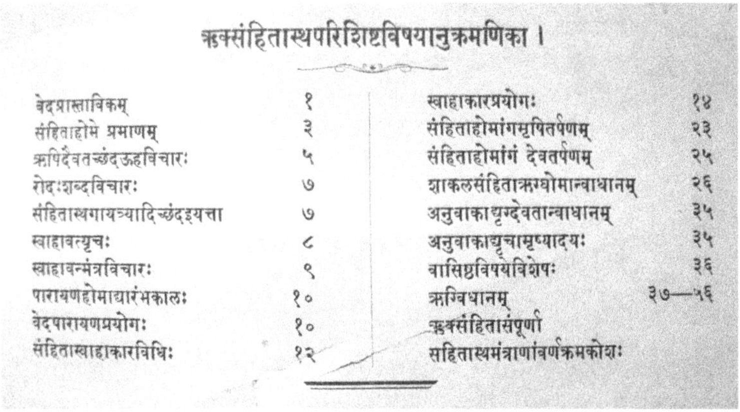

ऋक्संहितास्थपरिशिष्टविषयानुक्रमणिका ।

वेदप्रास्ताविकम्	१	स्वाहाकारप्रयोगः	१४
संहिताहोमे प्रमाणम्	३	संहिताहोमांगमृषितर्पणम्	२३
ऋषिदैवतच्छंदऊहविचारः	५	संहिताहोमांगं देवतर्पणम्	२५
रोदःशब्दविचारः	७	शाकलसंहिताऋग्घोमान्वाधानम्	२६
संहितास्थगायत्र्यादिच्छंदइयत्ता	७	अनुवाकाद्यृग्देवतान्वाधानम्	३५
स्वाहावत्यृचः	८	अनुवाकाद्यृचामृष्यादयः	३५
स्वाहावन्मंत्रविचारः	९	वासिष्ठविषयविशेषः	३६
पारायणहोमाद्यारंभकालः	१०	ऋग्विधानम्	३७—५६
वेदपारायणप्रयोगः	१०	ऋक्संहितासंपूर्णा	
संहितास्वाहाकारविधिः	१२	संहितास्थमंत्राणांवर्णक्रमकोशः	

Fig.14. *Sasvāhākaraprayoganirṇayā samantrakośā ca ṛksaṃhitā*, ed. Wāsudev Laxman Śāstrī Paṇśīkar, Bombay: Nirṇaya Sāgara Press, Śake 1832, AD 1910 (1911), table of contents

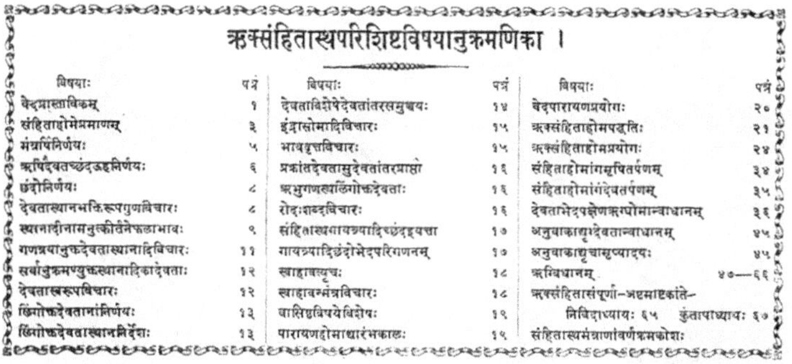

ऋक्संहितास्थपरिशिष्टविषयानुक्रमणिका ।

विषयाः	पत्रं	विषयाः	पत्रं	विषयाः	पत्रं
वेदप्रास्ताविकम्	१	देवताविशेषेदेवतांतरसमुच्चयः	१४	वेदपारायणप्रयोगः	२०
संहिताहोमेप्रमाणम्	३	इंद्रासोमादिविचारः	१५	ऋक्संहिताहोमपद्धतिः	२१
मंत्रर्षिनिर्णयः	५	भावृत्तविचारः	१५	ऋक्संहिताहोमप्रयोगः	२४
ऋषिदैवतच्छंदऊहनिर्णयः	६	प्रक्रांतदेवतासुदेवतांतरप्राप्तो	१६	संहिताहोमांगमृषितर्पणम्	३४
छंदोनिर्णयः	८	ऋभुगणस्यलिंगोक्तदेवताः	१६	संहिताहोमांगंदेवतर्पणम्	३५
देवतास्थानभक्तिरूपगुणविचारः	८	रोदःशब्दविचारः	१६	देवताभेदपक्षेणऋग्घोमान्वाधानम्	३६
स्थानादीनामनुत्कीर्तनेफलाभावः	९	संहितास्थगायत्र्यादिच्छंदइयत्ता	१७	अनुवाकाद्यृग्देवतान्वाधानम्	४५
गणत्रयानुक्तदेवतास्थानादिविचारः	११	गायत्र्यादिछंदोभेदपरिगणनम्	१७	अनुवाकाद्यृचामृष्यादयः	४५
सर्वानुक्रमण्युक्तस्थानादिकादेवताः	१२	स्वाहावत्यृचः	१८	ऋग्विधानम्	४७—६६
देवतास्वरूपविचारः	१२	स्वाहावन्मंत्रविचारः	१८	ऋक्संहितासंपूर्णा–अष्टमाष्टकांते– निविदाध्यायः ६५ कुंतापाध्यायः ६७	
लिंगोक्तदेवतानांनिर्णयः	१३	वासिष्ठविषयेविशेषः	१९	संहितास्थमंत्राणांवर्णक्रमकोशः	
लिंगोक्तदेवतास्थाननिर्देशः	१३	पारायणहोमाद्यारंभकालः	१९		

Fig. 15. *Sasvāhākaraprayoganirṇayā samantrakośā ca ṛksaṃhitā*, ed. Wāsudev Laxman Śāstrī Paṇśīkar, Bombay: Nirṇaya Sāgara Press, 1930, table of contents

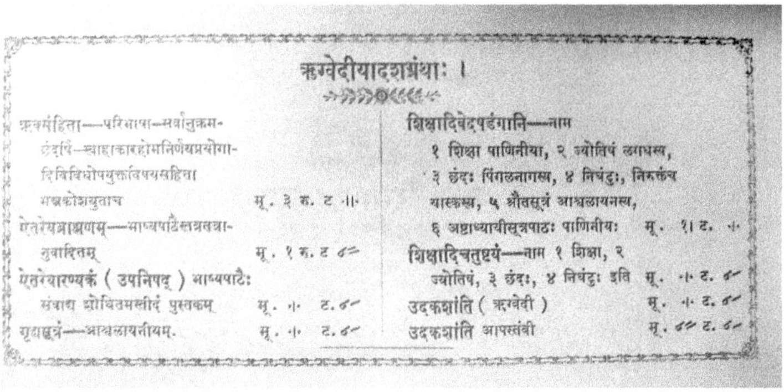

ऋग्वेदीयादशग्रंथाः ।

ऋक्संहिता—परिभाषा—सर्वानुक्रम-
छंदर्षि—स्वाहाकारहोमनिर्णयप्रयोगा-
दिविविधोपयुक्तविषयसहिता
मंत्रकोशयुताच — मू. ३ रु. ट ॥

ऐतरेयब्राह्मणम्—भाष्यपाठैस्तत्रतत्रा-
नुवादितम् — मू. १ रु. ट ८=

ऐतरेयारण्यकं (उपनिषद्) भाष्यपाठैः
संवाद्य शोधितमस्तीदं पुस्तकम् — मू. ।॰ ट. ८–

गृह्यसूत्रं—आश्वलायनीयम्. — मू. ।॰ ट. ८–

शिक्षादिवेदषडंगानि—नाम
१ शिक्षा पाणिनीया, २ ज्योतिषं लगधस्य,
३ छंदः पिंगलनागस्य, ४ निघंटुः, निरुक्तंच
यास्कस्य, ५ श्रौतसूत्रं आश्वलायनस्य,
६ अष्टाध्यायीसूत्रपाठः पाणिनीयः — मू. १। ट. ।॰

शिक्षादिचतुष्टयं—नाम १ शिक्षा, २
ज्योतिषं, ३ छंदः, ४ निघंटुः इति — मू. ।॰ ट. ८–

उदकशांति (ऋग्वेदी) — मू. ।॰ ट. ८–

उदकशांति आपस्तंबी — मू. ८= ट. ८–

Fig.16. A list of 'ten books of the Ṛgveda' – a folio from *Aitareya Brāhmaṇa*, ed. V.L. Panśikar, Bombay: Nirṇaya Sāgara 1925

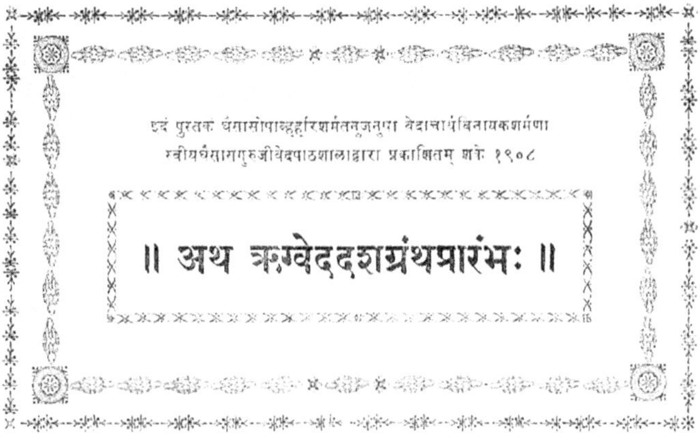

इदं पुस्तकं घैसासोपाह्वहरिशर्मतनूजनुषा वेदाचार्यविनायकशर्मणा
स्वीयघैसासगुरुजीवेदपाठशालाद्वारा प्रकाशितम् शके १९०८

॥ अथ ऋग्वेददशग्रंथप्रारंभः ॥

Fig. 17. *Ṛgvedadaśagrantha*, ed. V. Ghaisasa, Pune 1986

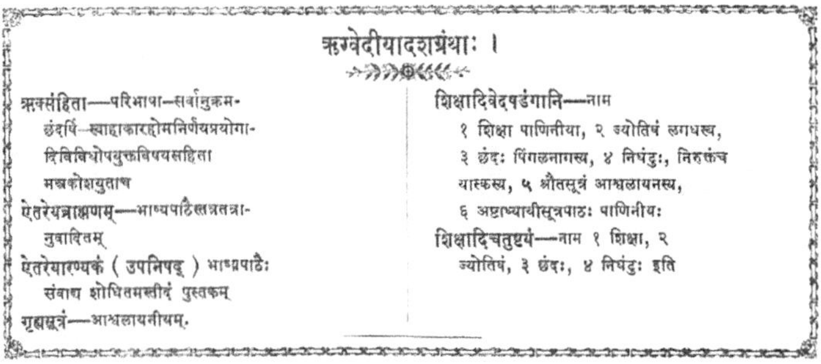

ऋग्वेदीयादशग्रंथाः ।

ऋक्संहिता—परिभाषा–सर्वानुक्रम-
छंदर्षि–स्वाहाकारहोमनिर्णयप्रयोगा-
दिविविधोपयुक्तविषयसहिता
मन्त्रकोशयुताच
ऐतरेयब्राह्मणम्—भाष्यपठितस्तत्रत्रा-
नुवादितम्
ऐतरेयारण्यकं (उपनिषद्) भाष्यपाठैः
संवाद्य शोधितमस्तीदं पुस्तकम्
गृह्यसूत्रं—आश्वलायनीयम्.

शिक्षादिवेदषडंगानि—नाम
१ शिक्षा पाणिनीया, २ ज्योतिषं लगधस्य,
३ छंदः पिंगलनागस्य, ४ निघंटुः, निरुक्तंच
यास्कस्य, ५ श्रौतसूत्रं आश्वलायनस्य,
६ अष्टाध्यायीसूत्रपाठः पाणिनीयः
शिक्षादिचतुष्टयं—नाम १ शिक्षा, २
ज्योतिषं, ३ छंदः, ४ निघंटुः इति

सस्वाहाकारप्रयोगनिर्णयः समंत्रकोशाच

॥ ऋक्संहिताप्रारभ्यते ॥

Fig. 18. *Ṛgvedadaśagrantha* (RDG), ed. V. Ghaisasa, Pune 1986 [reprinting SRS 1930]: a list of 'ten books' of the Ṛgveda (upper folio)

Introduction

Ever since the now classic *Printing Press as an Agent of Change* (1979), the notion of *print culture*, as explored by E. Eisenstein, has become a recurring idea and a point of reference, either taken for granted or questioned as a basic concept, to refer to the nature of transformations that print allegedly brought to human history as a new kind of communication medium.[3] More recently, the singular form of the collocation suggesting a uniform nature of such a cultural formation has been increasingly put to doubt in studies pointing to a need for more nuanced contextualization of different trajectories that culture(s) of print might take across varied socio-historical and geographical configurations. The same applies to the core idea describing the nature of the effect of the *print culture* as depending crucially on the shift from handwriting to printing. Other important conceptual framings of the nature of the socio-historical change highlighted rather a shift from orality to writing (Walter Ong, Jack Goody), while taking print as either an extension or amplification of the qualities, potentials, and limitations of writing. Earlier authors to reflect on print culture include M. McLuhan (whose inspiration in Eisenstein's ideas appears to be more often visible than the latter is ready to admit). McLuhan who contextualized its message, while locating it among other formulations, when he spoke of 'a culture based upon the printed book', 'typographic culture', and 'the role played by print in instituting new patterns of culture'; but also of other cultural formations, such as 'ear culture', 'auditory culture', 'visual culture', 'manuscript culture', 'electric culture', and 'alphabetic culture'. He did use the very collocation

[3] Eisentstein seems to have avoided the challenge of defining the concept of print culture as such while arguing passionately for the revolutionary impact of its appearance and for the acknowledgment of this impact in historical writing. Cf. Dane 2003: 13 – 'Eisenstein never defines what she means by print culture nor does she deal with the assumptions that term entails.'

print culture;[4] however, the latter one appears in *Gutenberg's Galaxy* often to be understood as a specific instance of a more general category of visual (or optical) culture which used—in McLuhan's view—to historically contradict the oral (or auditory) one in a radical, if not dramatic, way. He took print culture to represent one side of these binary and mutually opposing forces in cultural history.[5] In spite of the intuitive rather than systematic nature of his remarks, some of McLuhan's ideas seem revealing, or at least inspiring, in the context of the present study. Especially in how he saw the historical and mutually framing interrelationship of the oral and the written in manuscript cultures: 'Not only did this oral aspect of manuscript culture deeply affect the manner of composing and writing, but it meant that writing, reading, and oratory remained inseparable until well after printing.'[6] These, as well as other illuminating formulations by M. McLuhan, E. Eisenstein, R. Chartier, R. Darnton, and other more upstream authors in the field should, however, be taken with due caution here, given the sharply asymmetric histories of print culture development in Western Europe and South Asia. While German Lutheran printer-publishers of the mid-sixteenth century triggered a process leading to the mass consumption of printed books, at the same time, Jesuit publisher-printers on the south-western coast of the Indian peninsula neither succeeded at anything comparable nor aimed at it. And the early eighteenth century visionary project of the Danish-German Pietist missionary printers of Tranguelar failed to repeat the Lutheran experiment of opening the Bible to new readers by producing affordable copies of the former. Furthermore, the manuscript culture(s) heralded by McLuhan, which had almost been forgotten in Europe by the eighteenth century, continued in India well into the first half of the 19th century,

---

4 'Manuscript culture is intensely audile-tactile compared to print culture…' [McLuhan 1962: 28] and 'This book will try to explain why print culture confers on man a language of thought which leaves him quite unready to face the language of his own electro-magnetic technology' [McLuhan 1962: 30] with a conclusion on p. 31: 'We can now live, not just amphibiously in divided and distinguished worlds, but pluralistically in many worlds and cultures simultaneously. We are no more committed to one culture—to a single ratio among the human senses—any more than to one book or to one language or to one technology.' Other instances comprise 'fragmentation of the human psyche by print culture' [McLuhan 1962: 32].

5 'Since there can be no greater contradiction or clash in human cultures than that between those representing the eye and the ear, it is not strange that our metamorphosis into the eye mode of Western man should be only less agonizing than our present shift into the auditory mode of electronic man [McLuhan 1962: 68].

6 McLuhan 1962: 90.

parallel to print and performance cultures. Going back beyond McLuhan, we find his mentor Harold Innis, who, while commenting on cognate questions, seems to have preferred to speak of oral and written *traditions* rather than *cultures* and put them in the context of the evolution of civilizations and empires.[7] Innis's comments on the civilizational impact of print remained curiously influenced by his stress on the function of the material support in the historical development of successive new media and the historical empires' diverse capability in securing balance in the influence of different media on communication practices. Innis's bold and controversial thesis on the allegedly crucial role of the uneven development of print in British colonies, as a decisive factor in the eventual collapse of the British empire in the western hemisphere and its imperilment in the east, remains a challenge for historians and also a tempting avenue of interpretation for the present study.[8] Febvre–Martin, 1958, a classic in the field of book history, to which the present study also looks back for inspiration, does not rest on the concept of print culture. If *culture* appears in it at all, it is *culture écrite* or *culture livresque*, or 'the culture of the book', which mirrors the authors' preoccupation with the cultural object of the book rather than the gross civilizational processes. The latter remain continually at the background of the former, and the two stand out as profoundly related. The present study is meant to focus on the specific [printed] object of the Veda, and, while turning for inspiration to the above-mentioned authors, it remains related to the selective type of approach theorized some time ago by Roger Chartier. According to Chartier, apart from a more general reference to social change, we can regard print culture 'as the set of new acts arising

7 'The task of understanding a culture built on the oral tradition is impossible to students steeped in the written tradition' [Innis 1986: 59]. The relationship of print towards written and oral tradition looks peculiar in Innis, who imagined a conceptual place for it in a 'gap' between the oral and the written, which should probably not be taken in an evolutionary sense: 'The written tradition when dependent on parchment had been inflexible. Paper had expanded, in part, in relation to the gap between the written tradition dependent on parchment and the oral tradition. The printed word, at first strengthening the position of the written tradition by its emphasis on manuscripts, bridged the gap with the oral tradition later...' [Innis 1986: 150].

8 'The Empire was broken in part through the distorted effects of the uneven development of printing [Innis 1986: 158]. Innis's shortcut style makes immediate connection between the spread of print, the development of institutions, and theory: 'Inability to adapt English institutions to new circumstances lost the colonies in the Western hemisphere and imperilled the Empire in the east. Theory was unable to mediate between absolute dependence and absolute independence...' [Innis 1986: 158]. Parallel disequilibrium in print production in Europe led, according to Innis, to the French revolution. See Innis 1986: 159.

out of the production of writing and pictures in a new form. Personalized reading in private by no means exhausted the possible uses of print objects. Their festive, ritual, cultic, civic, and pedagogic uses were by definition collective and postulated decipherment in common...' [leading to the formation of] 'an interconnected network of specific practices that defined an original culture... .'[9] This understanding shall, however, be modified here by preferring plural *cultures of print / print cultures* to the singular *print culture* and in stressing the historical change that influenced them as much as they influenced it, in ways often still to be identified or better articulated. This understanding of print cultures shall be probed here through the lens of what Roger Chartier calls 'object studies' in an approach centred on a selected object put into perspective through showing its early printing history. This perspective shall favour 'a desire to understand the use of the materials we are investigating within the precise, local, specific context that alone gave them meaning.'[10] In this attempt to map the metamorphoses of the Veda entering the world of print in the hands of printers, patrons, and old and new users, I shall feed on the assumption that it is particularly promising to combine 'a description of formal elements (print format, page layout, the nature and placement of pictorial material) with an identification of the uses, implicit or explicit, that relied on those formal elements.'[11] While adopting this perspective, however, the present study shall also attempt to retain a wider historical perspective, by paying attention to institutions and processes, in order, among other things, to offer a contribution to the better understanding of the asymmetry in development that the introduction of moveable type to South Asia brought, in the early modern and colonial period, in comparison to Western Europe.[12]

The history of India has long been an object of seduction. In the past, this was to be found in two radically different conceptual attitudes: that of radical denial of historical thinking with regard to the entity circumscribed

---

9 Chartier 1989: 1.

10 Chartier 1989: 3. On the same page Chartier suggests possible contextual framing for such an approach enumerating ritual, political, and political-ritual contexts which, in the case of the present study, retain their validity, while being enriched with others, specific to time, place, and type of print culture that hosted the object under investigation.

11 Chartier 1989: 5.

12 The need for this avenue of investigation was indicated by E. Eisenstein herself: '...[O]ne must...explain why printing industries expanded so rapidly in Western Europe during the late fifteenth century and why the invention of movable type did not have similar consequences in the Far East. Furthermore' [Eisenstein 1979: 32].

as India and that of a vehement wrestling of one from, often fragmentary, epigraphical and other inscriptional data. Occasionally it would invite a middle-ground position, offering a possible conceptualization like that of 'other regime(s) of temporality.' The days of a macro-perspective, adopted to regard India as the forum of a unitary process of historical change to be represented by one single narration, seems to have receded slowly into the past. Yet a good number of books bearing titles such as, 'a History of India', still see the light of the day. However, recent decades seem to belong to more specifically outlined regional histories and to ever more conscious attempts to operate on first hand, mostly inscriptional, evidence and make conscious use of socio-historical and geographical concepts. The history of the book in India—which creates an immediate context for the present study—is no exception here, and it has been marked by similar basic problems of scale and choice of a unifying narrative. A pioneering study by Priolkar from 1958, concerned with the history of print in the Indian Subcontinent, remains a good point of reference. While a series of important studies on regional social and economic history have seen the light of the day in recent decades, the history of the book in India has been rather—as claimed by some—'in its childhood state of conceptualization,' or—as hold others—'virtually impossible ... purely in national terms, or within the parameters of the nation-state.' For a number of reasons that are well known to political, social, and cultural historians of India, any construction of a book history for the whole of the Indian peninsula remains a difficult, if not impossible, task. What still awaits conceptualization are the modalities of relationship between the specific types of textuality and their historical and spatial environments. Or, more generally: the nature of relationship between media and civilization. And this with an attention to forms of civilization in general and towards regional histories, geographies and power in particular. Nevertheless, a number of new inspiring studies proliferated in the last two decades, marking essential contributions to the field.[13] Most of the recent studies tend to focus on either literary fiction or popular mass printing in vernaculars, which has become a standard approach for book historians. A conspicuous absence of studies concerning printing

[13] Except for the above-mentioned Stark 2007, we need to notice more general volumes that introduced crucial concepts for the related fields of literary and print cultures, such as Pollock 2003, 2006, 2015; Gupta 2010, 2012, 2013; Blackburn 2006, as well as case studies such as Blackburn 1988; Ogborn 2007; Orsini 2002, 2009; Shaw 2007; Minkowski 2008; O'Hanlon 2010; Raman 2012; Venkatachalapathy 2012; De Simini 2016.

in Sanskrit marks the character of the dominant trajectory that the book history for India has been taking. A few contributions to the field to some extent compensate this imbalance [Rocher and Rocher 2012; Formigatti 2016]. A badly needed reference point, situating South Asian developments in that matter against those of Europe, may be, to some extent, found in the works that investigate the cultural history of reading in Europe, especially those by R. Chartier, G. Cavallo or, for different reasons, those edited or authored by C. Jacob [Jacob 2007, 2011; Giard and Jacob 2001]. The latter perspective connects also, even though not directly, to the areas explored by a new generation of scholars resuming the so-called Toronto school's interest in the mutual relationship between the rise, development, and fall of civilizations and imperial formations with the type and character of the dominant media that sustained them. This new interest draws partially from the re-appropriation of the conceptual frames of German *Kulturwissenschaften*, in what has been addressed by the category of media and cultural techniques and technologies.[14]

The printed book, in the shape familiar to us, came to India relatively early, in the middle of 16th century, but, after initial breakthrough events, it took a long time to establish itself as an accepted medium of communication. Long before that, India had known books in other forms than that of the codex, and written objects of different shapes and material forms circulated across local, regional, and transregional spaces of the vast areas of the Indian subcontinent.[15] Over several centuries since their first attested appearance in the early centuries CE, these spaces of circulation of written matter developed and changed and were used to being variously re-defined and re-organized in answer to new socio-political realities or religious movements. In the moment of their appearance in print, the cultural patterns of diffusion and actual networks of circulation they produced must have been well established and effectively tested through repeated social practices of patronized authors and scholars, professional and amateur scribes, paid copyists and appointed reciters, religious, scholarly, and literary codes and conventions of publishing and collective reading. The

14 See, for instance, Vismann 2013; Krämer and Bredekamp 2013; Siegert 2015; Young 2017; Peters 2015.

15 Over a several centuries long history of handwriting in South Asia, Indic manuscripts tended to adopt different shapes and formats according to different concepts than that of a codex. For a general review, see Wujastyk 2014; Ciotti and Franceschini 2016, Formigatti 2016.

history of their interactions in the early modern period and later has, to a great degree, only just begun to be explored systematically. A great many opinions have been voiced on the primacy of oral literature in India in the earlier phase of scholarly interest in this topic, often resulting in a stereotyped understanding. More resent fascination with the rich heritage of the manuscript culture(s) of India has tended to marginalize the role of print and argued for sophisticated and effective communication channels based on an infrastructure of professional scribes, copying practices, and bazaar writers, that could resist the onset of print a long time after its coming to India. The reasons for print's uneven, and often difficult career, while competing and interlinking with manuscript and memory cultures in India, are complex and have been rather briefly discussed without reaching final conclusions. There is little doubt that the arrival of print in South Asia must be seen against a history of several centuries of a multidimensional and extremely rich interaction between regional manuscript cultures and traditions of performance, that left an enduring and stimulating stamp on the development of print long after its introduction to India. In general, one should acknowledge that, over the length of time preceding the appearance of the printed book, as well as long time after, 'the interaction of the oral and manuscript traditions has had a far deeper and longer-lasting impact on the Indian imagination than any attributable to print.'[16] Still, in 1858, when not only Max Müller's *editio princeps*' of the Ṛgveda was underway (with the first two volumes already out), and the commercial printing in vernacular languages in several regions was gaining momentum, a Tamil author was referring to print as *eḻuta eḻutu*, 'the unwritten writ.'[17] As a new cultural order, print had, in many respects, to adapt itself to the economic and cultural realities of the Indian type of symbiotic correlation of writing and oral performance as well as to power relations associated with the communities of their users, who actively took over print with its new potencies in the process, that at first should be seen as inclusion and appropriation before giving way to the power of the latter. Whatever formula we choose in order to represent the consequences of the coming of print to South Asia, we cannot avoid addressing the problem of the nature of transition that led from the early modern knowledge and information order to the new one increasingly dominated by print, especially in its relation

---

16 Shaw 2007: 126.

17 Venkatachalapathy 2012: 215.

to the colonial state and the new public sphere. The transformations that affected the eventual nature of change in cultures and societies across the Indian Subcontinent, leading to regionally specific forms of modernity (as argued by some) initiated in the early colonial period, which remains the main time frame of this study.[18] But the still earlier beginnings of print in the Indian peninsula give this process a background that cannot be altogether avoided here.[19]

Most of the recent studies of the new wave of interest in the history of the book in India have turned towards literary works in vernacular languages or popular bazaar literature, increasingly focusing on the specificity and materiality of local practices of reading. For a reason hardly noticed at all, the history of the printed book in Sanskrit has almost escaped the attention of scholars, as did the history of various print cultures centred on Sanskrit books.[20] For reasons that may seem natural, almost no research had been done on the cultural history of print in relation to the Veda. This study aims at compensating for this situation, while changing the relation of the elements: I shall focus on the history of the printed Veda in order to see how it reflected the history of print and the development of print cultures. Print, printing, as well as printed objects may mean radically different things in different socio-cultural settings, as they no doubt did for the protestant missionaries printers of Serampore, government printers of Calcutta and King Sefoji II's printer of Tanjore, in the early years of the nineteenth century. This supposition accounts in part for the use of the plural in the title of the present study: cultures of print. This form was used intentionally also by other studies in the field, such as Johns 1999 or Ogborn 2007. The latter work also uses the metaphor 'empire of print'.[21]

---

18 For the ideas concerning colonial forms of knowledge and information order, see, among else, Cohn 1989, Baily 1996, Ogborn 2007.

19 For an attempt to conceptualize this historical moment of transition, see, for instance, Trautmann 2009: 5—'The early colonial period was a transition from one regime of knowledge based upon royal patronage and royal protocols of publication and canon-formation ... to a new regime of knowledge based upon government and university support of scholarship and the making of print editions circulating cheaply and in large numbers through markets.'

20 For general remarks on the tendencies in constructing the book and print culture history for India, see Stark 2007: Introduction. For remarks concerning the specific case of printed Sanskrit book history, see Formigatti 2016.

21 Ogborn acknowledges his inspiration from the ideas of Adrian Johns [Johns 1998) and calls for a focus on 'different forms of imperial printing or different *empires of print* [my

Though one of the concerns of the present study remains book history, it by no means aims to offer a history of the book in India, even just for the period of colonial domination. To write one for the whole of the Indian Subcontinent would be far beyond my capacity. As one of the recently voiced opinions has stated: 'No scholar would be so foolhardy to attempt such a project...' for an area with several languages (twenty-two officially recognized) whose literary histories often overlapped across regions.[22] The history of the book and book reading in Indian Subcontinent is made up of a variety of processes of uneven pace, endurance, and impact.[23] This may not sound surprising given the fact that, throughout its ancient, medieval and early modern history, the subcontinent has hardly ever enjoyed political and cultural unity, and has witnessed a rather shifting pattern of a huge number of political centres, with a tendency to develop macro--regional (South, Deccan and North) and regional varieties.

The allegedly gargantuan number of surviving Indic manuscripts attests to a long, rich, and diversified history of literary forms and genres, regional performance traditions, patterns of patronage and circulation that gave rise to variegated print cultures. Also the numerous, regional and historical concepts and modalities of material forms of literary genre identity across the many languages and scripts used in India, makes one feel quantitively overwhelmed. For this reason, the immediate focus of this study has been narrowed down to one single and specific type of text: the Veda. For many reasons, the case of the Veda may seem unusual and extreme in the history of the book in India. Believing that extreme cases sometimes create the space for articulating tendencies of a more general nature, I am taking this opportunity with the hope that examining and selecting examples of memory-cloning, hand-copying, and printing-publishing of the Vedic texts (especially the *Ṛgvedasaṃhitā*) may enrich the broader area of a more general book history of the early colonial period in India. The rich material and conceptual heritage shows that any understanding of the specifically Indic forms of print culture cannot be reached without simultaneously taking into consideration those of memory-cum-performance and manuscript cultures. This said, the present study derives from a conviction that

emphasis] as specific configurations of cultural and material practices that attempted to produce particular organizations of power and knowledge' [Ogborn 2007: 202].

22 Gupta 2012: 147. Nevertheless, the author of the quotation produced himself at least one such history as a contribution to the global history of the book. See Gupta 2013.

23 For a current notion of the 'nascent' book history in India, see Stark 2007; Orsini 2016.

only a combined in depth study into the textual, paratextual, material and socio-historical forms of the three main variants promises to contribute to a better understanding of the major historical processes that have shaped—and continue to shape—South Asian civilization.

Throughout its long history of formation, growth, canonization, endurance, continuity, remarkable preservation, and occasional loss and change, the Veda has passed through a number of different channels and *modi* of transmission in the hands of the various historical and regional communities of its guardians. Though the regionally scattered process of transmission within the various Vedic branches may have looked very different and over time could have resulted either in an astonishingly full, or rather partial, fragmentary preservation, some groups lost their capacity to continue in the process of transmission or completely lost the memory of the Veda in their custody. In general, however, a good number of Brahmin groups succeeded in retaining their capacity for the memory-based transmission of their respective Veda well into the early modern era, when a parallel and linked process of transmission in writing established itself on bigger scale. So was the case in the time of the growing use of print in the early colonial period, and some continue to do so to a remarkable extant even in the era of the digital archive. While, in this uneven and asymmetric process of transmission, the texts themselves remained amazingly stable, the modalities of transmission, as well as the concepts of the Veda and its textuality, changed and differed widely from community to community, with its guardians and users competing for their place in the changing social and political setting specific to the region and historical moment. These various communities happened to adopt different media for its transmission and would themselves change along with the different nature of these media. In the historical process of social transformation, some Brahmin groups redefined their link with the Veda and came to specialize in service professions, like those of court advisers, revenue administrators (Niyogi group), bankers (some Citpavan groups or Saraswata groups), or state policy makers (Dekkani Brahmins). In the course of this changes they distanced themselves from the Vedic transmission, which remained in the hands of other Brahmin groups, referred to for this reason by the name of 'Vaidika' Brahmins, although the term itself could take different meanings historically according to the region in question.[24]

[24] Roberts 1971; Frykenberg 1965; Hanlon and Minkowski 2008.

A recent appropriation within media communication and cultural studies of the Germanophone concept of *Kulturtechnik* (cultural techniques) developed some time ago by media theorists of German *Kulturwissenschaften* (by F. Kittler, among others), takes human speech or orality, as a form of medium to be understood through the concept of 'cultural technique.' From this perspective, orality as a cultural technique should be distinguished from cultural technologies, among which writing (and print) conspicuously appear.[25] From such a viewpoint, Vedic oral memorization—not to be confused with epic orality or any other form of memorization known to historians and anthropologists—would constitute, at least in some of its regional modalities, a form of durable inscription affecting not only the memory, but also the entire bodies of Vedic adepts. The latter would become carriers of the Vedic text inscribed through the memorization process operating a cultural technology of inscription.[26] Durability—one of the basic conditions for a cultural technology—appears to be an unquestionable feature of Vedic memorization, and it has proved its superior quality against writing in preserving Vedic texts in a number of known instances. If we agree that 'writing is a medium that extends memory', then the Vedic memorization of, say, the Kerala Nampūtiri tradition may be regarded as an extension of human memory through a particular technology of inscription on mind and body. The custom of venerating the Vedic memorization adepts, as 'inscribed' with the Veda has been noticed and recognized as such by modern scholarship (calling them walking tape recorders[27]), as well as early tradition, insisting on the veneration of their bodies as carriers of the Vedic gods.[28]

Through its long history, the Veda has meant different things to different people who would transmit it, perform it, use it, read it, comment upon it, copy it with their own hand, have it copied by professional scribes, or edit and print it. The concept of the Veda kept changing over time, and distinct ideas of the Veda might coexist, compete with each other, or overlap one another. No wonder, when it came to be edited for print and printed, the

---

25 For the concept of *cultural technique* and its meaning, see Peters 2015: 90–91 and Siegert 2015. See also.

26 More on the distinction between the cultural technique and cultural technology with respect to speech and writing, see Peters 2015: 262.

27 Witzel 1997.

28 For the concept of the person of the Veda knower as the carrier of Vedic gods, see Galewicz 2010b: 101.

editors happened to have different ideas of what it was they were about to publish. The expectations and reactions also differed. This is why the first part of this study concerns the Veda before print, and especially the concepts of the Veda, ideas about and images of the Veda, as well as the textual practices concerned with the process of the transmission of the Veda before going to print. To say, that before printing, the Veda used to be transmitted by memory and/or in handwriting is by far too little to make sense of the nature and consequences of such a bald cultural gesture as putting the Veda to print must have been in the first place..

While the circumstances of the early European [printed] editions of the Vedic texts remain relatively well known, it is not so with the early Indian editions. The former ones marked the history and its narratives of progress in the European philological interest into the intellectual and religious legacy of ancient India, It was appropriated by European academia and made part of the process of formation of the sub-discipline of classical Indology. As for the latter, only selected indigenous Indian editions had been acknowledged as forming part of the process. A great many of those, brought out by early 'native' Indian publishers, not only did not find their way in this history, that was written, at first, by Europeans for Europeans, but a number of them do not feature in library catalogues either in Europe or in India. If some of them made their way into bibliographical lists (especially Renou 1931—for some reason not included in Dandekar 1940–1986), the often dramatic circumstances of their production have never been included or made the object of a systematic study as such. The standard histories of Sanskrit literature, written in Europe and India from the mid-19th century up to the seventies of the 20th century, did not problematize the historical and political circumstances that either inhibited or disfavoured Indian native editions of the Veda to make part of this history. Colonial restrictions on native printing form only one part of these circumstances.

In line with the necessity of differentiating between various print cultures as the only way to make sense of print as an agent of change some historians have attempted to nuance the role of print by shifting the attention to its materiality and process, to paper and the mechanization of print. Among the latter a still stimulating but also warning voice belongs to Harold Innis: 'It would be presumptuous to suggest that the written or the printed word has determined the course of civilizations, and we should note well the warning of Mark Pattison that "writers with a professional tendency to magnify their office have always been given to exaggerate the effect of printed words.'"[29]

This book aims at charting the historical circumstances that stimulated and shaped the emergence of indigenous Indian print cultures in their relation to the heritage of the Vedic scriptural corpus. All that could gain momentum only after the Governor General, Charles Metcalf's, decision to ease the restrictions for owning presses by Indians in 1835.[30] Thus, the beginning of print capitalism and commercial printing, in the context of colonial India, should probably be gauged against the background of the colonial legal regulations of control. But also against the realities of the strong and functionally operative manuscript cultures and so-called script mercantilism.[31] Yet, this is by no means the only and sufficiently nuanced explanation. Rather, we need to look at a more complex picture. The same year, 1835, also saw the (in)famous speech by Macauley initiating a radical turn away from supporting education in indigenous languages in favour of English. Furthermore, the attitude of the Company and later British Indian Governments towards print was far from unambiguous. The Company's early policy of reluctance towards print and the printing press later came to be balanced with stimulating a controlled development, checked by legal regulations, combining licensing (the 1867 Act) with surveying and selective patronage.[32] Indigenous printer-publishers came to be regarded as agents cooperating in colonial policy and the alleged civilizing project of the empire as well as commercial competitors.

The principal focus of this study is an attempt to identify and map the scope of continuity and departure that marks the transition from the divergent manuscript cultures of pre-modern India to the new print cultures (plural intentional) that begin to take shape to an extent independently in a few distant areas of the Indian Subcontinent from the end of the 18th and the beginning of the 19th century. These new developments seem to bear rich traces of regional manuscript cultures and localized practices of communal and group reading, whether ritual or otherwise. The latter retained links to the performance traditions that preceded them and tinted their

---

29 Innis 1986 (1950): 5.

30 Priolkar 1958: 50.

31 For the concept of script mercantilism as a counterbalance for that of print capitalism, see Introduction to Pollock 2003.

32 Cf. Stark 2007: 26 which argues for three powerful mechanisms of state control: licensing, censorship and patronage.

shape with regional flavors, making early prints from Calcutta feature distinct marks from those of Bombay, Benares, Madras, or Trivandrum. This intentionally constructed area of interest feeds on the supposition that the modernity which took root on the Indian subcontinent at an uneven pace and in a fragmentary manner accommodated some important features of the pre-print book and the specific relationship between writing, reading, and memory performance.[33] Much remains to be done in order to identify and articulate the modalities and different regional trajectories that this development took over time, and to look for civilizational processes under such seemingly haphazard tendencies. The present study, however, is by no means meant to be a systematic overview of the subject. Rather, it serves as an introduction to the complex and fascinating history of the book in India conceptualized from a specific perspective.

From the early days of European trade, missionary, and colonial encounters with India, print had been seen by them as an instrument of social change and political empowerment. This must have been partly the heritage of the reformation and counter-reformation, which intensified the use of print, as well as the engagement of modern science with print and its alleged epistemological consequences. The instrumentality of printing had been recognized by early Jesuit and Protestant missionaries as well as by such institutions as the English East India Company, which, during its history, had shown a fluctuating and tense attitude towards the use of print within its Indian territories. In the early years of the latter, it was none other than Robert Boyle, who cherished serious plans of using print for a mission of evangelizing the heathens in India in his vision of a civilizational and modernizing project, which he saw as counterbalancing the purely commercial interest of the Company of whose Board he remained one of the directors. Boyle had hoped that 'pagan worship' might be overcome by printing and shipping to India ... 'a solid but civilly pennd Confutation of the Authentick Bookes wherin the Bramins religion is contain'd.'[34] As this example inevitably shows, a particular print culture

---

[33] Cf. HALL 2016. 90: Recent ... scholarship ... embraces the notion that knowledge of the written word in traditional religious and secular texts did not necessarily translate into readership, but that knowledge transfers based in traditional textual transmission, in oral recitations or in dramatic and dance rituals allowed illiterate and semi-literate audiences to share texts in communal reading sessions, in religious ceremonies, and in dramatic and musical performances.'

[34] OGBORN 2007: xx.

evolves and entails a specific concept of what print and printed matter should consist of, and what the very act of publishing in print means. To the Pietist Lutheran missionaries of the early 18th century, this all probably meant something entirely different than to the visionary Orientalist publishers from Calcutta, or to the indigenous printer-publishers from mid-19th century Bombay, such as Ganpat Krishnaji and Javaji Dadaji. In all the three instances, three different configurations of print culture were in operation, even though with time they gradually entered into closer mutual relationship. All three may be seen today as particular print cultures circumscribed by the dynamics of their specific clusters of practices of organization, production, circulation, reading, and sense-producing through print.[35] And, last but not least, all three shall be approached in the present study not exclusively from the perspective of print production but also, whenever possible, from the vantage point of print circulation and the modalities of print consumption and use, including the ways in which the latter ones influenced, situated, and determined the construction of meanings 'ascribed to texts.'[36] All of these would combine in different forms and varying degrees across the Indian Subcontinent to shape the modes of cultural experience of print in India as part of British empire, and also India as the continuing centre of the long developing South Asian civilization.

The kind of typology introduced by the present study suggests a concept of periodization in the historical development of different print cultures of the pre- and early colonial period. This, however, has been done for the immediate purpose of ordering the material for this study only, rather than as a proposition for historical periodization. The ordering principle adopted here is that of the ownership type (thus, also the agency) of the printing press: the missionary, the government, and the commercial presses. It is a simplified classification as, for instance, early presses of the East India company tended to be of a hybrid type combining government (East India Company) control and private ownership, while later on, publications initiated and controlled by goverment tended to appear through

---

35 Cf. a recent understanding of print culture in Colier and Connolly 2016: 5 as including 'production, dissemination and reading of printed material, as well as the creation of meaning through print.' The present study shall, however, differently position the relationship between the imperial and peripheral print cultures arguing rather for the coexistence of several varieties in partially overlapping spaces.

36 Colier and Connolly 2016: 6.

licencing processes rather than from government owned presses.[37] This simplified typology is meant to provide a conceptual framework for the understanding of the circumstances common to various regional development patterns during the pre- and early colonial era in India.

[37] Cf. a somewhat different classification in HALL 2016 who highlights a 'shift from the agency of Indian publications from the initial European missionary presses to a secular mix of Company, Company-licenced and private European- and Indian-owned presses' [HALL 2016: 109–110].

I. Objects, spaces and practices

No material culture ever evolves in void. And no space can be said to remain neutral to the developments of a material culture within it. The history of the book confirms it in many respects.

In order for the social practices of reading to be constituted over a specific historical period and space, some written objects must be circulated throughout this very space. Even though in a metaphorical sense, we can think or speak of a 'memorized book' and accordingly of reading from such a book, especially since certain regional Brahmin communities actually embodied the transmission of the Veda, it is the material form of the book with which I am predominantly concerned here. Accordingly, the memory-orality-performance complex, essential for an understanding of Vedic textuality as a specific type, shall be examined here from the point of view of its material and spatial situatedness and the consequences of this.

To the bewilderment of the first explorers of the remnants of the so-called Maurya empire, around the time of Emperor Aśoka, in the middle of the 3rd century BC, the initial finds of rock and pillar inscriptions turned out to represent a network of inscribed objects distributed over a huge area of subcontinental scale, from the present southern Karnaṭaka state in the south to the present Afghanistan in the north-west. Although they by no means can be regarded as books, we can hardly deny their medial dimension. The network of inscriptions set up within an apparently single project, spanning a relatively short period of time, appears to have had the function of communicating a cultural-political message of 'an empire on the rise' to a variety of different peoples inhabiting the vast tracts of the Indian subcontinent. To put into effect this earlier unprecedented and never--seen-before enterprise, the imperial chancellery of Aśoka had to invent and standardize a system of writing and deploy a communication network that could distribute and display in stone inscription what must have been actually composed several hundred miles away by the chancellery professionals in Aśoka's capital in Pataliputra. Though the evidence supporting this is lacking, it is difficult to imagine it involving anything other than a team of messengers, carrying either a memorized text or the same inscribed on a moveable object, to be dispatched to the often distant location of the imperial edicts.[38] Though neither the inscribed rocks or pillars, nor their intermediate form in the shape either memorized or inscribed, can be described as books in their moveable form, they form an immediate context against which it would be difficult to understand the appearance of objects deserving of the appellation of 'a book'.

With the area of interest for this study thus outlined, it is time to formulate a set of basic questions that shall animate our endeavour: Why was the need for publishing the Veda in print realized in India towards the middle of the 19th century and not in the 17th or 18th centuries? Were the circumstances the same (parallel) in Calcutta, Bombay, and Madras? What were the economic conditions that facilitated the indigenous Indian printed editions of the Veda? To what extent did, and to what did not, the printed Veda share the effects of modern printed matter? What were the reactions of traditional users to the printed Veda? Can we indicate what were the reading practices associated specifically with print? How did the practice of 'publishing' actually in connection with the type of textuality embodied by the Veda develop? How was 'printing' and 'publishing' conceptualized with respect to the Veda? Did there develop any distinct modes of reading connected to print among users of the printed Veda?

While attempting to identify and assess those elements which make for a culture of reading, we must remember that prescriptive passages, attested in some works, do not always come hand-in-hand with testimonies of actual practices. The latter can be gauged from sources of different status. One such source can be identified as formulas in colophons, stating or referring to practices concerned with the production, circulation, and handling of the book, that of reading being only one among many forms of dealing with the book.

38 For important remarks on the inscriptional practices and dissemination of texts composed in Aśoka's chancellery, see Tieken 2006: 74–75.

I.1. The book as an object circulating in space

Though at a point in time or for good one book might stay on a shelf and never move, books representing a text—whether memorized or inked (by handwriting, wood-block printing, typography, printing or digitizing)—would tend to travel and circulate in space. The trajectories of their movement would produce specific spaces of circulation, depending on the form of the practices of all those who took part in the book's composition, edition, production, proliferation, and dissemination. The same spaces would also be shaped by a variety of practices of those who made use of the book, according to reading protocols they believed proper and fruitful for a particular book in a particular socio-political situation and historical time. And last but not least, these spaces would shape—while being themselves shaped by—various concepts of the book promoted by its producers and publishers, and cherished or resisted by its consumers and users. Depending on such concepts and practices, the thus constituted spaces tended to differ as concerns the dominating principle of their organization. While some would authorize controlled and fine distribution through an institutionalized 'reading from memory' by professionals, others would favour patronized publication during congregational reading performances from (with the help of) a handwritten, or printed, copy, still others—a silent, solitary lecture. In other words, these spaces may be looked upon as specific functional orders. And this is, roughly speaking, the idea behind the title of the present book, which suggests as much a division line between the order of memory and the order of ink (metaphorically representing writing as well as printing) as their mutual coexistence and relationship that eventually gave a unique shape to the process of the development of regional cultures of print across the Indian subcontinent. No matter how strange it may sound, the memorized Veda used to circulate in space along with the communities of its guardians and users, with no written support, for many centuries, till *circa* 10th century AD, when the first attempts to write it down happened to have been noticed by Albiruni, writing from Kabul. This very circulation, either trans-regional, regional, or local at the moments of historical change, used to make its presence influential through the repeated collective practices of education, ritualized performance, and competition, specific to regional textual communities. While these practices continued and, to a degree, changed, the introduction of writing did not put an end to them. Rather, these multiplied channels of transmission and communication lived on parallel lives. Writing initiated new forms of circulation and other cultural practices, in a meaningful relationship to those ordered by memory and performance. The various modalities of this mutual relationship remain to be fully articulated. Print, with its promise of openness and liberation, proved to be instrumental in redefining old and creating new forms of mutual relationship between the oral and the written, while articulating new codes of inclusion and exclusion and triggering new regimes of control over its circulation in space as well as its duration in time. The period of the consolidation of the British imperial presence in the Indian subcontinent in the mid-nineteenth century saw the regionally developing print cultures influencing, and being influenced, by the circulation of the printed Veda to a varying degree and in different ways. To my best knowledge, the nature and consequence of this influence has not been systematically attended to so far by contemporary scholarship, thus making room for the present study. Being an attempt to make sense of the changes and transformations introduced by the appearance of the printed Veda in variously conceptualized editions in colonial India, the present study has to some extent to take into account the previous scholarship on European print cultures and hypotheses worked out in reference to the transformation period that allegedly took place within the historical period of the mature phase of mass printing, among else those concerned with the changing concepts of the Bible.[39]

I.2. The rebel book of the Veda

The backbone of this book on books is a history of a most unusual concept of the book that developed in South Asia with reference to the Veda. Even though the overall and simplifying approximation of the word 'book', used with reference to the Vedic corpus, may raise objections, this category appears promising, especially in the context of print cultures that inevitably tended to comprehend the Veda as consisting of 'book(s)', though variously

[39] One cannot resist the temptation to quote M. McLuhan: 'The new homogeneity of the printed page seemed to inspire a subliminal faith in the validity of the printed Bible as bypassing the traditional oral authority of the Church. It was as if print, uniform and repeatable commodity that it was, had the power of creating a new hypnotic superstition of the book as independent of and uncontaminated by human agency [McLuhan 1962: 144].

understood. One such functional approximation would be [a book of] scripture. And, historically, early encounters of Europeans with the Veda, whether real or imagined, did refer to the concept of either 'book' or 'scripture'[40]. However, it soon proved to be only misleadingly resembling other known historical scriptures. The concept of textuality behind the Veda seems rather different to that of most of other scriptures. It became the object of interest and speculation on the part of indigenous commentarial tradition and met with a number of different attempts at religious and philosophical interpretations and appropriations. Using the metaphor of 'the book', we may say that the Veda commenced as a memorized book and, in time—though reluctantly—incorporated its written and printed avatars, yet never broke the link with the sound, the rhythm, and the performance. The hand-copying practices developed original systems of representation not only with reference to linguistic phenomena such as sound modification (*sandhi*), but also for coding and decoding musical accents (*svara*). It followed the long history of the intellectual formation of its guardians: the diverse and often mutually competing communities of Vaidika Brahmins, who made it into the treasure trove of their group or family Veda. At the same time, in each case, the Veda remained a corpus of texts that, over its long history of transmission, has always evaded becoming part of a corpus of books. A corpus of texts that came to act as a rebel book of sorts, in that it continued to challenge the imagination of those who would attempt to understand their nature and message. Conceptually different either from the Bible or from the Qur'an, the Veda defies circumscription with the ideas transplanted from other book worlds. Just like other 'books' adopted to represent the final authority of a religious tradition, the 'book(s)' of the Veda happened to be revered and referred to without actual knowledge of its contents.

While the Veda had always been believed to be the paragon of a most stable and unchanging 'book,' the concepts of what the Veda was imagined to be, as well as the beliefs of what it should be, kept changing over time. The nature and trajectories of those changes were not without meaning and consequence for the print cultures that accommodated them for their use in the new media world of print.[41] Some of those concepts used to intrude on the very basic notions of textual integrity of one single

---

[40] See Baldeus 1703: 891, Halhed 1776: XIX–XXI, even Müller 1899: 169.

[41] For a survey of the changing concepts of the Veda and its textuality, see, for instance, Deshpande 1990, Galewicz 2010a, and, more recently, Larios 2017.

or multiplied Veda, and would address the very basic questions, such as whether the Veda had a personal (human or divine) author, or whether it had a beginning in time or had been eternal by itself, and whether it could be taken as an absolute and unquestioned authority in itself or only as a relational one. The concepts also addressed the material status of the Veda, articulating it, among others, as an 'amalgamation of sounds,' 'the sum total of *mantras* and *brāhmaṇas*', and 'the never perishing syllables.'[42] The regionally developed Brahmin textual communities took pride in understanding the true Veda to be their own: that is, the one experienced in their own specific textual practices in contradistinction to those of other Brahmin groups, either in the immediate neighbourhood or across mountains or rivers. Some of those communities attempted to translate these concepts into the new medium of print.

42 The problem of how to define the Veda remained one of the most important ones for the medieval commentator Sāyaṇa. For a survey of definitions of Vedic textuality in the works of the latter, see Galewicz 2010a: 177–79.

II. The Veda before print

Ne jamais perdre de vue qu'écriture est une fonction étrange, inhumaine, reflet de l'inhumanité du langage lui-même. Le langage, espèce domestique, redevient à travers l'écriture une espèce sauvage.

Baudrillard, *Cool Memories* V, Galilee 2005, p. 16

II.1. The beginnings: the travelling Veda

A new interest in isolated pockets of surviving Vedic ritualism in South India has given rise in recent decades to a ritual revivalism. Notwithstanding cases of reconstruction and innovation in its regional variations, it testifies to the sustained power and appeal of the ritual tradition that emerged roughly three millennia ago in the Northern part of the Indian subcontinent. In the centuries that followed, it spread east and south with migrant Brahmin communities who developed varied regional cultures of ritual performance for it.[43] All of them referred back to essentially one single textual tradition, preserved thanks to partially shared, sophisticated, and regular memory-cum-performance practices engaging organized collectives of individuals, for whom the preservation of the Veda remained a duty as well as a principle of social identification and self-assertion. Several centuries later, the regional varieties of Vedic ritual tradition came to coexist with and influence the new forms of belief and practice that we collectively refer to as Hindu. Before that, close to the appearance of Buddhism in the northern part of the Indian subcontinent towards the 6th and

[43] On early developments in Vedic schools' formation, see Witzel 2011. On the modern history developments and cases of re-appropriation of Vedic tradition in regional contexts, see, for instance, Larios 2017.

5th centuries BC, the already rich textual heritage of the Veda emerged as a systematized canonical collection of religious texts rearranged for ritual use. Most of them had been composed many centuries earlier, and continued to be transmitted through memory-cum-performance practices over a period of several centuries. All that accompanied a slow movement towards the east and south of the people who, in the Veda, call themselves *arya*, or 'the noble ones'. Their clans formed and changed alliances, fought among themselves as well as against others, with whom they also formed alliances in a process of a growing cultural synthesis. The Vedic canon, internally complex and multiplied, testifies to a religion which modern scholarship chose to name either 'Vedism' or 'Vedic Hinduism', which preceded post-Vedic Brahmanism and the later developed set of traditions labelled Hinduism. The Vedic textual corpus bears witness to repeated endeavours to rearrange and systematize a religious tradition with a marked emphasis on ritual practice of a decidedly elite character, in contrast with the emerging Buddhism. The late phase of this reworking process of oral canonization has been considered by some scholars as a redefinition in the face of the universal appeal of Buddhism [Bronkhorst 2011] or a challenge on the part of the written media of the neighbouring Persian Empire [Witzel 1997]. What emerged out of this process had been referred to as 'the Veda' (literally 'the [sacred] knowledge'). It came to be conceptualized as being divided at first into three—and later into four—parts, and accordingly referred to as the four Vedas. Along with an accompanying sense of unity, this four-part collection of texts of different origin and character became an important point of reference and source of authority for various communities of priestly functionaries and ritual practitioners, claiming their right of participation in the overall Vedic tradition. In addition to the earliest collection of mostly eulogistic hymns of the *Ṛgveda*, other Vedic texts express ideas about, as well as register and systematize various forms of ritual which they comment and speculate upon.[44] The Vedas, as fixed in the collective memory of their diversified practitioners, emerged near the time of the appearance of Buddhism, as a huge corpus, comprising various types of textuality represented by verse, prose, and mixed forms of different length, distinct history, time and place of origin, authorship, and purpose. All of them must have been selected out of a long tradition of performance and transmission practices within Vedic

44 For a general overview, see Witzel 2003.

clans, tribes, and 'schools'. All developed within, or have been later classified as belonging to, one of the initially three, and later four, acknowledged currents of Vedic tradition that came to be known as the Ṛgveda, the Sāmaveda, the Yajurveda, and Atharvaveda. All of them derived from a shared conviction about systematizing a particular, religiously useful skill, or knowledge (*veda*). Each of the four currents came to be represented textually by their own 'branches' or schools (*śākhās*).[45] The latter adopted a common organizational practice of completing their schools' repertoire with a set of texts emulating a paradigmatic arrangement into four classes of texts: the basic 'collection,' or Saṃhitā, in verse or short formulae; the Brāhmaṇa, or a ritualistic commentary in prose to the former; the Āraṇyaka, in speculative prose to be studied outside the village in wilderness; the Upaniṣad(s), or versed and/or prose dialogical texts, in search of a unifying principle of universe and new knowledge of a liberating character, to be taught to selected students. In the form we know it today, the Vedic corpus of texts represents the final result in a long process of amalgamation and rearrangement of various materials, composed earlier across a vast area from contemporary Pakistan to the plain of the Ganges in the east, and Nepal and Kashmir to the north and the Vindhya mountains to the south. This process must have been completed towards the 7th or 6th century BC, while later additions continued to be added until approximately the 4th century AD. Efforts towards systematization of practice were accompanied by the growing attitude that put the engagement with the very textuality of the Veda (on an oral-cum-memory basis) in the centre of ritual action of almost any kind. This amounts to the fact that Vedic ritualism is inseparable from Vedic textuality and performing the Vedic ritual must have meant, and still means, performing Vedic text and actualizing a Vedic type of textuality that realizes itself through performance. This performance engaged a professionally trained memory, according to procedures radically different from those known to have organized orally transmitted epic or folk narratives. The paradigmatic set of four distinct classes of Vedic texts, making each Vedic school, or *śākhā*, should better be made sense of as four distinct types of textual practices based on trained memory. Cultivated within families, clans, and schools as complementary ways of seeking power through verbal and bodily performance in composite liturgies, these textual practices gradually perpetuated in collective memory. They

45 For the early formation of Vedic schools, or *śākhās*, see Witzel 1997.

eventually came to be systematized and prescribed in the additional class of texts: the manuals of ritual procedure (*śrautasūtra*). The Ṛgvedasaṃhitā was compiled out of pieces of visionary poetry by authors who not only shared a belief in the ritual efficacy of their own art, or professional 'verbal behaviour' [Witzel 2003] and the power of ritual speech, but they must have regularly engaged in contests to prove its ritual efficacy in competitions that came to be regarded as religious practices themselves. The practices involved in composing Ṛgvedic hymns related to core concepts in the Ṛgvedic and were believed to be reflected and evoked through a successful poetic formulation. The best compositions, especially those of striking novelty, were believed to contain powerful formulations of *bráhman*, ready-made to activate the potencies of the Vedic gods and expected to affect reality. Their authors claimed the status of *brahmáns* (accent on the last syllable) or 'formulators' of these utterances. The most successful began to be preserved in a fixed form and were believed to repeat their functionality upon proper procedure. This required a belief in the potency of exact pronunciation and the enhanced development of memorization techniques and oral transmission with strict protocols of recitation. These important practices later developed regional inflections in response to social and political claims to control over the Vedic ritual. In effect, they juxtaposed oral transmission against writing for several centuries to come, with results even in contemporary practices of Vedic ritualists and communities of reciters. In the early Vedic context, failing to meet these protocols of exact reading from memory came to be sanctioned even with the danger of losing one's head[46].

[46] See, for instance, TS 2.4.12.1, BU III.9.26, ChU I.8.6-8 and 10.9-11.9.

II.2. The living libraries: the memorized Veda[47]

But a more important class ... are the Vaidikas... Learning the Vedas by heart ... is the occupation of their life. The best Rig-vedi Vaidika knows by heart the Samhitâ, Pada, Krama, Gatâ and Ghana of the hymns, the Aitareya Brâhmana and Âranyaka, the Kalpa and Grihya Sûtra of Âsvalyâna, the Nighantu, Nirukta, Khandas, Gyotisha, Sikshâ, and Pânini's grammar. A Vaidika is thus a living Vedic library.

R.G. Bhandarkar, quoted by F. Max Müller, 1878[48]

It has become a staple of the field to repeat the cliché about Indic literary traditions' predilection towards oral forms of literary performance and memorization as allegedly opposed to those characterized by a strong connection with writing. The Veda and its transmission would typically be indicated as paragon of this phenomenon. Not denying the overall reason for such opinions, I shall stress that the Vedic type of memorization as a principle of transmission and performance has always been something distinctively different from quite another type of orality that accompanied and formed the process of literary transmission, known either from classical epic literature or folk traditions. It formed early and had become, over time, standardized in principles within the traditions of transmission of each and every Vedic branch or *śākhā*. With the prolonged process of Brahmin groups' uneven migration towards the east and south, these traditions of transmission took on regional and local flavous, evolving, towards the second millennium, into regional cultures of Vedic transmission with a very differently configured relationship between the oral-memory order and the order of writing. Only very few of these processes had been textualized. Some of the communities that were active in this development survived till modern times and further transformed, before being explored with an ethnographic sense of documenting and understanding the living tradition.

The actual practice of Vedic memorization proved to be rather difficult to describe in detail. One of the earliest reports is Bhandarkar 1874.

---

47 A part of this section appeared in an earlier French version as Galewicz 2011c.

48 Müller 1878: 164. The section draws on my field work among Nampūtiri Brahmins in Kerala carried out between 2000–2015.

Several important contemporary studies [Staal 1961, 1983, 2008; Gray 1959; Howard 1986; Scharfe 2002; Deshpande 2011] divided their focus between the actual process and prescriptions from the classical texts and manuals.[49] Acknowledging this difficulty, the present account concentrates on maximum evidence from field study. The description, however, must remain fragmentary and incomplete for several reasons. When interviewed, the teachers, students, and expert reciters tend to favour the ideal model inherited by tradition, while actual practice observed happens to differ. A visitor to a Vedic recitation school belonging to the community of Nampūtiri Brahmins in Trichur, central Kerala, stumbles on a number of problems known all too well to ethnographers. It proves most difficult for a scholarly observer to keep his/her interference with his object of study within reasonable limits. This takes time and tends to blur the perspective, with practitioners asked again and again to do their routine practice. The burden of the traditional model and the expectations of teachers and students *vis-à-vis* a foreign scholar make them stage their performance so that the visitor gets the picture he or she came for. Nevertheless, experiencing and registering elements of the actual memorization process furnishes enough data to analyze against traditional manuals.

The primary aim of education at the Trichur Vedic school and education centre (referred to as Brahmasvam Maṭham) appears ideally to be the mastering of the complete *Ṛgveda saṃhitā* with its *pada* and *krama* versions and possibly also the two 'crooked' modes of recitation. Thus conceived, the whole process takes approximately up to six years and remains split into two broad stages or levels: the basic and the advanced.

---

[49] It is interesting to note the way in which F. Max Müller appreciated whatever he, having never been to India, knew about the oral-cum-memory practice of Vedic transmission. In his Lecture III [Müller 1878: 157], Müller assures that: 'They learn a few lines every day, repeat them for hours, so that the whole house resounds with the noise, and they thus strengthen their memory to that degree, that when their apprenticeship is finished, you can open them like a book, and find any passage you like, any word, any accent. One native scholar, Shankar Pandurang, is at the present moment collecting various readings for my edition of the Rig-Veda, not from MSS., but from the oral tradition of Vaidik Srotriyas.' In a postscript to the same lecture, Müller summarizes prescriptions for memorizing lessons extracted from the *Ṛgveda Prātiśākhya* and quotes correspondence from Maharashtra relating to the practices of Vedic memorization among Maharashtra *Brahmins* and their concept of *daśagrantha* or the ten 'books' as a complete corpus of the *Ṛgveda* to study—an idea foreign to the Kerala Nampūtiri Ṛgvedins and their specific memorizing tradition referred to here.

II.2.1. The basic level

The basic level of instruction comprises of only the first of the three basic modes, namely the 'continuous' mode of recitation (*saṃhitā*).[50] In order to accumulate and thoroughly store the entire collection of the *Ṛgveda-saṃhitā*—that amounts to 10,580 stanzas—in the memory, along with an effective skill of fine memory retrieval, students need approximately four years, several hours a day. Successive portions of the text are introduced in a systematic way, following a recurring pattern. Memorized quarters, half-stanzas, stanzas, groups of stanzas, lessons, and 'books,' are gradually stored in the memory, along with the markers of text division. As elsewhere in India, Nampūtiris use two different text divisions for the *Ṛgveda*, slightly adjusted:

1) into 10 'cycles' (*maṇḍala*) consisting of 'repetitions' (*anuvāka*), 'hymns' (*sūkta*), 'stanzas' (*ṛk*, *mantra*), and 'quarters' (*pāda*);
2) into 8 'eights' (*aṣṭaka*), comprising 8 × 8 = 64 'lessons' (*adhyāya*), 'groups' (*varga*) of stanzas, 'stanzas' (*ṛk*), 'hemistiches' (*ardharca*/*anta*), and 'quarters' (*pāda*).

The first was usually taken by academic discourse as being the historically earlier and 'meaningful' one, while the other was held as being later and 'mechanical.' The fundamental scheme of Nampūtiri *Ṛgveda* memorization makes use of the second system and, in the same manner, identifies basic repetition units other than units of sense. However, units of sense (hymns) appear to govern other structures of the memorization process.

A reader accustomed to the visual layout of the text may find it difficult to comprehend how a Vedic reciter is able to orientate himself, at a given moment, to the structure of larger text units; in other words, how he can fix coordinates for the passage he is practicing in a text as bulky as the *Ṛgvedasaṃhitā*. Neither is it easy to imagine how he can keep track of the passages already practiced or access a specific memorized passage in

50 For the meaning, see, for instance, DESHPANDE 2011: 91 – 'Pāṇini's definition of *Saṃhitā* 'euphonic combination' is given in rule 1.4.108 (*paraḥ sannikarṣaḥ saṃhitā*): 'Maximal closeness between items is called *Saṃhitā*.' This assumes that there are two sounds or words next to each other without any gap between them. The word *Saṃhitā* literally means joining...

case of a specific need. A number of orally and visually recognized indexes of the beginnings and endings appear to serve that purpose. They are represented by the table below.

II.2.1.1. Memorizing from the mouth of the teacher

During morning classes at the basic level (*saṃhitā*), a group of youngsters repeat after the teacher, and, according to a set pattern, recite a batch of ten successive hymns. The daily progress is marked by introducing one new and dropping one old, while a batch of ten *sūktas* always remains within the primary attention of students.[51] The batch is memorized at a gradual pace, quarter by quarter (*pāda*) first, hemistich by hemistich (*anta*) next. Each pace requires triple repetition of the teacher's words. This goes on for ten days, out of which, the first five are devoted to quarter by quarter repetition and the next five to the repetition of the same, at the pace of a hemistich. That makes a total of thirty repetitions of each hymn (*sūkta*), enunciated by the teacher in a double run.

II.2.1.2. Consolidating memory

In the next step, students proceed to perform a consolidating repetition of the same material at a longer stretch, with the teacher now only indicating units to be practiced by pronouncing their first words. The repetition unit is now one 'group' of stanzas. The teacher supervises the students repeating each group ten times, while marking the end of every completed unit with the 'tuft' (*kuṭuma*) index marker of the next one (see Table 1).

During the process, the memory of the Veda adept also records coordinates of single units within larger structures (*adhyāya*), while keeping track of the number of the groups (*varga*) and of the hemistiches (*anta*) through a finger count. Each unit thus appears to be assigned an address in the memory store by which it can be later accessed. When addresses are doubled (by the use of parallel classification), this adds to the security of the system. In this manner, 'addresses' of hymns and sets of stanzas are additionally encoded with a triple index of seer/deity/metre. The students

[51] This must be a model to be adjusted to exceptionally short hymns (only one stanza!) or long ones (thirty stanzas). Introducing *Ṛgveda* in *sūkta* units is believed to be essential and failing to do so, grave misconduct (M.J. Nampūtiri, personal communication).

Table 1. Verbal and bodily indices of beginnings and endings

Text unit in *saṃhitā*	Designation	Verbal index of beginning	Bodily index of beginning	Verbal index of ending	Bodily index of ending
pāda	quarter			modulation	
anta	hemistich (half-stanza)			*iti* repetition (pragraha)	next finger of the right hand
ṛc/mantra	stanza			*iti* repetition (*pragraha*)	
sūkta, tṛca...	a hymn or set of stanzas of common seer, deity, or metre	name of seer, deity and/or metre	touching three places on the body: head, chest and abdomen		
varga	a group of stanzas	OM	hands in *brahmañjali*	a quarter of the next (*kuṭuma*)	next finger of the left hand
adhyāya	a 'lesson'		*sūrya-nam-askāra*		
anuvāka/ōttū	'repetition'		*sūrya-nam-askāra*		
aṣṭaka first *varga*	an 'eight'		hands in *brahmañjali* on the right knee		
ōtikka	an instruc-tion	*virāmas tāvat*			hands in *brahmañjali*

Source: CG

accumulate successive units in their memory store, proceeding gradually by scanning the same hymn with shorter and longer units. When a mispronunciation creeps in, the teacher orders them to stop and repeat the affected unit.[52] Accordingly, each hymn (*sūkta*) is repeated 3 + 3 + 10 = 16 times daily. When multiplied by ten successive days, wherever a *sūkta* remains within the drilling batch, it has a chance of being repeated 160 times in total.[53] This number may be increased yet further, by refreshing drills during the Salutation of the Morning Sun (*sūrya-namaskāra*) rite, when

52 The same procedure is followed during a virtuoso performance in the Trisandhā cycle.

53 One interviewed teacher indicated 120 as the total number of repetitions.

a fairly long portion of one 'lesson' (*adhyāya*) gets repeated regularly in a repetitive cycle (twenty hymns on average). Thus, the basic memorizing process has each and every word of the *Ṛgvedasaṃhitā* repeated in a systematic manner, approximately almost two hundred times (not counting the self-practice of the students[54]).[55]

II.2.2. The advanced level

This level is marked with the introduction of two additional modes of recitation.

II.2.2.1. *Pada* and *krama*

A limited number of students continue with the next, advanced level of Vedic recitation.[56] Now 'word-for-word recital' (*pada-pāṭha*) is introduced, and this is possible only after a thorough appropriation of the bulk of the *Ṛgveda* corpus in its 'continuous' form. This means learning the same thing again, but in a form that ignores sound assimilation between every pair of words and involves certain grammatical operations (dissolution of compounds, etc.). In contrast with the 'continuous' flow of the *saṃhitā* mode, this can be heard more as a sort of staccato recital. Now, not only does the continuous text gets 'broken' into the 'original' word units, but some pitch accents fall on different syllables. This stage is also marked by the application of *mudrā* hand movements (see below). The unit of repetition now becomes one stanza, and the revision unit even stretches to one 'lesson' (*adhyāya*).[57] This is also the case in the third, still more complex, basic mode, the *krama*, which is a further modification, combining the principles of 'continuous' and 'word-for-word' modes into a 'step by step' algorithm. This serves to intensify the memory's concentration on the text and engages attention, which has to switch from one mode to another. By now, a set of three basic forms of representation of the *Ṛgveda saṃhitā* has

54 The self-practice drilling has been said to follow a decreasing number of repetitions for 15 days.

55 Whether the practice was similar in ancient India is not easy to determine: see SCHARFE 2002: 244–249.

56 As a matter of fact, even students who quit the school earlier may receive instruction in *pada* recitation to minor extent.

57 Cf. remarks on the concept of Latin *lectio* in SAENGER 1997: 264, 299.

been built into the memory of the Vedic adept. Now he will be able to learn how to bewilder and arrest the attention of connoisseurs[58] with the famous 'crooked' recitation modes to be performed by pairs of chanters squatting and facing each other from a close by. He will be ready to compete for titles at the famous annual Anyōnyam festival at the Kaṭavallūr temple or take part in the royal festival of chanting the Vedas known as *Muṟajapaṁ*, which takes place every six years at the royal temple of the erstwhile rulers of Travancore in the capital city of Trivandrum.[59]

II.2.2.2. The 'crooked' recitation modes

Few students master this sophisticated art of Vedic recitation thoroughly. The unit of training and recitation is one stanza within which an algorithm of progress and reiteration is to be executed by two performers in an altered, shifted or contradictory manner. As 'crooked' (*vikṛti*) modes are, by principle, further modifications of the three (*prakṛti*) ones, their memorization seems to be of a radically different level that requires appropriation of the rules for combinatory operation on the text. In a sense, the 'crooked' recitation modes represent operations on the elements of memorized text and its various 'reading protocols', with the help of interiorized rules. The two 'crooked' modes of reciting the *Ṛgveda*, practiced by Nampūtiris, are not taught separately, but introduced along with the 'step-by-step' (*krama*) mode as examples of its application and extension of its principles. Again, no written artefacts are made use of to assist during instruction or training. This demanding and respected skill is appreciated as a sophisticated art by accomplished Nampūtiris. School instruction in the 'crooked' modes remains fragmentary and is mirrored by their rare display during the senior reciters' competitions and ritualized performances outside the school context.[60]

The school's curriculum does not contain instruction pertaining to the meaning of the memorized texts. While teachers and some advanced students may have some knowledge of Sanskrit and Vedic words

---

58 Cf. remarks by M. Carruthers: 'One accomplishment ... greatly admired by both ancient and medieval writers was the ability to recite a text backwards as well as forwards, or to skip around in it in a systematic way, without becoming lost or confused. The ability to do this marked the difference between merely being able to imitate something (to reproduce it by rote) and really knowing it, being able to recall it in various ways' [Carruthers 2008: 21].

59 See Galewicz 2005a, 2010b.

60 For details, see Staal 1961 and Scharfe 2002, for social setting, see Galewicz 2005a.

or expressions, the semantic value of this most important component of the cultural identity of Nampūtiri Ṛgvedins remains outside the focus of education and community life. Now, what are we to think of the people who themselves toil by burdening their memory with bulky texts to be understood by somebody else? One possible answer to the last disquieting question was formulated some time ago by F. Staal: 'The reciters are ... not Vedic scholars. They are dedicated to the preservation of their sacred heritage for posterity. Without them, scholars of the Vedas would have nothing to be scholars of. Had the reciters themselves been scholars concerned with meaning, the original sounds might have long been lost.'[61] A few more questions remain, however, unanswered: is it possible to reconstruct a concept of memory at work in the Vedic memorization? What mental or bodily function have been imagined to be activated during the memorization of the Vedic text? What actually the Veda as the object of memorization has been taken for in the process?

II.2.2.3. The memory of the body and the embodied Veda

Only a careful observation of the Vedic memorization practice may show a degree of engaging the body of the Vedic student in the process. First of all, the body of every reciter should be ritually cleaned and marked. Any pollution incurred will result in a repetition of the ritual bath with purifying rites. Contact with outsiders, entering the space of memorization or recitation, is especially sensitive to pollution.[62] Complex rules regulate proper and improper times for recitation (season, day in a lunar calendar, time of the day, daily activity around). The same applies to place, arrangement of space, positioning of the body within it, and the posture of the body. All that appears to support the memorization process through radical differentiating the body of the Vedic reciter from that engaged in any other activity. The same should be said of correspondences established between the body of the reciter and specific activities of the teaching process. In addition to this, teaching systems developed that put thorough emphasis on the bodily apprehension of sounds, pitch accents and text

---

[61] Staal 1983: 30–31.

[62] Even contact mediated by objects should be avoided. If handed over by a reciter, an object needs to be received indirectly (dropped and caught), so that the purified body of the reciter and an outsider do not touch objects at the same time.

unit markers. In the practice of the Nampūtiri Ṛgvedins, the body of the new student becomes virtually imprinted with the memory of the crucial determinants of the proper articulation of the memorized text, while the teacher forces the head of the student down, up, and sideways, following the flow of pitch accents. These head movements need to be suppressed later with the progress of memorization. Some students find it difficult and tend to display traces of this practice further on in the learning process, which may reflect the power of bodily memory at work. Another element of engaging the body in the memorization process is finger-counting (Figure 1). Being positioned in a cross-legged posture allows two arms to rest on the knees and be free for the crucial action of supporting the systematic arrangement of the memorized text. The two hands engage in counting two different sets of text units. The number of groups (*varga*) counted with left hand may vary up to almost fifty, which must put a stress on the student's attention and memory, when forced to keep track of successive rounds of the five fingers' count! At the same time, the right hand has to count hemistiches (*anta*). Thus, the memory cursor keeps following the text according to the two different systems of coordinates imprinting on the memory a procedure of precise—double checked—locating of the passage to be retrieved from the memory stock. It appears to form part of a wider web of counter checks on the memory—a multiple security system. It is reinforced by means of scanning the collective memory of the community with a sort of anti-virus procedure, represented by competitions and the ritual recitation of the whole of the *Ṛgveda*, according to specific patterns of 'going over' (*pārāyaṇa*) the text. An important act of consolidating memory through bodily movements is the morning rite of salutation of the rising sun. Regular repetition of this gymnastic-cum-religious activity incorporates a thorough revision of larger units of memorized text, in a system that associates specific text units with particular bodily exercises. One is reminded of the monastic practices of medieval Europe and their use of 'rumination' or meditation on the memorized passages from the Bible during daily work such as gardening.[63] More advanced students learn more bodily gestures functioning as signs, or indexes, such as the marking by the loud sound of snapping two fingers (*miṭi*) an approaching *parigraha*, or a compound to be analyzed in *pada* or *krama* mode. Strangely enough, the same sound is used to signal a mistake by the performer taking part in

---

[63] Cf. Cavallo 2001: 98.

a contest (Figure 2).[64] Furthermore, breath control as a bodily skill plays an important role in memorization, and certain units of recitation are required to be pronounced in one breath, while others require breathing in and out at specific points.

By far the most spectacular bodily technique supporting memorization and memory retrieval efficiency are the hand movements known as *mudras*. This sophisticated system of bodily signs is introduced at an advanced level of learning. The Vedic *mudras* (Mal. Skt. *mudrā* = 'stamp', 'image', 'token') constitute an artificial sign system, encoding indications of the phonetic value of syllables, their pitch, and time.[65] These are executed with the right hand only and can effectively encode the flow of Vedic recitation in a way that it can be decoded by the students watching the teacher, or a co-performer, competing rivals, or an audience. With regard to Ṛgvedic *mudras*, each stanza can be represented silently, and classes happen to be revised in that form occasionally. The *mudras* are not supposed to be used in basic (*saṃhitā*) recitation and are introduced with 'word-for-word' recitation (*pada-pāṭha*). How compelling a process it is may be seen when elderly virtuosi happen to betray stray hand movements of *mudras* unconsciously, while reciting or listening to Vedic passages following non-mudra procedures. On the basic level of the 'continuous' recitation mode, a simpler set of hand gestures remains in use by teachers supporting spatial visualization of Vedic accents.

II.2.2.4. Learning by participation: community of practice

Much could be said with regard to appropriating the Veda through participation in its community of practice. The latter includes not only classmates, but past school adepts, virtuoso reciters, teachers, well known experts, and other individuals actively participating in the community's engagement with its heritage, through shared knowledge mobilized for its effective transmission and use. Other classes, training, long preparations, public performance or competition, regular and special occasions for the community to show off, or otherwise catering to the needs of wider community by group recitation in temples, at homes, or in institutions, are only some

---

[64] Cf. Galewicz 2005a: 568.

[65] As noted by Staal, unlike *mudras* used in other traditions of South Asia, 'Vedic *mudras* of Nampūtiris do not represent meanings, but sounds.' For description of *mudras*, see Staal 1983 II: 359–381. Cf. Gray 1959: 510.

of the *loci* where the knowledge is shared and learnt through participation. It is there, where one can see celebrated masters and identify their style, where one can test the competence of one's own memory and make oneself a name among the skilled practitioners. Many a day sees the Trichur school empty, with students leaving for festivities featuring Vedic recitation, competitions, ritual chanting, and events of Vedic sacrifice. It is only through participation that certain additional modalities of representation of the memorized text can be learnt. This is the case with a peculiar manner of chanting known as *koṭṭu*. Its name means 'drumming'; however, no drums—but a rhythmical humming sound (of recitation)—is to be heard, albeit executed through nostrils kept closed with two fingers of the right hand. This results in an articulation unintelligible to outsiders. Yet the participants have to know not only how to decode the coordinates of the started passage, but also how to immediately identify the stanza and continue with it when the initial reciter stops. Another peculiarity of this chant is its chain pattern and fixed rhythm: It is heard only immediately before food for a feast for Vedic reciters is served. The feasting itself happens to be part and parcel of the ritualized sessions of recitation. A *koṭṭu* recitation may happen during Trisandhā, Vāram, or Anyōnyam and is believed to be ritual 'food-purification.' Its progress is marked stanza by stanza, following the *krama* mode. Each has to be completed in one breath, and often the voice of a performer takes on a dramatic tone when he runs short of it. To participate in *koṭṭu* is a challenge, since the reciter who starts, picks up another of his choice to continue by finger pointing. If *koṭṭu* makes up a part of competition during the festival of Anyōnyam, two rival parties are engaged and, after a few stanzas played within one's own party, the 'ball' is suddenly transferred to the other side, whose team has to keep their attention alert in order not to miss or mistake one stanza for another.

II.2.2.5. Collective memory

A striking feature of Vedic recitation (and memorization) is that it tends to work (better) in a group. This seems to give the performers more self-assurance. Among Nampūtiris one can see it also in the sophisticated 'crooked' modes of chanting, where two reciters not only support one another, but stimulate their respective hold on memory by reciting the same lines in a contradictory, altered or shifted arrangement of elements. Furthermore, during self-revision drills, students can be seen practicing in pairs with two boys facing each other. This tendency is to be seen across India, as noted by Scharfe: 'Vedic brahmins prefer to recite in pairs; for two do not only know more than one; two that recite together know more than the same two reciting separately.'[66] Among Nampūtiris, this tendency is also seen in ritualized public recitations. One of the simple rituals, for which Nampūtiris are invited to recite the *Ṛgveda* in its entire 'continuous' form, is the Lakṣārcana ('Ten thousand Offerings'). This requires fifteen performers taking turns, so that it requires a team of ten reciters to carry on the recitation, not unlike in sport games of volleyball or hockey. Roughly the same number of chanters is required for the much more demanding Trisandhā ('Triple Combination'), although only five reciters at a time are considered a minimum to mobilize collective memory sufficiently to carry it over through a long, multi-session cycle.[67]

Against this predilection, the most demanding appear to be recitations that require individual memory to work more or less alone, as in the sacrificial ritual. Even this, however, is remedied by the presence in the sacrificial arena of a supervising expert ready to indicate and remedy mistakes. The same holds true for periodical contests in chanting, where awards are given to individuals courageous enough to perform without feedback from others but checked by the audience and a rival party. At certain levels, *mudras* hand movements, executed in front of the reciter, are of great help to memory if decoded properly, at others, they are not allowed. Not only errors of pronunciation, pitch, timing, and mode of recitation, but also mistakes in reproducing the structure of the text passage and specific pattern of its performance, are seen as a grave matter of general concern for the collective memory of the community. This is shown in vivid emotional reactions, disputes over correct judgments, and often long repetitions of units affected by the spotted error. The concept of collective memory at work among Nampūtiris seems to derive from a pan-Indian Vedic imperative of 'personal study' (*svādhyāya*).[68] The idea, long discussed by commentators and philosophers, addresses the problem of different 'protocols of reading' the scripture. While initially conceived of as a solemn and solitary duty, daily contact with the scriptural text of the Veda was later developed into the double duty of learning and teaching the Veda, that was to bind every Brahmin male. The unique

[66] Scharfe 2002: 26.

[67] For a description of these ceremonial recitations, see Galewicz 2010b.

[68] For a discussion on this important concept, see Malamoud 1977 and Killingley 2012.

Nampūtiri reworking of this idea took shape in the periodically performed ritual called Trisandhā. Trisandhā appears to form a curious extension of the teaching-learning pattern of Vedic transmission through memorization. Its basic structure closely resembles the teaching process: the performers seem to—imitate a Vedic class by their manner of sitting, and one by one alternate in the role of a teacher facing a group of pupils. Furthermore, the very pattern and discipline of this ritual recitation of the *Ṛgveda* recreates the process of memorization. To make it more demanding, however, it is not a simple mimetic act, but rather a modification of the schooling procedure with its mnemonic devices arranged in a manner requiring constant alert on the part of the participants. Its recitation discipline follows a complex daily pattern and covers the whole of the *Ṛgveda* recited in three primary modes.[69] The performance of a 'crooked' mode may also occur. By custom, it falls during a meal taken together by the participants, who are supposed to pay attention to mistakes while eating. Since 'going over' the *Ṛgveda*, according to the adopted pattern, is rather time consuming, Trisandhā stretches to a several month cycle of recitation sessions and remains a considerable effort for the community to complete.[70]

An additional flavour to the collective construction of Vedic memory is given by the agonistic dimension of the rituals and festivals engaging recitation of the *Ṛgveda*. Though actually not in current usage, a vivid memory persists of a genuine context, in which the announcement of a Trisandhā by one of the two Ṛgvedins' associations almost inevitably triggered a risk of the rival party arriving at the spot to test the art and memory of the organizers. This competitive structure survived in a somewhat petrified shape in the Anyōnyam festival.[71]

The important concept of periodically refreshing the collective textual memory can only be mentioned in passing due to limited space. This is the idea of a ceremonial 'going over' (*pārāyaṇa*) the whole of the memorized corpus of the *Ṛgveda* by a group of best reciters representing the community. At least three institutions developed by the community of Nampūtiri

---

69 Performers of Trisandhā, witnessed by me in 2005, got into heated argument on points of recitation pattern and procedure. They never referred to the *Trisandhāparipāṭi* manuscript. Comparing their practices with the prescription of this manual, supplies further proof for the power of collective memory. See Galewicz 2010b.

70 Cf. Pisharothy 1928: 706–707 and Govindan Namboodiri 2002.

71 See Galewicz 2005a. For a historical instance of a feud between two rival factions of Nampūtiri Ṛgvedins, see Haridas 2018.

Ṛgvedins ensure that the memorized text of the *Ṛgveda* is periodically refreshed in its entirety. Apart from the aforementioned Lakṣārcana and Trisandhā, the third continues to be organized, albeit in a much reduced form, by the royal Padmanabha temple in Tiruvānatapuram, closely connected to the former kingdom of Travancore. As such, it still retains the air of a spectacular royal event and represents an important display of the power and authority of the learned communities pursuing the Vedic tradition in Kerala. One should note that to 'go over' the entire textual body of the *Ṛgveda* can take quite some time, ranging from approximately a week, in the case of one basic mode of recitation realized in a simple linear pattern (the Lakṣārcana and simple Muṟajapam), to several months in the case of the three modes of recitation and the specific, non-linear pattern of progress in the Trisandhā (Figure 3).

II.2.2.6. Remembering and forgetting

The Vedic memorization system, as sketched above, appears to be marked not only by things to be memorized, but also by things to be cleared from the memory during the process. Such is the case with head movements being of great help in the very initial phase of memorization. Enforced on students' bodies in beginners' classes, they have to be suppressed, forgotten, and discarded as soon as the memory gets accustomed to and retains the flow of pitch accents. The moment when they should be abandoned is said to be decided individually for every student. As shown in interviews, it may come fairly soon, even by the end of mastering the first batch of ten hymns.[72]

Another challenge for the already-built memory of the Vedic student is a demand to forget that the *Ṛgveda* he memorized with so much effort and time at the basic level is the only form in which it may appear. This happens when he advances in his study and proceeds towards memorizing the other two of the three basic forms of the text, or modes of its representation, namely the 'word-for-word' (*pada*) and the 'step by step' (*krama*). Henceforward, his image of the *Ṛgveda* corpus is to be reinvented so that it is comprised of different forms of the same: the *samhitā-pāṭha* (of the *Ṛgveda*), the *pada-pāṭha* (of the *Ṛgveda*), etc. In due course, he will be forced to discover that the whole memory of any fixed form of Vedic text, memorized during

[72] Personal communication by Dr. M.J. Nampūtiri, 2009.

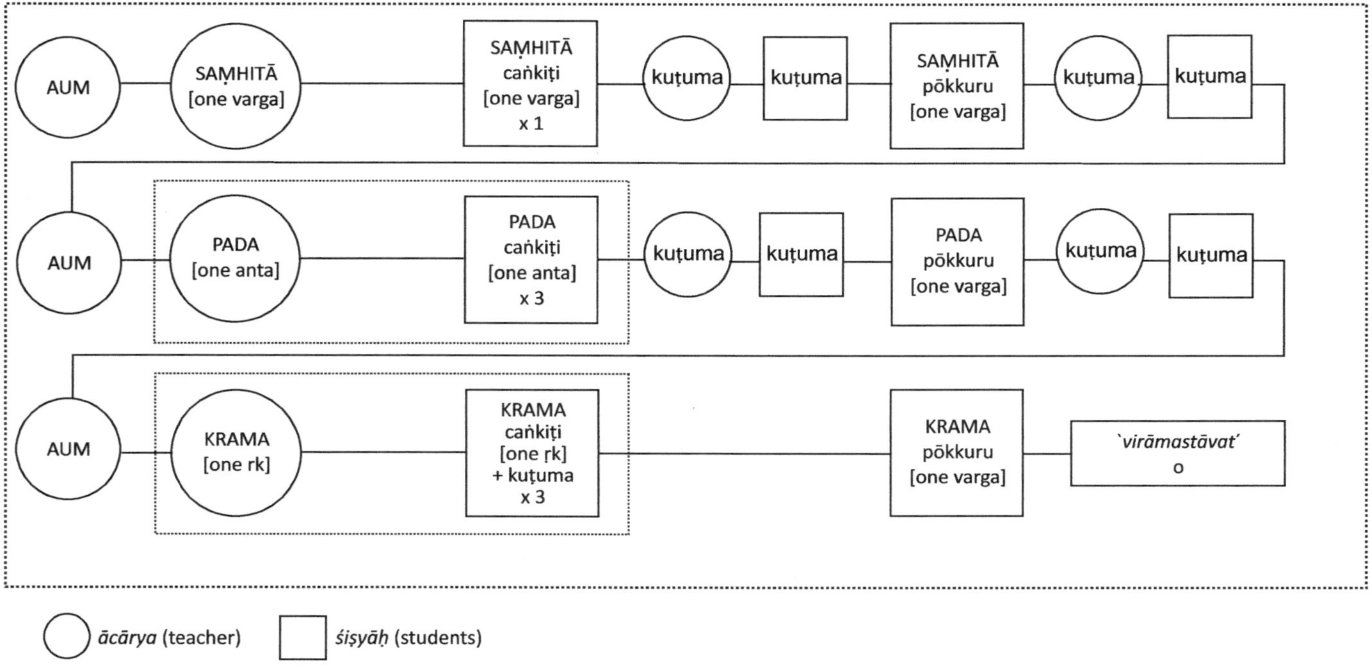

Fig.19. TRISANDHĀ – recitation sequence scheme

the years of apprenticeship, has to be suspended in order to give way to yet another form of representing the *Ṛgveda* text when it comes to reciting *Ṛgvedic* mantras during solemn (*śrauta*) Vedic sacrificial ritual. This demanding type of Vedic recitation is not taught at schools but forms the object of separate instruction from heads of certain Nampūtiri families (Vaidikan), who have the hereditary responsibility for preparing and supervising the performance of Vedic sacrifices. Even though the performers representing the Ṛgveda on the sacrificial ground will draw from the memorized *Ṛgvedasaṃhitā*, they will make use of particular selections of stanzas arranged in a specific way and will have to abandon pitch accents (*svaras*), otherwise believed to constitute the gist of the Veda. Here, with some minor exceptions, Vedic mantras are to be recited in monotone (*ekasvara*).

II.2.2.7. The memory of the system

As indicated above, the Vedic memorization process, adapted from classical manuals and developed to suit the local context, appears to make use of a fairly complex meta-language of classification made of categories of text division units, indexes, modes, and patterns of recitation. The same classification is resorted to when the memorized Veda is to be accessed in order to be put to public performance, ritual, or contest use. As such, it provides systematic access to the treasured past of the community stored in the corpus of the *Ṛgveda* and crucial to the community's identity.[73] Its formal characteristics and innermost logic and coherence make it an organized system of knowledge, effective in oral practice. To its participants, it may also be seen as an internally coherent, albeit closed, information system made of structured elements.[74] The memory of such a system remains effective within the joint, wider context of neighbouring Nampūtiri communities, concerned with the preservation of two other Vedas.[75] Taken together, they deserve the metaphor of a 'living library', composed of systematically

---

[73] Cf. contemporary research into the role of classifications in knowledge production. According to a recent study: 'Classification schemes always have the central task of providing access to the past' [Bowker and Star 1999: 255].

[74] Incidentally, this text division system of the *Ṛgveda*, combined with memorization discipline in wide use across influential Brahmin communities, had been made a clever use of in the grand imperial self-promotion project of the early Vijayanagara empire of the mid-fourteenth century. See Galewicz 2010a.

[75] Perhaps, this kind of memory, distributed among several nexus areas, was once a must and later an alternative for the need of 'using a centralized external memory source such

archived canonical texts of the Veda, preserved along with the procedures of their performative implementation, even though most members of the community today seem not to make any specific use of the resourses of the library they take so much effort to guard against oblivion.[76]

II.2.2.8. A perfect memory with suspended sense

A tradition of memorizing, deprived of an accompanying system of transmitting the meaning of the memorized text, may indeed seem bizarre.[77] Although reasons for that could be many, some ideas of the Mīmāṃsā school of Vedic interpretation may well have contributed to this. One of them is the belief that the Veda is possessed of the inner power of 'illuminating other things as well as itself.'[78] Another one is the doctrine of 'ceremonial perfection' (*saṃskāra*), promoting the view that the Vedic text needs to be constantly refined through a never-ending process, focused on securing its perfect form and structure, rather than meaning.[79] This type of development in the ideology accompanying the modelling of the 'protocols of reading' the scriptural texts is not quite absent from the history of reading the Bible in medieval Europe. Let it suffice to recall the testimony of Saint Augustin, who strongly recommends to everyone studying the Bible to commit the text to memory, even if one cannot understand the sense of the passages.[80]

---

as the library at Alexandria ...' [Bowker and Star 1999: 261]. For a more recent approach to classification and list making, see Young 2017.

[76] The metaphor, used for the first time in 1874 by R.G. Bhandarkar, albeit with reference to an individual Vaidika Brahmin [Scharfe 2002: 27]. More on this metaphor, see Galewicz 2005a. Other metaphors concerning contemporary Vedic recitation include: a 'walking Rig-Veda MSS' [Shankar Pandit quoted in Scharfe 2002: 25] and 'tape-recording' [Witzel 1997]. Incidentally, some of Nampūtiri Vedic virtuoso reciters remain members of quite another community of practice related to efficient memory work, namely, a tradition of chain recitation and a game-like collective performance of literary verses known as *akṣara-śloka*, or the 'undying verse'. Its exponents boast of retaining in memory a few thousand stanzas in three different languages. See Galewicz and Sudyka 2005, 2012.

[77] Cf. following remarks by K. Pomian: '*...chaque écrit est forcément lacunaire: on ne saurait jamais tout noter et il est des choses qui ne laissent pas décrire... C'est pour cette raison, semble-t-il, que même dans des sociétés qui connaissaient déja l'écriture, il fut interdit ... de mettre par écrit les récits de l'au-déla ainsi que du passé le plus ancien... La mémoire collective n'existe plus uniquement dans et par les mémoire individuelles. Elle existe aussi ... dans les images et les textes qui, avec le passage du temps, perdent, les unes et les autres, leur intelligibilité immédiate*' [Pomian 1999: 281–282].

[78] See VBhBhS: 15.

[79] See Galewicz 2003.

[80] St. Augustin, *De doctr. christ.*, II, ix, 14 quoted in Cavallo 2001: 97.

The kind of memorization represented by the Vedic model differs from those of other textual traditions by concept and practice. While it is not always easy to articulate this difference in modern categories, an old distinction developed within the orthodox Hindu tradition itself might be of help in its understanding. This tradition draws a clear division line between that part of the Vedic heritage which can be 'directly heard' (*Śruti* = heard tradition) in its original form (understood as 'revelation'), and another one that can be known only through 'remembrance' (*Smṛti* = remembered tradition).[81] Both were used practically and referred to as foundation and justification for 'the Hindu way of life.' Of the two, the former was usually taken and sought after as the ultimate source of authority. The latter was respected, as derived from a presumably lost, degenerated, or otherwise imaginatively misrepresented Veda; in consequence, it was also believed to be authoritative, albeit in a secondary degree, as only in 'remembrance'—i.e. as not having a directly perceptible Vedic form.[82] The former was further believed to have no human author (*apauruṣeya*), while the latter was seen as a creation of humans, who somehow articulated what was 'remembered'. As a result of this fundamental distinction, developed some time in the first centuries AD, probably within the philosophical circle of Mīmāṃsā, the heritage of the first was given a religious sanction of being handed down only through oral channels of transmission. These were believed exclusively to secure its unique, perfect, and genuine sound-and-rhythm form.[83] The second, on the contrary, did not require that strict regime of transmission and could lend itself to processes of reformulation, gloss, and paraphrase. It soon incorporated within its fold traditional epics and religious narratives as well. As a result of this basic split, the latter gave rise to a rich variety of linguistic and regional versions, believed somehow to 'remember'/register the same 'true story'. The 'heard' Veda, however, remained singular in its perfect and immutable form, requiring direct representation in the only possible linguistic form of Vedic Sanskrit. It is this form, rather than the content, that very early became the concern of proper transmission within respective Brahmin families and, with the course of time, in Vedic recitation schools. In this sense, while the Veda means 'knowledge', what is to

81 For the history and concept of the juxtaposition of *Śruti* and *Smṛti*, see Pollock 2005.

82 Cf. remarks by S. Pollock: 'The controversy over how we are to explain the unavailability of the Vedic texts whose memory *smṛti* preserves is long and complex' [Pollock 2005: 51].

83 See Colas 2001: 320: '*La bonne prononciation du mantra prévaut souvent sur son sens.*'

be memorized in a Vedic recitation school comes down to an interiorized and bodily remembered appropriation (*prāpti*) of a full textual competence in the repertoire of one's family Veda.

To understand the Vedic case better, it is necessary to reflect on the uneasy problem of what actually was the scope, aim, and use of memorization in the traditional Vedic model and its interpretations. Incidentally, this very topic happened to form the object of heated argument among the exponents of the leading school of Vedic hermeneutics. While some authors insisted that the primary aim of memorization was the grasping of sense, others tended to see it in a quite different perspective. The discussion was summarized towards the middle of 14th century by Sāyaṇa, a polymath and author of extensive commentaries to major Vedic texts patronized by Vijayanagara empire. In his commentaries, Sāyaṇa insists on the need of penetrating and rescuing the 'extraordinarily deep' (*atigambhira*) meaning of the Vedic text and ridicules masters of recitation who remain content with the memorized text only.[84] At the same time, he advocates the necessity of a genuinely oral memorization of the Veda, disqualifying the use of written artefacts for that purpose. He also insists that the basic injunction to study the Veda, that binds every Brahmin, should be interpreted as the duty of artful memorization, not as the duty of comprehending the meaning. How should we understand that? What did Sāyaṇa have in his mind? For a commentator genuinely committed, as he must have been, to the aim of supporting the weakening Vedic tradition, there were two extremes to be avoided: a discontinuation of the Vedic sacrifices on the one hand, and fragmentary transmission of the Veda on the other. The former was risked by advocating the view that Vedic memorization aimed at understanding the text, rather than at its competent recitation required for performing rituals. The latter might result from the memorization process, limited exclusively to the recitation competence necessary for Vedic rituals to continue, since only the portions that find ritual application would be transmitted. Sāyaṇa took pains in giving a clear rationale for the need of memorization of the entire corpus of the Veda, as necessary for the whole of the Vedic heritage to be preserved. His views on where to locate (or relegate), and how to tap into, the meaning of the memorized Veda draw from the Mīmāṃsā school of hermeneutical interpretation. This topic, hower, remains, outside the shape of the present study.[85]

---

84 See VBhBhS: 49 and Galewicz 2010a: 232–236.

85 Sāyaṇa elaborates on this problem among else in his RSBhBh [see VBhBhS: 109]. For a discussion of this topic, see Galewicz 2010a: 245–256.

II.3. Performance and spectacle: the ritual Veda

Except for the Veda for transmission, consisting of particular Vedic texts to be stored and continually re-memorized in collective memories within the Vedic branches, there has always been a Veda for ritual. And for the Mīmāṃsā school of exegesis, this was the ultimate Veda. The idea of a ritual Veda or the textual body of the Veda understood as corresponding to that of the Vedic sacrificial ritual (*yajña*) can be seen as an operative concept in the Vedic commentaries by Sāyaṇa and probably derives from ChU 4.16.1. It has been understood as tripartite, like the old concept of the 'triple knowledge' (*trayī vidyā*).[86]

The concept of the ritual Veda, as articulated by the late medieval commentator, may be understood not as the sum total of its many texts but as the Veda consisting of the textual competence of the three main *śrauta* ritual functionaries. They represented on the ritual ground by the three Vedas, the *Ṛg-*, the *Yajur-* and the *Sāma*, coupled with the 'mental' competence of the fourth—that of the Brahman priest—in theory representing the *Atharvaveda* as the fourth Veda. This understanding was given the shape of a formal definition, in which the Veda stands as a sort of 'triple domain of verbal competence' (*adhvaryava*, *hautra* and *audgātra*) translates into the three domains of Vedic ritual competence of the three principal officiants in the *śrauta* ritual spectacle who are said to be 'perfecting the course of the sacrifice having the form of speech.'[87] The Veda remains here conspicuously threefold, with the *Atharvaveda* not included. Its textual body is made of performing competence of the professional ritualists and based exclusively on the ritually usuful and partially modified selections from the textual domains of the three Vedas. As such it does not cover the entire textual body of the Veda. Its transmission does not secure the reproduction of the textually complete Veda. This very risk seems to have

[86] In most instances, where the idea of the unity of the Veda surfaces in Sāyaṇa's own wording, or in quotations used by him, the formulation does not refer to the *Atharvaveda*, thus (seemingly) excluding it from the body of the Veda, which has one common meaning. On the other hand, we should remember that Sāyaṇa is also credited with a commentary on the AS with an introduction in which, among other things, he comments on the concept of the *trayī vidyā* [Galewicz 2010a: 147].

[87] *vāgrūpaṃ yajñamārgaṃ saṃskurvanti*, while the Brahman priest is said to be perfecting the course of the sacrifice having the form of thought: *manorūpaṃ yajñamārgaṃ saṃskaroti* [RSBh (M) I: 2, 13; VBhBhS: 13, 28–29]. See Galewicz 2010a: 178–179.

been of major concern for Sayāṇa and proved its detrimental effects on the integrity of the Veda over time.

II.4. Scribes and scripture: the handwritten Veda[88]

For a long time, it has been common to think of the corpus of Vedic literature as fashioned by or exemplifying primarily an oral culture of transmission. While several aspects of orality in the historical process of the preservation of the Vedic corpus have gained the attention of scholars, questions relating to the motives for copying of Vedic texts in writing have hardly ever been asked.[89] In spite of a strong ideology that distrusted writing as a means of the preservation of the Veda, Vedic texts used to be copied widely on birch bark, palm leaf, and paper from 11th: century onward. A good number of manuscripts survived, testifying to the copying of the Veda as an important cultural practice. It took a variety of regional inflections and went through transformations over time while featuring uneven and shifting distribution over geographical spaces and varying types of links to Brahmin groups, religious communities and structures of patronage.

One of the preserved Vedic manuscripts in the custody of the Bhandarkar Oriental Institute Library features a colophon formula that reads: *śivaprasanno 'stu lekhakapāṭhakayoḥ pārvatīyutaḥ* [MS No 381 of *Atharvaveda Saṃhitā*, DC Poona 1916: 382]–'let Śiva, united with Pārvatī, be favourable both to scribes and to reciters/readers.' A similar idea can be seen in the colophon to MS No 738 of *Aitareya Brāhmaṇa*, catalogued in DC Tanjore 1928: 501–*lekhakapāthakayoḥ śubham bhavatu*–and another version in a colophon to MS No 297 of *Śatapatha Brāhmaṇa*, catalogued in DC Poona 1916: 223–*leṣakapāṭhakayoḥ kalyāṇaṃ bhūyāt*–'Let prosperity be with scribes as well as with reciters.' Parallel instances can be traced in a number of colophons to manuscripts of various Vedic (and other Sanskrit works), and it probably belonged to a common stock of formulas used by professional copyists as well as those venturing into the world of

88 A part of the material covered by the present section appeared in an earlier version in Galewicz 2011b.

89 Most studies contented themselves with taking for granted the general reason for copying as rooted in the need for rescuing the supposedly dying out oral tradition, notwithstanding the rather self-evident fact that it would be extremely difficult to refer to some general pan-Indian situation in this respect at any given historical moment.

handwriting on a more casual basis. The formulation seems to specifically express a dichotomy of two worlds usually set apart and contrasted: that of oral performance or transmission and that of writing/printing. It has been noted that for the pre-modern Indian context in general, and the Vedic texts in particular, the relationship between the oral and the written rather tended to remain complementary rather than contrasting. A number of historical sources, in the form of letters or reports by European travellers, merchants, and colonial officers, refer to the practices of 'reading', 'studying', and 'reciting' the Veda by Brahmins from written 'books'. Only some acknowledge a diversification of these practices among various regional Brahmin groups. These important testimonies differ in value from case to case and generally show the need of presenting the observed phenomena in categories intelligible to European readers.[90] The nature of that relationship remains still, notwithstanding the rich scholarship, far from sufficiently articulated. And to understand the nature of this relationship seems to be one of the keys to correcting our often incomplete image of knowledge transmission in India. Several questions in need of answering include: what did it actually take to publish a work, did it mean the same thing for the world of *kāvya* and for that of *śāstra*? What did this entail in terms of reading the work aloud, on the one hand, and circulating copies, on the other? What sort of editorial practices could be resorted to? What were the modalities of handling the books as material objects by their copyists, correctors, owners, reciters, readers, commentators, and other users? What sort of social transactions were triggered by manuscript books, and what were their aims and functions? Additionally, we would like to know why did the manuscript culture of pre-modern India prove to be so strong in its defiance of the world of print and why did it leave traces in, for instance,

90 See, for instance, a note by Francis Buchanan, who toured Southern areas of Mysore State around 1805: 'The greater part of the Vaidika Brahmans here, although they employ much of their time in reading the Vedas, or eighteen Puranas, do not pretend to understand either. They get a copy of some portion of either of these books, and every day employ a certain number of hours in reading it aloud, which they perform with a most disagreeable cant, and twang through the nose. This, however, they consider as sufficiently meritorious to entitle them to the love of god, and the veneration of men; and a large proportion of their countrymen are of the same opinion' [Buchanan 1807 II: 65]. Cf. also a more informed note in Bhandarkar 1874: 138. The earliest outside evidence as to the complex relationship between memory and writing comes from Albirūnī, who mentions having heard, while in India (1017–1030 AD), of the Veda being committed to writing, by a Kashmiri Brahmin named Vasukra. See Müller 1891: 34. The earliest negative evidence to the tense relationship between the order of memory and writing comes from Mahābhārata VIII, which condemns those who would dare to make profit on writing the Veda down and circulate it.

the appearance, form, and shape of early printed books that linger on even today? We should keep in mind that, to copy a text, did not always necessarily involve writing it down, and to circulate a text did not necessarily mean distributing its hard material copies. On the other hand, preferring memory as safe medium for the purpose of transmission did not always preclude the use of written, or later printed, copies of the same text by members of the same textual community.

A special case within the much wider spectrum of Indian manuscript culture of the pre-modern era is furnished by the cultural context and ideology of the traditional transmission processof the Veda. Changing historical circumstances of this process tended to expose radical insistence on refraining from the use of writing, while, at the same time, making room for the practice of producing manuscripts of Vedic texts for purposes that remain not quite clear today. The so-called Vedic memorization—being a case apart in itself[91]—involved, in its model shape, the virtual cloning of the text, or reproducing its memory image, just as much as did its re-writing. The reasons and motivations for the two ways of cloning texts may have, however, differed considerably, as may the actual use or application of the two different sorts of copies. The much discussed case of the oral transmission of the Veda probably still needs a further revaluation from the perspective of the pragmatics of education. We need to learn more on the purpose that the process of transmission in a specific, historically and geographically situated brahmin community actually served. And whether any regionally observed transmission actually catered for something like a genuine need for general transmission, or rather answered more practical needs that have not been fully identified by modern scholarship. Is it not the case that all education systems prioritize perpetuating themselves as a system supporting the social status quo? From an individual or family perspective, the teaching of the Veda should satisfy religious needs, such as those formulated in later Vedic texts, like that of T.Ā. II, as shown some time ago by Ch. Malamoud.[92] From a community perspective, such teaching could fulfil other functions too.

Further exploring the complex relationship between the memory cloning and manuscript copying through studying seemingly minor details of material culture or instances of verbal formulas framing the texts proper,

---

91 As stressed, among else, by J. Bronkhorst [2002].

92 See Malamoud 1977.

can still reveal little known aspects of the once flourishing world of Indian manuscript culture(s). This world may be mostly gone today but its elements still happen to linger in a sort of afterlife within pockets of contemporary print culture as well as across the electronic media.[93] This relationship must have taken different shapes for different literary and manuscript cultures, taking distinct regional variations, and probably remained culturally and politically sensitive.

A preliminary review of motives for copying Vedic texts is proposed here as they are represented in colophons to a selection of extant manuscripts of Vedic texts. The review offers a tentative categorization and is purposefully informed by the contrastive nature of the ideology inscribed within the tradition of Vedic transmission that precluded, discouraged, or banned the copying of Vedic texts through writing. This instance exemplifies perhaps once again a dichotomy between theory and practice, or a powerful normative and a lived-in world, attesting to what Jan Heesterman once called 'the inner conflict of tradition' that—in his words—used to provide 'a driving force behind Indian civilization.'[94] How should we understand the *intentio auctoris* behind the words of a colophon to MS No 134 of *Ṛgvedasaṃhitā*, in DC Tanjore, 1928, I: 77, by a copyist, who, having completed a copy the 4th *Aṣṭaka* of the *Ṛksaṃhitā*, proceeds to quote the famous lines of the *Pāṇinīyaśikṣā*, listing a figure of a reciter reading from a written copy (*likhitapāṭhaka*) among the six 'worst' (*adhama*) instances of Vedic recitation to be avoided altogether?[95] The paradox of the two seemingly irreconcilable attitudes is more than obvious and indeed paradigmatic, when written into the same material object of a Vedic manuscript. From what follows in the same manuscript, we may infer that the copyist himself hints at the situation of reciting the Veda from a written manuscript without recuperating for its (inevitable) mistakes, as the most precipitous of the uses that might befall to his work. Again, taking refuge in a common stock formula, the copyist feels obliged to address, if not bequeath, his

93 What I have in mind is the gigantic national projects of digitization (continuing to be a fashionable expression) and otherwise rescuing the seemingly unlimited number of manuscripts, with the idea of reviving and stimulating national, regional, or religious feelings, and fuelling mass imagination with respect to once elite and now misleadingly open access to this presumed treasure-trove of Indian cultural heritage, often jealously guarded from foreign eyes.

94 Heesterman 1985.

95 *gītī śīghrī śiraḥkampī tathā likhitapāṭhakaḥ| anarthajño 'lpakaṇṭhaś ca ṣaḍ ete pāṭhakādhamāḥ* || PŚ 32 ||

manuscript to those learned ones who know how the written text before their eyes should be rectified/purified (*pariśodhanīya*) with what they remember as those deserving the qualification of 'the noble ones' (*ārya*).[96] The formula seems to exemplify the 'power of memorized tradition', as embodying an ideal never to be caught up with in writing as well as a symbiotic relationship between the two. In this respect, one should note that some colophons to Vedic manuscripts refer explicitly to the act of 'correcting', while indicating the name of the 'proofreader'. Mentioning the name seems to testify to no mean significance being given to the action of correcting the inevitable errors of (re-)copying.[97]

Now, it could be argued that Vedic education used to (and to some extent still does) do well for centuries, if not millennia, without resorting to writing and physical objects as vehicles (if a man's memory is not such a thing), even explicitly refraining from doing so. After all, it is the authority of *Pāṇinīyaśikṣā* that warns against resorting to writing, and that of *Mahābhārata*, which condemns to hell those who profess or make their living by writing down the Vedas (were there actually some who did so?).[98] Well into the era when writing was widely used for literary purposes in India, we still hear of authoritative condemnation of writing used with respect of the Veda.[99] Even a few centuries after Vasukra's bold enterprise (the 10th century?), it was Sāyaṇa, the imperial commentator, who strongly advocated against using written copies in studying the Veda as *svādhyāya*.[100] The same

96 *hastasya doṣān matibhramāśca nyūnātiriktaṃ likhitaṃ mayātra |*
tatsarvam āryaiḥ pariśodhanīyaṃ prāyeṇa muhyanti hi ye likhanti || 3 ||

97 See, for instance, MS No 223 of *Ṛgvedasaṃhitā* in DC Tanjore 1928 I: 223—… *sāriṅgadhara-sutamahādevena idam pustakam śodhitam* ('corrected by Mahādeva, son of Sāringadhara').

98 Aśvamedhika Parvan 106, 92: *vedavikrayiṇaś caiva vedānāṃ caiva dūṣakāḥ | vedānāṃ lekhakāś ca te vai nirayagāminaḥ* || ('Those who make money on the Vedas are wicked and sinful/those who commit the Vedas to writing are bound for hell.')

99 Kumārila: *Tantra-vārttika* I 3 [p. 86], p. 123.20 in K.V. Abhyankar's edition. It is Kumārila, who, in the 7th century, 'reasserted (in writing, of course) that learning the Veda from a concrete text-artefact—"by means contrary to reason, such as from written text"—could never achieve the efficacy of the Veda learned in the authorized way, "by repeating precisely what has been pronounced in the mouth of the guru"' [quoted in Pollock 2006: 83, fn. 23]. Even still in the late 14th century, albeit for different reasons, Sāyaṇa warned (in his *RSBhBh*) against using written artefacts in memorizing the Veda. Cf. Scharfe 2002: 8. fn. 2 referring also to Al-Bīrūnī, who 'reported in the eleventh century: "They do not allow the Veda to be transmitted to writing."' More on avoiding putting the Veda into writing, see Bronkhorst 2002: 800; Kane 1941: II, 348–349.

100 Müller: I, 14, l. 15: *kratuvidhayo hi viṣayāvabodham apekṣamāṇās tadavabodhe svādhyāyaṇ viniyuñjate | adhyayanavidhiś ca likhitapāṭhādi vyāvṛtyādhyayana-saṃskṛtatvaṇ svādhyāyasya gamayanti | ata ubhayopādānāt tatsiddhiḥ* || ('As the injunctions to perform sacrifice do

means, however, that the written versions must have been at hand and, no doubt, consulted when needed during other occasions and other types of textual lecture than that of *svādhyāya*.[101]

In his third lecture, from the series published in London in 1878, under the title 'On the Origin and Growth of Religion', F. Max Müller (whose first edition of the *Ṛgvedasamhitā* had been completed four years earlier in 1874 wrote: 'These men ... know the whole Rig-Veda by heart, just as their ancestors did, three or four thousand years ago; and though they have MSS., and though they now have a printed text [he probably refers to his own edition?], they do not learn their sacred lore from them.'[102] We may only guess whom Max Müller, who had never been to India, could actually have had in mind. In fact, such figures must have been imagined on information probably concerning a group of Brahmins from Maharashtra, since at least some of his informants had written letters to Müller from there. And referring to his own so-called critical edition of the *Ṛgvedasaṃhitā*, he may have remained chosen to remain silent of the early printed editions of Vedic texts that had started to appear in Mumbai in the second half of the 19th century, through the initiatives of local Indian printer-publishers, among whom Ganapat Kṛṣṇaji, Janardāna Mahādeva Gurjara and Nirṇaya Sāgar Press remain the best known today. Still earlier they were preceded by the pioneering work of Rev. John Stevenson who published an edition of the beginning part of the *Ṛgvedasaṃhitā* with the American Missionary Press in Bombay in 1837. A number of these early editions opted to appear in an oblong shape of the *pothī* book. One of the early printing initiatives continuing this line was, for instance, *Ṛgvedasaṃhitā*, published in Mumbai in *pothī* form by Janardāna Gurjara—a printer-editor in *Śaka* 1822, 1900 AD. This beautiful specimen of Devanagari print mentions earlier editions and other early printed Vedic texts, such as the *Ṛgvedamantrasaṃhitā* and *Āśvalāyanagṛhyapariśīṣṭa*, that must have begun to appear from 1867, i.e. seven years before the famous *editio princeps* of Müller was completed (1874),

indeed require the knowledge of their dominion [of application], for this knowledge they apply *svādhyāya*. And as the injunction to study excludes reading from written words, they understand "perfection of study" as the *svādhyāya*-study. So, in the appropriation of both of them lies the attainment of this [result of ritual perfection]'.)

101 Keeping this in mind may help to understand the function of printed copies of the *Ṛgvedasaṃhitā* in Malayalam script, kept by teachers in the *Brahmasvam Maṭham* in Trichur, otherwise boasting of a teaching system based exclusively on memory and oral transmission (observed by the present author during his field study in Kerala in 2008 and 2010).

102 Müller 1878: 156.

by Janardāna Mahādeva Gurjara, a printer-editor from Mumbai. Incidentally, one of them, *the Ṛgvedamantrasaṃhitā*,[103] in another early printed edition by Vasudeva Laxmana Pāṇśīkar, features a passage by the editor, that refers to the necessity of double checking the print with the memory of the savants, i.e. with the oral transmission that not only still continued, but was still held in undiminished respect by the editors of printed books, just as it had been by the copyists for the past few hundred years.

This presumably extraordinary focus on memorization in Indian textual practices, reiterated in early European reports from India, soon became one of the cultural clichés with which to represent Indian civilization as a whole. As a cliché, it more often than not passed without much attention, both to its concept as well as its actual practice. Succeeding scholarship usually related it to the debate on orality versus literacy in cultural development and quite often uncritically took for granted an evolutionary development from the former to the latter. The epitome of this reportedly marked feature of Indian civilization has often been believed to be the so-called Vedic oral tradition, or Vedic memorization.

It is most often agreed that, for around two millennia, until manuscripts of Vedic texts probably started slowly to appear at the beginning of the second millennium AD, the Vedas had been transmitted orally by way of a process that could perhaps be described as 'chain memory cloning'. Even afterwards, their transmission, although rationally systematized, must have remained[104] in principle oral among a number of Brahmin communities (albeit not always and not everywhere to the same degree), while interfering in many ways with the medieval manuscript culture in its regional varieties. As mentioned above, oral instruction and memorization, as opposed to reading, was still recommended by authoritative commentators well into the era of the wide use of manuscripts on Indian subcontinent. According to Sāyaṇa (middle 14th century), proper Vedic memorization is not feasible by 'reading the written.' And yet, an imagined opponent in one of Sāyaṇa's works argues that the 'visible effect' (*dṛṣṭaphala*) of memorizing the Vedic syllables could also be imagined for a reading of the written text in one's own way, that, at the time, would have been the custom—as he

103 It is to be seen even in its 2009 reprint by Anamela Prakaśan (see Prastāvanā). Cf. remarks by M. Winternitz: 'There are several MSS. and lithographed editions of a *Mantrasamhita* of the *Rigveda* (which does not, however, belong to the *Aśvalayana-Grhyasutra,* but is of a more modem character)' [Winternitz 1897: xi, fn. 4].

104 This point was rightly stressed several times, among others, by J. Bronkhorst [2002].

says—among followers of Ayurveda medicine. However enigmatic it may look, it remains clear that Vedic memorization was nothing like a memorization through habituation or learning by participation, but a memorization through deliberate effort and with specific aims to fulfil. The latter meant a rationalized system of instruction, training, refining, refreshing, and testing, through meticulously followed procedures. These technical procedures are most often believed by contemporary scholarship to have been designed and deployed in order to guarantee an immutable form for the Vedic texts transmitted. A religious sanction given to this system transformed elements of its structure into rituals of their own. In practical terms, however, different regional Brahmin communities developed their own distinct ways of handling their proper parts of Vedic heritage in a manner marking their own distinct identities.

From the beginning of the secon millenium at least, Vedic texts have been copied and recopied also well as in writing. The idea of a sudden deterioration of of the oral transmission in the times of Al Beruni might perhaps be defended for the northern part of the subcontinent. In general, a parallel stream of written transmission seems to have slowly constituted itself, in uneven distribution across the subcontinent. It culminated in the well-known 19th century printed editions by European scholars, based exclusively on manuscripts, and a number of far less known Indian editions, some of which claimed to have drawn from specific regional oral traditions too.[105] The two streams must have interfered with one another—conflicting, emulating, reflecting and merging in an mutually dependent regimes of textuality—to be measured each time against the varying background of the historically situated socio-economic context and the never ending status game on the part of communities claiming the exclusive right to handle the heritage of the Veda in the most proper way. The very nature of the actual ways these two regimes functioned side by side still awaits articulation and conceptualization. A contribution to this seems to be promised by studying the motives for copying the Vedic texts in writing. The picture of what could the reasons and motivations for ordering handwritten copies of the Veda in specific situations be is far from complete. The same pertains to the motifs for bringing the Veda in print to the newly emerging public sphere of the colonial India in specific, regionally situated historical moments.

---

105 See, for instance, introduction to PAṆŚĪKAR 1930.

It is not easy to find a measure for assessing a historically grounded attitude towards the practice of writing down the Vedas or cloning Vedic manuscripts against the normative exclusion of such gestures from the realm of accepted attitudes vis-à-vis the legacy of the Vedic scripture. One such possibility opens itself by turning attention to an important cultural complex represented by what seems to have constituted not only an ever-present topic in the *dharma* literature, but a veritable cultural institution of *vidyādāna*, or a 'ceremonial gift of knowledge'.

A paramount merit of the act of *vidyādāna* is thus summarized by *Devīpurāṇa*:[106]

> *vidyādānāt paraṃ dānaṃ na bhūtaṃ na bhaviṣyati |*
> *yena dattena cāpnoti śivam paramakāraṇam ||*
> 'There has never been and shall never be a higher gift than the gift of knowledge
> Through it [only] one attains the presence of Śiva—the primal cause of everything.'

This aphorism happens to have been singled out and juxtaposed with other similar ones in a most interesting work representing a rather underestimated genre of (*dharma*) *nibandhas*, or digests (on *dharma*). A few passages quoted in a *nibandha* called *Kṛtyakalpataru* (The Heavenly Tree of Meritorious Deeds), compiled by Lakṣmīdhara around the 12th or 13th centuries CE, deserve attention with respect to problems signalled above.[107] Chapter 5 of the *Kṛtyakalpataru*, true to its name (*Dānakāṇḍa*), happens to be devoted entirely to the *dharma* of gift-giving, or to what I would style as the 'art of gift giving.' Lakṣmīdhara specifies a hierarchy of gifts, among which a series of major gifts (*mahādānas*) is headed by the 'gift of land' (*bhūmidāna*). This position of land-giving as most revered among major gifts finds confirmation in the vast epigraphic evidence from the middle ages and pre-modern era. Curiously, with regard to the hierarchy that he himself admits—as noted by Rangasvami Aiyengar, editor of *Kṛtyakalpataru*—Lakṣmīdhara devotes a disproportionate scope of space in his treatise to 'the gift of knowledge' or *vidyādāna* (Section 12 in Book 5).[108] Significantly enough, Lakṣmīdhara opens the section on *vidyādāna* with a quotation from *Agnipurāṇa* reading [*Kṛtyakalpataru*, *Dānakāṇḍa*: 200]:

---

[106] *Devīpurāṇa*: 202. For a more systematic survey of the concept of *vidyādāna*, see Simini 2016.

[107] See Dash 2007: 83.

[108] Aiyengar 1941: 110.

sarveṣam eva dānanāṃ brahmadānaṃ viśiṣyate
kāryaṃ tu gomahīvāsastilakāñcanasarpiṣām[109]
'Among all gifts to be given the gift of *brahman* stands aloof conspicuously
Even among those [made of] of clarified butter, money, sesamum, land or cows.'

The term *brahmadāna* itself also appears in earlier authorities on *dharma* (YājSmr) and, according to Lakṣmīdhara, it should be understood as the 'gift of the Veda' (*vedadāna*).[110] Yet most of the citations offered by him concern *śāstras*, *purāṇas*, works on *dharma*, or, at best, *vedāṅgas* (to name something closer to the Veda proper). In the introduction to his edition of *Kṛtyakalpataru*, Aiyengar voiced doubts as to whether the 'present transcripts of *śāstric*, *purāṇic* and other works ... was applicable also to the Veda.'[111]

According to *Hayaśīrṣa*, a text of Pañcarātra tradition, among different *vidyās* recommended to be donated to a *brāhmaṇa* and praised as meritorious acts, there is no Veda proper. What we can see, however, are *vedāṅgas*, the auxiliary limbs of the Veda (sometimes taken as 'keys' to the knowledge of the Veda):

vedāṅgān lekhayitvā tu yo dadyāt brāhmaṇarṣabhe |
sa tu svargam avāpnoti yāvat āhṛtasaṃplavam ||[112]
'One who will have the *vedāṅgas* written down/copied
and donate them to an outstanding *brāhmaṇa*
shall indeed enjoy heaven until the final deluge sets in.'

The passage leaves no doubt that the *vidyā* to be given as a gift should be put into writing first. The absence of the Vedas among *vidyās*, to be offered in the highly meritorious act of *vidyādāna* stands out all the more conspicuously when we note that a hierarchy of *vidyās*, suggested by *Hayaśīrṣa*, introduces a good number of various areas of knowledge.[113] Naturally enough for the work in question, the most important branch of knowledge, or *vidyātama*,

---

109 The *śloka*, as pointed by Aiyengar, is to be seen also in *ManuSmṛ* IV.233.

110 KK *Dānakāṇḍa*: 202.

111 Aiyengar 1941: 110–111.

112 Quoted in Dash 2007: 83.

113 *yo dadyāl lekhayitvā tu pañcarātraṃ dvijottame* | *sa vidyādānapuṇyena vāsudeve layaṃ vrajet* || *purāṇaṃ lekhayitvā tu ye dadyāt brāhmaṇe naraḥ* | *sa vidyādānapuṇyena vāsudeve layaṃ vrajet* || *rāmāyaṇaṃ bhārataṃ ca yo dadyāt dvijapuṅgave* | *sa vidyādānajaṃ puṇyaṃ prāpya viṣṇau pralīyate* || *yo dharmasaṃhitāṃ dadyāt lekhayitvā dvijottame* | *sa vidyādānajaṃ puṇyaṃ samagraṃ prāpanuyān naraḥ* || *vedāṅgān lekhayitvā tu yo dadyāt brāhmaṇarṣabhe* | *sa tu svargam avāpnoti yāvad āhṛtasaṃplavam* || [quoted after Dash 2007: 83].

proves to be that offered by the Pañcarātra. Omitting the Veda altogether may seem, at first, somewhat strange in the light of a standard list of 'knowledge disciplines' (*vidyāsthānas*), repeated throughout medieval *dharma* texts in sets of 14 (or 18) *vidyās*, among which Vedas are usually enumerated first.[114]

A number of medieval authors dealing with *dāna* include references to *vedadāna*—this is the case, for instance, of a passage quoted by Lakṣmīdhara from *Devīpurāṇa* [*Dānakāṇḍa*: 209]:

> *vedavidyāṃ naro datvā svargo kalpatrayaṃ vaset*
> 'a man who makes a gift of knowledge of the Veda
> will dwell in heaven for three eons.'

The passage, however, fails to specify whether it is the gift of a written copy of a Vedic text or rather a gift of teaching the message of the Veda, a sort of *upadeśa* on the meaning and purpose of the Veda to be transmitted by a teacher to a selected pupil.[115] The same authority goes as far as enumerating the entire traditional set of fourteen *vidyās* as objects of meritorious gift-giving. Among them, the four Vedas, along with their six *aṅgas*, are specifically mentioned [*Dānakāṇḍa*: 207], but, again, no direct hint at producing written copies of any of the Vedic texts proper can be seen. After all, is it not that the most meritorious act of donating knowledge (*vidyādāna*)—as admitted by the traditional authorities—may be achieved in three distinct ways: as the gift of a book, as the gift of an image of the Goddess of Learning to be worshipped, or, as the gift of teaching? Such is the opinion of Nīlakaṇṭha in his *Dānamayūkha*:

> *evaṃ trividham vidyādānam pustakadānaṃ pratimādānaṃ adhyāpanaṃ ceti*[116]
> 'Threefold may be the gift of knowledge: gift of book, gift of image, and teaching.'

All in all, an act of ceremonial gift giving of knowledge might become—as indeed is shown by epigraphic evidence—a gesture of power infused with cultural, religious, and political meaning.

---

114 Cf. *Yajñavālkyasmṛti* 1.3: *purāṇanyāyamīmāṃsādharmaśāstrāṅgamiśritāṃ | vedān sthānāni vidyānāṃ dharmasya ca caturdaśa ||*. The same list also happened to have been elaborated on by Sāyaṇa [see Galewicz 2010a: 227].

115 Cf. Sāyaṇa's *Bhūmika* to his *Ṛgvedasaṃhitābhāṣya*, in its closing part, referring to the gift of *vedavīdyā* by a teacher to a student [see Galewicz 2010a: 265, 271].

116 As quoted in Dash 2007: 84.

One of the modern examples of the powerful concept of *vedadāna* at work can be indicated in the initiative of an influential and ambitious Vaidika of Maharashtra, who, in 1986 AD, decided to circulate printed copies of a compendium called *Ṛvedadaśagrantha* and, through this act, initiated on a regional scale something comparable to a new canon formation for the *Ṛgveda*. The enterprise proved to be of no mean consequence since field study shows that most of the *veda pāṭhaśālās* of western and central Maharashtra, and some transregionally, soon adopted this textbook specifically for daily use, as the most authoritative one for basic Vedic study. At the same time, it is also significant that this very compendium remains little known or studied in reality. A look into the introductory and closing formulas of the publication leaves little doubt that the book was conceived as a gift of knowledge, although the term *vidyādāna* does not appear there.[117]

Taking into consideration this conspicuous absence of the Veda among *vidyās* to be donated as *vidyādana*, one should, however, differentiate between various purposes for preparing written copies of the Veda. There is little doubt that it must have been a different thing to memorize the Veda as a *brahmacārin* and to teach it as a teacher, and yet more different to study it along with a commentary, without mentioning the practical implementation of Vedic mantras within a ritual context, be it *śrauta* or *gṛhya* or otherwise. Each situation entailed contact with a different Veda of sorts. Thus, written copies, potentially addressing these different situations, should not necessarily look the same and be the outcome of one and the same process. We may probably expect motives for copying the Veda to be functionally different in matching different cultural contexts.[118]

If, and this is on evidence, manuscripts of the Veda began to be widely produced (and circulated?) what could be pointed to as motives or reasons for this? The highly valued cultural gesture of the gift of knowledge, understood as a religiously meritorious and socially elevating act, could probably be one such important opportunity for distributing written copies. The fear that the precious Veda could be lost, so emphasized in modern scholarship, may have also been another reason, but there does not seem to be much

117 For more on the case and concept of *Ṛgvedadaśagrantha*, see Galewicz 2012, 2014.

118 A case apart and telling example of such circumstances can be seen in the copying of the (complete) Veda, commissioned around 1783 in Jaipur by Col. Polier, who subsequently donated the set of copied Vedic texts to the British Museum. See Bendall 1902; Polier 1809, and Section IV.2 below.

in the indigenous writing to testify to this, even though it is tempting to admit and take for granted that the history of putting the Veda into writing proceeded along rational lines on the subcontinent scale. There is, of course, the testimony of Al-Beruni, but, important though it is, this cannot substitute for evidence from within the tradition. We need to look for traces of motives for preparing written copies of the Veda within the extant copies themselves. After all, one can hardly imagine copying a valuable work of traditional knowledge for no purpose at all.

To begin with, I am inclined to imagine that the act of copying must have been aimed at either self-study (personal or in family), a *vidyādāna*, or at producing a copy by a specific order. Another important motive to be taken into consideration is 'data migration'—recopying decaying manuscripts in a collection, whether those belonging to a family, school, temple, or monastery. Furthermore, the act of copying should probably be perceived as a complex one, involving a patron commanding the copy and acting either as a donor or as an owner, a copyist and a recipient and, in the end, a user. The recipient did not have to be a person—it could be an institution such as a temple or a monastery (*maṭha*). Although many of these aspects can be said to be true for the manuscript culture of India in general, other agents and acts involved in the process (correctors, *svarakaras*—see below), should be identified as specific to the culture of Vedic manuscripts. A case apart must be that of dictating a passage, part of a Vedic text, from memory, in order for it to be written down by a professional scribe or be written down from memory by a Brahmin, who, for some reason, would decide to do it with his own hand.[119]

The reproduction, copying, and cloning of traditional texts may take various forms and practices, and fulfil different social functions or individual needs. It seems that an anthropology of the cultural gesture of copying/cloning/disseminating the material substance of the Veda should probably be imagined as different thing from an anthropology of gift-giving, even if the gift is that of 'the knowledge of the Veda.'

---

119 A most interesting aspect of this hypothetical culture of Vedic manuscripts is circulation. In what sense and in what circumstances could a production of a written copy of a Vedic text in an early-modern regional context of the Indian Subcontinent be imagined as an act of 'publication'? For a general idea of contemporary methodological problems of approaching similar phenomena, see, for instance, Darnton 2005; Chartier 2003, 2004. An excellent introduction to the problems of understanding medieval manuscript cultures is Dagenais 1994. For the reasons indicated above, Vedic manuscript culture needs a specific approach and specific questions in relation to the parallel oral cultures of transmission and use.

A casual survey of descriptive catalogues shows that most extant manuscripts that can be used for evaluating possible purposes for copying the Veda in writing (cloning the Veda in a written form instead of doing it in the traditional way) are not very old, so the image that comes to mind, out of several selected instances, may hold some validity for the early modern and colonial era circa 1650–1850 AD. This cursory review shall, naturally, be limited to selected examples, showing strong cases that may suggest some tendencies. A more systematic survey is needed to actually draw more valid conclusions.

While most (though not all) patrons and actual copyists of Vedic manuscripts remain humbly anonymous, the instance of a manuscript of *Ṛgvedasaṃhitā*, listed as No 33 in the Tanjore Sarasvatī Mahal Library [DC Tanjore 1928 I: 22], containing RS I.1.1–8.26 and dating from 1787 AD, offers lavish details concerning the time of the preparation of the manuscript as well as the persons and responsibilities involved. After details concerning the astrological moment selected for the completion of the copy, the (sub-) colophon to MS No 33 provides the elaborate name of the patron and the owner of the book as well as the name of the copyist, being, in this case, the son of the former.[120] While elaborate statements recording the astrological time of completing a manuscript are far from rare, it is by no means usual that a detailed description of a probably carefully selected and auspicious astrological moment is supplied to locate in time a related but distinct act, indicated by the past participle *svaritam*.[121] This should probably be understood as the act of supplying the already prepared copy with proper accents (*svaras*).[122] I am tempted to consider it as a cultural gesture of infusing the potential text (i.e. the copy without *svaras*) with life—such a contention might probably account for its having been recorded by the scribe (or his patron) as an act at least as important as that of preparing a copy of the

---

120 *plavaṅgasaṃvatsare māghamāse śuklapakṣe caturdaśyāṃsaumyavāsare prathamāṣṭake aṣṭamo 'dhyāyaḥ | ṛgvedasaṃhitāyāṃ aṣṭamo 'dhyāyaḥ || paurāṇikopanāmarākṣasabhuvanakara-vāsudevadīkṣitātmaja jīvarāmadīkṣitatanayagovindabhaṭṭasūnukamalākarabhaṭṭasutena likhitam idaṃ pustakaṃ kamalaākarabhaṭṭasya | plavaṅgasaṃvatsare māghamāse kṛṣṇapakṣe pratipattithau bhṛguvāsare kamalākarabhaṭṭasya putreṇa svaritaṃ* || [DC Tanjore: 22]. The owner of the MS indicated in the colophon is Kamalākara Bhaṭṭa to whose credit a whole range of manuscripts had been prepared, as evidenced by extant MSS in the collections of Saraswatī Mahāl Library.

121 The presiding deity of the *tithi* called *pratipad*—the first lunar day of the waning moon—is said to be either Agni or Brahma and is considered good for all types of auspicious and religious ceremonies.

122 I thank Saraju Rath for suggestions in that matter.

main body of the text proper. Perhaps an amplified interpretation of this case could also be possible through extension: *svarita* as the effect of the act of making the written copy fit to resound with Vedic *svaras*. It is evident that, in order to mark the already copied body of the inscribed text formed of strings of characters standing for syllables (*akṣaras*) with proper Vedic *svaras*, the person who was supposed to execute it had to recite the text prior to the marking or had to have it recited by somebody else in his presence. The same also seems to amount to the fact that the copy was either done from another copy that was unaccented, or it was a dictated copy. It might also be considered appropriate or necessary to supply/check *svaras* anew with a new copy, in order to check the correctness of the Vedic text in question, i.e. its compliance with the family's oral memory.[123] The detailed information concerning the auspicious time of marking the *svaras* allows for a probably telling remark: the moment of supplying the *svaras* is different from the date given in the same colophon as that of the completion of the copy. It seems to indicate an independent role ascribed to the act of supplying correct *svaras* to the copied Vedic text. A simple calculation allows us to infer that the act of marking the *svaras* took place two days after finishing the copy of the basic, unaccented text. This sort of power control and decisive check, executed by the memory over the writing, seems to provide us with a due perspective to look at the manner in which the two were interrelated. Such an interplay seems appropriate for the situation of the copying of an accented Vedic text, which, in order to sound correct, had to be performed with all the required accents and articulation If not, the two distinct sets of detailed time qualifications, supplied by the scribe of the MS, would not make much sense. In the case of the above mentioned MS, the person indicated in the colophon, as the one who was to supply the *svaras* ('making the manuscript fit to sound'), happens to be the same person who prepared the unaccented copy two days earlier. This might indicate, with additional strength, that the two acts were considered not only technically separate, but also ritually distinct.[124] Another MS of the

---

[123] A better understanding of this mutual interplay between the written and the oral (memorized) seems crucial for our contemporary attempts at making sense of manuscript cultures. This should probably refer to the materiality of specific regional social practices connected to the production and use of manuscripts.

[124] There is a considerable amount of literature regulating the practices of copying manuscripts carrying scriptural traditions, conceived as a ritualized process, attested from the early second millennium across several distinct regional and religious traditions. For a survey, see Simini 2016.

Ṛgvedasaṃhitā in the same group, said to have been owned by the same patron, no doubt differentiates between the person of the scribe and that of the accent-maker (MS No 66 in DC TANJORE 1928 I: 40, dated to 1770 AD and containing RS II.1.1–8.27). This is also true for MS No 101 [DC TANJORE 1928 I: 80], containing RS III.1.1–8.26, copied by Moravyāsa, son of Nirajivyāsa but accented (*svarita*) by the son of Kamalākarabhaṭṭa (perhaps the same as the scribe and the *svara-kāra* of the MS referred to above). There is also a visible graphic mark of difference: accents are marked in red ink (second half of 18th century). Yet another instance of a manuscript giving a separate name for an accent maker, or *svara-kāra*, is MS No 419 in DC TANJORE 1928 I: 255 containing *Ṛgveda-padapāṭha* III.[125] A curiosity, catalogued in the 1887 catalogue of Sanskrit Manuscripts in the library of India Office—the bulky copy of the *Ṛgveda saṃhitā* in two volumes, containing four *aṣṭakas* each—features only fragmentary accentuation distributed unevenly over the initial parts of the first *aṣṭaka*, the rest being left unaccented.[126] Out of twenty six complete or partial handwritten copies of the *Ṛgveda* registered in the same catalogue, twelve bear no accent, thirteen are accented throughout, and one accented fragmentarily.[127]

Coming back to the DC TANJORE MS No 33, one cannot fail to note formulas also to be found in manuscripts of other areas of Sanskrit literary heritage, not necessarily Vedic, thus testifying to the common context of Indic manuscript cultures. A slightly specific shade of meaning in a Vedic textual context is the same colophon featuring a set of four common stock *ślokas*, used in a function close to a propitiatory formula neutralizing undesired effects of possible errors that might have crept in during the copying.[128] They no doubt establish an important connecting link between the oral and the written. The two needed each other in a complementary way: the wise ones (*budhāḥ*), who already are familiar with (the memory image of) the text will forgive any of the listed scribal errors when they spot them (p. 1):

---

125 Other instances of colophons registering the acts of supplying the MS with *svaras*: MSS No 454 and 455, *Ṛgveda Padapāṭha*, DC TANJORE 1928 I: 277; MS No 463, *Ṛgveda Padapāṭha*, DC TANJORE 1928 I: 283; MS No 626, *Ṛgveda Saṃhitā Bhāṣya*, DC TANJORE 1928 I: 402.

126 The complete copy of the *Ṛgvedasaṃhitā* in two volumes, catalogued under Nos 1690–91, features only the following parts accented: Aṣṭaka I. 1–5, and I.6.1–3, and parts of Ādhyāya 7 and 8. See C INDIA OFFICE 1887: 1.

127 See C INDIA OFFICE 1887: 1–3.

128 It was F. Max Müller, who had already noted a group of manuscripts with colophons, including similar formulations and remarked rather straightforwardly that '...the writers of manuscripts ... complain frequently of the hardships and difficulties of their work' [I: xii, fn. 5].

bindudurlipivisargavīthikāśṛṅgapaṅktipadabhedadūṣaṇam |
hastavegajamabuddhipūrvakaṃ kṣantum arhatha samīkṣya vai budhāḥ || 1 ||

and the noble ones (*ārya*) will know how to correct (*pariśudh*) the text if they find it corrupted; that is, by not complying to the image, they must keep in their memory (p. 3):

hastasya doṣān mativibhramād vā nyūnātiriktaṃ likhitaṃ mayātra |
tatsarvam āryaiḥ pariśodhanīyaṃ prāyeṇa muhyanti hi ye likhanti || 3 ||
'Whatever errors of shortage or surplus I happened to make due to failures of hand or unstable mind all that shall be rectified by the noble ones. So, let the scribes be forgiven.'

This motif, to be seen in many other colophons, remains highly suggestive of the type of relationship between the oral and the written.[129] At the same time, the scribe does not fail to secure his work with an imprecation against those who would mistreat the book produced with so much labour (p. 2). It also seems to have functioned as stock, formulaic expression, considered proper for the act closing or sealing the production of a manuscript copy:

pustakaṃ likhitaṃ yatnair anekair yan mayā hare |
hartum icchati yaḥ pāpī tasya vaṃśakṣayo bhavet || 2 ||

The verse reminds one of formulas closing royal *praśasti* inscriptions, especially land grants, as well as contemporary legal statements threatening trespassers, not necessarily with fines or imprisonment, but with dire consequences in the afterlife.

The sub-colophon to MS No. 33 concludes with a homage to a specific deity and by the very act may suggest not only a religious affiliation of the copyist or the patron (Śrīvidyā tradition?), but also a religious aspect of the very act of preparing a copy of the Veda. Here, the deity to be honoured with the *hastalikhita* Veda is the famous goddess Mahālakṣmī of Kolhapur and her divine consort: *śrī kolhāpuramahālakṣmyai namaḥ* || *sāmbasadāśivāya namaḥ* ||.

129 A simple question inevitably imposes itself: why should the wise ever need to read the manuscript if they know its contents? Is there a proofreading what is meant here, or a written copy needed as an *aide-memoire* only? The various types of relationship between the oral and the written remain to be studied and articulated.

A group of manuscripts deposited in the Tanjore Saravatī Mahāl library feature devotional *ślokas* matching pictorial decorations of mostly *pauraṇika*-type folk Hindu legends, suggesting a valuable work of art or devotional gift, rather than a copy for practical reasons [for instance MSS No 34–41, DC Tanjore 1928 I: 22–27]. The pictorial representations bear no apparent relationship to the Vedic text they adorn. A composite nature of such an artefact must have required a team of artisans to work for a final effect and a patron and perhaps a middle man to arrange for separate elements to be made. Furthermore, the non-Vedic *ślokas* attached could be added by someone other than a copyist writing down the text proper (in this respect very short—one *adhyāya* only—but meant as a series with manuscripts containing succeeding *adhyāyas*: after the colophon a few words from the next *adhyāya* are added by the copyist).

An interesting instance of a formula hinting at the context and purpose of copying can be seen in the colophon of MS No 101 of *Ṛgveda Saṃhitā* [DC Tanjore 1928: 80]:

> *idaṃ pustakaṃ nīrājivyāsaputramoravyāsena likhitaṃ svārthaṃ parārthaṃ ca* |
> *rākṣasabhuvanakaropanāmakamalākarabhaṭṭasya sutena svaritaṃ* ||

The patron of this manuscript happens to be the same as in the case referred to above. Therefore, the mention of the *svara*-marking/voicing (*svaritam*) of the text, of the copy by his own son, sounds familiar. The two accusatives of the first half of the stanza seem to suggest the purpose of copying to be a complex one, made up of some unspecified personal benefit (*svārtham*) to fulfil as well as a benefit of others (*parārtham*).

It should be noted that a certain, probably quite substantial, number of copies of major Vedic texts survived thanks to commentaries that included the commented text, which thus happened to have been copied alongside. Copying and donating *bhāṣyas* no doubt counted the much appraised *vidyādāna*, with no traditional reluctance towards writing down the Veda itself.

A colophon to a manuscript of a *bhāṣya* commentary on *Taittirīya Saṃhitā* [MS No 110 in DC Madras 1904 I.2: 158] seems to indicate that it might have been considered an immediate religious custom to copy a Vedic *bhāṣya*, otherwise perceived probably as *vedavidyā*: knowledge of the Veda.[130]

130 The colophon reads: ... *rāmācaryasya putreṇa śrinivāsākhyasūnunā vidyāraṇyasya bhāṣyasya likhitaṃ kṛṣṇatuṣṭaye* ('... it has been copied/written by the son of Rāmācarya Śrinivāsa in order to satisfy *Kṛṣṇa*').

As such, it must have been appreciated as a gesture of the proliferation of *śāstras*, manuscript copies of the latter most often being praised as objects of *vidyādāna*. Here, no hint of a gift is directly expressed. One cannot imagine, however, the copying of a valuable work of traditional knowledge for no purpose at all.

samāptaśca dvitīyaḥ prapāthakaḥ || rāmācāryasya pu(pau)treṇa śrīnivāsākhyas-ūnunā | vidyāranyasya bhāṣyasya likhitaṃ kṛṣṇatuṣṭaye || samapto 'ayam kāṇḍaḥ ||

Yet, we cannot be sure whether, and to what extent, if at all, the formula containing the words '[this section of] the *bhāṣya* [credited to the sage] Vidyāraṇya has been written to the satisfaction of Kṛṣṇa' expresses a direct declaration of a religiously meritorious act of producing a written copy of a Vedic *bhāṣya* or any text deemed to be worthy of respect on religious grounds.

A cursory survey of colophons, in search for such and the like formulations brings, however, more differentiated results that: For the reason of clarity they might be subsumed under the following tentative headers:

A. The general well-being of the world around (probably imagined as stimulated by the beneficial effect of the Vedic recitation performed with the help of the written copy).

sūpāṭhena paropakārārthe likhitam
'...copied for the benefit of others through proper recitation' [*Atharvaveda-jaṭāpāṭha*, MS No 383, DC Poona 1916 I: 220, dated: Śake 1593]

śubham astu sarvajagatām
'Let all be prosperous' [*Ṛgvedasaṃhitābhāṣya*, MS No 640, DC Tanjore 1928 I: 416]

Śrī anahīlapurapattane ... śrī anantasuta vrajabhūṣaṇena ... likhāpitam idam paropakārāya
'copied for the benefit of others upon order by Vrajabhuṣaṇa, son of Śrī Ananta in the city of Anahilapura' [*Atharvavedasaṃhitā*, MS No 365, DC Poona 1916 I: 268, dated: Samvat 1753]

śrī | śubham astu | kalyāṇam astu [*Atharvaveda Saṃhitā*, MS No 379, DC Poona 1916 I: 278]

śubham astu | iti maṅgalam bhavati; śivaprasanno 'stu lekhakapāṭhakayoḥ pārvatīyutaḥ | śubhaṃ |
'let the benevolence of *Śiva*, united with *Pārvatī*, be both with copyists and reciters/readers' [*Atharvaveda Padapāṭha*, MS No 381, DC Poona 1916 I: 279]

iti navamaṃ khāṇḍaṃ samāptam ... lekhakapāṭhakayoḥ śubham || kalyāṇam astu || śrīgaṇeśāya namaḥ || [*Atharvavedapadapāṭha*, MS No 383, DC Poona 1916 I: 280, dated Saṃvat 1669]

The next example shows similar closing formulas of benediction, supplemented with a wish for 'freedom from diseases' (*ārogyam*):

śrīr | kalyāṇam astu | ārogyam śubham bhavatu | lekhakapāthakayoḥ śubham bhavatu |
'Let there be prosperity! Let there be freedom from diseases! Let there be good fortune for copyists and reciters alike!' [*Atharvavedabrāhmaṇa*, MS No 825, DC Tanjore 1928 II: 561].

This, and similar formulations, suggest the copy was prepared in order to be actually recited with/from (not only to please a deity) and symbolically expresses the interdependence of the written and the oral, in the case of the Veda, which requires a trained reciter, irrespective as to whether he has or has not a written copy at his disposal.

B. The fulfilment of a religious aim/gaining religious merit.

B.1. Pleasing a deity with the act of completing a copy of a Vedic text.

idaṃ pustakaṃ bhānūpanāmakagaṃgādharaśarmaṇo yajamānasya sāhāyyena peṇḍase ityupanāmnā śrivardhanagrāmasyasarvatomukha[so]*mayājinā 'nantaśarmaṇā kāśyāṃ saṃpāditaṃ | tena śrīvedapuruṣarūpī parameśvaraḥ prīyatām*
'this book was produced in Kāśi with the help of the patron, Yajamāna Bhānu Gaṅgādhara Śarman ... by Sarvatomukha Somayājī Anantaśarma Peṇḍase.[131] Let the Supreme Lord, in the form of *Śrī Vedapuruṣa*, be pleased with it' [*Ṛksaṃhitābhāṣya*, MS No 607, DC Tanjore 1928 I: 383]

[131] One of the prominent lineages of *Maharashtra brāhmaṇas* of the *Deśastha* group.

> *bhānūpanāmakagaṃgādharaśarmaṇo yajamānasya sāhāyyenedaṃ pustakaṃ peṇḍase ityupanamnā 'nantadīkṣitaṃta(tena) sarvatomukhayājinā saṃpāditaṃ tena śrīvedarūpayajñanārāyaṇaḥ prīyatām ...*
> 'With the help of the patronage of Bhānu ... this book was produced in Kāśi by Anantadīkṣita Sarvatomukhayājin Peṇḍase. Let Lord Yājñanārāyaṇa, in the shape of the Veda, be pleased with it' [*Ṛksaṃhitābhāṣya*, MS No 609, DC Tanjore 1928 I: 385]

This MS, as the one above, belongs to a group of manuscripts with similar—but not identical—colophons. Here, the deity seems to be linked to the sphere of activity of the Vedic sacrifice patron (*yājamana*), who, apparently, gave his patronage to the preparation of the copy.

> *...tena śrī vedapurāṇapuruṣaḥ prīyatām*
> '...Let Lord Vedapurāṇapuruṣa be pleased with it' [*Ṛksaṃhitābhāṣya*, MS No 617, DC Tanjore 1928 I: 393]

A manuscript from the same group as the two above and with a similar colophon. The reason why Vedapurāṇapuruṣa is indicated as the deity to be pleased here, instead of those deities mentioned in the two other manuscripts is not clear—perhaps it had something to do with a different patron?

> *śrīparadevatāprītyai* [*Ṛgveda-padapāṭha*, MS No 437, DC Tanjore 1928 I: 266]

B.2. Paying honour to a deity / satisfying a deity / securing the benevolence of a deity.
Some manuscripts feature the names of deities specific to regions, places, or households.

> *iti dvitīyāṣṭake aṣṭamo 'dhyāyaḥ | asmatkuladaivatāmbārpaṇam astu || idaṃ pustakaṃ nirānivyāsaputramoravyāsena likhitam* | [*Ṛgveda Saṃhitā*, MS No 66, DC Tanjore I: 40, dated 1770 AD]

> *kṛṣṇatuṣṭaye* [MS No 110, DC MADRAS 1904 I.2: 158 (already mentioned above)]

> *śridattatreyārpaṇam astu*
> 'Let it be an offering to Dattatreya' [MS No 461, DC Tanjore 1928 I: 418]

vedapuruṣāyārpaṇam astu
Let it [the copy] be an offering to Vedapuruṣa.' [*Ṛksaṃhitābhāṣya*, MS No 14, DC POONA 1916 I:15]

nṛsiṅhāya namaḥ | *vakratuṇḍāya namaḥ* | [*Aitareyabrāhmaṇa*, MS No 70, DC POONA 1916 I: 61]

śrīkedareśvara prasanno 'stu [*Ṛksaṃhitābhāṣya*, MS No 610, DC TANJORE 1928 I: 386]

dattatreyārpaṇam astu [*Ṛksaṃhitābhāṣya*, MS No 635, DC TANJORE 1928 I: 412]

śrīkedareśvaraḥ samarthaḥ
'[Let] Lord Kedara prosper!' [*Ṛksaṃhitābhāṣya*, MS No 636, DC TANJORE I: 413]

śrīśivacaraṇāravindabhramara sadā tava śubham astu [*Ṛksaṃhitabhāṣya*, MS No 642, DC TANJORE 1928 I: 419]

B.3. Indicating the presence of a deity in the process of copying (?).
The evidence of a number of Vedic manuscripts seems to shed light on the practice of securing divine assistance in the difficult task of the faithful reproduction of a Vedic text in a written manuscript. This appears to be the message in the following colophon of a manuscript of *Ṛgvedasaṃhitā*, from Tanjore Sarasvati Mahal Library, although it may also refer to the spatial circumstances of copying, either in the house of a Brahmin named after a deity or a deity itself:

śaṅkaranārāyaṇasannidhau śaṅkaramahādevagṛhe ... kamalākarabhaṭṭasūnurāmeṇa likhiteyaṃ ...
'This was written by Rāma, son of Kamalākara Bhaṭṭa, in the presence of Śaṇkarnārāyaṇa, in the temple of Śaṇkaramahādeva' [*Ṛksaṃhitā* V.1.1–8.36, MS No 165, DC TANJORE 1928: 96]

A similar message, here indicating the vicinity of the temple of Lord Narasiṃha, is given in the following colophon:

dharmapurinarasiṃhakṣetrasannidhau ātmārtham ... likhitam
'written in the vicinity of the temple of Dharmapurinarasiṃha for one's own purpose...' [*Ṛgveda-padapātha*, MS No 415, DC TANJORE 1928 I: 253, dated 1663 AD]

> *kedareśvarasannidhauayyārappasvaminaḥ anumatena mayā likhitam*
> 'copied by me, with the permission (*anumatena*) of Lord Ayyārappa in the vicinity/presence of Lord Kedara' [*Ṛksaṃhitābhāṣya*, MS No 647, DC TANJORE 1928 I: 424]

B.4. A separate group of Vedic manuscripts happens to be associated with actual contemporaneous religious circumstances through extra-textual graphics; for instance, representations of Śiva, occasionally supplemented with *dhyānaślokas* of non-Vedic origin, supply the link between the Vedic text and the Hindu/(here) Śaiva reality: see, for instance a group of RS MSS No 166–175, with pictorial representations of Śiva, registered in DC TANJORE 1928 I: 96–101.

C. Manuscripts produced under royal patronage.

C.1. Some copyists (or their clients) apparently deemed it important to indicate a royal location for the act of copying of their Vedic manuscript. See, for instance, MS No 311 or *Ṛgveda Saṃhitā*, DC TANJORE 1928 I: 178, referring to the 'palace' (*rājagṛha*) and 'court of justice' (*dharmasābha*) as the location where the preparation of the copy took place. Thus, the manuscript produced had the double sanction of the proximity of the king and the vicinity of Lord Kṛṣṇa (Venugopala):

> *rājagṛhe dharmasābhāyāṃ veṇugopalasaṃnidhau likhitam idam pustakam*
> 'This book was written in the Court of Justice, in the presence of [deity named] Venugopala...'

The manuscript was copied in the city of Taṅjapaṭṭana (Tanjavur?) and contains the whole of *aṣṭaka* 8. It is dated to 1819 AD.

> *rājarājasya candicandāvarendrasya dharmarājasya ayyārūpasvaminaḥ anumatenedaṃ pustakaṃ jayarāmabhaṭṭena likhitaṃ kāśyāṃ kedā(re)śvaraghaṭṭe ... śrīkedareśvara prasanno 'stu*
> 'This book was written with the consent of Rājarāja Candicandāvarendra Dharmarāja Ayyarūpasvamin by Jayarāma Bhaṭṭa in Kāśi, on the Kedareśvara Ghat. May Lord of Kedāra be of benevolent mind' [MS No 610 in DC TANJORE 1928 I: 387, dated 1829 AD]

The following example of a colophon, from the same group of manuscripts, amounts to an instance of a veritable *praśasti* to the patron king:

śrīrājarājendracandicandāvarendrabiḍaujaojasatkarmadharmapālakaduṣṭabidāraka śatrubhayakāraka | śrīśivacaraṇāravindabhramara sadā tava śubham astu [*Ṛksaṃhitābhāṣya*, MS No 642, DC Tanjore 1928 I: 419]

śrīrājarājendrasya candi candāvarendrasya mahārājasya vedabhāṣyasyedaṃ pustakaṃ kāśyāṃ kedareśvarasannidhau ayyārapp(rūpa)svāminaḥ anumatena mayā jayarāma-bhaṭṭena likhitaṃ
'This book of the *vedabhāṣya* of Śrī Rājendra Candicandavarendra has been copied in Kāśi in the presence of Lord Kedāra, with permission of Ayyārūpasvāmin, by me, Jayarāma Bhaṭṭa' [*Ṛksaṃhitābhāṣya*, MS No 647, DC Tanjore 1928 I: 424]

D. Manuscripts copied with the intention of obtaining a specific effect (understanding, powers..., aid in studying/teaching).

D.1. Copied in order to acquire powers (*siddhi*).

siddhyartham likhitaṃ [*Atharvavedasaṃhitā*, MS No 375, DC Poona 1916 I: 275]

D.2. Copied for personal benefit and the benefit of others:

idaṃ pustakaṃ... bhaṭṭena likhitaṃ | svārthaṃ parārthaṃ ca | [*Aitareyāraṇyaka*, MS No 71, DC Poona 1916 I: 61]
...liṣitaṃ [likhitam?] *duvedodarājena ātmakāryyārthaṃ* || [*Aitareyabrāhmaṇa*, MS No 64, DC Poona 1916 I: 55]

E. Copied with the purpose of recitation/reading/future studies/recitation.

E.1. Copied for the purpose of one's own studies (*svapaṭhana*).

śrī mūlajī tatsutaprabhūjīyena likhitaṃ idaṃ pustakaṃ ātmapaṭhanārthaṃ svayaṃhastena likhitaṃ...
'Copied with his own hand by Prabhūjī, son of Mūlajī, for the purpose of his own studies' [*Gāyatrībhāṣya*, MS No 436, DC Poona 1916 I: 315]

ātmapaṭhanārtham [*Sāmaveda Saṃhitā Padapāṭha*, MS No 112, DC Poona 1916 I: 94]

E.2. Copied for the purpose of studying/reciting of others, most often one's sons/family members:

> *putrapautrādīnām paṭhanārtham likhitam*
> 'copied for the sake of study/recitation of son and grandsons...' [*Sāṁavedasaṃhitā*, MS No 103, DC Poona 1916 I: 88, dated Samvat 1582]

> *ṣaṭbhrātṛpaṭhanārtham likhitam*
> 'copied for the purpose of study of the six brothers...' [*Āraṇīpadapāṭha*, MS No 121, DC Poona 1916 I: 99]

A similar concern with the education of brothers is voiced in another MS, which gives a specific name (of the recipients of the copied manuscript?). The colophon reads that the MS had been prepared in Vairāṭanagara in Samvat 1706, in order to be recited from by the brother of the scribe (?), to be well known (by this act of preparing a copy) in his residential town of Maphalīpura...:

> *vairāṭanagaramadhye maphalīpuravāstavyaṃ*[a] *ābhyantaranāgarajñātīya śrī harajīsuta-kumarajīkenyabhrātṛkeśavajīpaṭhanārtham stobhasya pustikā*[ṃ] *lilikhe* [*Stobhāḥ*, MS No 143, DC Poona 1916 I: 114].[132]

> *jośī sukharāmeṇa likhitaṃ ... someśvarasutanāṃnā paṭhanārthaṃ*
> 'copied by Sukharāma Joshī for the sake of recitation/study of the son of Someśvara' [*Uhyagāṇa*, MS No 236, DC Poona 1916 I: 175]

A similar formula to denote persons can be found in other manuscripts:

> *keśavajīsutaratanajī likhitam ... gīradharajī prabhujī paṭhanārtham* [*Stobhāḥ*, MS No 144, DC Poona 1916 I: 115, dated Samvat 1772],

a colophon to MS No 150 of *Naigeyapariśiṣṭa* (Sāmaveda), DC Poona 1916 I: 119, gives a combined purpose and reads:

> *nānīyasutarāmakṛṣṇenāyaṃ likhitaṃ putraśivarāja tathā śivarāma paṭhanārtham tathā paropakārāya puṇyārthaṃ likhitaṃ*

---

[132] The reading of this (and a number of other) colophon remains, however, doubtful.

> 'This has been copied by Rāmakṛṣṇa, a son of Nānīya, for the sake of recitation/study of *Putraśivarāja* and *Śivarāma* as well as for the merit-gaining of others' [DC Poona 1916 I: 150]

A parallel wording can be seen in colophons to MS No 168, *Ārṣeyabrāhmaṇa*, DC Poona 1916 I: 130, and MS No 173, *Vaṃśabrāhmaṇa*, DC Poona 1916 I: 133. A great source for indications concerning the motives for copying proves to be MS No 129 in DC Poona 1916 I: 104, containing the *Āraṇyakagāṇabhāṣya*. The manuscript seems to feature more than one colophon, probably by different copyists: it is not only the studies/recitation, but also understanding/making sense (*svāvabodha*) and enlightening that is mentioned explicitly as the purpose (*artham*) of the act of copying (*likhitam*): *likhitam svāvabodhāya narendrāśramayoginā ... ātmabuddhiprakāśahetoḥ śiṣyāṇām laghubrātṛnām ... svena ... āraṇyakabhāyam likhitam* [*Araṇyakagānabhāṣya*, MS No 129 DC Poona 1916 I: 105, dated Samvat 1709].[133]

A case apart is MS No 291 of *Śatapatha Brāhmaṇa*, DC Poona 1916 I: 219, featuring a colophon that appears to refer to a situation of copying to the satisfaction and joy of a Vedic teacher of a copy ordered by Lilādharabhaṭṭa. [?] (*uddhava*): *vārānasyāṃ lekhaka upādhyāya uddhavena likhito yaṃ granthaḥ* || *lilādharabhaṭṭena likhāpito yaṃ granthaḥ* |

F. Gift-giving/donating of a MS.[134]

A certain number of Vedic manuscripts register hints at the act of manuscript gift-giving or otherwise transferring the right of proprietorship.

F.1. A gift to a spiritual preceptor – *ācārya*:

> *idaṃ pañcamāṣṭakaṃ ... vāsudevena likhitaṃ māce gaṇanṛsiṃhācāryāya* [*Ṛgvedasaṃhitā*, MS No 162, DC Tanjore 1928 I: 94]

---

[133] It appears that all the manuscripts with colophons indicating the purpose of studying are actually accented, which seems pretty natural. On the other hand, manuscripts of secondary Vedic texts, containing non-*śruti* works, appear to feature similar formulas: e.g. MS No 273, DC Poona 1916 I: 205 (*Śuklayajuḥprātiśākhya*), dated Samvat 1607: ...*gaṅgogadādhara-paṭhanāya paropakārāya ca prātiśākhyam alekhīt*).

[134] For a more systematic study on the concept and practice of the gift of knowledge, or *vidyādāna*, in connection with manuscript copying, see Simini 2016.

F.2. A gift to an unspecified person (a Brahmin?).[135]
An instance of a colophon registering a donation of the manuscript is MS No 427, DC Tanjore 1928 I: 260, stating simply that the manuscript copied on such and such day had been given by Bāhekaraśeṣabhaṭṭa to Kamalākara, otherwise known in the Tanjore collection to have been a patron of the copying of a good number of Vedic manuscripts towards the end of 18th and beginning of 19th century. This manuscript contains *Ṛgveda-padapāṭha* IV.8.

An interesting instance is MS No 411 (*Gopathabrāhmaṇa*) dated Śaka 1751, DC Poona 1916 I: 300, which registers a gift of a *Gopathabrāhmaṇa* manuscript—an *atharva* text—to a *paṇḍita* knowledgeable in *Atharvanic* lore, by the person who copied it with the purpose given as *svārtham* and *paropakārārtham*—suggesting that the gift giving of a Vedic manuscript could be counted as meritorious to oneself as well as to others in general: *vināyakena likhitam svārtham paropakārārtham ... idam pustakam atharvavidbāpūbhaṭṭasya dattam.*

F.3. Manuscripts accepted as gifts.
A separate case should probably be indicated by the formula reading: *gṛhītam idam pustakam* ('hospitably received by...'), MS No 455, *Ṛgveda Padapāṭha*, DC Tanjore 1928 I: 277.

F.4. Other types of gift.
A case of a friendly gift can be seen in MS No 426, *Ṛgveda Padapāṭha*, DC Tanjore 1928 I: 259:

> *doro jagannāthabhaṭṭasyedaṃ pustakam | idaṃ pustakaṃ prītisnehābhyāṃ jambunāthāya tena dattam*[136]
> 'this book belongs to Doro Jagannatha. This book has been given by him to Jambunātha in expression of friendship and affection.'

---

[135] An ideology of gift-giving, most interesting and important in itself, cannot, for the sake of space, be referred to here, though it forms the core of the KK Dānakāṇḍa and many earlier normative texts of *dharma*, which usually carefully distinguish between not only objects to be donated as gifts and suitable circumstances and aims, but also among persons of givers and recipients, the latter ones headed by *brāhmaṇas* [see Aiyengar 1941].

[136] The editor of the DC Tanjore 1928 I supplies the following remark: 'The MS belongs to one Doro Jagannātha who is said to have presented the same to his friend Jambunātha [DC Tanjore 1928 I: 259].' We may only surmise whether it is the same physical object that was gifted to Jambunātha by his friend or another copy of the same, i.e. *Ṛgveda-padapāṭha* IV.1.1–8.32 (J.L. Collection No. 103).

The manuscript catalogued as MS No 130, dated Saṃvat 1718, of *Ūhagāna*, DC Poona 1916 I: 130, features a colophon which does not explicitly mention the act of giving but features two stanzas in praise of knowledge (*vidyā*, an object of *dāna*[?]), quoted from *Nītiśātaka* of Bhartṛhāri and, following a common stock verse about a book (of knowledge?), speaking to his owner (receiver?) in order to be guarded against misuse in the hands of others:

> *adyeha śrīsūryapuravāstavya ābhyantaranāgarajñatīya* || *travāḍī śavajīsut travāḍīgabala svayaṃ likhitam idaṃ pustakaṃ* || *śubhaṃ bhavatu* || *śrīr astu* ||
> *tailādrakṣe*[j] *jalādrakṣe*[d] *rakṣe*[t] *śrathalabandhanāt* |
> *parahastagatā*[d] *rakṣet evaṃ vadati pustikā* || ...
> *vidyā nāma narasya rūpamādhikaṃ pracchannaguptaṃ dhanaṃ* ||
> *vidyā bhogakarī yaśaḥsukhakarī vidyā guruṇāṃ guruḥ* ||1||
> *vidyā bandhujano videśagamane vidyā paraṃ*[ā] *daivataṃ*[ā] ||
> *vidyā rājasu pūjyate nahi dhanaṃ vidyāvihīnaḥ paśuḥ* ||2||
> 'On this day this [handwritten] book has been copied with his own hand by Travāḍīgabala, resident of Sūryapura, well known in the town as the son of Travāḍī Śavajī. Let there be Prosperity!'[137]
> 'Protect me against oil [spill], protect against water, against oppression of cover protect me,
> Protect me against falling into alien hands—thus speaks the book.'
> 'Knowledge indeed is the highest shape of man, his hidden secret wealth;
> Knowledge—she grants wealth and fame and happiness, Knowledge is the Guru of the Gurus;
> Knowledge is a friend in a trip to foreign land, Knowledge indeed is Goddess Supreme
> Knowledge is honoured among kings, not wealth, man with no knowledge is a beast.'

G. Special cases of patronage of manuscript production.

A case apart, to be indicated in the context of the purpose of the copying and dissemination of the Veda, is, by no means, the early Vijayanagara rulers' project of *vedārthaprakāśa*. As I have argued elsewhere, in order to fulfil its aim as a means of solidifying the image of empire, it needed the

---

137 Travāḍī (Tivari?), or Trivedī, became the well-known name of a wealthy Gujarati family of Brahmin city bankers active in Surat at the beginning of the 18th century, also in Maharashtra [Haynes 1987; Torri 1991].

bhāṣyas to be circulated along with the text of the Veda, probably targeting the centres of Vedic learning. This is suggested by the distribution of colophons marking the *bhāṣyas*, especially that to the RS, as a result of patronage on the part of either Bukka I (later *bhaṣyas* also Harihara II) and the religious authority of Vidyātīrthamaheśvara, represented through Sāyaṇa's brother, Mādhava. A key to this ideology is provided not only by colophons, but also by the introductory formulas to the *bhāṣyas* (*maṅgalacaraṇas* and *śāstrāvataraṇa*), shared by most of the extant manuscripts.[138]

A case that should be highlighted here is made by the existence of both accented and unaccented copies among extant Vedic manuscripts.[139] If we judge the question of the possible use of unaccented copies of Vedic texts against the textual practices of a contemporary Brahmin community, the image we will find may be different in the case of different communities of users, since actual practices of handling manuscript copies may differ to a considerable extent. If we take the example of the relatively well documented Nampūtiri Ṛgvedins of Kerala, with their textual practices, we may observe that, in the process of education, the basic *adhyayana-svādhyāya*, or memorization training through self-study, is still nowadays generally done with pupils in principle denied any access to written sources during the memorization process. This pertains to all levels of instruction: the basic *saṃhita-pāṭha*, *pada* and *krama-pāṭha* as well as the two *vikṛtis* practiced by them—the *jaṭā* and *ratha*—all require an accented text and are to be executed not only using *traisvarya*, but with a modulation neither known nor practiced by other Brahmins in other parts of the subcontinent. No doubt, even accented copies, in their case, would not be of much help. Their educational and memorization techniques seem indeed—as F. Staal[140] once noticed—to have been developed, not in spite of the absence of writing, but because of this absence. Some traits of their recitational style seem not to exemplify at all the prescriptions and recommendations known from *Ṛgvedaprātiśākhya or Pāṇinīya Śikṣā* and could be contrasted with the

138 On circumstances of producing and circulating Vedic *bhāṣyas* in 14th century and framing devices in Sāyaṇa's *Ṛgvedabhāṣya*, see Galewicz 2010a.

139 A possibility that unaccented copies were aimed not for daily recitation of *svādhyāya* but for *śrauta* ritual use, where, in most of the cases, the type of recitation recommended is that of *ekaśruti*, or monotone, could be accepted only in those cases where we have a copy of a text in a redaction matching the procedure of a particular *śrauta*—or *gṛhya*—ritual and cannot be accepted for unaccented copies of *saṃhitās*, especially that of RS, that actually do occur.

140 Staal 2008: 279.

recitation practices of members of other Brahmin communities.[141] On the other hand, one should take good notice of the full scale of the regionally developed textual practices employed in the service of the Vedic re-memorization. Taking again the instance of the Nampūtiri Ṛgvedins, a variety of such practices may be found. All of them used to fulfil important social functions, but, at the same time, worked as efficient procedures for guarding the collective memory of the Veda.[142] One of them is a ritual cycle called the Trisandhā, during which the whole of the *Rksaṃhitā* is recited *in extenso*, according to different modes of recitation and a specific algorithm or pattern, which is not supplied with any known written copy of the *Ṛksaṃhitā*. Some other social institutions of that kind are those known by the names of Anyōnyam and Muṟajapam, to which I referred elsewhere.[143] Other communities of Brahmins, throughout the subcontinent, developed other varieties of 'reading protocols,' especially those referred to by the general term of *pārāyaṇa* or 'going over the entire text,' usually in a process of concatenated sessions of recitation given more or less ritualized character. At the same time, we should note that, while in principle no written copies are used in the education process in the still functioning school of Vedic recitation in the Keralan city of Trichur, the teachers do keep copies of *Rksaṃhitā* in Malayalam script at hand in case their memory fails them (however reluctantly they admit to doing so). An altogether different case is that of the community of Daśagranthis of Maharashtra (here, the community in the sense of a 'community of practice'): the widely used compendium named *Ṛgvedadaśagrantha*, though treated with utmost reverence, appears not to be followed in practice—in a series of reviews with Daśagranthis, most of them admitted not only not to follow the sequence

141 I am reminded here of an observation made by David Shulman [2007]. Shulman notes a custom among a group of Andhra Ṛgvedins, who happen to put a little receptacle with lime juice on the head of the Vedic reciter supposed not to spill a drop while sounding the Veda and thus testifying to the absence of the 'shaking of the head' (*śiraskalpiti*)—one of the six vices of Vedic recitation according to *Pāṇinīya Śīkṣā*.

142 The uniqueness of the culture of oral transmission of the Veda lies perhaps in its specific technology of cloning the memory, not only individual but also group memory, and I believe it is the latter that was crucial to the ongoing process. Where the existence of scholarly communities in the sense of self-contained and self-reproducing ecosystems of transmission (endowed with social institutions for proofreading and antivirus cleaning procedures) began to fade away, some of their exponents, left alone, might have accepted writing as an alternative: a substitute, albeit imperfect, to the method that once seemed the only possible and logically sound one.

143 See Galewicz 2010b.

of texts making up the compendium in their daily or occasional *pārāyaṇa* practices, but also of not being aware of certain texts actually present in the compendium (here the quasi-tantric chapter named as the *Yāmalāṣṭaka-tantropaniṣad* inserted after the *Ṛgvidhāna*).[144] Thus, a picture suggests itself, that written copies must have been rather rarely, if ever, used as a direct source for reading practice. Their use must have remained limited to a sort of aide-memoire, and their users, if there were any, only those who already memorized at least some part of the text.

At the same time, one needs to admit that, all other reasons aside, there is a strong logic to the historical reluctance towards writing as means of preservation of the integrity of the Vedic textual tradition: in fact there has never been (and this still holds true) a system of notation in use that could register all sound and rhythm phenomena needed to reproduce a Vedic passage in its full *traisvarya* (in practice, there are usually more than just three *svaras* performed in *Ṛgvedic* recitation, not to mention *Sāmavedic* chants) shape. Whatever systems of graphically noting the Vedic accents were used, all of them remained only a rough approximation and, in actual practice, needed a guide to show the way. This is visible in contemporary practice of Vedic recitation, that differs a lot regionally even if the same written source for education/performance might happen to be used by Brahmins from separate regional communities.

The asymmetry between the inscriptional and oral textual practices has been rightfully noted by Siniruddha Dash:

> ...the recognition in the Dharmaśāstra-s and the Purāṇa-s of the gifting away of manuscripts as an act of great merit had, down the ages, a very beneficial effect in the production of manuscripts ... it is not as if every manuscript was copied for presentation or was attended with all the paraphernalia of the ritual.[145]

The copying of religious texts with the intention of ceremonial gift–giving of the produced manuscript should be recognized as most beneficial and important cultural institution, that helped propagate the high image of scholarship. But it must have been paralleled and complemented by silent copying for private use, preparing copies as religious acts conceptualized differently than *vidyādāna*, not to mention producing copies for sale

144 See Galewicz 2012, 2014.

145 Dash 2007: 94.

(from the very admonitions against doing so in early sources—for instance *Mahābhārata*—it can be inferred that copies of Vedic texts were also offered for sale here and there and some of them, like the illustrated manuscripts of *Ṛgveda* in Sarasvatī Mahāl library, must have constituted prized objects of desire on the part of the rulers and, perhaps, also of the wealthy).

The manuscript culture of medieval and premodern India, however, probably does not represent the type of richness exemplified by the manuscript culture and art of calligraphy known by the Islamic world.[146] It seems to exhibit another, far different sort of ideology behind writing, copying, preserving, managing and circulating manuscripts as objects of value, though there is evidence that, in some areas, manuscripts acquired the function of valuables used in financial transaction such as, for instance, paying back debts or deposits against loans.[147] Some colophons to Vedic manuscripts also suggest a kind of personalized relationship of possession towards manuscripts as material objects as well as the importance of the act of preparing a written copy with one's own hand.[148]

The wide evidence of extant Vedic manuscripts with no accents noted on them suggests that at least some part of the manuscripts must have been copied for a different aim than reading, either as a pious act leading to a gesture of *vidyādāna* or as an aide-memoire for Vedic teachers to be kept ready at hand in case their memory fails them. If it actually was some sort of *vidyādāna*, our understanding of this gesture should, however, be cautious enough to take into account the main points of the classical *dānadharma*, with its fear of reciprocity and its demands on the status of the recipient.[149] Thus, to offer only one reference perplexing enough for our context, Manu VII.85–86 lists a hierarchy of gifts corresponding to the status of the recipient: an [ordinary] *brāhmaṇa* and another qualified as 'knower of the Veda' (*vedavid*) are sharply differentiated, and a gift to the former is believedd to have a sixteen-fold *puṇya*, while, for the latter, it is a hundred-fold *puṇya* of religious merit. Of what use, we may ask,

146 A remarkable introduction to the world of Islamic manuscript cultures remains Houari Touati, *L'armoire à sagesse. Bibliothèques et collections en Islam*, Paris: Aubier, 2003.

147 See most interesting remarks to that matter in Dash 2007: 228–229.

148 See, for instance, a colophon to a MS of *Ṛgvedabrāhmaṇa* [DC Tanjore II: 825]: *muddibhaṭṭanasutagurunāthena svahastalikhitam | bhagnapṛṣṭhakaṭigrīvastabdhadṛṣṭir adhomukhaḥ | kaṣṭena likhitagrantham yatnena pratipālayet || bhāskararāyadīkṣitīyam ||*

149 The early brilliant study on gift giving by Marcel Mauss [1924] idealized this institution for the Indian context and this fact has been noted by scholars, such as Parry 1986 and Michaels 1997.

could a written copy of a Vedic text be for a *vedavid*, considered himself to be a receptacle of Vedic scripture?

The oral and the written seem to have engaged in many intricate and indeed fascinating ways throughout Indian intellectual history, while differing widely regionally. The practices of the first public readings of written manuscripts of *kāvya* works, of which we have heard, is but one example of this.[150] The case of the Veda is different for obvious reasons and nothing like public reading could, in regular circumstances, be imagined to have been ever performed. However, historical references to *vedaghoṣṭhi*, or something like competitive artful performances of the Vedic recitation, as well as contemporary remnants of ritualized competitions in Vedic recitations, call for an articulation of a Vedic example of public performance. Such instances make the interrelation between the oral and the written, in the context of local Vedic traditions, even more interesting to explore, as these have been marked by additional traits differentiating them from the otherwise common contexts of *śāstra* and *kāvya* literary cultures.

We still need more anthropology oriented historical studies of social practices and cultural gestures of writing and reading including the modalities of handling manuscripts as cultural objects. Only more case studies may give more justice to the historical and geographical differentiation of several manuscript cultures and may help us see the working the network of relationships between what was oral and what was written, what was aural and what visual.

II.5. The Veda commented upon

A series of early printed editions of *Ṛksaṃhitā* and other primary Vedic texts, that came out from Indian publishing enterprises in the middle and late 19th century, confirmed, in the medium of print, the imperial status of the commentaries to the bulk of eighteen Vedic texts prepared under the auspices of the early Vijayanagar empire by Sāyaṇa—a status already long-established within the ecumene of Sanskrit learning and the information order composed of the regional manuscript cultures. The 19th century also saw a heated debate among European philologists over the value of 'native' commentaries to the Veda, which went hand in hand with a romantic

150 See Pollock 2006: 87–88.

search for the earliest commentary possible as allegedly representing the closest distance in time between the Veda and the commentator's world, to guarantee a continuity of concepts and ideas within an intelligible context. While, in the eyes of European philologists, the commentaries by Sāyaṇa were neither early enough to genuinely represent the world of the Vedic *saṃhitās* nor were they in any intellectual sense better than those by Uvaṭa (6th c. ?) Skandasvamin (7th c. ?), Bhaṭṭa Bhāskaramiśra (12th c.), Ṣaṭguruśiṣya (12th c.) or any other commentators that preceded Sāyaṇa in time, the sheer bulk of extant manuscripts outnumbering the others (especially in the case of commentaries to the RS) as well as the aura of 'the commentator' accompanying Sāyaṇa in the hands of traditional Sanskrit scholars with whom the philologists may have been in touch, convinced some of them to follow suit and edit Vedic texts along with the commentary of Sāyaṇa.[151] A number of general features marking Sāyaṇa's commentaries might also be indicative as reasons for his success too. None of the three main pre--Sāyaṇa commentaries[152] on the *Ṛgveda* feature a theoretical introduction that might parallel, not to say, rival the *Ṛksaṃhitā Bhāṣya Bhūmikā* in its form, scope, or purpose. No doubt valuable commentary by Skandasvāmin features no introduction proper, while a passage coming after the first line of the commented text serves this function to a limited extent. The *bhāṣya* by Udgītha appears to have survived only in portions with nothing like an introductory part. The *Vyākhyā* by Veṅkaṭamādhava features a thirty-stanza preface with no apparent ambition, however, to discuss theoretical problems pertaining to the textual, ontological and epistemological status of the Veda, the validity and shape of a commentary on it, or the logic of efficient and legitimized procedures of obtaining the meaning and message of the Veda as a whole. None of the earlier commentators seem to have aimed at a totalizing textual experience of the Vedic discourse as apparently Sāyaṇa did in his RSBhBh.[153]

151 Until recently we had very few studies concerning either Sāyaṇa's predecessors, such as Skandasvāmin and Mādhavamantrin, or those who followed him, with the important exception of the 17th century commentator Nīlakaṇṭha Caturdhara [see Minkowski 2002]. While some early commentarial works, like *Nirukta* or *Bṛhaddevatā* (BṛD), attracted the attention of earlier scholars as supposedly representing a point of view closer to the Vedic material on chronological grounds, it is only recently that the commentarial genre of *Bṛhaddevatā* has been acknowledged and studied in its specific form [see Patton 1996]. This situation has recently been improving inter alia by a new interest in Vedic commentaries, like Skandasvāmin's work, on the part of such scholars as Silvia d'Intino.

152 See Vishva Bandhu 1965: 3–6. For a general survey of pre-Sāyaṇa Vedic commentaries, see Gonda 1975: 40–41; Kunhan Raja 1936; D'Intino 2016, 2008.

153 More on Sāyaṇa's totalizing commentary, see Galewicz 2010a.

II.5.1. The imperial commentary

In spite of the status of the highest scriptural authority that the Veda claimed for itself through its guardians or/and orthodox thinkers and very often received in religious and philosophical debate in medieval India as a type of textuality, it was not easily associated with political power. Whatever we may have in mind while indicating the predilection of some historical Indic kings and dynasties for supporting their own claims with executing so called Vedic royal rites, no instance is known to me of the idea of the Veda being made into an object of control, in order to be used for the consolidation of political power before the 14th century AD and the inception of the kingdom named Vijayanagara. In an unprecedented and totalizing project of commenting upon the meaning of the whole of the Veda (*vedārthaprakāśana*), the first rulers of Vijayanagara did not only order and patronize the composition of a series of long authoritative commentaries to most important Vedic texts, but had the basic idea of their association with the project of the totalizing commentary inscribed into the prefaces, introductions, and colophons framing each and every textual unit of the eighteen bulky commentaries to the eighteen different Vedic texts.

Seventeen out of eighteen main commentaries[154] were composed during the rule of Bukka I: two hundred within a span of twelve years, sometime between 1365 AD and 1377 AD.[155] All of them were framed with recurring versified preambles and colophons that recycle the same information: each commentary was meant to form part and parcel of the general enterprise of commenting on the whole of the Veda.[156] Such a picture must have been designed to impress everybody by the totalizing completeness of its aim.

---

[154] For the list of works attributed to Sāyaṇa, see Galewicz 2010a: Appendix 1.

[155] For a list and dating of particular commentaries by Sāyaṇa, see Galewicz 2010a: Appendix 1.

[156] The standard recurring formula to in colophons ending text units and divisions reads RSBh (M) I, p. 549:
iti śrīmadrājādhirājaparameśvaravaidikamārgapravartakaśrīvīrabukkabhūpālasāmrājyadhuraṃdhareṇa sāyaṇācāryeṇa viracite mādhavīye vedārthaprakāśe ṛksaṃhitābhāṣye prathamāṣṭake 'ṣṭamo 'dhyāyaṃ samāptaṃ.
'Here ends the eighth *adhyāya* in the first *ogdoad* in the Light on the
Meaning of the Veda, the *bhāṣya* on the *Ṛgvedasaṃhitā*, set along the line
of [the ideas of] Mādhava, composed by Sāyaṇācārya bearing the burden
of [exercising] the rule of the illustrious brave *Bukka*, King of Earth,
Promoter of the Way of the Veda, the Highest Lord, illustrious Great King of Kings.'

A distinction between particular commentaries and the commentarial project as a whole can be traced in the choice of vocabulary visible mostly in the preambles and other framing structures of the commentaries proper.

The success of Sāyaṇa's commentaries on the Veda, written in the second half of the 14th century, must have been heavily influenced by the royal *kulturpolitik* of the rulers of the early Vijayanagara. Whatever be the reason, at least one of a number of works produced by Sāyaṇa under the royal order managed eventually to establish itself as a sort of a canonical commentary. This is his commentary to one of the four main Vedic *saṃhitās*, namely, the corpus of the *Ṛgveda*—the oldest of the collections of texts making up the Vedic canon. In fact, the commentary by Sāyaṇa was neither the first nor the last.[157] Yet, not many more managed to survive until our times. Moreover, the links established once between the basic work—that is, the collection of *Ṛgveda* hymns—and the text of the commentary, did not cease to exert their powerful authority half a millennium later, when F. Max Müller, while working on the first printed edition of the *Ṛgveda*, could not help but publish it along with that very commentary by Sāyaṇa. In the latter case, the author of the commentary had been given the traditional title of *ācārya*, which, from early times, was attached to his name, indicating the highest respect and social prestige.

By the time Sāyaṇa answered to the call by King Bukka I to initiate the project of composing new Vedic commentaries around 1365, his brother Mādhava must have already been a well-known religious figure and the author of a number of influential religious and philosophical treatises. Sāyaṇa too must already have shown himself as a skilful author of scholarly works in several different disciplines, such as poetics, medicine, grammar, religious literature, the science of ritual, ethics, etc.[158] Introductory stanzas to one of them, known by the name of *Puruṣārtha-sudhānidhi*, contain a story about his brother Mādhava convincing King Bukka to listen to Sāyaṇa's work.[159] His *Ṛgvedabhāṣya-Bhūmikā*,[160] or an Introduction to the

---

157 For an overview of Vedic commentaries, see, for instance, GONDA 1975: 39–42.

158 Among those were: *Subhāṣitasuddhānidhi* (an anthology of verses from *kāvyas* & *śāstras* arranged under four headings: *dharma*, *artha*, *kāma*, and *mokṣa*), *Alaṃkāra-sudhānidhi* (an unprinted. manuscript in the Oriental Institute Mysore), *Ayurveda-sudhānidhi*, *(Mādhavīya) Dhātuvṛtti*, *Yajñatantra-sudhānidhi*, *Prayaścitta-sudhānidhi* (=*Karmavipāka*), *Karma-vipākaprāyaścitta-sudhā-nidhi* (*Dāridraya-roga-pratikriyā*, see col. C.C.: 67).

159 *Puruṣārtha-sudhānidhi* 8–11. See MODAK 1995: 12.

160 This work happens to be referred to also by the generic names of *upodghāta* or *upakramāṇika*.

commentary on the *Ṛgveda*, has been conceived as part and parcel of the major *bhāṣya* commentary to the *Ṛgveda* collection, one of an impressive number of regular commentaries to different texts which make up the Vedic canon. The scale of such a project clearly made a claim to completeness on the part of the author and his mighty protectors. This claim was most probably communicated through the wording of the declaration inserted in the opening preamble, which spoke about a commentary to (the whole of) the Veda (*vedārthaprakāśa*).[161] As such, it may have been perceived as an impressive royal act of cultural promotion. And this probably was its aim.

To begin with a reflection on the use of strategies for textual authority in Sāyaṇa, it is essential to remind ourselves that the texts commented on by him constituted primarily what went by the name of *śruti*, or revealed tradition, that could be 'listened to and heard'[162] in the Veda as a whole, and only secondarily, in particular Vedic texts in themselves. This perspective is consciously put into relief and, I would say, played upon in the opening verses and chapter/section ending colophons of his commentaries to particular Vedic texts.[163] The inner architecture of his work ensures that the reader meets time and again the formula for declaring commentary on the whole of the Veda: *Veda-artha-prakāśa* ('shedding light on the meaning and purpose of the Veda') or *Veda-vyākhyāna* ('an explanation of, or commentary on the Veda'). It is also in his *Introduction to the commentary on the Ṛgveda*, that the Veda as a whole is stated as the formal object of his work taken as a traditionally acknowledged genre of *vyākhyāna*—a scholarly commentary (*vyākhyānasya vyākhyeyo vedo viṣayaṃ*).[164] This is done while discussing the nature of a scholarly commentary as constituted by four components, or 'topical tetrad,'[165] and proving one's expertise in meeting requirements, as well as declaring formal elements of a valid scholarly commentary as such. Assuming the whole of the Veda to be a unity capable of being commented upon needs, however, a definition somehow coming to terms with the existence of a multitude of different Vedic texts. First of all, the constant reference to the project of commenting on the Veda as a whole

---

[161] See VBhBhS 1958: 11. Similar declaration is repeated in all versed preambles to the Vedic commentaries attributed to Sāyaṇa.

[162] On the meaning of *Śruti*, see Pollock 2005, Galewicz 2010a: 228.

[163] On the inner architecture of Sāyaṇa's commentary see Galewicz 2005b: 335 and Galewicz 2010a: 145–152.

[164] See RSBhBh, Müller 1983: 17.

[165] For this rendering of the term *anubandhacatuṣṭaya*, see Minkowski 2005: 240.

must have been implying an intention of completeness—a fact which could impress prospective readers. Secondly, each and every versified preamble to each particular commentary by Sāyaṇa contains a short narrative relating the sequence in which subsequent Vedic texts were taken by him in order to be commented upon. The sequence had been given a proper rationale each time, with reasons for the precedence of commenting on one text over another. In that way, a hierarchy was introduced among the Vedic texts, which gives the impression of a well-planned project and a deep knowledge of the whole of the Veda behind it. This, notwithstanding the fact, that all Vedic texts were never, and probably could never, be commented on by Sāyaṇa. Thus, it is possible for Sāyaṇa to give a reason for a choice of hierarchy in the order of commenting, for instance, a reason for commenting first on the text of *Ṛgveda*, on the basis of a quotation from *Ṛgveda* itself, which, from our point of view, amounts to an anachronism, but, from his, is meeting the rules declared as governing the valid commentary on the Vedas. One basic rule is the presumed *svataḥprāmāṇya* of the Veda as a whole—the unquestionable source of authority in the matters of *dharma*. This is also understood as the inner capability of the Veda to explain not only things external to it but, also—'as the example of moon and the sun shows'—to elucidate its own text.[166] From this perspective, a passage from—what is in our view—the historically earlier collection of *Ṛgveda* may well be interpreted as referring to the later collection of *Yajurveda*.[167]

The well-known and accepted injunction to study the Veda pertains within the perspective adopted by Sāyaṇa to something which the opponent of his arguments understands as memory training only. Sāyaṇa takes the same as a necessary text appropriation and textual mastery through an exclusively oral experience of the education, in close contact between teacher and pupil—a mastery indispensable for further study with the help of the fourteen 'strongholds of knowledge.' According to the commentator, it is another injunction, this time called *śravana-vidhi*,[168] which pertains to the duty of acquiring access to the knowledge of the meaning of the Veda. As its very name suggests, however, it is an injunction to 'hear,' i.e. to acquire the knowledge (*jñāna*) from someone else rather than directly from the textual experience. This should be someone who is eligible for

166 VBhBhS 1958: 15. See Galewicz 2010a.

167 See Müller 1983: 1, 27; Galewicz 2010a: 81.

168 VBhBhS 1958: 43.

investigating knowledge himself on his solitary way to the 'secret of the meaning of the Veda.' For whom then is the search for the knowledge reserved?

It is in line with the Uttara Mīmāṃsā or Vedāntic point of view, when Sāyaṇa admits that knowledge of the Veda is not the same as knowledge about the meaning and message of the Veda. The latter proves to have been composed at a lower level, corresponding to the knowledge of *dharma*, and a higher one—corresponding to the knowledge of Brahma—the ultimate principle of reality. Any personal investigation into the Brahma portion of the meaning of the Veda is, according to Sāyaṇa's *Bhūmikā*, reserved for individuals who deserve the appellation of Paramahaṃsa[169]—spiritual teachers and renouncers of public life. Himself a householder and the father of three sons, Sāyaṇa could not project his image as that of a Paramahaṃsa. In order to legitimate his right to compose a valid Vedic commentary, he needed the authority of a Paramahaṃsa behind him.[170] Here, the connection with his brother Mādhava, a charismatic religious figure apparently qualifying as Paramahaṃsa, comes to the fore as a cleverly designed strategy. It is worked upon through constant textual projection of the link by the way of declarations and authoritative quotations from Mādhava's in the body of the *Bhūmikā*.[171] Emphasizing this link, Sāyaṇa's commentary has been actually called *mādhavīya* and was probably targeted to reach the well-educated elite of Brāhmanic circles. In a project actively promoted by the rulers of early Vijayanagara, it aimed at influencing the interplay of power and religious authority in distant provinces of the empire to come.[172]

From the closing words of the introductory part of his commentary to the *Ṛgvedasaṃhitā*, we also learn that his commenting upon the textual tradition of the *Ṛgveda* had actually started, not from the *saṃhitā*, or the basic collection of hymns, as we would most naturally expect, but from

---

169 The prestigious title meaning literally 'the high flying [wild] goose' and symbolizes a person committed to a solitary pursuit into the realm of highest spiritual knowledge. See Galewicz 2010a: 124.

170 Perhaps, this might be the reason why much later editions of the *Ṛgveda*, even those well into the age of print (and electronic media) tend to secure an accepting voice of a respected renunciate (*Saṃnyāsī*), displayed in introductory paratextual spaces: such is the case of the 1986 edition of the *Ṛgveda Daśagrantha* [see Galewicz 2014].

171 Sāyaṇa quotes usually from *Jaimīnīya-nyāya-mālā* and the quotations are in the form of versed maxims of his brother given in support for his opinions. See Galewicz 2010a: 123–125.

172 I am developing this idea in Galewicz 2010a: 76–90, 123–126.

the *Brāhmaṇa* and *Āraṇyaka* 'portions' of that tradition. The latter were clearly taken by him as constituting the whole of the *Ṛgveda*, understood as a Ṛgvedic *śākhā* (lit. 'branch' or 'school' of the Veda), or the tradition of that particular Veda, comprised roughly of mantra and *brāhmaṇa kaṇḍas*, just as the Veda understood as one whole. From such a point of view, the *Ṛgveda* represents and reflects the structure of one coherent Veda, systematized and rationalized by the commentary aiming at showing its mastery over Vedic 'scripture'. This unitary Veda is presented by the commentary as a source of unquestioned authority in the matter of *dharma* meant not only as the order of the Vedic sacrificial system, but also as an ideal cosmic order, and its mundane reflection strived after by the *dharmic* ruler—the king consciously shaping his domain with reference to the ideal order of *dharma* rooted in the Veda itself. In this totalizing project of commenting upon the whole of the Veda, a sort of representation of this whole by the parts had been adopted, textualized, and presented by Sāyaṇa, in a way meant to impress the reader through its mastery over the powerful source of authority rooted in the concept of one homogenous Veda. Its purpose was to be able to show oneself as a master of this representation meant to wield power at least over those textual communities of Vedic teachers who played important social roles in the Brāhmanical education system. Through this system, one could influence numerous collective bodies of Brahmins holding power over rich and powerful temple complexes, temple towns, and monasteries, as well as those rural areas administered by Brahmin groups directly and those others for autonomous administrations.

It is far from sure whether all (if any) of the verses of the opening preambles to the Vedic commentaries actually come from Sāyaṇa himself and not from the editors of his work.[173] As mentioned above, these verses reappear in all eighteen different commentarial works of Sāyaṇa in a slightly modified shape. A certain number of them also appear at the end of each important section of the Vedic text commented upon.[174] The intertextual character of those verses is shown in further relief, with evidence of its first stanza also being used in the works of Sāyaṇa's brother Mādhava.[175]

173 For a discussion of this topic, see Galewicz 2010a: 159–167.

174 For a general discussion on the authorship and location of these verses, see Galewicz 2010a: 159–174.

175 For instance, in his *Jaiminīya-nyāya-mālā-vistara*, with important remarks by the author himself in the introduction to the author-commentary section of the work. See Galewicz 2010a: 126–130.

Furthermore, other authors make use of it, some even two centuries later, such as the famous grammarian Bhaṭṭoji Dīkṣita (in his *Vedabhāṣyasāra*).[176] These complex phenomena await further study in the context of general editorial practices in medieval India, which may shed interesting light on pre-modern Indian concepts of textual integrity and authorship. In the perspective of this study, they must be taken into account as further evidence of the complex character of the process of constructing the textual authority of scholarly commentary like that of Sāyaṇa's, a process to which the person of the author contributes in a relatively limited part, the rest being supplied by editorial work, the text production process, dissemination and circulation, and perhaps also promotion. If these suppositions hold true, the texts ascribed to Sāyaṇa and other authors of the time should be seen as revealing of the actual working of contemporary editorial ideology. Due to the lack of sufficient historical data, it cannot be determined which and how many influential religious centres of the time could the copies of Sāyaṇa's commentary actually reach. From the extant manuscripts deposited in modern libraries, it stands to reason that Sāyaṇa's works were copied in different Indic scripts, which suggests transregional circulation. We may infer from this fact, that his commentaries must have been distributed over several linguistic areas of the once vast empire. Whether the fact that the Vedic commentaries and the name of their author succeeded over time and history to establish themselves as 'canonical' was actually a matter connected to imperial cultural politics or other circumstances is, naturally, open to criticism.

The historical circumstances of the *vedārthaprakāśana* project and its actual deployment on the body of the commented scriptural texts, at least in the case of the RS, suggests a triggering of the process of substituting the authority of the canon with that of the canonical commentary.[177] Needless

---

176 See GALEWICZ 2010a: 129.

177 In his vision of the unitary Veda drawn by Sāyaṇa, especially in his introduction to the commentary on the *ṛksaṃhitā* [RSBhBh] he reestablished and reorganized, for the purpose of great imperial project of commenting on the Veda (*vedārthaprakāśana*), the old model of *vedāṅgas*, 'once developed for the preservation of the Vedic "scripture" and later turned into *śāstras*. With the new commentary, the Vedic legacy has been redefined with the ideas of influential religious thinkers to suit political aspirations of the kingly patrons. It is a holistic vision, and the Veda after Sāyaṇa will no longer be the same, not in the sense of its textual shape, which should not change, but as a type of social and cultural experience, regulated by methodological norms, now legitimized by the form of a canonical commentary' [GALEWICZ 2010a: 118].

to say, that in contradistinction to the polyvalent and visionary content of the *Saṃhitā* itself, the latter became an instrument, if not controlling the reception and use of the canon altogether, then at least of securing efficient means of channeling and circulating additional content, extraneous to the canon itself, and related to the imperial cultural politics. A process of this kind was, in itself, nothing new for the Hindu religious tradition at large: the taking over of Vedic legitimacy by later textual traditions known by the generic name of Smṛti must have been basically parallel, through its claiming to substitute, essentialize, summarize, extend, recover and simplify the Veda, although completely outside history, and in the guise of timeless tradition itself. Yet, the case of the 14th century Vedic commentarial project is specific, in that one is inclined to see fewer effects of long term cultural processes and more of purposeful cultural/political action deriving from a definite historical context. This does not mean, however, that it should not be judged against such cultural background from which it must have drawn inspiration. Skilful play with elements of this background must have formed part of the claim for the canonical legitimacy of the royal commentary, which would actually compete with and take over the legitimacy of the canonical Veda itself.[178] This impressive work, initially meant to support the legitimation of the early Vijayanagara rulers, came to be itself legitimized by the imperial idea and eventually survived the empire itself, while attaching itself effectively in the transmission process to manuscript copies of the commented texts in a way that, for many, came to constitute a necessary connection between the two. The world of the printed Veda proved, in many instances, to have taken this for granted.

II.6. The Veda in the empire of writing

It was Harold Innis who told us in 1950 how to think and about empires and civilizations through the categories of media communications. Harold Innis was one of Marshall McLuhan's predecessors and mentors.[179] Some of Innis' ideas strike us as ready model tools of analysis when trying to make sense of the type of communication medium a palm-leaf manuscript might

178 More on this idea, see Galewicz 2010a: 155–158.

179 The seminal work by Innis, entitled *Empire and Communications*, was published in 1950 by the University of Toronto Press.

for the growth and sustenance of represent South Asian empires, such as the one called Vijayanagara (1346–1565). In his second book entitled *Bias of communication*, Innis argues that 'a medium of communication has an important influence on the dissemination of knowledge over space and over time and it becomes necessary to study its characteristics in order to appraise its influence in its cultural setting.'[180] However, it is the crucial link between the medium, the genre, and convention of circulation that might be revealing when identified and articulated. In this particular instance, one can indicate a few: the Vijayanagara empire begins when the use of paper was becoming more and more popular to the north, where Persianate elites held power and controlled the media. But the climate in the south does not favour paper: the subtropical zone with monsoon rains and micro-fauna make it difficult for paper to last more than a few decades. Much better, in this respect, fared another support: palm-leaf, which, as a medium was never just a piece of leaf from a palm. It was rather a carefully processed young leaf from two specific varieties of palm tree, seasoned with oil and ingredients and cut to a regular size. Manuscripts made with it could stand this unfavourable climate for two centuries, very few made it up to four or five. To keep the collections or archives lasting, palm-leaf books needed to be recopied once every two centuries.[181] The inscribed leaf remained flexible but crispy, vulnerable to break at the edges; the manner of writing needed a skilful and trained hand: each sign (usually a syllable) needed to be precisely incised with an iron stylus in the usually one millimetre thick surface, carefully, in order not to cut it through, as leaves were inscribed on both sides. The first reading needed soot to be applied over the surface; such inscribed palm-leaf folios used to be bound together in a book—with a string put through two or sometimes three holes, bored in the surface of the folios; the act of reading consisted of unbinding the whole and proceeded by putting on stack the read folios before the reader. To close the book amounted to putting the folios back in the right order and stringing them together. This made it highly likely for a palm-leaf book to lose a folio or two whilst being circulated or to fall apart and never be rearranged properly. In order to guard against that, the parts or chapters of the book used to be supplied with a conventionalized formula, usually stating the name of the chapter (its title) as well as its topic and position in

---

180 Innis 1986: 33.

181 For a succinct outline of the nature of Indic manuscript cultures, see Wujastyk 2014.

the sequence. This also used to be the location of credits: the name of the author and/or that of the scribe as well as that of the munificent patron who had made the copying possible. Larger-sized works, copied onto the medium of palm-leaf folia, rarely made it possible to circulate the complete works of, say, religion or philosophy in one single bundle. This made the situation of making a connection between successive bundles a necessity. All of these peculiarities of the palm-leaf media had been cleverly made use of by the early ambitious rulers of Vijayanagara in order to communicate the message of the new empire. One way in which the new empire chose to communicate was through a huge project of writing (and circulating) scholarly commentaries on the religious canon of multiple works called the Vedas. This project took several years and remained unprecedented in its scope and ambition.[182] The colophons of chapters and other parts of each and every copy of each and every work had been supplied with a proper formula in the place where a colophon could be expected by their readers or listeners. This formula highlighted the legitimization of the kings, in reference to the connection to the meritorious act of recopying the Veda and producing commentaries in line with the ideas spread by an influential religious figure of the time. The same formula was to be repeated at the end of each chapter, thus giving the message the appearance of being doubly sealed by both imperial and religious power. This peculiar enterprise proved effective, both over space and time. What is now left of the project are copies in several scripts, distributed over a wide space, which exceeds by far the territory of the former Vijayanagara empire. And, along with the copied clones of the work, the formulas ending the chapter, though having no purpose any more, survive intact, testifying to the power of the skilful use of this particular medium, by an empire that made a point of mobilizing different media in order not only to cope with the lack of proper pedigree on the part of its founding dynasty, but, first and foremost, with the radically different audiences it had to address. Probably temple inscriptions had more chances to appeal to devotees and pilgrims while palm-leaf manuscripts to the scholarly and opinion-making circles based in monasteries (*maṭha*) often making part of temple complexes, some of them, rich, and influential. The rise and fall of Vijayanagara still puzzles historians. To the best of my knowledge, no study of the Vijayanagara empire concerned itself in any measure with Harold Innis' ideas on empires

182 For the historical circumstances of the project, see Galewicz 2010a: 76–90.

and communications. At least one, the best-known intuition of Innis, seems capable to shed more, light on the otherwise rich data concerning the life of the empire that had vanished. It is this concept of light and heavy type of media. In order to extend its imperial control over its new conquests in South India, the rulers of Vijayanagara had to depend on effective communication. The epigraphic evidence strongly suggests that at least two parallel channels of communication must have developed in support of the imperial project made of multiple centres of power: that of a heavy medium of temple inscriptions and that of a light medium of *tālapatra* or palm-leaf manuscript.[183] Both proved to be effectively mobilized in the project of communicating the mission of the empire. And both attested to Innis' qualifications of either durable in time or light enough to travel through the expanding space of the empire on the rise.[184]

---

183 For another perspective of looking at this problem, see Galewicz 2010a.

184 See Innis 1986: 5.

III. The coming of print to Indian subcontinent

It was as if print, uniform and repeatable commodity that it was, had the power of creating a new hypnotic superstition of the book as independent of and uncontaminated by human agency

Marshall McLuhan, *The Gutenberg Galaxy*

III.1. The missionary, the government and the commercial printers

Though the earliest history of printing on the Indian subcontinent is not a direct concern of this study, a cursory survey of the key events and early trajectories of its development may supply the necessary historical context for the slow and regionally diversified rise of regional and communal print cultures. And the latter can be made fuller sense of only against the background of the former. In a simplified typology, we may see the uneven development of print cultures across different regions of the Indian subcontinent with the help of three broad categories of printing enterprises: the missionary, the government and the commercial printers. For most of the formative period of the colonial era on the Indian subcontinent, the three represented three different concepts of the power of print, the concepts that influenced one another and sometimes overlapped, while shaping the unique history of Indian print cultures developing against the background of a struggle over at first trade, and later, of colonial domination of the resources of the vast areas of the subcontinent. The three developed three ultimately different cultures of print, with three different kinds of expectations towards the demand on printed matter on the part of their prospective readers. For the missionary—and in this case, I mean Protestant missionaries who dominated the second phase of print development–it was the inherent power of the word of the Lord, believed to inevitably work on everyone who chanced only to be exposed to its inner truth through intelligible, printed text. It implied a sponsored or semi-commercially organized circulation. Its maps arose out of trajectories drawn by the travelling preachers. Its objects were taken for the embodied word of God and printing itself as the work of such embodying, which resulted in the ceremonial act of bringing about the printed word of the Lord.[185] As we shall see, the same act of printing was a totally different thing in the eyes of those who decided to have their Vedas printed.

III.2. Preachers, printers and pundits

We may remember ... how much the Art of Printing contributed to the Manifestation of divine Truths, and the spreading of Books for that End, at the Time of the happy Reformation ... with Thanksgiving to Almighty God.

Bartholomeus Ziegenbalg to George Lewis[186]

The alleged, and much commented upon, link between the reformation and print as an agent of change, proved to be a tempting historical concept which, however, needs to be nuanced against historical and geographical circumstances of the specific culture(s) of print under consideration. In the context of South Asia, it were not the Protestants but the Jesuits who first introduced print to the Indian subcontinent. The way they did so reflects as much their connection to the type of political power represented by the Portuguese *Estado*, as did the type of engagement with the book and printing, that remained specifically Jesuit, in contrast to the use made of it later by the Lutherans in Tranquebar.

---

185 Cf. Ogborn 2007: 208, who highlights the moment of the completion of the Bengali New Testament, which 'was bound and placed on a communion table in the chapel, "and a meeting was held of the whole mission family and the newly baptized heathen, to acknowledge their gratitude to God for the completion of this important work..."'

186 From a letter dated 7 April 1713, to George Lewis, the Anglican chaplain at Madras, on the occasion of successful printing outcome of the newly established printing press donated to Tranquebar Mission by the London based Society for the Propagation of Christian Knowledge (SPCK), as quoted in Sweetman 2004: 24.

III.2.1. The Jesuit printers of the western coast

Printing, as such, started in the Indian subcontinent relatively early, with the first printing press established in Goa by Jesuit missionaries. All that happened rather accidentally, since apparently the press was virtually seized from the vessel that was transporting it elsewhere (it was originally destined for Abyssinia). In 1556, it was installed in the College of Saint Paul and put to work by Jesuits. Soon, two presses were in operation in Goa and, between 1556 and 1581, they produced a total of eight books in five different languages (Latin, Portuguese, Ethiopian, Konkani and Tamil), all but one in Roman script. The one exception was the 1577 catechism in Tamil script, of which, however, not even a single copy has survived. The earliest extant printed matter produced in India, in an Indian language using an Indian script, is from 1578 and comes from Kollam (Quilon) on the western, Malabar coast, today's Kerala. It is doubly titled as *Tampirāṉ vaṇakkam* (Tamil: 'Let the Lord be praised') or *Doctrina Christam en Lingua Malauar Tamul* and, as its title suggests, it is a translation from Portuguese to the Malabar variety of Tamil by Henrique Henriques, possibly of a reworked version of a Portuguese catechism by João de Barros, published in Lisbon in 1539.[187] Otherwise known as the 'small catechism' it had been published in 1578 AD by a press run by Jesuits at *the Collegio do Saluador*, in a Portuguese fort, built in the coastal town of Kollam. Quite another and much longer work of 127 pages by Henrique Henriques, one sometimes referred to as 'the big catechism,'[188] had been printed under almost the same title of *Doutrina Christã* or *kirisittiyāṉi vaṇakkam*, also in the Portuguese possessions in Kerala, in the place referred to as Kouchim (Kochi, or Cochin), at the Collegio de Madre de Deus in 1579.[189] The same author is credited with yet two more titles printed within the Jesuit sphere of influence in South India. In 1580, his *Confessionario* (Confessionary) of 214 pages had also been printed in Cochin. The circumstances of the editing and printing of his *Flos Sanctorum* (Lives of Saints), a voluminous work of 669 pages, published in 1586, remain somewhat ambiguous. It could also have been printed in

---

[187] Blackburn 2006: 34; Priolkar 1958: 9. For a different view, see Üçerler 2013: 109.

[188] Županov 1999 64.

[189] It was a translation of *Doctrina Christa* by Marcos Jorge published in 1561 (Baretto Xavier and Zupanov 2015: 226). Priolkar 1958; Blackburn 2006.

Cochin.[190] According to other opinions, it appears that either the fonts for its printing had been prepared or the printing itself had been done in Punicale (Punnayiakayal) on the south-east coast of Coromandel in the enclave then in possession of the Portuguese.[191]

It is difficult to measure the impact of these early printed Tamil Christian books. At that time and place, the books must still have been perceived as wonder objects in the hands of those very few who happened to come into contact with them, who were not necessarily those who knew how to read them. They must have been very often read collectively, in group readings and listenings. We may infer this from reports by Jesuit missionaries and collaborators with Francis Xavier's work; in the 1540s, Xavier is said to have distributed 'a written copy of a catechism in each village he visited', so it could be sung from in groups 'on every Feast day.'[192] Some of those objects must have found their way into the hands of local, traditional scholars, in most cases hailing from local Brahmin groups. In an annual letter of 1600, by a Jesuit to his superiors, we find a short mention of the distribution of newly printed Tamil Christian books into the 'interior, where pundits admired the novelty...'[193] We know of early printed books by Henrique Henriques put on display in the churches of the Parava Christians of the south Coromandel coast.[194] Incidentally, the latter ones proved to be quite active in the initial phase of the history of the book in India: two Christian books edited by members of their community were printed in Romanized script in Lisbon in 1554.

The early phase of print in India includes also the printed works of the English Jesuit, Thomas Stephens (1549–1619). His *Discurso sobre a vinda de Jesu Christo*, published in Roman script, appeared in print at 1617.[195] We know that his famous *Kristapurāṇa* was printed thrice in Goa, in 1616, 1649, and 1654, but no copies of its first edition survived. What does survive are copies of his *Doutrina Christam em Lingoa Bramana Canarim*, a catechism printed in Roman script in the college of Rachol, south Goa, in 1622 and one single copy of his Confessionario, apparently printed in 1580 in Cochin, at Collegio da Madre de Deus.[196]

---

190 Blackburn 2006: 44.

191 Lach 1977: 496.

192 Blackburn 2006: 37.

193 Blackburn 2006: 37.

194 Blackburn 2006: 37.

195 Chakravarty 2017: 119.

196 For the circumstances of this find, see Barretto Xavier and Županov 2015: 229, fn. 87 and Shaw 1982.

Quite a different printing enterprise also deserves pride of place among the Jesuit institutions: It is believed that, in 1602, 'Jesuits established a Syrian press at Vaippikkotta located near Chendamangalam in Ernakulam district.'[197] Most probably, Christian religious material was printed there, not in Malayalam but in Syriac. However, none of those books have survived. According to Stuart Blackburn, the printing press at Vaipikotta (not far from Ambalakad) seems to have produced at least one book in Syriac typeface.[198] If this is true, it testifies to early initiatives to use print as an instrument for mobilizing and asserting the social standing of the religious community of Syrian Christians.

As mentioned above, the now defunct but once very active Saint Paul's Seminary in Ambalakad (Ampalakāṭu), later known as Sampallor (Sampallūr), appears to have operated a printing press and to have used newly made fonts in Rome (around 1670) for the publishing of DeNobili's catechism in three volumes in 1677—almost a hundred years after the works of Henrique Henriques. After several decades of operation, the Jesuit press at the Saint Paul seminary in Ambalakkad, as well as the seminary itself, had been destroyed by the invading armies of Hyder Ali in 1781. It was there, where one of the most important book of the time appeared in print in 1679—the first Tamil-Portuguese dictionary by Antem de Proenca (1625–1666)—another Jesuit and Tamil scholar.[199] It was also in the same seminar of Saint Paul of Ambalakad where somewhat later a German Jesuit scholar, proficient in several languages, remained active for some time—Johan Ernst Hanxleden (1681–1732).[200] For some reason, none of his Tamil works or scholarly treatises came out in print from this still active printing press. Paradoxically again, some of his Malayalam writings (*Puttanpāna*, *Caturantyam*) entered into wide circulation not through print but within the traditional regional networks of manuscript copies and oral performances, with an effect far exceeding that made by the printed works of the Protestant missionaries on the eastern Coast of Coromandel.

The slow decline of the Jesuit printing towards the end of 17th century reflects, in some measure, the rapid decline of Portuguese political power, eclipsed first by the Dutch in Kerala, and later on by the British, who

197 http://keralaculture.org/printing-press/292 [accessed on 15 Nov 2017].
198 Blackburn 2006: 39–40.
199 Blackburn 2006: 43.
200 More about Hanxleden, see Vielle (forthcoming).

reduced the effective operations of the once most powerful Portuguese to their core territories in Goa. Deprived of their coastal base, the Roman Catholic missionaries operated inland in technical conditions of marked disadvantage when compared to those of their rivals in the South, the Protestants. Over the entire 18th century, the not so long before so active centres of Jesuit printing in Goa, Kollam, Cochin, and Ambalakad appear not to have produced a single book, not only in Tamil, but in any other language.[201] The decline of the political power of *the Estado* translated into logistical and technical difficulties for the Jesuit printing presses—a lack of good Tamil fonts and a shortage of printers with sufficient knowledge of Tamil.[202]

To this early phase of printing in India also belongs the only partly successful attempt at setting up a printing press in Surat by an enterprising Indian close to the British. Probably using Gujarati typefaces, a number of religious Hindu texts were either planned or actually printed there towards 1671;[203] however, the printing was soon abandoned, and we do not hear about the operation of printing presses in this area except for the British Courier newspaper press until the arrival of the American Mission Press, which started operating in 1817.[204]

With its new authoritative capabilities and potential for a wide audience, print remained an important tool for various missionary enterprises throughout the subcontinent: among others, the first print in the Malayalam language and script prepared by Father Clemens Pianus was printed in 1772 in Rome, under the auspices of the institution named Sacra Congregatio de Propaganda Fide, with the Malayalam title *Saṃkṣepa-vedārtham* (*nasrānikaḷ okkuṃ ariyeṇḍunna*), which, because of its Sanskrit looking main title, might have been mistaken for a commentary on the Veda. But the

---

201 Blackburn 2006: 44; Priolkar 1958.

202 Blackburn 2006: 44.

203 Blackburn 2006: 40; Priolkar 1958.

204 In this year a tract in Marathi containing a translation of the Gospel of St. Mattew appeared from the American Missionary Press. See *Memorial Papers* 1882: 77 and Hazen 1913: 8–10. The two English newspapers, the Bombay Courier and the Bombay Gazette apparently start to appear from 1790 and 1791 respectively from the Courier press. See Naregal 2017: 161. Other attempts at printing in Marathi or Gujarati characters occured away from Bombay, among else in Serampore (1810) and in the Maratha enclave in the distant southern kingdom of Tanjore where Serfoji II published on a press locally established with the help of Danish missionaries around 1804 the *Balbodh Muktavali*, a Marathi translation of Aesop's fables which appeared in 1809 and used a Devanagari fount designed in cooperation with Charles Wilkins. See Nair 2011; Naregal 2017: 162.

Jesuit printing establishments in India cease to be active by the late 1600s, with no lasting response from the indigenous Indian side. The new printed objects produced from Jesuit presses must have at least provoked curiosity from the established communities of learning and knowledge, such as those operating across Kerala, along a network of houses of traditional scholars of Nampūtiri Brahmins, as well as in monastery-cum-education centres like the complex of three *maṭhas* in Trichur. A feeble echo of that may be heard in the Jesuit correspondence that made it to our times; in an annual letter of 1600, by a Jesuit missionary to his superiors, a short mention can be seen concerning the distribution of newly printed Tamil Christian books into the 'interior, where pundits admired the novelty...'[205]

It is an uneasy question to answer, when we ask what effect the Jesuits had on printed books in terms of stimulating interest in the new medium of print among Indians. Scattered reports mention interest expressed by the pundits. Except for a vague echo concerning the Mughal court, we don't hear much on that matter, which probably reflects Jesuits' own bias in forming questions (this perhaps can exemplify Harold Innis' thesis of the vicious circle closing the possibility and readiness of media-appraisal). However, some indirect hints tell the story of the disinterest of those in power. Thus, a Jesuit-Dominican short visit to the court of the Sultan of Bijapur in 1569 resulted in a gift of a (most probably printed) book to the Sultan. The Jesuits had been sent to Bijapur's court by the archbishop of Goa on a sort of a diplomatic mission. They reported to have offered the Sultan of Bijapur. In fact, the Jesuit accompanied a Dominican, Antonio Pegado, and both travelled as representatives from the archbishop of Goa, with whom the sultan wanted to be on good terms for political reasons. They offered the Sultan of Bijapur 'a copy of Aquinas's *Summa contra gentiles*'. The sultan is said to have impressed them with a good manners of his court. Apparently he himself remained unimpressed by the gift he received.[206]

---

205 Blackburn 2006: 37. For the actual value of Jesuit correspondence as a historical source in the light of numerous editorial interferences with the textual matter and succeeding re-editions of the letters, see Županov 1999.

206 Rubiés 2001: 322 referring to a letter by Goncalo Rodriguez in *Documenta indica* V: 141-2.

III.2.2. German Danish evangelists on the Coromandel coast

A second phase of the early printing on Indian subcontinent appears to belong to the Protestant missionaries on the opposite side of the Indian subcontinent, the eastern Coromandel coast.[207] While Jesuits are credited with introducing the printing press to the Indian subcontinent around 1556 AD, it was the establishment of Protestant missions a century-and-a-half later that triggered processes which, in the longer run, came to be acknowledged as harbingers of change in the sense of a deep transformation in communication patterns. These processes allegedly brought social and civilizational change, deserving, in the opinions of some, the appellation of 'media revolution' caused by print as an 'agent of change.'[208] However, the beginnings and early decades of Protestant printing activity proved to be far from revolutionary in their results. As late as 1811, we still hear of a lack of printed Bibles in the south, and a pressing need for a printing press on the part of the Protestant community in the southern kingdom of Tanjore, whose court boasted at the time of possessing a printing press itself to the dismay of the Protestant missionaries.[209] The Jesuits controlled the printing presses over the 16th and 17th centuries but the Lutheran Protestants took over at the beginning of the 18th century and made printing in Tamil their own speciality. By so doing, they put to work the earlier experience of the German Lutherans in printing Luther's Bible, first in Wittenberg and later in other German towns, as well as the later Pietist systematization of those experiences in the Halle education project of August Francke. The early success in the 16th and 17th centuries in the use of print German Protestant reformers contributed to the onset of a belief in an intrinsic connection between Protestant ideology, the transforming power of the 'Word of God', and the technology of book printing.[210]

---

207 A confused adjectival use of Malabar/Malabaric(k), with reference to the language of the eastern part of the southern Indian subcontinent, recurred throughout missionary writings from the 16th to the 18th century.

208 See, for instance, McNeely and Wolverton 2009: 173.

209 For the complaints of a local Protestant congregation lacking a 'single complete copy of the Bible', see Buchanan 1811: 63. The same source contains complaints about the printing press remaining in the hands of 'pagans' instead of the Protestant missionaries.

210 See McNeely and Wolverton 2009. An extremely rich recent scholarship on early Protestant missions in South India, drawing from several editions of missionary letters, reports and other documents, leaves almost no room for new discoveries, and this chapter

While there can be little doubt indeed 'that the book was one of the great forces for change in sixteenth-century Europe' (and that Reformation lay at the centre of this) and that 'the connection between the book and the Reformation seems so obvious that it needs little extra comment',[211] it may not be that obvious when it comes to examining how the printed book and print technology actually fared in the hands of missionaries continuing the early call of the Reformation in the changed geographical, historical and socio-cultural circumstances.

In one of his later formulations, Andrew Pettegree argues that '... the book looms large in all explanations of the appeal of the evangelical cause—a view shared, it must be said, by the reformers themselves.'[212] Indeed, when we try to make sense of the early association of European print cultures with Protestantism and the later consequences of this, it is sometimes important to put into perspective how the Protestants themselves conceived of print. This is somehow possible either through retrieving their own words or by showcasing those of their social practices in which the book stands prominently as the tool of action and change. With reference to the latter, Elisabeth Eisenstein, who herself quotes Richard Altick, says that: 'The Evangelicals ... believed that the grace of God could, and did, descend to the individual man and woman through the printed text.'[213] This view did not necessarily have to appeal to others, labelled as heathens, whose sensibilities may have been nurtured by quite different sets of preconceptions and cultural realities. These would be formed by and concerned with written and printed objects of an altogether different shape and cultural concept—objects circulating in an altogether different way and in spaces differently defined and circumscribed. The case at hand here is the so-called Tranquebar mission in the Danish enclave in South India, which began in 1706 AD.

The ideas and concept of European Reformation, as it manifested itself in the activities of the Protestant missionary press establishments in South India, may certainly be visible in the pattern of missionary work in the

draws from multiple studies, while focusing on those primary sources which may have something to tell as concerns the topic of print and conceptual images of the function and aim of printing, cherished by the early missionaries. For a critical overview of this scholarship and their sources, see Sebastian 2015: 4.

211 Pettegree 2004: 785.

212 Pettegree 2005: 128.

213 Eisenstein 2011: 153.

Tranquebar mission. However, the contemporary understanding of the role of the printed book in the later phase of the Reformation needs a historical relocation of the assumed straightforward role of the book in the hands of protestant missionaries, as an agent of change powerfully influencing societies in the manner proposed some time ago by Elisabeth Eisenstein.[214] First of all, we need to argue for the reasonability of the plural cultures of print instead of the singular print culture postulated earlier by Eisenstein and reproduced in an array of studies following that choice. We must admit that '...the dynamics of the book industry varied very markedly from country to country' in Europe itself,[215] not to mention in other further removed areas with a radically different historical experiences and an altogether different configuration of social and political forces at work.

Another formulation by Pettegree, forged in relation to the historical situation of the 16th century reformation in Europe, can, with some probability, be extended to that of the Reformation exported overseas, where it proved that '...the book did not function as an autonomous agency, but within the context created by the intermingling of a whole range of communication media.'[216] It is this very context, which appears to have been rather radically different for pre-modern Europe and the early modern Indian subcontinent in its regional variety found in the southern areas of today's Tamil Nadu. First of all, we have to acknowledge the probability of a radical difference in the scope and impact of the manuscript culture in its regional varieties across India. Recent estimates put the figure of approximately thirty million manuscript works still extant in libraries, private collections, and the ancestral homes of traditional scholars and literary connoisseurs, as representing a still greater figure of written objects in multiple languages and scripts and varied material forms and shapes in circulation.[217] For the immediate purpose of this study, we should consider the sociohistorical context of coastal Tamil Nadu and the wider space of the Tamil ecumene, along with its interrelationships with those of Sanskrit, Telugu, and Malayalam.

---

214 E. Eisenstein herself appears to have modified her early formulations in her later works, where she puts more emphasis on the later stage of the development of mass-printing, as being qualitatively distinct from the print technology itself.

215 Pettegree 2004: 787.

216 Pettegree 2005: 128.

217 Estimate to be seen in Pollock 2003 and 2007. For a more 'conservative' estimate, calculated within the Indian Government Manuscript Mission, presupposing a number of seven million, see Wujastyk 2014. For a critical reassessment of the former calculation, see, among others, Formigatti 2016.

Processes that were later named 'a media revolution', also triggered new regional cultures of print. To them goes the credit for profoundly influencing and actually shaping the use of print for regional and trans-regional projects of social and cultural change as well as those of imperial consolidation later on. The legendary Tranquebar Mission Press, founded by Bartholomeus Ziegenbalg in 1712, was a work of missionary zeal by a Pietist. At the initial stage, it was the Pietist ideology that gave impetus to this pioneering establishment and the prominent case of the printing press started by the Lutheran missionar in the remote Danish enclave of Tranquebar (Tarangabādi). In spite of unquestioned success animating future developments it remained itself, by and large, confined to the missionary project, with no effect to be measured in terms of a media revolution that one might expect from the print project of that ambition and scale. It is only later, in a third phase in relation to the reconstitution of the colonial power by means of a new hold on education and knowledge control, that the process of spreading the new print culture gained momentum but remained uneven, rather fragmentary, and regionally limited–varying in degree in different parts of the subcontinent. In that later phase, it was Bengal that took the early lead with the exceptionally busy Baptist Missionary Press, started by the visionary William Carey towards 1800 in Serampore, another Danish enclave located at a distance of fourteen miles north of Calcutta. The early enthusiasm of Baptist missionary printers remained limited by the reluctance of the British East India Company to allow missionary work in the territories under its control.[218] Only when this changed did print gain momentum on Indian soil.

Due to the East India Company's policy of not allowing missionaries on territories controlled by the company, none of the otherwise extremely active English Protestant missionary institutions could set their foot on Indian soil before 1806, when the regulations changed. An option to circumvent this regulation proved to be Danish possessions in India. The first of them was Tranquebar, otherwise known as Tarangambādi, in South East Tamil Nadu, between the French enclave of Pondicherry to the north and the then Portuguese station in the port city of Nagapattinam to the South. In the first two decades of its activity, between 1712–1730, the Protestant's printing establishment in the Danish enclave of Tranquebar

[218] This policy changed with the 1813 East India Company Charter, which lifted the ban, while introducing the so-called 'pious clause' allowing a frame for cooperation between the Empire (Company) and missions.

produced as many as 117 different printed books in multiple languages, and nearly tripled this number by the end of the century.[219] Among the printed books were bibles, gospels, catechisms, grammars, dictionaries, and almanacs. Their languages included German, Dutch, Latin, Danish, and Portuguese, and later increasingly English, but most of these books were printed in Tamil.[220] Thus, after a rather modest output of printed books from the presses operated by Jesuits during the whole of the 17th century, which saw not more than a handful of books printed, the Lutheran Protestants of Tranquebar became unquestioned leaders in the use of print, and especially in the printing of Tamil books, for a long time.[221] Yet, paradoxically, the increasingly better standard of Tamil types used for printing did not stimulate an improved standard of Tamil language, which used to be ridiculed by their rivals in South India, the Jesuits. On the other hand, due to changes in the political situation, much weaker progress in printing can be seen on the part of Jesuits in the 17th and 18th centuries.[222] After the successes of late 16th century, the Jesuit printing establishments faced serious technical problems with their presses, until new font arrived from Rome and a new generation of printers eventually resumed their work, thus ending a long gap. This came along with scholarly works on the Tamil language and serious efforts for standardization, which, in many cases, had been assisted by the old medium of manuscript writing and circulated within the ecumene of a regional manuscript culture. Both developments took place within spaces that partly overlapped on the eastern coast and looked back to different traditions of the use of print, represented by the Jesuits and Lutheran Protestants. Both aimed at expansion from their base territories in European enclaves. The two, however, conceived of print, its aims, and its functions in a rather different way.

In 1620, the village of Tranquebar was acquired in a lease for 86 years for the Danish Crown, by the Danish Admiral Ove Gjedde, who signed an

---

219 Blackburn 2006: 51.

220 Blackburn 2006: 47; Priolkar 1958.

221 The institutions that organized and supported early missions in Tranquebar were the The Danish royal house, The Franke Foundations (Die Stieftungen August Hermann Frankes) in Halle (1695–) with the East India Institute (Ostindische Missionsanstalt), the Society for Promoting the Christian Knowledge in London, and later the Mission Board in Copenhagen [Liebau 2017: 84]. 'Like August Hermann Francke who was a professor of Oriental languages at the university, the later directors of the Hall Orphan-House were also connected to the local university' created by the kings of Prussia [Liebau 2017: 82].

222 Blackburn 2006: 48; Priolkar 1958.

agreement on behalf of the King of Denmark with the ruler of the Tanjore Nayaka Kingdom, by the name of Raghunatha Nayaka.[223] The kingdom was a successor state to the once powerful Indian empire of Vijayanagara, whose previous tributaries gained independence towards 1550 AD, especially after the defeat of the Vijayanagara armies by a coalition of largely Muslim armies in 1556. Now, the circumstances of this Danish acquisition are quite interesting and telling. They are connected with a shipwreck fatal to most of the crew of a Danish vessel, part of a Danish expedition to Ceylon, which, on the way, engaged in sea battle with the Portuguese by the Coromandel coast of south India. The ship had been destroyed by the superior Portuguese fleet and most of the crew killed or taken prisoner with two victims heads even said to have been put on wooden poles and exposed on the beach of Karaikal, a port controlled by the Catholic Portuguese, south of Tranquebar. The fourteen survivors of the shipwreck went ashore and had been taken to Tanjore and shown to the king, who is said to have them with due respect, apparently regarding new Europeans in his territory to be in his interest. As a result of the negotiations that followed, the Danes had been offered the right of establishing a fort and a trading station on a piece of land twenty-five km long, along the coast, some distance south of Madras and trading privileges comparable to those enjoyed by the Portuguese in their enclave in Karaikal further the south. This was granted in exchange for a yearly tribute and functions to fulfil in the ceremonial exchange of gifts and privileges that constituted an important part of the Nayaka kingdom's political structure, which provided an immediate political and cultural context for the operation of the Trnquebar mission.[224] Through a treaty with the Hindu Nayaka king of Tanjore, the Danish built a fort named Dansborg, where the seat of the Governor was to be located together with a trading factory, around which evolved a local urban centre.

The Danish merchants in Tranquebar, just like their English colleagues to the north, wanted no Danish priests in their territories. However, King Frederick IV's chaplain insisted there should be a Lutheran presence in Danish settlements. As a compromise, Frederick IV invited the Pietists to send out priests to Tranquebar. The 23-year-old Bartholomaeus Ziegenbalg

---

[223] Hudson 1993; Liebau 2017.

[224] The story tells us a lot about how Protestant-Catholic relationships might appear in extreme cases. It also shows us other things, for example, how it came about that the Danish acquired land for their trading factory, which later came to host Pietist missionaries. For details, see Hudson 1993.

and the 29-year-old Heinrich Plutschau were suggested by their teacher Lange from Halle and answered the call. They probably did not know where they were heading for until coming to Copenhagen, as the king's plans clarified slowly and there didn't seem to be much difference between sending his missionaries to work in the New World, New Guinea, Madagascar, or Indian Tamil Nadu. Ziegenbalg had had no opportunity to prepare himself for his Indian mission in any sense of the word. He had probably never studied anything that was known of India during the time before he came to Tranquebar. He also had not had the opportunity to study any language except Danish, which he did only when already onboard a ship of the Danish East India Company.[225] When they arrived in India in July 1706, they founded the first formal Protestant mission in Asia. Almost immediately after arriving, Ziegenbalg took to learning languages, at first Portuguese, but very soon Tamil. He also made it a routine of his to discuss religion with Tamils, at first a local schoolmaster, later on with local Brahmins. After a very short time, he radically changed his views about whom he was encountering in India. This began with an early expectation of a 'barbarous people' but—to his growing astonishment and bewilderment—his interest grew in their learning, knowledge and religious institutions. During this process, he decided (and this appears to be a decision by a true Lutheran Reformist) that the best way to understand what he was dealing with was to study the indigenous texts in the original languages. For this reason, he started to collect Hindu writings and soon formed a collection, later to be known as *Biblioteca Malabarica*.[226] It has been estimated that, in his writings, he referred to at least 170 Hindu titles of his collection. Most of these must have been at first procured or hand-copied for him on order, by the elderly schoolmaster who figures prominently as the most frequent source for his early information on Tamil Hinduism.[227] Furthermore, in an early letter of 1706, Ziegenbalg mentions using 'Malabar scribes', whom he had 'sent into the country to buy Malabari books.'[228] His collecting and subsequent study of original textual sources made him an exceptional textual scholar among other contemporaries writing on India.[229] As Sweetman

225 Sweetman 2014: 306.

226 For the evaluation of the contents of the collection, see Gaur 1967; Zvelebil 1974; Jeyaraj 2005; Sweetman 2012, 2014.

227 Sweetman 2014: 309.

228 A letter by Ziegenbalg published in Book No 16, quoted in Gaur 1967: 67.

229 Sweetman 2014: 308.

convincingly showed, Ziegenbalg's understanding of Tamil Hinduism, as can be seen in his major published works, was formed under the influence of one particular Tamil Hindu textual source, namely the *Tirikālaccakkaram*. In his *Genealogie* and other works, Ziegenbalg refers to this very text as the source for his description of the allegedly monotheistic character of Hindu belief.[230] Ziegenbalg appears to have been considering translating (and probably publishing) its text.[231] This would add an additional dimension to the otherwise acknowledged ideology of print, that accompanied his and his patrons' policy and actions. A fundamental belief in the transformative power of the printed 'Word of God' accompanied not only the motivations of the Ziegenbalg's team in Tranquebar, but also shaped the framework for the broader missionary politics of Protestant institutions formed in Europe. It derived from the historical experience of the early Reformation's use of print in 16th century Germany and presupposed the inherent link between the power of the Gospel in the vernacular and print. It also took for granted the feasibility of repeating the Wittenberg phenomenon of mass printing among 'heathens' overseas. A short passage from a printed circular by a Danish association for the promotion of missionary work in the East Indies shows this more than clearly:

> We joyfully remember upon this Occasion, on the happiest Effect of Luther's Reformation; since by this Means we have recovered the free Use of the Holy Scriptures, and the liberty to read them in our own Language, whereby we our Selves are enabled to search the Sacred Oracles, and to know the Will of God revealed in them.... It must be acknowledged to be a very great Blessing to the Malabar Heathen, to have the Gospel laid before them in their Native Tongue...[232]

The unambiguous belief in the eventual effect to be brought about by the circulation of printed objects revealing the 'Word of God' is more than conspicuous here:

> As soon as the Effect of the Portuguese and the Malabarick Printing Press shall appear by furnishing the Heathen with a Sufficient number of Printed Copies

230 Sweetman 2004: 19.
231 Sweetman 2004: 12–38.
232 Downing 1715: 10.

> of the Word of GOD ... we shall have a fresh and signal Occasion to Praise the Lord's most holy Name ...[233]

A further piece of correspondence, which, as the two preceding ones, had also been rather thoroughly edited before having been translated and published in print and circulated by 'the Society for the Propagation of Christian Knowledge', attests to the consequences of the Protestants' variety of faith in the power of print:

> We may remember how much the Art of Printing contributed to the manifestation of divine Truths, and the Spreading of Books for that End, at the time of the happy Reformation ... O Living God, grant that the Christians here in India, and the Multitude of Gentiles, may, with Hearts full of Gratitude, become sensible of this great Benefit, and receive with Joy that Word of Life which is, and shall be laid before them, printed in their own Languages...[234]

These and cognate ideas must have been an important source for Ziegenbalg's efforts for establishing a printing press capable of producing (and subsequently circulating) the vernacular Bible and other religious texts. In this context, his interest in Tamil Hindu writings and plans for translating some of them look as enriching as Lutheran print ideology centred on the Gospel. However, after a rather short period when Ziegenbalg remained active in writing on Hinduism, he decided to refocus on practical aspects of his mission establishment. Initially, Ziegenbalg organized the Tamil congregation on Sundays at his own house and let the same house be used as a school on other days. The services were held in Tamil and Portuguese, which was the lingua franca at that time. Since the Zion Church that existed in Tranquebar faced growing tension between the European community and Tamil converts, Ziegenbalg helped in organizing a new church in 1707. The church was named 'the New Jerusalem Church', after the Francke Foundations in Halle, which was considered to be the New Jerusalem. The registers of the church indicate that most of the congregation were servants of Europeans, former converts from Roman Catholicism, children, and women. The majority of them came from the lowest strata

---

233 Downing 1715: 11.

234 From a letter of 1713 by B. Ziegenbalg as quoted in Venkatachalapathy 2009: 132.

of Tamil society at that time.[235] Later on, after a powerful storm struck Tranquebar in 1715, destroying the city, a new church had to be built and consecrated under the same name of New Jerusalem Church in 1717.[236] Not only the naming of the churches, but also the reports sent by Ziegenbalg and others to Halle suggest a strong and enthusiastic commitment to the Pietist ideals of awakening and education in a project of building a new, reformed society out of the hard working community, a society imagined as a chosen people. In a more general fashion, the reports and letters sent to Halle by Ziegenbalg and others from Tranquebar (even if most often censored and re-edited)[237] indicate the eager deployment of strategies of educational work, otherwise known from the extraordinary experiment of August Francke's (1663–1727) alleged transformation of what used to be the 'decaying salt-mining town [of Halle] into a New Jerusalem', centred in a 'walled cluster of over forty buildings dominated by imposing Baroque edifices', that made the effectual machine for perpetuating piety and profit.[238] Pietists 'shared with other evangelical Protestants, like Puritans and early Methodists' a severe moral code, a desire to uplift the poor, and a missionary zeal and enthusiasm.[239] Pietists refrained from the supposedly sterile and stiff style of worship, seen in traditional Lutheran churches, and preferred meeting in private circles, often at home, in order to 'pore over the Bible' in a distinct type of reading practice that was believed to be leading to experience scripture in a direct and emotional way. We find this practice highlighted in Ziegenbalg's letters, showing his own house in Tranquebar used for such a cause on Sundays, in addition to other days, when it was said to have been used as a school—another basic cause of the Pietist movement being improvement through education, strengthened by their own inventions in daily educational process and schooling practices, such as a class roster, arranging writing desks in rows, and raising hands for questions.[240] Though young when starting his Tranquebar adventure,

---

235 Fenger 1863: 36. For a brilliant analysis of the social stratification in Tranquebar Mission church congregation, see Hudson 1993.

236 Fenger 1863: 105.

237 Virtually each and every piece of correspondence, even private letters, were directed to Halle first to be read and edited, if necessary, before being forwarded to addressees or before being published as materials serving the cause of attracting new sponsors and convincing new converts.

238 McNeely and Wolverton 2009: 168.

239 McNeely and Wolverton 2009: 168.

240 McNeely and Wolverton 2009: 169.

Ziegenbalg must have been well-acquainted with the Pietists' methods and inventions and, for that reason, suggested as a candidate to the Danish by his teacher. A number of letters written by Ziegenbalg had actually been published (probably after thorough re-editing) and included in the Pietists' media machine for spreading the news and attracting support. In some, he admitted assistance on the part of native Indian scholars.[241]

Like other evangelists, the Pietists also leaned heavily on Luther's German Bible to do their missionary work. Now, in the changed circumstances of missionary work among non-German speaking 'heathens', a translation of the Bible was a 'must do'. We do not know to what extent Ziegenbalg was aware that the missionaries worked among people whose historical experience remained multi-lingual and multi-cultural.[242] Ziegenbalg himself immediately began using a local variety of spoken Tamil and used to be seen among school children attempting the vernacular in order to learn Tamil, which he apparently did in an amazingly short time. But Tamil, not to mention its polyglossia, multiple varieties, and registers was just one language, albeit, no doubt, spoken by most of the people. Apart from this, however, the cultural reality of the land had been formed by the intellectual and religious output, be it texts or performances, of other languages: Marathi, Telugu, Sanskrit (and to some extant maybe also Malayalam). To these, we must add a rather different reading practices as well as practices of 'publishing' and circulating written texts in regional varieties of manuscript culture. As concerns the latter, we must note that Ziegenbalg recognized its potential for teaching the gospel, and he is said to have employed a team of thirteen efficient copyists, that could produce enough to keep a few hundred or maybe thousand copies of tracts in circulation.[243] This example from Ziegenbalg's life shows how, in a different historical and social situation, the relationship between the order of the manuscript and the order of the print

---

241 In a letter written in 1708, Ziegenbalg speaks of two vocabularies of the Malabar language prepared by him, in which he was assisted by Indian scholars and poets who remained at his house for four months.

242 According to Liebau 2017: 84, 'It was common for the early workers of the Dannich-English-Halle Mission to have had a theological-philological training' but Zieganbalg and his companion did not have any specific training in Indian laguages. Their motivations for self-teaching and dedication to learning of new languages was exceptional and due to their Pietist formation. Cf. Liebau 2017: 83—'The first missionaries trained in Halle were brought up in a strict Pietistic tradition, or they have reached a deeply interiorized Pietistic feeling through a subjective experience of edification.'

243 Hudson 1993: 8.

could take a different shape entirely from that known from the first decades of Protestant Lutheran evangelism in the 16th century Germany. The press and its products had to cope with and adapt themselves to the most complex of cultural environments, created not only by generations of trade between Europeans and south Indian kingdoms, but also involved in a hierarchy of tributary relations to sovereign powers to the north and a fluctuating and shifting balance of power among the polities of the south, with the kingdoms of Madurai and Travancore to the west of Tanjore and Muslim polities to the immediate north, as well as the competing Europeans: the Portuguese, the Dutch, the French and, later, the British. Perhaps, it is in some sense true that the little pamphlet which Ziegenbalg printed first at this newly established press in 1713 'inaugurated the modern era of Tamil book-printing and printing in Indian languages as a whole.'[244]

Ziegenbalg was keenly aware that, in order to attain his missionary objectives, he needed a printing press. He made repeated demands for a printing press in his letters of April–June 1709. The Danes forwarded the appeal to London to the Society for Promoting Christian Knowledge (SPCK). The SPCK, not allowed a foothold in India by John Company's merchants, was only too eager to help. Eventually, the SPCK, set up in London in 1690, answered the call and came forward to help under the recommendation of the Rev. A.W. Boehme (the German chaplain to Prince George of Denmark). In 1711, the society sent the mission some copies of the Bible in Portuguese as well as a printing press with pica types, paper, ink and other accessories along with a printer to operate it. The ship was held up by the French near Brazil, and the printer Jones Finck was arrested but later released. Finck soon succumbed to fever near the Cape of Good Hope. When the SPCK consignment arrived in Madras in 1712, the printer was missing. Fortunately, a German soldier in the Danish Company's service knew something about printing and was recruited, and this is how the press started functioning. Johann Heinrich Schloricke, 30 years old at the time, printed the Tranquebar mission press's first publications in 1712/13 in Portuguese. With this, printing in India got its second wind, and this marked a new phase of the career of print in India.

Ziegenbalg, however, was convinced that the Mission's work would not prove successful without a printing press capable of producing books and other literature in Tamil. He arranged for drawings of the Tamil alphabet

---

[244] Gensichen 1967: 34.

characters to be made and sent them back to Halle, requesting the production of Tamil typefaces there. The Tamil type arrived in Madras on 29 June 1713, together with three Germans, who were to galvanise the press and printing when they got to Tranquebar by the end of August. In September/October 1713, Johann Gottlieb Adler, a type founder, printer and mechanic, his 14-year-old brother Dietrich Gottlieb Adler and the 27-year-old Johannes Berlin, a bookbinder and printing assistant, used the Halle Tamil type, to print the first 'Malabarick' publication since the Portuguese had put a stop to printing in Tamil c. 1612.

The type prepared in Halle, however, proved to be inconveniently large and impractical. It quickly devoured the mission's limited paper stock. While more paper was sought from London, Johann Adler began cutting a new and smaller Tamil type in June/July 1714, and cast it using, according to legend, the lead covers of tins of Cheshire cheese that were regularly sent out by the SPCK. Using this type, Johann Adler completed the printing of the New Testament in Tamil (Pudu Etpadu) in July 1715. Adler's type foundry was set up in Porayur, on the outskirts of Tranquebar. In 1715, he started a paper mill in the same village, the government meeting half the costs and the mission the rest. He then opened a printing ink manufacturing unit nearby. All three were the first printing material 'factories' in India.[245] The Tranquebar mission press was now virtually self-sufficient, and this was to help it remain active for another hundred years. However, after 1817, there is no report of this press functioning.

Ziegenbalg continued to work on the translation of the Old Testament to Tamil and by 1719, the year of his death, he had finished the Old Testament up to the Book of Ruth. The remaining work was completed by another German missionary, Benjamin Schultze, and published in Tranquebar in 1723. Philip Fabricius, also a German, spent twenty-four years on a new, improved translation of the Bible, which was published in 1777.

Strangely enough, by the time the mission press in Tranquebar had started working in a regular way, Ziegenbalg probably had in his collection

[245] No estimation is known to me, however, to what extent this locally produced paper was actually used for printing in Tranquebar. The price of imported European paper and the insufficient quality of 'country paper' remains one of the major issues for the huge printing projects of the Serampore Mission and continues to be a major hindrance in developing commercial printing in India till the second half of the 19th century. For a general situation in 19th century Northern India, see Stark 2007: 66. See also Gode 1969a and Gode 1969b.

a fairly good number of Indic manuscripts, which he passionately gathered in the first years of his days in Tranquebar. The palm-leaf manuscripts did not seem to have been a popular and easy to acquire commodity in early 18th century Tamil Nadu, rather, quite the contrary. In order to acquire them, he must have found his way to private or institutional collections, which may have been rather reluctant not only to part with their possessions, but maybe even to show them to Ziegenbalg. At least two such collections were, at that time, 'at hand,' not further that 20–30 km away from Tranquebar. And, as rightly remarked by Sweetman, only very few '...elite scholars would have had access to those which did exist, such as at the Śaiva maṭams (Sanskrit: *maṭha*) at Tiruvāvaṭuturai and Tarumapuram [...]. Although Ziegenbalg never explicitly mentions either maṭam, there is reason to believe that at least a part of his manuscript collection was derived from the libraries at the Tiruvāvaṭuturai and Tarumapuram maṭams'.[246]

The collection which he managed to gather was later turned into what came to us as *Bibliotheca Malabarica*. For our immediate purpose, we should note that there is no indication left concerning any idea of editing some of them in print. Printing indigenous knowledge would probably be, in Ziegenbalg's (and that of his superiors in Halle) opinion, an act of putting wrong thing in the machine for spreading the gospel, which, for the Protestants, the printing press must have primarily been.

In the meantime, printing—in the words of a contemporary Indian journalist—'not only continued in Tranquebar, but also spread to Madras, Tanjore and later on to another Danish settlement, Serampore, near Calcutta where it flourished.'[247] The pioneering printing enterprise of Ziegenbalg eventually resulted in the native Tamil printing project of Arumuga Navalar,[248] who set his first press near Tiruvannamalai and named it the Preservation of Knowledge Press (*vidyā-anubalana-yantra-śālā*).[249] Relocated later on, the press served as a powerful tool in the hands of the Tamil *Śaiva* renaissance movement against Christian missionaries, printing and circulating several booklets written by Navalar himself and his Tamil Brahmin collaborator.[250]

246 Sweetman 2012: 29.
247 The *Hindu* 2016 [online version], Chen, 'The Legacy of Ziegenbalg'.
248 Hudson 1993: 58.
249 Hudson 1993: 41.
250 Hudson 1993: 44.

Besides his translation and missionary activities, Ziegenbalg worked on other ideas of his own that he came up with after the experience of his missionary work. But his works never got published during his life. There was a Ziegenbalg–Hale controversy: 'A.H. Francke categorically refused to allow publication of one of Ziegenbalg's two main works, the *Genealogie der malabarischen Gotter* (written in 1713), because 'the missionaries were sent out to exterminate heathendom in India, and not to spread heathen non-sense throughout Europe.' It was not until 1867 that this work was 'officially' published in an essentially unabridged, though not very reliable, edition.[251]

In his letters, Ziegenbalg proves to be ruminating over an idea of a spiritual and intellectual encounter, albeit based on a concept of 'Christian awakening.' As he wrote: 'The Indians no longer understood the true, lost origins of their own religion; this is why they needed to be reawakened by Christianity.'[252] Ziegenbalg found the potential for such a reawakening lying in the forgotten depths of their own traditional wisdom; indeed, he even found a certain implicit anticipation of true monotheism therein.[253] Unfortunately, Ziegenbalg had no knowledge of Sanskrit, and probably also no first hand access to intellectual and religious treatises in high literary Tamil. He must have based his ideas on the opinions of intermediaries that he had hired to assist his translation work. The press he established appears to have continued until the early 1800s. In the meantime, another printing enterprise emerged to the north of Tranquebar.

When, in 1761, the English attacked the French colony of Pondicherry, they seized the printing press from the French governor's house along with its typefaces (and the printer, DeLong) and transferred the spoils to Madras. Johann Phillip Fabricius, a German-Danish Missionary and a Tamil scholar, convinced the English to hand over the press on condition that the press would meet the demands of Fort St. George with due diligence.[254] In 1762 itself, the Society for Promoting Christian Knowledge press published a calendar and several Tamil books, 'pre-dating the books printed in Calcutta and Bombay at least by a decade.'[255] The French press had been initially installed at Vypery but, around 1766, it was returned to Fort St. George, which resulted in the establishment of the Government Press in Mount Road. The

---

251 Sweetman 2004: 21; Halbfass 1988: 47.

252 Halbfass 1988: 48.

253 Halbfass 1988: 48.

254 More 2004: 80.

255 Blackburn 2006: 58. Cf. More 2004: 80 who dates this event to 1761.

Vepery Press was renamed as the SPCK Press...[256] It would be interesting to gauge how the printed matter, issued from Tranquebar and SPCK press, actually circulated. Though there is more evidence to this than we have with reference to the imprints from earlier Jesuit establishments, these are not sufficient for a well-balanced assessment. One important instance is the story of a transformation and eventual conversion of a young man from Tanjore (Thanjavur), told by Fenger in his history of the Tranquebar Mission. The story includes details of handwritten and printed books in circulation in early 18th century Tamil Nadu. One of the characteristics of this print circulation it hints at is that even small printed books by Tranquebar Mission were, for the most part, beyond the reach of common people, even if they happened to be literate. Another telling piece of information, from the same source, is that referring to a copy of Tamil Bible, that had been presented as a valuable gift to the French Governor of Pondichery. We may infer that at least some of these were objects of prestige rather than textbooks actually used among the people. Apart from stories like that included in Fenger 1863 and sacred Missionary reports, we do not have enough evidence to assess what effect Bibles, printed in Tranquebar, had on the Tamil people. Even missionary sources, as late as those of 1811, indicate that cases of families, or even whole local congregations, who could actually afford a copy of a printed Tranquebar Bible must have been rare.[257] The latter source also brings telling reports on the project of publishing a new translation of the Bible into Malayalam, printed in Bombay, and a most interesting report by the protestant author on the reasons for publishing in print a Bible in Syriac, on the basis of an old manuscripts preserved in Kerala. The reasons, or motives, for printing the Syriac Bible, given by Buchanan, are as follows:

1. To do honor to the language, which was spoken by our blessed Savior when upon earth.
2. To do honor to that ancient Church, which has preserved his language and his doctrine.

---

[256] This press was sold to the American Board of Commissioners for Foreign Missions (the American Board Mission or ABM) in Çintadaripet in the mid-19th century. After ABM left India in 1886, the press returned to the hands of SPCK and was renamed the Diocesan Press, that still exists today [Blackburn 2006: 58].

[257] '[T]here were upwards of ten-thousand Protestant Christians belonging to the Tanjore and Tinavelly districts alone,who had not among them one complete copy, of the Bible' [Buchanan 1811: 62].

3. As the means of perpetuating the true Faith in the same Church for ages to come.
4. As the means of preserving the pronunciation, and of cultivating the knowledge of the Syriac Language in the East; and
5. As the means or reviving the knowledge of the Syriac Language in our own nation.[258]

However, for a project actually approaching anything like 'mass printing' of the Bible in Tamil, we need to look to William Carey's Serampore Mission Press, far away to the north of Tranquebar and Tamil Nadu. Towards 1813, Serampore Press undertook a commission from the Calcutta Auxiliary Bible Society to produce new Tamil typefaces and print five thousand copies of the Tamil Bible at a price competitive to that offered by Tranquebar and Vypery presses. This was possible mainly through reducing the size of print, thanks to a newly cut smaller Tamil typefaces.[259] The new Tamil Bible printed in Serampore could take the shape of 700 pages in octavo. As had always happened before, and many times subsequently, the size of the font and the price of paper remained two decisive factors in shaping the actual impact of printing projects in India.[260]

III.2.2.1. Missionary printers and cultural encounter

It seems of interest to signal a historical paradox of something that should probably be judged as a failed cultural encounter. The German Danish missionaries seemed to be little interested in Sanskrit and its heritage, which may seem logical from the point of view of Protestant ideology centred on the vernacular gospel. Around the time of Ziegenbalg's arrival to Tranquebar, in the nearby area of Kumbakonam, some 60 km inland, west of

---

258 Buchanan 1811: 116. On translations of the Bible to Indian languages, see Israel 2010.

259 *A Memoir for Serampore Translations* 1815: 18–19. On Bible translations into Indian languages, se Israel 2010.

260 From a report of 1813, it is clear that the problem of overpriced imported paper and inadequate local produce still remained grave in the first decades of the 19th century: 'It is impossible that the Scriptures can be diffused sufficiently among the nations, if copies are printed only on paper brought from Europe: the high price of it will render this impracticable [*A Memoir for Serampore Translations* 1815: 22.].' For some statistics showing the growth of the paper industry in the United Kingdom between 1800 and 1900, see Innis 1986: 159 'Total production of paper in the United Kingdom increased from about 11,000 tons of hand-made paper in 1800, to 100,000 tons in 1861, of which 96,000 tons were machine-made, and to 652,000 tons, of which 648,000 tons were machine-made in 1900.'

Tranquebar and within the same political organism that Tranquebar had been included by the tribute paying agreement with kings of Tanjore, there flourished an extraordinary intellectual institution: a village for *paṇḍitas* or traditional intellectuals, founded and patronized by the then Maratha king of Tanjore (the Marathas took over Tanjore in 1671), by the name of Śāhaji. The ruler donated a village to a group of forty six traditional scholars with the aim of promoting intellectual pursuits. 'In the years to come, the scholars of this college would produce a flood of literature on all aspects of the arts and sciences, including linguistics, theology, philosophy, law and ethics, drama and medicine.'[261] The texts that were produced, as an effect of this important act of traditional patronage of the righteous Indian king, entered the region-specific space of circulation, proper for the regional manuscript culture with its bias for the specific writing technique on preformatted palm-leaves and its modalities of publishing (first reading at the court), circulating, and re-copying. 'The manuscripts of much of this work are today housed in Thanjavur library. Many of these works have been printed; an even greater number are still in manuscript, unpublished, and are yet to be integrated into contemporary scholarship.'[262] Some of those works must have been written in the years when Tranquebar mission and its printing activity took place. However, no mention, either of the presence of the missionaries or of the allegedly revolutionary technology of print, found its way into the corpus of these writings. And vice versa—no mention of either the existence of such a centre in the nearby village nor any of the work produced there appears to have been indicated in the sources available for the history of the mission, such as reports and other correspondence or Ziegenbalg's own writings, at least in the form in which they came down to us after having been edited in Halle by August Franke and his successors at the Pietist centre.[263]

Something of the encounter must have impressed one of the later successors to Śāhaji, the then king of Tanjore, namely King Serfoji II, who, apparently inspired by his tutor, a Dutch missionary, decided, towards 1802, to establish a printing press in his capital. The Rev. Christian Fredrich Schwartz, a Dutch missionary, was appointed as the teacher and guide of

---

261 Wujastyk 2012: 4. For early Indian paper production, see Gode 1969a and 1969b.

262 Wujastyk 2012: 4.

263 On the nature and status of Pietist missionary reports and letters and their editorial re-shaping, see Liebau 2017: 21–23 and Sebastian 2015: 54.

the young Serfoji II. Serfoji was 'trained and tutored in St. George school Madras under the direct supervision of the Rev. Schwartz and, in the course of time, became a scholar.'[264]

Under the rule of Serfoji II, Tanjavur (Tanjore) became a centre of learning. His library, successively known as the Saraswati Mahal Library, boasted of a growing collection of manuscripts and printed books. To this enlightened figure of the ruler, already limited by the growing power of British East India Company, we owe the beginnings of one of the richest manuscript libraries in contemporary India, housing reportedly around 500,000 manuscripts, out of the estimated gargantuan number of thirty million works believed to be still extant across India in libraries and private collections, only one million being catalogued.[265]

What is interesting, in the context of the coexistence of different media of writing in that part of the Indian subcontinent, is the evidence from the very end of 19th century and beginning of 20th, showing that manuscript culture among traditional scholarly families was, to some extent, still in operation. Eugen Hultzsch, an intrepid explorer, paleographer, and traveller in search of manuscripts gives, in his 1905 report, a vivid description of the family collection of the descendants of one of the scholarly families of *brahmanas* that had benefited from the royal donation, showing that not only a rich variety of works in Sanskrit has been written in the past, but that a few works continued to be authored and written on palm leaves still in the second half of the 19th century. Only some of them had been locally edited and published in print by 1925. Hultschz lists in his reports two rural family collections of Kodaṇḍa and Rāmasubba, counting up to a hundred manuscript works in each. One of those families has kept remnants of this collection in their ancestral home till today.[266] Studies concerned with manuscript distribution[267] show that titles featured in these collections reappear in other collections (Kanchi, nearby villages) across Tamil Nadu, indicating a network of circulation yet to be established and described. 'This literary and intellectual persistence demonstrates the family's lasting intellectual engagement in serious scholarship and its participation in a philosophical discussion over centuries that stretched

264 Cf. Blackburn 2006: 78.

265 For an account of Serfoji's collecting passions and the establishment of printing press, see Nair 2005 and 2011.

266 See Wujastyk 2012.

267 Zysk 2012.

from Tiruviśainallūr to Thanjavur and Kanchipuram.'[268] In the opinion of Wujastyk: 'The documentary evidence abundantly supports this community memory, as well as the extensive networks of Sanskrit scholarship and intellectual exchange that resulted from Śāhaji's endowment and that were still alive and active in the early decades of the twentieth century.'[269] No traces of this apparently vivid and intensive networks of exchange of Sanskrit knowledge can be traced in the report of Tranquebar missionaries who flourished nearby and who must have occasionally visited the king's court in Tanjavur and met with the Sanskrit culture no doubt present there.[270]

We could expect a sort of clash between the introduced print technology and the regional variety of manuscript culture, based on pre-formatted palm-leaves, with its technique of writing. In the latter one 'the dried leaves are cut to equal lengths, drilled for the string binding, boiled in water, dried again and then buried in sand before a final polish with conch shells. A *śalāka* (Sanskrit: metal stylus) was used to inscribe the text into the thin pre-formatted leaf surface on both sides, a rather demanding technique.' In order to be read for the first time, it had to be smeared with soot (lamp) or 'washed with a mixture of charcoal and vegetable juice to add contrast to the letters. The finished leaves were smoked over a fire and coated with juices to provide protection from insect damage.'[271] This technique served an extremely effective manuscript culture with professional scribes, the whole economy of market services, which Sheldon Pollock dubbed 'script mercantilism', in contrast to print capitalism, and which was capable of circulating hundreds and, in extreme cases, thousands of manuscript copies of texts, which is proven by the gargantuan number of extant Indic

268 Wujastyk 2012: 250.

269 Wujastyk 2012: 251.

270 Cf. Liebau 2013: 94 where Liebau agues that 'The missionaries ... hadly had any contact with this [Brahmins] section of the local society. Apart from this, only a few missionaries learned Sanskrit.' Some opinions indicate the major difference between the conversion strategy of the Jesuits who often focused their attempts on Brahmins, and the Tranquebar missionaries who targeted rather lower strata, be it the Paṟaaiyār, or śūdras. See Liebau 2013: 219, fn. 155.

271 http://designtraveler.wordpress.com.[accessed on 29 Nov 2017]. Cf. an eyewitness description by a Protestant missionary from late 18th century quoted in Liebau 2013: 389, fn. 177: 'They are seated while writing and place the left hand, with which they hold the leaf, on the raised left knee; the hand rests on the knee and holds the leaf firmly: the right hand holds the stylus that should be long and heavy at the top.The leaves on which they write should have a double layer so that the stylus does not go through the surface.'

manuscripts in library and private collections in India and around the world, only one in thirty of them having been catalogued.

This was not the end of the Tamil and other translations of the Bible into Indian languages. Dr. Buchanan reported in his memorable journey in 1806, that there was a 'great cry for Bibles.' People followed him pleading: 'We don't want bread or money from you, but we want the Word of God.'

A few notable facts concerning the early years of the Printing Press of Tranquebar seem to provide an outline of the idea of print in the hands of Lutheran evangelists in Tranquebar: Ziegenbalg never published in print his major work in the Missionary press. It was published after editing by German and Higginbottom for the Christian Knowledge Society Press in Madras in 1867. Two years later, German brought out his English translation, also by Higginbottom. I know not of any trace of Ziegenbalg's reflecting on the possible project of bringing any of his collected 'heathen' books into print, either through his printing press or any other in Europe. A strong connection between print, printing, and the spreading of the gospel in Lutheran form made it unthinkable to use the printing press in any other way, except, perhaps, for a little profit that might be turned into the upgrading of the mission. It is, perhaps, an irony of history, that Ziegenbalg did seriously consider translating into German one specific Tamil book of his collection, which he held in the highest esteem and from which he took most of his ideas included in his 'Genealogy of Malabar Gods'. This can be safely inferred, thanks to a discovery of Albertine Gaur, published in 1967, from Ziegenbalg's own remarks under the title of this book in the catalogue named *Verzeihnis der Malabarichen Bücher*, that was sent overseas with some handwriting of his to Halle and subsequently published:

> Once I had it in mind to translate this work into German but I could not help wondering whether this was really advisable. It would cause a lot of unnecessary speculation and only distract people from more important things. But I am still keeping my mind open whether or not I should do this translation.[272]

On considering translating into German and possible reactions to it (in Germany?), he must have had in mind publication in print. We may

[272] Gaur 1967: 88. On the same page, Ziegenbalg expresses his hesitation regarding the possible reception of such a translation (he must have thought of publication): 'If the scholars in Europe got a chance to read it they would hear strange and unprecedented thing.'

ask a rhetorical question: why did he not think of publishing it in his own missionary press in Tranquebar? Naturally, rather not in German.[273]

'Thus it seems that in 1726, only eighteen years after the composition of the *Verzeichnis der Malabarischen Bücher*, not more than twenty six of the manuscripts Ziegenbalg had collected with so much effort during the first years of his stay in India were still in the possession of the Tranquebar mission.'[274] Out of the at least one hundred and seventy texts mentioned on lists sent to Europe, some were sent to Denmark in early 1700, as specimens, along with the lists of the collection; some were shifted to Madras; but the bulk of the collection was probably dispersed irretrievably. For the immediate topic of this study, it is of interest what one of Ziegenbalg's letters home suggests, as far as his intention of procuring a copy of the Vedas is concerned. It is true that all the missionary reports, and letters—even private ones—reached Halle first, where they were probably heavily edited, and we should take it into account while judging their historical value. Moreover, they kept appearing in print in German, Danish and English, in redactions that differed much among themselves.[275] One of his relatively early letters, as we know it in Brgen's redaction, written before his printing press was established, suggests not only his intention, but actual steps taken towards copying 'the remaining three' of the Vedas.[276] Another letter edited by Joachim Lange has Ziegenbalg ask his old schoolmaster to arrange for copying 'the remaining three of them' and concludes that he failed to do that because it would be 'against their [those who possessed the manuscripts] law.'[277] It would be, of course, pure speculation to say that, if Ziegenbalg—with his unprecedented interest and collector's instinct—actually lay his hands on whatever Vedic texts he could find, then it may have had some chances to find its way, in some sense at least, into the writings he deemed proper for print and distribution. It is almost beyond doubt, that,

---

[273] However, his own 'Genealogy of Malabarishen Gods' came to be published a hundred-and-fifty years later, in 1867, in German in Madras, at the Christian Society for Propagating Knowledge Press with Higginbotham as distributor. Only two years later, its English version appeared in the same place. See Germann 1867 and Metzger 1869 respectively.

[274] Gaur 1967: 89.

[275] For a general assessment of this phenomenon, see Liebau 2017; Sweetman 2014: 309.

[276] Sweetman 2014: 309.

[277] These remarks are brought to light in Sweetman 2014: 308–310. See also Sweetman 2014: 309: 'While Ziegenbalg asked the schoolmaster to transcribe the remaining three of these for him: "he could not bring himself to do it, for it would be against their law to allow a Christian to have access to them."'

if he eventually had some Vedic texts transcribed for him, he would never have cherished any idea of putting them to print. The very idea of doing so would be as foreign to them as it was for those who used these texts, though the reasons could have been altogether different.

For the main interest of this study, the question of the impact of print remains to be answered: can we today speak, in any sensible way, of a transformative influence of print in the shape it took in the hands of the early 17th century protestant missionaries of Tranquebar? If so, on whom and in what way? The printed book must have been considered a weapon of sorts, and a modernizing, if not civilizational instrument, by the very Protestants who thought it worth the effort to operate a press under conditions that were unfavourable at the least. This can be seen in the published missionary correspondence, where the book appears as an object of interest and a tool for missionary action. In one such report, dated 5 March 1714, not more than two years after Ziegenbalg had started his printing enterprise, we hear of 'heathens' coming to Ziegenbalg's house with a request that he give them 'some Printed Books, such as they had seen in the Hands of some of their Neighbours.'[278] Whatever value we may ascribe to the this early English rendering or paraphrase of the original, we must admit the independent value of this document for the prospective donor and patrons of the missionaries among the English subjects to whom it was directed. The picture of 'heathens' coming from a distant city to communicate their hunger for 'printed books' could prove communicative enough to gain support among fellow English Protestants for Ziegenbalg's printing project in far-away Tranquebar.[279] A few important hints to the missionary's views (probably lifted up by the Halle editors) towards the nature of their printing enterprise can be identified in the answer given to the above quoted words by 'one of the missionaries:'

> Tis not, said I, to raise your Admiration, that we are come here from our own Countrey, and print these Books with so much Cost and Pains-taking; but to the

---

278 Philipps 1718: 241.

279 For a critical evaluation of the Halle Protestant sources, see Liebau 2017; Jeyaraj and Young 2013, who warn against paraphrase rather than translation by Phillips [Jeyaraj and Young 2013: 5]. See also Sebastian 2015: 55–'Ziegenbalg was a missionary who was a part of a well-established system of communication that was centralized in Halle, from where it reached out to other parts of the world, including England and colonies of North America.'

> end we may spread among you the Knowledge of the True God, and that your selves may read the Words of Eternal Life.[280]

The same missionary interlocutor also pointed to the mission's policy of distributing the printed matter 'without Money and without Price.' This economy of evangelization, however, later proved to have been complemented by initiatives that looked much more like print capitalism, when the Missionaries started the printing of almanacs.[281] In the longer run, the protestant missionary concept of print showed hints of changing into a more economy-oriented initiative. But also, in this avatar, it does not appear to have competed successfully with the traditional networks of circulation of texts and ideas. On the other hand, one should point to some continuation of the Pietist way of using print in Tamil Nadu; the best candidate, however, does not appear till the mid-19th century, and it is the use made of a printing press for advocating the promotion of *Śaiva* ideology by Arumuga Navalar.[282] Some influence on the operations of printing presses, established in Vypore and later in Madras for the SPKN, could also be demonstrated, as well as the more direct effect on the project of the setting up of a press by the Maratha court of Serfoji II in Tanjore around 1802.[283] While this separate instance did not produce much output nor did it stimulate any follow-up; by the early 1800s, the missionary printing initiated in Tranquebar had moved to the growing new urban centre of Mirai/Madras and its satellite villages. Although, in terms of size, this was a far cry from the urbanity of the then contemporary Calcutta, Madras had, especially after the College St. George was established there in 1812, almost everything needed to develop a new market for the printed book. It took, however, another five decades for this to develop or, rather, to burst out suddenly in a multitude of printing enterprises and journalism.

In spite of much of modern scholarship's pointing to the later missionary mass printing in Serampore of the early 1800s, print did not prove to be an agent of revolutionary social or civilizational change on the Indian subcontinent before the middle of the 19th century, and the reasons for this are complex and interesting—one theory on offer[284] links the circumstances

---

280 Philipps 1718: 241–42.

281 See Blackburn 2006.

282 See Hudson 1993. See Weiss 2016.

283 See Blackburn 2006: 78 and Nair 2011.

284 See McNeely and Wolverton 2009.

of the developments in Halle after Napoleon closed the university in 1806 and the British trying to control information and media after the 1857 Sepoy uprising, that gave impetus to the indigenous printing establishments.

Out of the competitive impact of the process initiated by protestant printing in the service of evangelization, there emerged indigenous printing initiatives on the part of Hindu communities. One such initiative was the Kalvi Kalanciyam Press (Caturveda Siddhanta Society) at Salai Street, George Town, Madras, that commenced its work by protesting against missionary activists.[285]

III.2.3. The media revolution of Serampore 1800–1837

In this later phase of the history of print on the Indian Subcontinent, it is Bengal that took the early lead, with the exceptionally busy Baptist Missionary Press, which was started towards 1800 in Serampore (Śrirampur) by the visionary William Carey and his associates. As with the earlier instance of Tranquebar, it was once again a Danish enclave located at a distance of fourteen miles north of Calcutta, and this circumstance reflects the uneasy relationship between the missions and the company in the earlier phase of the empire building.[286] The inventiveness and enthusiasm of the early Baptist missionary printers remained, at first, checked by the reluctance on the part of the company's executives towards allowing missionary work on the territories under its control, deriving from a fear of social unrest. Only when these initial attitudes began to change did print gain momentum on Indian soil. The unprecedented energy of the Serampore Baptist publishing project soon came to constitute a paradigm to follow by later indigenous printing-cum-publishing enterprises. Within the early decades of the 19th century, from 1800 to 1837, the translation and printing enterprise set up by the intrepid little bunch of Baptist missionaries, in what was at first a tiny Danish enclave, produced a stunning number of 21,200 books in almost forty languages. Even if the quality of some of these suffered from the dazzling speed of their production process, the scale of this phenomenon, at least in the opinion of some, brought a veritable media

---

285 Blackburn 2006: 112.

286 Due to the official ban for the operating of missions within the territories of the East India Company. This situation changed in 1813, when a new company charter lifted the ban, while introducing a formula of cooperation between the company and missions under the so called 'pious clause.' See Sweetman 2015: 11.

revolution to the northern part of the Indian subcontinent.[287] The character of this revolution should, however, be understood today in a slightly more nuanced way, as proposed by C.A. Bayly:

> The conceptual revolution which the Serampore missionaries and 'padres' of the educational establishment had hoped to spread through small books, became a print bazaar in which vast numbers of standardised texts of popular devotional works and epics spread a generalised Hindu or Muslim consciousness to the respectable people of the urban and rural worlds. 'Print capitalism', in Benedict Anderson's formulation, gave many existing communities of knowledge the capacity to operate on a wider scale. It was midwife to intellectual change, not in itself the essence of that change.[288]

This important formulation retains its force, while the present study takes a bit different perspective. Initially, the main field of Serampore printing activities concerned the circulation of translations of the Bible, at first, often parts of New Testament. The circulation frequently depended on the activities of travelling evangelists, who journeyed to provinces under the control of the company and distributed copies of the Evangels free to people whom they considered heathens. This important aspect of print history in India has been reflected in the rich missionary literature made up of extensive reports, memoirs, registers, and correspondence, which most often underwent the process of thorough editing before being published and circulated in Europe and America, with the aim of attracting pious sponsors to the cause. Some of these gave evidence to the peculiar effects of these practices of circulation, in which the 'English books', as they were often called, irrespective of the language they were printed in, happened to be treated as material objects of curiosity rather than texts carrying meanings worth considering. In extreme cases, this attitude lead to the use of the printed text for purposes quite foreign to the intention of the publishers, such as wrapping or waste.[289]

Other missionary institutions initiated the use of print in order to meet their immediate needs connected to missionary work, sometimes in frantic attempts at distributing free copies among the 'heathens'. The operation of

---

287 McNeely and Wolverton 2009: 189.

288 Bayly 1996: 376.

289 See, for instance, Gupta 2016: 349.

one such a press is mentioned in the Sixth Report of the Calcutta Committee of the Church Missionary Society in the *Friend of India* (itself printed by Serampore Mission Press) in 1824:

> During the past year 17,150 Tracts and School books have issued from the Committee's press for the use of schools, and for distribution by the Missionaries.[290]

At least in the first two decades of the century, the new mass printing projects suffered badly from material impediments: inflated prices of imported paper, unstable quality of paper made in India and faltering quality of types. All of them had a high impact on the costs of production and greatly increased prices that effectively kept printed matter beyond the means of common readers, even if such an entity existed. In the case of printing Bible translations into vernacular languages, the minimum economic basis of the production process could be secured exclusively, thanks to the global network of protestant fund-rising institutions. Reports show that income from the actual sale of the printed copies could often account for less than 1% of the total costs incurred.[291] The perennial deficiency of cheaper paper still remained the main obstacle for later commercial printing in the hands of Indian entrepreneurs. Yet, the unprecedented enthusiasm, combined with missionary zeal and belief in civilizational progress, even if this eventually brought grave financial shortcomings, did result in the dazzling figures of print production indicated above. It gave rise to a network of relations with patrons, commissioning agents, distributors, other publishers and printers, the government institutions included, and set a number of standards in organization and distribution for the commercial printing to continue in the next few decades. How far missionary printers and publishers engaged in publishing projects focused on Sanskrit religious texts remains an uneasy subject to judge. Apart from the cases of commissioned printing jobs accepted by missionary printing facilities, there were also cases of publishing projects initiated, stimulated by, or actively joined by the missionary institutions. Such an example was the project of publishing the Sanskrit *Rāmāyaṇa*, carried out by the Serampore Mission Press

---

290 *Friend of India*, Vol. VII (1824): 29.

291 See, for instance, *A Memoir of the Serampore Translations* 1815: 26–7 which features the figure of 52 Sicca Rupees, representing the sale of Bibles against the figure of 28,516 Sicca Rupees of the total cost of translating and publishing.

between 1806 and 1810, after an agreement and financial grant on the part of the Fort William College. For his part, William Carey seems to have developed a genuine interest in Sanskrit studies, which was also the case with other missionaries of the time involved in the printing revolution, such as John Stevenson of the Presbyterian Church of Scotland, who worked in Maharashtra and made a name for himself as an original editor and translator of Vedic literature and a linguist exploring Indian vernaculars.[292] His pioneering edition and translation of the initial part of the *Ṛgvedasaṃhitā* appeared in a lithographed version made by the American Mission Press in 1833, and his better-known translation of *Sāmaveda* appeared in London in 1842. The type of excuse or rationale for their association through print with the religious literature of the heathens given by Carey and Stevenson appear quite similar. Carey presented his justification in the correspondence to his superiors by declaring his intentions as focused on exposing the 'mysterious sacred nothings ... which have maintained their celebrity so long merely by being kept from the inspection of any but interested Brahmans,'[293] while Stevenson wrote in the preface of his 1833 edition that:

> Should this small tract be useful in opening up the meaning of those ancient writings, and leading the native youths to compare them with the simple and sublime system of Christianity, the translator will not esteem lost the time he has expended upon it.[294]

The latter, active two decades later, accomplished what Carey only dreamed of when writing in 1802:

> I have long wished to obtain a copy of the Veda; and am now in hopes I shall be able to procure all that are extant ... If I succeed, I shall be strongly tempted to publish them with a translation, pro *bono publico*.[295]

---

292 See his frequent publications in the *Journal of the Bombay Branch of the Royal Asiatic Society*: among else Stevenson 1841, 1844, 1853. For details, see Galewicz 2019.

293 Quoted in Rocher and Rocher 2012: 77.

294 Stevenson 1833: V. A parallel formulation can be seen in his *Principles of the Murathee Grammar* that appeared the very same year (Stevenson 1843a: vi): 'If this attempt should facilitate the progress of those who are endeavouring to sow the seeds of useful knowledge, and teach the Natives of the Murathee country the principles of Divine Science, the author will esteem all his labour well bestowed.'

295 Smith 1902: 157–158 quoting a letter by W. Carey dated 17th March 1802. Carey's dream met partial fulfillment: his *Grammar of Sunsgrit Language* of 1806 included on pp. 902—906

Though involved in passionate missionary work, the two took an active part in what amounted to the modern race for the unearthing and opening to the public of the long concealed and withheld Veda with the powerful means offered by the printing press.

III.2.4. Later missionary print cultures

III.2.4.1. The Baptist Mission Press, Calcutta 1818

New opportunities opened before the missionaries after the renewal of the East India Company Charter in 1813. The new charter stipulated that the Company should add to its declared goals one of 'religious and moral improvement', through accepting missions provided they operate according to so-called 'pious cause'. The company was also forced to accept the funding of an Anglican bishopric in Calcutta.[296] Thus, an early idea of Boyle, one of Company's directors and shareholders, took legal shape. In practical terms, however, the Company retained the power of silencing and extruding unwelcome voices, which it took advantage of.

Founded in 1818, the Baptist Mission Press eventually amalgamated with, or rather took over, the Serampore Missionary Press in 1837, when the latter's heavy debts put it in danger of being closed. It was here, where, in 1849, one of the early printed editions of the Vedic texts was printed, namely E. Röer's *Bṛhadaraṇyakopaniṣad*, Bibl. Indica (printed by J. Thomas at Baptist Mission Press).

III.2.4.2. The American Mission Press of Bombay 1817–1856

After initial troubles with Company's authorities the Americam Baptist Mission started formally in Bombay from 12 February 1813.[297] The beginning of its press' operation is usually dated to 1816 and the arrival of Rev. Horatio Bardwell.[298] In 1817 a tract of Scripture, the Gospel of St. Matthew as well as

the *VajuSuneya or Oopunishut Eesha Vasyu belonging to the Yajoos Vedu*. See Carez 1806, Gildemeister 1847: 2.

296 For particular and consequences, see Sweetman 2015: 25—'...the Company was forced to accept the establishment of an Anglican bishopric in Calcutta and the insertion in its charter of the 'pious clause,' first framed twenty years earlier, insisting that the company had a duty to promote the 'religious and moral improvement' of the Indians.'

297 *Memorial Papers* 1882: 92 and Diehl 1986: 206.

298 *Memorial Papers* 1882: 77.

'a harmony of Gospels' in Marathi got printed from a wooden press.[299] The operation of the American Mission Press is said to have gained momentum thanks to its self-taught setter, who, later on, instructed one of the first and most successful native printers, by the name of Śeth Jāvajī, who established his own printing press enterprise and foundry in 1867 in Bombay.[300] Soon the American Mission Press in Bombay 'printed for everybody'.[301] It was here, in the American Mission Press in Bombay, where one of the first ever mechanically reproduced integral Vedic texts appeared in AD 1833.[302] This came out as a lithographed Devanagari text of an initial part of the *Ṛgvedasaṃhitā* (RS 1.1–35), unaccented, along with excerpts of Sāyaṇa's commentary attached and a Marathi rendering facing the 'original' in the right column of the two-columned text printed vertically.[303] This shape must have been a consequence of incorporating the oblong, *pothī* manuscript-like, folios on which the Devanagari text had been handwritten. Manuscripts of that format must have been in circulation in Maharashtra and one such handwritten copy must have been either acquired or prepared specifically for Stevenson as

---

299 *Memorial Papers* 1882: 92–93.

300 Priolkar 1958.

301 Diehl 1986: 208: 'Virtually all Society publications ... were their products; Bible Society orders (whether British, American, or local), as well as Tract Society 12mos, were printed accord ing to contract. Much government work...'

302 The little earlier *Rig-Vedae Specimen* by Rosen, published in 1830 in London, important as it was, contained only a modest selection of hymns printed in unaccented Devanagari with a Latin translation. See Rosen 1830. J. Stevenson did not know about Rosen's work till his own translation appeared in 1833. See Stevenson 1833: Preface.

303 The beginnings of the lithographic press in Bombay connect to the person of Robert Macdowall appointed in 1824 a superintendent of the Company's lithographic press service for the Bombay Presidency (the so-called Lithographic Office). The Company planned to furnish its offices with lithographic presses mainly in order to meet its needs for uniform administration documents and blank forms. The first batch of six litho presses was shipped to Bombay from England in 1824. The pioneering use of lithographic press in India belongs to Nathaniel Rind, a surgeon in Bengal who brought the first lithographic press from Edinburgh and put it to use of the Company around 1822 in Calcutta where it was apparently used for printing of revenue survey maps, country plans, etc. [Shaw 1993: 1, 9]. Apart from serving the administration needs, the Lithographic Office of the Bombay Government catered widely and free of charge to the Native School Book and School Society and its education projects. For a detailed assessment of the early use of lithographic press in Bombay, see Shaw 1993. See also Diehl 1986. After the short-lived but ground-breaking and influential early carrier, the lithographic presses were handed over to the government agencies involved with the government education policy. Apart from the government establishments, also the missionaries found lithographic press a useful technology used mostly for fast and short tract campaigns. The American Mission in Bombay and the Scottish Missionaries were apparently the first to use it for mass tract printing. See *Memorial Papers* 1882; Diehl 1986: 208; Shaw 1994.

a basis for his lithographed edition.[304] Judging by the colophon ending to the first part containing the text of the *Ṛksaṃhitā* 1–35, it may have been copied/hand-written/prepared for lithographed print by a Christian convert. Curiously, it featured a title that misleadingly referred to something other than the *Ṛgveda* proper: *Trividyā Triguṇātmikā Sabhāga.*[305] Its second part had been titled with an English equivalent of the former as *The Threefold Knowledge* and brought an English translation of the Sanskrit text of the original with a preface and notes by the author, the Rev. John Stevenson.[306] It is interesting to note that this early edition came from the hand of a missionary working for the Scottish Missionary Society, whose education policy strictly banned, from any use within their fast developing schooling network in Maharashtra, books of this sort, as can be seen in a report declaring that, in their schools, 'all Heathen Books are excluded, and no instruction relative to Hindoo superstitions is allowed.'[307] The second part of the publication contains an English translation with a preface in which J. Stevenson suggests a rationale for his printed edition of the Ṛgvedic hymns. The official tone of the Preface makes this clear for the readers whom he expects to be 'native youths' that the published text of the Veda will speak by itself and loose in comparison to the 'simple and sublime system of Christianity.'[308]

However, the beginning of the Preface shows the author as not only a missionary, but a philologist with a keen interest in the emerging project of editing and translating the Veda by the European philologists of the

---

[304] The Rev. John Stevenson is reported to have arrived in India in 1823 and to have been directed, along with another missionary, to start a new station in Hurnee, 80 miles South of Bombay, on behalf of the Scottish Missionary Society. See *Missionary Register for the MDCCCXXV*: 71. Later on, his name reappears in the Missionary Register as being active in Pune (Poonah) and touring Maharashtra. He was reported, among other things, to have stayed for some time at 'Punderpore, a celebrated place of Hindoo pilgrimage, where he ... distributed three bullocks' load of Tracts and portions of Scripture...' [*Missionary Register* for MDCCCXXXIII: 93].

[305] A British Museum copy, which I refer to here, features a partly legible handwritten note to its title page. It is dated 1836, i.e. three years after the date of publication, and, as far as I can decipher, it reads: 'This [is] a rare and curious translation of a book that the Hindoos venerate above all others and have for a long time held too sacred to be ... to any but those of their own class (?) ... initiated into the priesthood...' [Stevenson 1833: frontispiece].

[306] A missionary, if not proselytising, bias of the scribe, whose written transcript had been adopted as the basis for the publication, stands out from a concluding set of beneficiary stanzas in Sanskrit (occasionally broken) and Marathi. See Stevenson 1833 I: 60. (I thank Dusan Deak for offering a working translation from Marathi of this passage.)

[307] *Missionary Register for the MDCCCXXV*: 70.

[308] For full quotation of the passage, see fn 294 above.

time.[309]In addition to its curious title, the whole work reveals a specific architecture that accommodates three different typographical orders while being divided in two parts.[310]

The Bombay American Mission Press, whose operation proved to be seminal for the future development of the early indigenous printing in Bombay, acquired its lithograph probably before 1825 and put it to efficient use in the time when production and use of Devanagari character types were still facing serious technical and logistic difficulties.[311] However, the use of lithograph proved to be problematic in the climatic conditions of coastal Maharashtra. Scottish missionaries active in primary education in Marathi region deplored the fact that handwritten copies occasionally withstood the climate much better than the lithographed copies.[312] The same Scottish Missionary Society operated its first lithographic presses already before 1825.[313] A report by the Bombay Station of the Scottish mission records the effective operation on its lithographic press in Bombay for the year of 1832.[314] Also missionaries in other regions found it more than useful to make effective use of lithographed copies of their tracts to be distributed freely while remaining reluctant towards producing lithographed copies of the Bible. The latter case was avoided probably on the basis of the fear of impermanence that could possibly be effected by lithographic copies that apparently were seen as lacking the permanent status of regular print

309 See Stevenson 1833 II: iv.

310 A colophon-like set of verses concluding Part One indicates that it may have been either copied/hand-written in preparation for the Stevenson's lithographed edition by a Christian convert, or intentionally fitted by Stevenson himself with a sort of Protestant Christian "confession of faith." Its positioning at the end of Part One along with a Marathi version of the same appears to be mirrored by the English version in Part Two which strongly suggests a translation from Sanskrit/Marathi to English. The whole exhibits a composite character: not only Part One is lithographed from the handwritten source while Part Two appears to have been typeset. Part Two has been fitted with a Devanagari text of the *vedāṅga* of *jyotiṣa*, namely the text of *Lagadhajyotiṣa*. The colophon-like conclusion to Part One contains an indication to the overall message of the whole: its headline declares the verses to be excerpts from Christian scriptures. However neither the Sanskrit nor the Marathi version or the supposed English translation identifies the source of them.

311 For a report on the circumstances of the lithographic press in service of the Scottish Missionary Society and work commissioned with its lithographic press by American Mission in Bombay, see *Missionary Register for the M DCCCXXV*: 71. For cicumstances the introduction of lithograhphic press in Bombay, see also Diehl 1986: 206 and Shaw 1993 and 1994 II.

312 See *Missionary Register for the MDCCCXXV*: 70–71.

313 See *Missionary Register for the M DCCCXXV*: 70.

314 *The Oriental Christian Spectator* Vol. IV (1832): 74.

deemed proper for the eternal truth of the Scripture.[315] The fast growth of the printing activities of the American Press saw its establishments towards the beginning of 1840ies as possessing 'materials for printing to any extent required, in English, Sanskrit, Marathi, Guzarati, Hindustani, Persian, Arabic, Zend and Pelvhi, besides several small founts of other kinds of type to be used in printing extracts, quotations, criticisms, &c.' employing at peak working periods as many as '125 men and boys.'[316] From 1825 it started also its own type foundry and introduced improved smaller fount by 1836.[317] After two decades of busy operation, due to fast growing printing industry in Bombay, the American Mission Press establishments were sold. But its experienced staff proved to be instrumental in instructing new generations of printers, setters and book binders that took part in the emergence of the indigenous printing industry in Bombay.

III.2.4.3. The London Missionary Society Press in Surat 1820

In his standard study on the early printing presses in India, Priolkar (1958) does not include this enterprise in his regular narrative, and we learn of the activities of this press from a specific chapter in his study concerned with the East India Company's opposition towards the spread of print in India that benefited from the new 1813 East India Company Charter lifting the ban on the operation of missions in the Company's territories.[318] According to Priolkar,

> Messrs. V. Fyvie and Skinner, two Missionaries of the London Missionary Society, came to Surat in 1815 and by 1817 they had translated the whole New Testament into the Gujerati language. In 1820 they set up a printing press and before the end of 1821 they printed the Gujerati New Testament in eight parts. It seems that the Gujerati types used for this Bible were brought from Calcutta.'[319]

---

[315] On the paradox of avoiding the use of lithographic press for producing copies of the Bible in India, see Shaw 1994.

[316] *Memorial Papers* 1882: 93.

[317] *Memorial Papers* 1882: 94.

[318] For the particulars and consequences of the new charter and its 'pious cause' formula, see Sweetman 2015: 25.

[319] Priolkar 1958: 114 quoting *The Oriental Christian Spectator*, Vol. LXIV (September), Bombay 1854, pp. 339–401.

The London Missionary Society appears to have been active with early printing in a number of locations across Bombay Presidency and elsewhere in the sub-continent. One of these is reported to be the operation of the Bellary Tract Society founded as early as 1817 and said to have supplied as many as 26734 copies of tracts between 1817 and 1823.[320]

III.2.4.4. The Basel Mission Press, Mangalore 1841

A case apart, the printing press of the Basel Mission, set up in 1841 in Mangalore, on the northern tip of Malabar coast (present western Karnataka), soon came to function as a commercially successful enterprise attracting, among others, commissioned orders from the Government of Madras, busy in producing colonial knowledge of an ethnographic kind in the form of surveys and assessments of the vast areas under the jurisdiction of the British presidencies of Madras and Bombay.[321] The press remained under the control of the Evangelical Missionary Society of Basel in Switzerland, commonly called Basel Mission, founded in 1815 at the initiative of German and Swiss Lutheran and Reformed Churches. The Basel Mission sent its first missionaries to the Malabar Coast in 1834.[322] The establishment of the press was assisted by Rev. James Bailey of the Church Missionary Society who had experience with establishing a printing press in Kottayam, in the territory of the princely state of Travancore.[323] The beginnings of this establishment is marked by the successful operation of the lithographic press which proved to be especially efficient in the climate of Mangalore said to be far less oppressive to that of Bombay. First tracts and parts of scripture as well as Luther's catechisms translated into Kannada by the Basel Missionaries were lithographed still in Bombay in 1841 but already the next year a small lithographic press is said to have been started in Mangalore to print Lord's Prayer in English, German, Kannada and Tulu.[324] The first major work in Tulu being a translation of St. Matthew's Gospel was lithographed from the same press later that year and following this the whole New Testament in Tulu appeared in successive parts up to 1847. In 1842 the Mangalore station acquired from Madras its second, superior lithographic press and expanded its activities into the

---

320 *Missionary Register for the M DCCCXXV*: 72.

321 On the operations of the Basel Mission Press, see Shaw 1977 and Sebastian 2015.

322 Sebastian 2015: 176.

323 Shaw 1977: 154.

324 Shaw 1977: 155.

realm of government commissions and education materials. It is here where Hermann Gundert came to oversee the printing of his own early Malayalam hymn works.[325] After acquiring the second press in 1842 the Missionaries continued to print tracts and portions of the Scripture in Kannada, Tulu and Malayalam languages. In 1845 they opened a second press at its station in Telicherry, further south on the Malabar Coast. It would largely cater to the needs of the other Basel Mission stations in Kannur and Calicut by printing books and tracts in Malayalam. Both presses published schoolbooks, liturgies, but also periodicals. The Telicherry press issued in 1847 the Malayalam New Testament by Heinrich Gundert.[326] The lithographic presses remained in operation for several years and were not replaced with a letter-press until 1851 when a delegation from the Mission headquarters arrived with the equipment, a set of new Kannada founts and a printer experienced in stereotyped printing which he practiced in Stuttgart.[327] In 1853 both lithographic and letter-presses were reported to operate parallelly. The printing establishment of the Mission continued to expand and by 1902 it was reported to have eight press units operated by an oil-powered engine where 'books can be printed ...in 10 different languages in six various characters.'[328] A parallel development of type foundry and book binding facility combined with the scholarly activity of the missionaries made Basic Mission stations in Mangalore and Telicherry into an important printing and publishing centre for several decades to come. The translations, editions, printing and publishing operations of the Basel mission are reported to have been paralleled by the vocational training and employment given to converts and local population. The success of Basel Mission remains strongly tied to Pietist ideology as far as it concerned not only the organization principles of the missionary work and education with printing press in its centre, but also in its general focus on the work of upbringing of the individual and the collective. The cultivation of high respect for work and self-discipline looked for inspiration to the visions of ideal community inhabiting an ideal polis as depicted in Joachim Valentin Andrea's Christianopolis (1619). Influenced strongly by the teachings and experience of August Francke of Halle, Pietists—as aptly summarized in a contemporary study—'demanded spiritual rebirth from an individual

---

[325] Shaw 1977: 156.
[326] Shaw 1977: 158.
[327] Shaw 1977: 159.
[328] Shaw 1977: 160.

while professing deep care for the well-being of the collective.'[329] One more important dimension of the Basel Mission activities remains linked to its missionaries' training at an important centre of academic learning of the 19th century Europe, namely the German University of Tübingen. At least three influential figures of missionary scholars, namely Heinrich Gundert (1813–1893), Gottfried Weigle (1816–1855), and Hermann Moegling (1811–1881), received their training in Tübingen where the modern discipline of Indology took shape among else under the inspiration of Rudolf Roth, a leading scholar of the Veda. All the three left their stamp on the scholarly work done and published in print from the Basel Mission in Mangalore. The combined activities of the Basel Mission Press establishments are believed to have influenced the 'perceptions of cultural and ethno-linguistic identity' and to effectively stimulate the processes of standardization of regional vernaculars: Kannada, Malayalam and Tulu.[330]

III.3. The Empire in print and the ethnographic state

> *Captain Sydenham ... wishing to gratify a desire expressed by the Nizam* [of Hyderabad] *to see some of the appliances of European science procured for him three specimens, in the shape of an air-pump, a printing press, and the model of a man-of-war...*[H]*e was censured for having placed in the hands of a native Prince so dangerous an instrument as a printing press.*
>
> J.W. Kaye, *The Life and correspondence of Charles, Lord Metcalfe*, Vol. II, London 1854, p. 248

The early printing initiatives of Jesuits in Goa and Malabar almost coincided in time with the last decade of the powerful Vijayanagara empire (1346–1565), which not only bordered, but, at least nominally (through a chain of tributary binds), controlled the coastal areas of Portuguese settlements and those of Jesuit missionary activities. The political elites of the very much cosmopolitan Vijayanagara must have come into touch with printed materials. This must have been especially the case with the rulers of Vijayanagara's successor states (Nāyakas), who could not fail to have had contact with the Jesuits and their printed books and, after 1712, with the

[329] Sebastian 2015: 181.

[330] Sebastian 2015: 177–178.

Protestants' books on the Coromandel Coast. But, almost no trace is left of their interest in print before 1800 AD. As was the case with the Mughal empire to the north, whose rulers happened to express an interest in European books, but did not care to take over and adopt printing to any extent for imperial use in their dominions. Neither did the East India Company make much use of print or make it part of its empire building before the last decades of 18th century.[331] With a limited capacity for transport on long distances, the use of printed matter remained costly and rare, and, except a set of printed rules and regulations introduced in an attempt to give some unity to scattered British enclaves just before 1700, all the administration was done and circulated in handwritten copies and is said to have remained so up to 1755.[332]

One might be tempted to look for straightforward and simple ties between the power-seeking new company's land empire in Bengal and print technology. But ready-made formulae projected from European history could be misleading, if not confusing. The often taken-for-granted presupposition concerning print and printed matter may obscure the reality in which the fixed nature, stability, and reliability of print had to be worked out of situated circumstances. And to understand the complex reality of empire building in reference to the the development that print took involves, among other things, an understanding of the active role that the company took in shaping the place of print in the service of the empire and modernity, the two being often believed to go hand in hand.[333] The process of making the empire must have involved mobilizing as well as controlling print on different levels of the newly reconfiguring society. The latter, in the form of legal regulations, initially hampering the development of either missionary or indigenous print on the Company's territory went, in compliment, to the former, in the shape of government printing houses. They not only served immediate needs of the growing administration, but

---

331 For an instance of a book gift by Jesuits to Sultan of Bijapur, see Rubies 2014: 204. The first Company government press started to operate in Madras in 1766 after a press had been captured by the British from the French. The beginnings of the Calcutta Company's government press is usually dated to 1778.

332 M. Ogborn puts it straight while saying that 'By 1755 it remained the case that any "Publications"—circulars or notices—produced by the Company in India were composed and copied by hand' [Ogborn 2007: 199].

333 Cf. the formulation of Ogborn for whom 'Understanding Company printing in India involves situating it within the contested processes of doing imperial politics' [Ogborn 2007: 201].

also took the mission of providing standards in the name of the company's governments. Although, from 1772, the structure of administration gave precedence to the Calcutta government over the other two Presidencies, the actual forms the government press took in each of the three differed considerably. The differences were due to the largely different histories of the company's expansion. Out of the three, the first printing establishment was in Madras, thanks to the combination of two factors: the protestant printing activities in Tranquebar and the printing press captured by the British from the French in Pondicherry in 1761. The latter resulted in the press having been taken to Madras and put under the SPCK in Vepery (outside Madras) curatorial, with close links to Fort St. George.

1778 saw the Honorable East India Company install its first printing press in Calcutta as a solution to the pressing need 'to cement the Empire.' Miles Ogborn[334] shows how the Company's commercial-cum-colonial machine was able to continue, thanks to the circulation of written and printed objects. The study by Ogborn appears to have added a more focused view of the actual material forms of the expanding network of the empire, mediated through the agency of a commercial mega-company, to the to the earlier study by C.A. Bayly which articulated the working of the Empire and its information.[335] But the history of the introduction of print into the British territories in India appears to corroborate also a thesis formulated around 1950 by a theoretician of media and communication studies, Harold Innis, who pointed to a regularity in the historical development of events resulting from the introduction of a new revolutionary medium as well as to its contradictory effects in a longer perspective for the development of nationalism or parliamentarianism.[336]

In his study on the early printing in Calcutta, Graham Shaw enumerates as many as forty printers, who, in the period between 1770 and 1800, catered almost exclusively to the booming English journalism addressed to Europeans in Calcutta and Bengal. Any additional printing activities they did were custom made office forms and, increasingly, almanacs. This early commercial printing was often seen by the Company's government

---

334 Ogborn 2007.

335 Bayly 1996.

336 See, the reworked formula by G.C. Lewis in Innis 1986 (1950): 167 ("The effects of printing on nationalism have been conspicuous in common-law countries. 'Success of a representative system of government has been materially influenced by the invention of printing,' but its limitations have again been largely a result of printing").

with a suspicious eye and publishers and printers happened to face various forms of attempts to control their activities.

An often-stressed delay in the more massive onset of print in India, in comparison with Europe, has been explained either by technological backwardness or colonial control and restrictions. We must remember, however, that European powers aspiring to colonial control over parts of the Indian subcontinent, and later on the one that eventually took the upper hand in this race, were part and parcel of the process, since they themselves made the choices that determined future developments. We should not forget that, in Europe, the gradual spread of printing and its pushing the older handwritten regime was a highly uneven and fragmentary process. As Innis' visionary study notes,[337] even Paris, one of the future centres of printing, at first experienced a delayed process in that matter, with print introduced there not earlier than 1469.[338] The reasons for the time shift could be notably different in different historical-economic and cultural--religious configurations of the place or region in question. In the longer run—according to the overwhelming vision of Innis—the consequences of an imbalanced development of the medium of print over the vast spaces of the British empire contributed to its eventual disintegration.[339]

Several patterns of print development introduced by the British under the aegis of imperial projects that got published through government press continued to influence the local and regional print scene. Such was the case, for instance—as argues Fiona Ross[340]—of the indigenous Bengali type founders, who remained heavily influenced by early Wilkins' font until the second half of 19th century. The first attempt by an indigenous press to design a Bengali type was made towards 1858 by the Girisa Vidyaratna press. This attempt illustrates the change in the evolution of regional print cultures, from the moment when classically trained Sanskrit pandits began to enter the world of editing and printing.[341] The project of imperial printing, envisioned first by William Bolts and put to early practice by

[337] Innis 1986 (1950): 167.

[338] Innis 1986 (1950): 144. The circumstances of the later coming of print to Paris are thus given by Innis: 'The influence of copyists and illuminators delayed the introduction of printing in Paris until 1469, but the delay and the control exercised by the university favoured the introduction of Roman type early in the sixteenth century.'

[339] 'The Empire was broken in part through the distorted effects of the uneven development of printing' [Innis 1986 (1950): 158].

[340] Ross 1999: 125; see also Hatcher and Ross 2001: 637.

[341] Hatcher and Ross 2001: 638.

Halhed and Wilkins towards 1788, involved a huge amount of labour and determination in the decision-making involved in the difficult process of the standardization of Bengali script. As Miles Ogborn argues, 'Imperial printing became possible, therefore, on the basis of these prior indigenous standardizations of Bengali.'[342]

The ambition of mobilizing print's alleged potential for stability, permanence, and uniformity, to go with wide dissemination for the service of the empire, entailed a risky and extremely complex process of shift, adjustment, and change, which, in effect, was to produce a new quality—from script through reading practices to audience. Printing a bigger number of copies had the power of disseminating either a new order or a new mess. The risk started with the founding of a new typeface for difficult Indian scripts in a nascent technology, through a task of selection of the medium of the right translation (vernacular register), to constructing a new kind of audience ready to accept, acquire, or receive the new physical shape of texts, and many other aspects of the long chain connecting the composition and production to circulation and reading practices. Printing had to envision and secure a new economic basis for its ideas. When triggered, the process might fail or miscarry and turn against the initial intention, as was the case of the early project of Bhim Ji Parekh in Surat and Bombay towards 1674, or an attempt a century later at stabilizing the imperial information circuit through the project of a new Bengali font by William Bolts, which, after much enthusiasm, ended up idle, suspended, and never to resume.

III.3.1. The infernal machine

The nineteenth century saw an unprecedented speed in the development of technologies which proved to be seen as serving the immediate goals of the fast growing British empire. The steamship, telegraph, new weaponry, and other improved technologies, among them mechanized print, proved to be new powerful vehicles for the imperial idea—the growth of global trade—but also a threat for the empire. 'Technologies empowered the metropole but also ... strengthened the periphery.'[343] The British government policies adopted in face of these new developments kept changing. While the general attitude of *laissez-faire* favoured free entrepreneurship on a growing imperial, if not

[342] Ogborn 2007: 247.

[343] Kubicek 1999: 248.

global, scale, 'successive governments ... were persuaded that technological and economical imperatives required an interventionist approach to safeguard British interests.'[344]

The later, post-1770 policy of the East India Company and its governments towards print appears to have gone up and down in its colder and warmer eye on printers and their activities in its Indian dominions. Part of this policy also extended to its choice of publishers, printers, and publications in England. Selected publishers in London had been given priority in publishing books ordered or patronized by the Company, while selected publications enjoyed official credentials by the Company positioned on the title page.[345] As noticed by Ogborn, print 'could change what the Company was, and it could change who considered it part of their concerns ... it could ... "destroy the *Credit* of the *Company*".'[346] The latter could and actually did happen to be influenced by the content, form, and time of public dissemination of news from Indian dominions of the company, and could and did affect the price of the Company's stock as well as the expectations of its stock owners. For this reason, the company developed its dedicated policy for gathering, dispatching, archiving, ordering, and assessing the intelligence flow from India to East India House in London. With a growing demand on the transparency of the company's business transactions in India on the part of the public interest and parliamentary agency, the company's directors developed a sophisticated policy of control over the news transferred to parliament as well as to the public. According to Bowen, the directors of the company 'were powerless to prevent the outward flow of information to government and parliament, but they were at least able to exert some degree of control over the release of news to the stockholders.'[347]

This overall policy affected the shaping of the company's Indian institutions' policy towards print and control over publications and press. Its early attitude seems to have been particularly influenced by the troublesome activity of the Calcutta-based British owned printers, publishing English newspapers that fed critical opinions predominantly to the British of the

344 Kubicek 1999: 257.

345 Selected publishers and printers had been granted privileges of using the title 'Booksellers to the East India Company', as apparently was the case with Black, Parry, and Kingsbury in Leadenhall Street [Buchanan 1807, title page]. Selected publications used the imprint 'Published Under the Authority and Patronage of the Honourable the Directors of the East India Company.' See Buchanan 1807, title page, Müller 1849, title page.

346 Ogborn 2007: 155.

347 Bowen 2006: 163.

Calcutta Presidency. Therefore, the first phase of the attempts to control print and printers did not concern either native printers—since there weren't any—or printing for Indians, because the early journalism catered for the British, very often with the news from the metropolis. Another face of this early stage was shaped by those incidents by the missionary printers, that provoked in the agents of the company a strong fear of a possible violent reaction on the part of their Indian subjects.

In a report on the activities of the British Residency in the native State of Hyderabad by J.W. Kaye, that was published in 1847, we read unauthorised gift made to the Nizam of Hyderabad of a printing press for which he is said to have been officially 'censured' for putting in the hands of a native Prince a dangerous instrument.[348]

The fear of the disruptive powers of print was not one-sided—quite the contrary. Most of the anxiety of the early company's governments of Bengal had been directed towards English printers operating in Calcutta in connection with English journalism addressed to the English population of Calcutta. This anxiety translated into the editors and printers being legally persecuted, sued in courts, imprisoned, and expelled from the territories of the company—as Bolts, Hicky and many others were in the last decades of the 18th century. The restrictions on printing and the independent press were strengthened during war-time under the governance of Wellesley and continued from 1799 to 1813, also including the previously deployed ban on missionary printing. The long debate that followed, contained ideas concerned with the founding of a government press as a powerful agency, capable of controlling the confusion on the danger of part of independent printers. Besides, one actually started under the supervision of Wilkins during the governance of Warren Hastings—it was Lord Wellesley who drew an extensive plan for a government press of truly imperial dimensions: '...a government press would "effectively silence" Calcutta printers judged both potentially seditious and "Useless to literature and to the Public."'[349] The Directors to the Company, however, remained unimpressed by this imperial vision, mostly because of the unnecessary costs and extension of the press jurisdiction involved in it.

---

[348] Kaye 1854: 248. Cf. Priolkar 1958: 127.

[349] Ogborn 2007: 264.

III.3.2. The Government Press and imperial typography

Government presses, as a separate category of printing press in colonial India, started operation in the three presidencies in different time and circumstances. The first printing press controlled by the English East India Company was war booty. It had been captured from the French Governor's house when the English took over Pondicherry in 1761, during the Seven Year War.[350] The captured press was relocated to Madras, and it was put to operation there by a French printer, overseen by two Protestant missionaries of the Society for the Propagation of Christian Knowledge (SPCK). In 1766, this press started to officially work under the label of the Government Press in Fort St. George in Madras.[351]

While the Madras presidency developed as an important centre for government printing, it was Calcutta that eventually emerged as the centre for the Company's government-shaped and controlled use of print.

By the second half of the 18th century, the development of a land empire out of the English East India Company's possessions in the Indian subcontinent had put print in a historically specific context. We can see print and printers involved in colonial government operations on different levels in the process of making the empire. It is visible in the three separate strands of print development at that time, which were often contradictory, but all sensitive to the policy of the new Indian empire on the rise. One of them can be seen against the perceived need to introduce and sustain, through regular involvement in the Government's agency, in the printing of authoritative documents to be circulated in the newly constructed map of the empire by way of free distribution to Government outposts, officers, and employees.

This meant a sudden and risky shift from the hitherto scribal written documents to printed-to-order circulars an other paperwork, which, to a high degree, made the life of the empire. The double potential of print as a powerful means, ready either to support or to downgrade and undermine the empire, made the Company's governors in India take several controversial steps toward securing control over the development of print

350 See Blackburn 2006: 58 and Ogborn 2007: 199. An earlier instance operation of a Company printing press in Bombay around 1678–1723 remains conjectural.

351 Ogborn 2007: 199; Blackburn 2006.

media in India in general and in Bengal in particular. When, a century earlier, Bhim Parekh in Surat had attempted to put print into the service of rescuing the traditions of the Brahmins in cooperation with the East India Company; and when, half a century earlier, the Protestant printers were busy printing the Tamil bible and other texts in Tamil from Tranquebar; and when the SPCK press had just commenced operations near Madras, in post-1773 Calcutta, the government of the company still perceived the printing press as more of a 'threat to the Company's authority than an instrument of its power.'[352]

Measures of control and prohibitive regulations introduced by the Company were initially directed mostly against early print enthusiasts and later against independent English printers, who happened to be censored, persecuted, and expelled from the company's territory back to England. These acts of control and violence triggered a heated argument in England and India, that took up several different forms of press and book publications. The famous early case of this heated argument was made by William Bolts, a merchant, who, while attempting to fight for the free trade opportunities against the monopoly of the company, highlighted the Company's inhibitory policy towards print in the 1760s. Having been expelled from British Bengal for his disruptive actions and 'turbulent character' by Governor Harry Verelst, Bolt devoted the rest of his life to fighting his case in the courts and press. His publication, in 1772, of *Considerations on Indian Affairs*, met with a considerable response and contributed to the new legislation of 1773. This response had to be taken into account by the then new Bengal Council and new governor general Warren Hastings. The issue of print stood conspicuously in the preface of Bolt's publication.[353]

The history of early printing in Calcutta differs considerably from that of the two other presidencies for several reasons. Calcutta and Bengal were the places where the English East India Company had consolidated control over its extensive Bengal possessions, and Calcutta took the lead in the initial phase of the new presence of the company as a territorial empire, which soon resulted in the establishment of the administrative supervision of the Calcutta government over the governments of the two other presidencies. This leading role of Calcutta, along with its job offering administrative and trade institutions, attracted a larger European population,

---

[352] Rocher and Rocher 2012: 203.

[353] Bolts 1772. For the quotations and comments, see Ogborn 2007: 204–205.

which provided the space for the onset of English journalism. According to Graham Shaw [1981], the last decades before 1800 saw as many as forty printers working in Calcutta and its environs, almost exclusively for Calcutta's English journals. Their additional activities included commissioned orders for the government and, increasingly, almanacs—the genre that soon came to dominate indigenous printing in Calcutta. The printing process is said to have remained relatively expensive for the reason that most of the equipment and materials had to be imported from Europe. This situation, along with the sudden outburst of journalism increasingly critical to the Company's policies (with a leading role of James Hicky's Bengal Gazette),[354] convinced Warren Hastings, the then Governor General, to opt for establishing a Company's own printing press rather than ordering job from outside. This press started operation in 1778, under the supervision of Charles Wilkins, first in Maida, 175 miles north from Calcutta, then shifted to Calcutta in 1781.[355] This is believed to have been the result of a personal initiative by Warren Hastings among whose other initiatives the foundation of the Asiatic Society of Bengal in 1784 is also counted.[356] The operations of the press grew rapidly, while the policy behind its functioning kept changing, as, did its relationship to missionary and independent printing enterprises as well as the legal environment for all printers and publishers to pursue their profession under the government of the company.

The beginnings of the category of government press, introduced here in order to highlight a specific type of agency, should be seen in the early initiatives of Warren Hastings, the then Governor General of the British Settlements in East Indies, stationed in Fort William, the major establishment of the East India Company in Bengal. He came up with an idea of arranging for a translation of a source texts for laws of Hindu customs and publishing them in print for the use of English courts in India. The company had enjoyed a monopoly over trade with India under periodically renewed charters by the British Parliament after the first one had been issued on 31 December 1600, when Queen Elizabeth granted the monopoly over trade with the east to the East India Company. In the words of one

---

354 For the controversial history of James Hicky's Bengal Gazette, see, among else, the recent Otis 2018.

355 Some sources give 1779 as the year when the press was to be shifted to Calcutta.

356 Jasanoff 2005: 61 and Priolkar 1958: 51. Cf. Hall 2016: 94–95, who argues for 1776 as the beginning of the government press in Hooghly. See also Diehl 1968: 335 who locates the beginning of the press at Hooghly in 1778, indicating its shifting to Calcutta by 1779.

of the foremost historians of Hindu law, 'initially the British were unconcerned about the laws of India. But the gradual transformation of trading companies into colonial powers created a responsibility for the British to adjudicate disputes between their Indian subjects.'[357]

Following the initiative of Hastings, a commission of ten pundits was assembled in 1773, with a view to 'summarize all that is essential of the classical Hindu law in a code.'[358] Such a code was ready in 1775, and it was subsequently translated from Sanskrit (under the title of *Vivādārṇavasetu*) to Persian, and next to English. The translation had been bequeathed to the British grammarian, Nathaniel Brassey Halhed, and was published in London in 1776 (with a second edition also in London in 1781).[359] It is in the preface to this edition, where Halhed refers to the Veda by the curious form *Beid*–probably borrowed from Prince Dara Shikoh's Persian translation of Upanishadic texts–a specimen of which Halhed inserts in his preface.[360]

---

357 ROCHER 2012: 78.

358 ROCHER 2012: 79.

359 See HALHED 1776 and 1781, see also ROCHER 2012: 79. See PRIOLKAR 1958: 51 '"A Code of Gentoo Laws or Ordinations of the Pundits" was printed in London, presumably for want of printing facilities in Bengal.' Cf. HALL 2016: 94–95. Contrary to Priolkar, Hall suggests that Halhed printed his translation in 1776 'on the first Bengal press that he had set up in Hugli (Hooghly)...' [HALL 2016: 94]. He argues that this first Indian edition was the one that had been 'provided to India-based administrators' and that a 'private luxury edition was subsequently printed in London for the East India Company promotional distribution there' (HALL 2016: 95). If this was true, it would make the precedent for the later similar use made of another luxurious edition, which is of primary interest for this study, namely the set of the edition princeps of the *Ṛgvedasaṃhitā* by F. Max Müller (published in London in 5 vols., 1849–1874). The luxurious character of this edition and its promotional function was mentioned by Müller in the introduction to his second, Indian edition, of 1890. See MÜLLER 1890: Lii.

360 HALHED 1776: XIX–XXI. It is introduced on page XVIII by the following passage referring to the four Vedas by the form *Beid*: 'an Explanation of it is here inserted from Darul Shekuh's famous Persian Translation of some Commentaries upon the Four Beids, or original Scriptures of Hindostan; The Work itself is extremely scarce, and perhaps of dubious Authenticity; and it was by mere Accident that this little Specimen was procured.' Earlier in the same Preface another instance of the same appellation can be seen in the following curious formulation: '...the same confidential Reliance, which we put in the Divine Text upon the Authority of its Divine Inspirer himself, is by their mistaken Prejudices implicitly transferred to the Beids of the Shaster' [HALHED 1776: XIII]. On page XXV an attempt at understanding the nature of the Veda can be seen: 'In the Four Beids [the original and sacred Text of the great Hindoo Creator and Legislator Brahma] the Length of the Vowels is determined and pointed out by a musical Note or Sign, called Mātrāng [implying one whole Tone] which is placed over every Word; and in reading the Beids these Distinctions of Tone and Time must be nicely observed.'

The 1776 *Code of Gentoo Laws* not only contains the earliest specimen of a Vedic text published in printed (double) translation. It also introduces Devanagari alphabet, specimen of Shanscrit "ashlogue" (*śloka*) in various metres and an extract from *Manusmṛiti.* It also includes a fragment from an alleged commentary on the *Reig Beid* (Ṛgveda) by a Bisesht Mahaamoonee, with an English rendering. It comes probably from *Mahāvākyavivāraṇa* ascribed to Śankara.[361] Halhed's *Grammar of the Bengal Language*, printed two years later in Hooghly, north of Calcutta, in 1778[362] remains an early achievement of the art of printing in its introduction of the first Bengali typeface, invented and manufactured by Charles Wilkins, then the superintendent of the Hooghly Press, with the major help of Joseph Sheperd and a Bengali blacksmith–Pancānan Karmakār–who was later to make a name for himself as a skilful type founder.[363]

Halhed and Wilkins pioneered the difficult task of producing a Bengali typeface to be used in printing. As was the case earlier with Jesuit and Protestant printers, the inventing and implementing of Bengali typefaces involved complex processes of modernizing and standardizing Bengali

---

361 In the Preface to the French translation of the Codes that appeared in Paris in 1778, its author ruthlessly points out to the misattribution of the verses cited in the original as part of the Vedas. It is often assumed that the first book to feature Devanagari characters is *Alphabetum Brahmanicum* (Rome 1771). Occasional examples can be seen also in *Alphabetum Grandonico-Malabaricum* by Clemente Peani (Rome 1772). An instance of early Devanāgarī in print from India is "On the Orthography of Asiatic Words in Roman Letters" by William Jones in *Asiatick Researches* I (Calcutta 1788). It features a passage from *Bhāgavatapurāṇa.* Still another was the 1796 John Gilchrist's *Grammer of the Hindustanee Language*, printed in Calcutta at Chronicle Press. Among the earliest integral works printed with Devanagari were probably the following: the *Hitopadeśa* printed by William Carey in Serampore in 1803–04, *Theses of Students of the College of Fort William* (1803), Colebrooke's *Sanskrit Grammar* (1805), W. Carey's grammars of Marathi (1805) and Sanskrit (1806), W. Carey and J. Marshman's *Ramayuna of Valmeeki* (1806), *Carey's A Grammar of the Sungscrit Language* (1806) with appendix of probably the first genuine Vedic text in print: the *Īsavāsya Upaniṣad*, as well as sixteen Sanskrit works published for the Fort William's College by Bābū Rām's Sanskrit Printing Press between 1807 and 1815. The series contained Hindu legal texts and is believed to have set a pattern for Sanskrit printed books in the form of oblong shape of paper manuscripts with most information in the colophon and no title page. [see Rocher and Rocher 2012: 75; Formigatti 2016: 104]. Wilkins' Devanagari typefaces, produced in 1795 were used for his Sanskrit Grammar printed in London in 1808. The Grammar served mainly the education purposes at Hayleybury College, Hertford. A great fire consumed Wilkins' house in England along with his equipment and typefaces [Ogborn 2007: 241]. There must have been a second set developed by Wilkins thereafter .

362 Halhed 1778: title page.

363 See Diehl 1968: 337.

regional script and posed a grave technical difficulty for printing technology.[364] In their project, they benefited from the crucial assistance of local munshis and pundits, of whom we have largely incomplete knowledge.[365] Charles Wilkins supervised the project as a nominated superintendent of the government press that operated from Hooghly until 1779, before moving to Calcutta. Charles Wilkins had to return to England where he set up a private printing press and workshop in his own house and continued with work on developing a satisfactory type set for Devanagari, the task that he treated as a major challenge and took on with due sophistication, since to him 'the study of the shape of Indian characters was an important intellectual project.'[366]

Thus, after the initial debate and mixed opinions on the need for a government patronized press on the part of Bengal Council, the last two decades of the 18th century saw a virtual flood of routine printing ordered by different departments of the Bengal Government. It seems that the ideology for this move had been supplied in the preface to the Halhed's Grammar of the Bengali Language. The preface points to the supposed ultimate source of major Asian languages in Shanscrit (Sanskrit) in the spirit betraying links to the Romanitic version of early Orientalism.[367] The grammar was published as the first major printing work heralding the new Honorable Company Press to start the same year, 1778, incidentally the same that saw the printing of *Ezour Vedam* in France. Both publications, albeit each in different fashion, marked European imperial ambitions to a new hold over the Indian past and its languages.[368] The government press of Calcutta

---

364 A parallel development appears to have been going on in the newspaper presses of the time and at least one, namely the Chronicle Press in Calcutta, is said to have been working and actually prepared a few sets of vernacular types around 1789, allegedly including Devanagari. See Shaw 1981: 32.

365 See Ogborn 2007: 242 who mentions one such person, whom Halhed referred to as 'an intelligent Brahmin' and who was paid for his assistance by Governor Hastings.

366 Ogborn 2007: 241.

367 In Halhed's vision '...the Parent of almost every dialect from the Persian Gulph to the China Seas, is the Shanscrit; a language of the most venerable and unfathomable antiquity, which although at present shut up in the libraries of Bramins ... appears to have been current over most of the Oriental World; and traces of its original extent may still be discovered in, almost; every district, of Asia' [Halhed 1778: iii].

368 Halhed includes elements of imperial ideology in a straightforward way in his Preface: 'The English, who have made so capital a progress in the Polite Arts, and who are masters of Bengal, may, with more ease. and greater propriety, add its Language to their acquisitions; that they may explain the benevolent principles of that legislation whole decrees they inforce; that they may convince while they command' [Halhed 1778: ii].

must have been, in the eyes of Bengal government, more closely connected to the core of the British imperial project, whose heart was Calcutta, than the other two government presses in Madras and Bombay. The latter two, however, operated within imitative but also much more competitive frames, expressing imperial ideas in their own respective ways, deriving from different regional characteristics.

The type of print culture sustained by the government press depended heavily on the direct patronage of the Company, which entirely sponsored or substantially aided the circulation of the printed matter by subsidies, commissioned job, ordering copies, or subscriptions forced on, or suggested to, its office position holders and army officers. It operated in a tied relationship to government agencies and their publishing policies. Its selection of titles depended largely on the personal choices of the decision-makers. Thus, the titles of Sanskrit works printed between 1806–17 in the Bābūrāma's Sanskrit Press working on commision from the Fort William College reflected the personal interests of Henry Colebrooke and his mission of 'ushering Sanskrit literature into the age of print'.[369] At the same time, as the case of Bābūrāma's press shows, government controlled presses, like the Honorable Company Press in Calcutta itself, remained hybrid, semi-subsidized, and semi-commercial enterprises.[370] In the longer run, government presses tended to morph away from the Government-controlled publishing agencies that commissioned printing job increasingly, and at first predominantly, with missionary presses, which must have been considered a means for securing control over the whole process of editing, printing, and publishing, in those cases where the printed matter might be sensitive to Government policies and effective administration. Such was the case of the huge 'Vedic project' initiated at 1847 by the Calcutta government which eventually saw through the government-controlled edition process and missionary presses a range of Vedic texts proving the imperial hold over the Veda as the core part of Indian cultural heritage.

After the turbulent years of restrictions on independent printers under Governor Welsley in 1799–1813 and his largely misconceived plans for

369 Rocher and Rocher 2012: 76.

370 See Rocher and Rocher 2012: 221–'These forms of patronage and finance shaped the patterns of dissemination and distribution. Copies of legal codes were sent to the provincial courts as well as those in Calcutta, and the intention was that Halhed's Grammar would be sold to Company servants across Bengal. Printing was part of the creation of a new imperial geography of authors, texts, and readers.'

transforming the Bengal government press into an institution of power and authority of an imperial dimension, the government printing press establishment, with its then thirteen press units, was taken over in 1815 by the Military Orphan Society.[371] This shift resulted in the fast growing process of splitting competencies between publishing and printing, while the Government and its agencies retained and consolidated important instruments for influencing the new public space through the power of the print medium as well as controlling the government's own policies of publishing, but also of regulating and containing the independent printers and publishers within the frame of the imperial project.[372]

As far as the immediate object of this study is concerned, no publishing project initiated by one of the three presidencies agencies and their government presses saw the Veda in print before the so-called 'Vedic project' had been adopted by the Asiatic Society of Bengal in 1847.[373] Even the pioneering project of Devanagari editions of a series of Sanskrit works, commissioned by Fort William's College and printed by Bābū Rām's Sanskrit Printing Press between 1807 and 1815, did not involve an edition of any of Vedic texts.[374] On one hand, this might have been due to the legacy of the influential opinion of H. Colebrooke, published in 1805, or simply reflected his personal interests and choice while proposing the titles to be published to the College Board, but on the other, may simply have shown how heavily the success of the publication projects depended on the direct patronage, or other forms of financial support, on the part of subsidized government institutions like Fort William College. The latter, in turn, reflected very much the tensions in the power relationships accompanying decision-making inside these institutions and between them and the Bengal government and company's directors in London. The most frequent form of supporting Sanskrit publications by authors remaining in the service of the Company's

371 Ogborn 2007: 264.

372 The general shift towards overseeing the outsourcing printing jobs rather than maintain government printing units did not mean the end of control and the Office of Superintendent of Government Pronting remained in operation still in last decades of 1800s. See, for instance, Gough 1878.

373 Early translations by Colebrooke in *Asiatick Researches* vols V, VII and VIII (1805) include *Gayatri Mantra* (RS. 3.64), RS 7.43, 10.125 and 129, fragments of *Aitareya Brāhmaṇa* and *Āraṇyaka, Yajurveda Vājasaneyi Saṃhitā , Bṛhadāraṇyaka Upaniṣad, Taittirīya Saṃhitā, Taittirīya Upaniṣad, Chandogya Upaniṣad.* His sources included manuscripts collected in Benares by R. Chambers and W. Jones, Polier's collection, General Martin's transcript and his own acquisitions (Colebrooke 1808: 428, 469).

374 Rocher and Rocher 2012: 75. . A notable exception was.

institutions or outsiders (for instance W. Carey's Sanskrit Grammar 1806) remained subscription to an agreed number of copies.[375] Occasionally, heads of government institutions involved in publication projects attempted to cooperate with the leading missionary publishers in order to stimulate and influence the emerging market for Sanskrit printed matter.[376] Such was the case for W. Carey and H.T. Colebrooke, who acted as advisors on the committees of Fort William College and later the Asiatic Society, and subsequently participated in the project of publishing the Sanskrit *Rāmāyaṇa*, that was printed by Serampore Press between 1806 and 1810. The latter, however, remained uncompleted due to the lack of further support on the part of the college committee.[377] In spite of rather lower editorial standards that Bābū Rām's Sanskrit Press was believed at the time to represent, the seventeen Sanskrit titles, mostly grammatical and law digests, published during 1806–1817 are believed to have set the pattern for Sanskrit publications in print among else in their choice of an oblong shape in imitation of Sanskrit manuscripts still in circulation. Not denying the influence of these publications, we must remember that the operation of later decades indigenous printers, especially from Bombay area, shows that the choice of the shape and format, be it that of the codex or the oblong *pothī*, were influenced also by other factors, and the same publisher happened to issue the same Sanskrit title in two different formats depending on the kind of readers he would target with it.

How the process of establishing government presses in the service of the British presidencies came to be imitated, and, to an extent, emulated, by the so-called native Indian states has remained virtually unexplored. One exception is the establishment of King Serfoji II's press in the Maratha kingdom of Tanjore towards 1804, where printing of Sanskrit texts in Devanāgarī had been pioneered independently. Among the titles were Annambhatta's *Tarkasangrāha* (1811) and *Dīpikā* (1811), Visvanatha Pancānana Bhattācārya's *Karikavalli* (*Bhāṣāpariccheda*, 1812), Māgha's *Śiśupālavadha* (1812) and Cokkana Kavi's *Kumarasambhāvacampū* (1814). They were implied by king Seroji as textbooks for his newly set college named Navavidyā Kalaśālā. We know that 1836 saw the beginning of the Government Press

[375] On constant policy fluctuations and tensions in decision making within Fort William College and other company institutions, see Rocher and Rocher 2012: 65–76.

[376] Rocher and Rocher 2012: 76.

[377] Rocher and Rocher 2012: 77.

in Tiruvanantapuram, in the southernmost kingdom of Travancore, under Maharāja Svāti Tirunāl.[378] Other sources (*Travancore Manual*) mention the first publication of this establishment as being the Anglo-vernacular Calendar of Travancore for the year 1015 of the Malayalam era, corresponding to 1835–1836 AD.[379] Whatever the truth of this, in 1836, Svāti Tirunāl, the then ruler of the Kingdom of Travancore, introduced a new code of regulation for the state. It was printed at the Kottayam Mission Press, but soon after the same ruler is reported to have decided to start a government-controlled press. In 1838, a press had already been set up and was being operated by Samathanam Maistry, 'who was one of the first batch of workmen trained in the Nagercoil [Mission] Press' (in operation since 1820). The first Superintendent of this Government Press was Rev. Sperschneider.[380] It is in this princely state Government press where later on an important series of editions of Vedic texts appeared between 1929 and 1942, among others, K. Sāmbaśivaśāstri, ed. (1929), *The Ṛksamhitâ: With the Bhâṣya of Skandasvâmin and Dîpikâ of Veṅkaṭaṁâdhavârya.* A bit later, in 1864, came the establishment of the Government Press in the Princely State of Mysore. These—often originally mimetic enterprises patronized by Indian rulers, or native Princes as they used to be named by the British—proved to be successful instruments in the regionally specific policy of princely statecraft.

III.3.3 Print, catalogues and native knowledge

Towards the end of the 19th century, a number of intrepid scholars set off for the Indian interior in quest of manuscript sources of the indigenous knowledge, that had been rumoured to remain with 'native gentlemen' and traditional institutions. Their quest followed a new British Indian Government initiative of 1868 to allocate new funds for a project envisaged as holding out the promise for 'many ... uncontemplated practical uses.'[381] The project, unprecedented and not repeated again until the digital age, was fuelled by a European idea of representing the indigenous knowledge

[378] http://keralaculture.org/printing-press/292 [accessed on 21 Nov 2017].

[379] Nagam Aiya 1906: I, 389. The following note in Travancore State Manual points to a somewhat later date as well: 'This was the first Code of Regulations of Travancore and it was printed at the Kottayam Mission Press, as the Government Press was not then established' [Nagam Aiya 1906: I, 489].

[380] Menon 1878: 418. Cf. http://www.swathithirunal.in/rlinsti/press.htm [accessed on 20 Nov 2017].

[381] For the text of the government announcement, see Gough 1878.

of India through a conceptual blend of the academic discipline of philology and an imperial ambition to control the totality of the native knowledge systems. It added substantially to a new frame for Asian Studies in general and Indology in particular, while articulating the imperial ambition to rationalize and control the totality of native knowledge. The project continued and aimed at confirming the then conceptualized role of Sanskrit philology as a major and dominating scholarly paradigm, centred on written material artefacts in the shape of manuscripts, conceived as representing the vast and mostly neglected treasure of the knowledge of the past. The findings and reports of the scholars involved in the project helped in developing new libraries, supplied ideas for defining principles for organization and for producing printed representation in the form of descriptive catalogues and research institutes, thus framing a part of Asian studies in a way that must have seemed—at the time—to be holding good forever. The paradigm and its historiographical presumptions were soon to be seriously challenged.

This entirely new initiative of the British to vastly finance scholarly expeditions into the Indian interior is believed to have been stimulated by a letter written by Pandit Radhakrishna, a leading Indian intellectual attached to a princely court allied with the British. The so-called Simla Act of 1868 marks a major change in the policy of the central British government of India towards its own role and involvement in the process of representing the heritage of the indigenous knowledge of India. It should be seen, however, as one of the steps undertaken in order to reconstitute the new form of colonial presence in India, while acting upon the dire consequences of 1857, a turning point in the political history of British India. In many respects, the events of 1857 caught the British unprepared, revealing blind spots in the government apparatus of intelligence gathering and the fragmentary character of the intelligence processing system. They marked a major failure of the colonial administration in deploying the efficient information networking and data assessment needed to properly identify and recognize major components of the powerful social processes that shaped the complex societies of the Indian subcontinent at times of change.[382]

Against this roughly sketched background, the British government's decision of 1868 to initiate an extensive manuscript search leading to

[382] For a general overview of reconfiguration of the British imperial information order of the time, see Bayly 1996.

establishing major collections should be seen as a recognition of the government's active involvement in the process of representing Indian traditional knowledge systems through planned collections of manuscript artefacts. These collections came to be organized according to preconceived and controlled principles, that is, according to procedures perceived to be modern. Within roughly half-a-century, when the government retained its funding scheme, a relatively limited group of 'collectors'—at first almost all of them European—set off into the interior to identify traditional collections of manuscripts, track their records, copy or draw the title lists, make purchases, and commission copies.[383] They were helped by 'native' assistants and agents, who proved to be indispensable in not only identifying local collections, but also in approaching often reluctant, if not unfriendly, owners or curators. Stories of the many vicissitudes of the search make up a substantial part of the reports that came to be regularly produced by the 'collectors' appointed by the government and subsequently also published.[384] The manuscript search tours resulted in an attempt at mapping the world of indigenous knowledge networks, of which traditional collections made up a substantial part. The rapidly growing major government collections that emerged from the activities of these collectors were to be housed in in the offices of the provincial governments, with the apparent intention of their being directly associated with the three administrative centres of the British rule in Calcutta, Madras and Bombay. However, they soon had to be transferred to specialized institutions constituted for that purpose.[385]

Before this new turn, several early collections of Indian manuscripts offered for sale on the antiquarian market and subsequently left India to form important parts of European libraries.[386] While more collections ended up

[383] The 'collectors' included such scholars as Georg Buhler, Franz Kielhorn, Peter Peterson, Luis Rice.

[384] For the account of the manuscrit search tours, see, among else Bühler 1868 and 1880.

[385] See Belvalkar 1916.

[386] One of the first of this kind was a collection of around one hundred sixty volumes sent by the French Jesuit Mission in Karnataka to the King's library in Paris in 1729–1735. 'Most of them were MSS written in Sanskrit, Telugu and Tamil languages, which nobody in France could read at that time' [Colas 2012: 69]. Another, and a much bigger one, must have been a fine collection of Sanskrit MSS (c. 1800 MSS) gathered in 1774–1779 by Sir Robert Chambers, Supreme Judge in Calcutta. In 1842 the Government of Prussia succeeded after 14 years of negotiations started by Wilhelm von Humboldt, an important figure for German revolution in education, to purchase it and the collection had been deposited in the then Königlische Bibliothek in Berlin. A catalogue of this collection had been published in 1854 by Weber and served later as one of the models for the catalogues of new

in Europe, the systematic search triggered by the 1868 Simla act was aimed at forming, enriching, or complementing library collections that were to be patronized by the British Indian Government and to remain in the possession of Imperial British India and its institutions. The search and the cataloguing mobilized several leading philologists and Orientalists of the period. They made their choices and accepted presuppositions that, in the long run, profoundly influenced the course of Asian studies.

One such presupposition was that indigenous knowledge could be accessed in an unmediated way by, first, acquisition, amassing, archiving (topped with printing descriptive catalogues), and than by studying the dislocated and securely stored hand-written copies of *śāstric* treatises and other works making traditional knowledge systems,[387] and that such a study was possible and feasible without the intermediating figure of a traditional Indian scholar, a *śāstri/paṇḍit*. Another was a strong bias for Sanskrit manuscripts, that resulted in a considerable asymmetry in representing knowledge in other idioms. Yet another premise was that indigenous knowledge can be taken as the sum total of its written artefacts, as a fully textualized body, which entailed that it could be assessed, measured, evaluated, organized, and disciplined, and what followed, that it could be mastered and controlled. This also entailed an allegedly non-problematic and necessary step on this path—that the written artefacts should be shifted to new centralized localities, stored, and organized in a systematic way—so that they could help create new *lieux de savoir*.[388] Many of these presuppositions and biases were the result of different concepts of knowledge, its production, and its representation cherished by the authorities, early collectors and later cataloguers. They still remain to be articulated as it is far from clear. The most pressing questions in that matter include the following: what the authorities, founding bodies, collectors, and cataloguers actually attempted to find and collect, what they thought they eventually unearthed and retrieved and for what purposes,

Indian libraries. Another early collection, though of different character and scope, was formed during 1796–1806 by Col. McKenzie who worked as Surveyor general of Madras and later for the whole of British India. He is believed to have spent L15.000 for collecting manuscripts, maps and antiquities. His collection had been purchased by the East India Company. It counted about 8000 hand-written copies of predominantly Sanskrit texts and was subsequently catalogued in 1828 by H.H. Wilson. It forms an important part of the Bodleian, India Office and other British libraries.

387 Minkowski 2010.

388 Certeau 1975; Jacob 2007 and 2014.

and whether the process can be seen as one that affected something like a major reconfiguration of knowledge? In the repeated voices of scholars involved in the grand project of systematic search for manuscripts, which they articulated in their reports, one can hear the urgent need for drawing and publishing in print appropriate catalogues that could open the newly formed collections to 'the public'. The prospective authors of such catalogues, at first, were imagined to be European scholars only.[389]

The manuscript search tours resulted in the amassing of thousands of hand-written copies believed to represent indigenous knowledge. In the second stage of the process, a new generation of Indian scholars were also included. Their input to the process proved to be crucial in many ways. Soon came the disquieting question concerning the method of preservation and organization of access; thus, the idea of descriptive catalogues systematically compiled and edited according to appropriate standards of philology and textual criticism, as best for representing the treasures of the big government collections, had already come to light already by the end of the 19th century. This idea was fuelled, in part, by the emulation of the catalogues of Sanskrit manuscripts compiled earlier in Europe, especially Germany and England. At first, the authorities accepted the opinion that such catalogues should be produced in Europe rather than in India. While a number of collections of Sanskrit and other Indian manuscripts that were moved to Europe remained without descriptive catalogues long thereafter, even to the present day, the beginning of the 20th century saw a series of ambitious projects for compiling descriptive catalogues in India itself. Some of these reflected the early enthusiasm and discontinued after the first volume had been published. But a good number succeeded in producing up to as many as thirty-five volumes, prepared in successive years, and outlived the idea of surveying and mapping the empire and cataloguing its possessions.

The extensive search initiated and deployed by the British government of India in 1868 was not the first but was, no doubt, radically distinct in being planned and systematically performed for almost half-a-century through regular tours into the interior. The scale and scope of this initiative probably deserves to be described as 'the scanning of the intellectual landscape in search for the handwritten artefacts representing indigenous knowledge.' The force that powered the project must have been, in some measure, at

---

389 See Gough 1868.

least related to the colonial need for domination. But, this also led to the more general necessity to know and understand the epistemological other. The resulting process of cataloguing may perhaps be seen as having been driven by the need to organize and conceptually master the intellectual space in a way much resembling that of mapping through triangulating, which helped us to understand and master physical space.[390] This entailed an ambition for completeness in charting usually three kinds of collections: family, royal, and institutional (traditional schools, monasteries and temples).[391] And such ambition can be read from the reports on those search results that aimed at mapping at least the collections remaining, at that time, in private hands.

This and other facets of a mass shift towards producing and publishing descriptive catalogues around the beginning of the 20th century probably reflects the nature and the way of conceptualizing Indian modernity, or the modernity that allegedly was coming to India. There has recently been offered two distinctly contradictory historiographical models for Indian modernity. The dominant one underscores a radical rupture and discontinuity between the old order of the indigenous Indian *episteme* and the modern organization of knowledge in educational and research institutions controlled by the government. This stresses the colonial character of the processes leading to radical relocation, by displacing of the manuscripted artefacts from their original contexts to new localities with a view to securing political and civilizational domination. The other one points to the contrary—a continuity of the process of reorganization of knowledge—which had already been well underway as an original Indian type of early modernity and which had made itself historically noteworthy during the period between 1450 and 1750, postulated as an early modern period of Indian history.[392]

The dislocation of knowledge through new collections does not necessarily refer to the supposed rupture in the allegedly traditional and unchanging world of the Sanskrit knowledge, but rather to the creation of new types of centres, which aimed at reinventing knowledge for a radically different use, while encouraging distinctly new scholarly practices by new and different agents. Already the early finds with their breathtaking

---

390 See Jacob 2007.

391 Minkowski 2010; Zysk 2012.

392 Pollock 2007; Minkowski 2010; Houben and Rath 2012.

number and distribution called for a super-catalogue and one such produced by the very end of 19th century by Theodore Aufrecht remains still in use. After the period of the explosion of descriptive catalogues in the beginning of 20th century the Aufrecht's *Catalogus Catalogorum* had been seen as in need of urgent complementation or replacement by a new one, drawn by Indians in India. Thus an idea of *New Catalogus Catalogorum* was born in the thirties and first volume appeared in 1937.

It may seem that this unprecedented enthusiasm for rediscovering indigenous knowledge on the part of the British and their agents should be represented as a definitive and irreversible move towards reshaping a part of the cultural heritage of older India into something that the British imagined represented true indigenous knowledge.[393] But we must remember that the intrepid European scholars and the modern(izing) Indians that joined them needed and actually based their search on indigenous traditional scholars—various *paṇḍits* and *śāstris*—who thus lent not only their hands, but also knowledge and concepts thereof, to the task. To a minor extent, the new project for past knowledge to be recovered was to be their choice.

The new 'cartography of disciplines', built by the cataloguing effort, on the conclusion of the enthusiastic work of the 'collectors', shows mostly native Indian concepts and categories for the representation and classification of knowledge disciplines. If historical forms, processes, and social practices of knowledge production are going to remain within the future frame of Asian studies (whichever way they reconstitute themselves), should remain concerned—one way or another—with the burden of knowledge produced not only over the centuries of Indian manuscript culture transmission, but also during the initial upsurge of modern institutions, that proved so eager to organize and control it by publishing descriptive catalogues that represent different historical ways of forming and conceptualizing ambitious collections. When examined more closely, the regional and 'local pragmatics'[394] behind these different projects may offer important insights into the original and distinct ways of knowledge production and representation as well as its historical relationships to centres of power and authority.

---

393 Earlier local projects of cataloguing Indian collections did happen, but they did not bear the stamp of a systematic government-designed plan. See, for instance, *A descriptive catalogue of the Oriental library of the late Tippoo Sultan of Mysore*, by Charles Stewart (Cambridge, 1809) and *A catalogue of Sanscrita manuscripts presented to the Royal Society* by Sir William and Lady Jones (London: Royal Society, 1798).

394 Sengupta and Ali 2011: 4.

Descriptive catalogues also appear to constitute an interesting instance of the way in which 'western science was adapted and woven into preexisting, precolonial epistemologies.'[395] The way they arranged and organized their subject matter also reflected basic rules of modern cataloguing, which had evolved in Europe. At the same time, however, it testified to the pragmatics of the indigenous ways of representing contents and of classifying knowledge adapted by the catalogue editors. The catalogues show Indian 'modernity' as an original hybrid form, distinct from British or any other form of modernity that might be imported to India by the colonial state and its functionaries. The knowledge structures embodied by the descriptive catalogues appear to be 'dialogically produced',[396] as the effect of the encounter with, and (often creative) appropriation by, the newly formed Indian disciplinary professionals of the field. Whatever it may mean, the Veda forms a prominent category—both in terms of the architectural hierarchy of the catalogues as well as in the quantity of all the extant catalogues—from the time that they were neatly printed in a finalizing act of framing (and freezing) of the allegedly complete edifice of ancient traditional knowledge.

III.3.4. The ethnographic state in print

An array of publications documenting territorial 'surveys' and stamped with the authority of 'Government Press' or 'Printed for the Government' begins to appear towards the end of the 19th century, at an uneven pace and number, in the three Provinces of British India. Though animated by a centralized decision taken in Calcutta, they intensify to a different degree in Madras and Bombay. In part they remain conceptually complemented by the series of censuses that happen to be initiated in the same period. Also by the huge regional survey projects of decisive cartographic impact, given a similar form of authoritative 'government printing', with a strong suggestion of final acts of imperial embracing and control.[397] All this appears

[395] Sengupta and Ali 2011: 6.

[396] Sengupta and Ali 2011: 8.

[397] For an account of the huge project of triangulation and map making of western parts of Indian Subcontinent, see Insley 1995. For a history of associating empire and writing (inscription), see Peters 2015: 279 ('The Christmas story in Luke 2 begins with Caesar Augustus ...decreeing ... that the empire should be inscribed—into a database.') and Vismann 2008: 48–61.

to be a culmination of a process that had started already in last decades of the previous century, when the directors of the Company had begun to demand, from their Indian subordinates, more detailed land surveys and maps in order to maximize 'the advantages gained from the recently acquired' provinces, as was the case in a letter by the company's directors, dispatched to Calcutta in 1765.[398]

The post-1858 British Indian Empire engaged in a vast operation of self-representation through government-printed or government-sanctioned imperial maps, economic resource surveys, and ethnographic descriptions of lands and peoples across vast areas of British possessions in India. Some projects planned by the General Government in Calcutta remained only projects on paper, some were suspended half-way when they proved to be unfeasible, but a good number went all the way through the process and produced the new type of imperial knowledge sanctioned by the permanence of Government-approved print.[399] As aptly summarized by Bowen:

> the increasingly well-regulated paper empire they [the Company's directors] created inside East India House acted as a surrogate for the territorial empire that had been established on the subcontinent, and they hoped that the order they imposed upon the former could be projected on to the latter through the application of high standards of accuracy and attention to detail.[400]

For several reasons, the Madras presidency came to stand out conspicuously, with its huge Government-inspired projects of surveys that produced bulky printed volumes of ethnographic descriptions. They were penned by government revenue collectors or other officers having access to the necessary data. Some of the descriptions took the appellation of 'manual',

---

398 Bowen 2006: 175. For a more general policy of the company towards producing systematic surveys of its possessions, and other forms of knowledge production, see Bowen 2006: 174–81.

399 This process had commenced roughly a century earlier along with the need for assessment of the new land acquisition for the Company with respect to its revenue potential. Cf. Bowen 2006: 175 – '... the practical demands of revenue collection, military-policing operations, and political administration drew the Company into new spheres of inquiry in India. At the most basic level, those in London needed to know about the territory and resources that had been secured, and this could only be achieved through extensive fieldwork of the type that began in earnest during the late 1750s and early 1760s, when Hugh Cameron and James Rannell were charged with surveying new lands brought under Company control.'

400 Sengupta and Ali 2011: 180.

suggesting an exhaustive treatment of everything that should be known as concerned a given area. These manuals began to form important points of reference not only for the British policy makers, but also for the native intitiatives for several varieties of cultural memory revival. William Logan's *Malabar Manual* of 1887 and the nine volume *Castes and Tribes of South India* (1909) by Thurston testify to the huge project of ethnographic knowledge production of a systematic and stabilizing claim.[401] The author of the latter served in the capacity of superintendent of the newly-formed Government Museum in Madras, and his gargantuan publication bears the imprint of the inventory-like concept behind its construction. This process soon found its continuation imitated (not without a spirit of emulation) by native Princely States, which competed in projects of finalizing descriptions of their possessions. The state of Travancore saw several government publications of this character, such as the *Travancore State Manual* (1906) by Nagam Aiyya; the neighbouring state of Cochin saw the publication of Ananta Krishna Iyer's *Castes and Tribes of Cochin* in 1906. Results include Brahmins with their allegedly hereditary possession of the Veda who started to feature in these and the like publications as 'tribes' or 'castes'. Their textualized knowledge in the form of the Veda suddenly changed status into the ethnographically documented indigenous knowledge made of regionally distinct customs and practices to be described rather than published in its original textual form or its translation into intelliginble modern languages. The new order of printed knowledge planned to fix new and stable points of reference and appeared to represent a final step at substituting the previous native paradigms of knowledge production and circulation in the process in which, according to Bayly:

> ...the diffuse pieces of information brought by news writers and runners, and once filtered and organized by the mind of the aged diwan or clever munshi, were now ordered into files, and processed through official publication and the Anglo-Indian press, giving news a formality and fixity previously unknown.[402]

---

401 Cf. General remarks by Veena Naregal on the nature of mutual links between I, imperial philology, geography and etnology (NAREGAL 2001: 45): 'Philology and Ethnology had comparable concerns...: create a cognitive order that was a systematic empirical reconstruction of native ways.' 'Relying on technics of objectification, enumeration, measurement, and classification, the emerging fields of philology, geography and ethnology aimed at...'

402 See BAYLY 1996: 372.

III.4. Indian commercial printing after 1835 (new beginnings)

The year 1835 saw a change in the company's Calcutta Government attitude toward restricting print and opened opportunities for native enterprise in this area. Paradoxically, the same year witnessed Lord Macaulay's infamous speech on the value of Indian indigenous knowledge. Macaulay's views triggered a process that resulted in cutting the company's funds for supporting native forms of education in traditional schools like madrasas and *pāṭhaśālās*, that encouraged Persian, Sanskrit and regional vernaculars, in favour of English medium instruction in a new system of education adopted from Britain.

Another part of the context of the ongoing development towards mass printing in the biggest regional centres is supplied by the introduction of lithographic press. We know that six lithographic presses had been shipped out to Bombay on the Dunira by June 1824.[403] This laconic statement in an English East India report represents a move on the part of the British Bombay government to cope with its costly printing services and the brief but rich career of lithography on the Indian subcontinent, particularly popular in the printing of Urdu texts.

> The one printing technology that did strike a cultural chord, particularly with Muslim communities, was lithography, introduced to South Asia in the 1820s... This was precisely because it enabled the printed book to imitate the characteristics of the manuscript which still held cultural authority.[404]

In contrast to most studies, which took for granted that it was typography print that successfully competed with the manuscript culture, Shaw convincingly suggests that, in the case of India, it may have been rather lithography that appealed more successfully to the expectations of the traditional manuscript culture. According to Shaw:

> It was the arrival of lithography, more than typography, which introduced the concept of printing as an alternative method of book production to the traditional

403 Shaw 1993b.

404 Shaw 2007: 127.

patrons of the manuscript scribes—rulers and their courtiers, rich merchants and religious institutions, etc.[405]

Probably a number of early Persian works to appear in print were published in Bombay thanks to the introduction of the lithographic press. This is the case of an edition of the *Gulistan* believed to be printed at Bombay about 1826. However, 'the earliest Bombay edition otherwise known is that lithographed by R. Prera for the Bombay Native Education Society in 1833.'[406]

In Calcutta, the development of indigenous commercial printing took a trajectory that was characteristic of its specific socio-political situation. As remarked by Ogborn:

> The first indigenous vernacular presses of the 1810s and 1820s were run by men of the scribal high castes, such as Bābu Rām and Gangākīshor Bhattachārya, who had already been teaching, writing, and printing didactic works in Sanskritized Bengali in association with the English. These scholar-printers, and the nouveau riche *abhijāta* aristocracy that sponsored their printing of the works of Brahminical high culture, formed the basis of attempts to purify Bengali language and literature in the early nineteenth century. By the 1850s they were being joined and superseded in this reformism by a new *bhadralok* professional, service, and rentier class.[407]

Not much later, in 1857, more than half a million books were reported to have been printed in Calcutta.[408] Most of them, however, were cheap prints and pamphlets produced in tiny enterprises around the Batala area, representing largely, though not exclusively, a lower level of literary ambition and technology development, a far cry from the *bhadralok* class directing Bengal Renaissance. It was their activity, however, which shaped much of the future development of mass print, that showed the double-edged power of print technology in general. The developing vernacular journals widely criticized colonial authorities, and the fighters of the 1857 uprising used to destroy British printing presses as tools of colonial oppression.[409] In the post-1857 India, which had officially been taken over by the British Crown, the press was still viewed by the British as an instrument of civilizing and modernizing

405 Shaw 1994: 5.
406 Shaw 1993b: 10.
407 Ogborn 2007: 267.
408 Ogborn 2007: 267.
409 Ogborn 2007: 268; Bayly 1996: 241.

potential on the one hand, and a powerful tool of sedition on the other. It is in this historical context, that the first indigenous attempts at publishing the hitherto oral or privately handwritten Veda saw the light of the day.

The concepts behind several projects of printing the Veda looked altogether different. While the growing print industry after 1850 and the accompanying new reading practices should perhaps not be best described through the much-used concept of 'print revolution', another form of change was definitely triggered and resulted in several developments of both social and cultural character.[410] The apparently limited case of the Veda happens to be quite instructive in that matter. One of the effects of the eventual lowering of prices towards the 1860s was the increased output of printed religious texts and the galvanization of communal emotions around religious beliefs and identities. The person and work of Dayānanda Sarasvatī offers an instance of a case, which involved a new concept for the Veda and the novel idea of its textuality and social function, that involved a printing project inspired, to some extent, by the practices of Christian missionaries, predominantly the Protestants with their specific attitude towards print and reading. The processes of mobilization of religious feelings towards sharpening the borderlines of communal identity accompanied Dayānanda's tours around the northern and western provinces. The tours involved initiating local branches of Brahmo Sabhas and featured Dayānanda using the old traditional intellectual-cum-religious institution of debate. Debates with predominantly local orthodox Brahmin communities used to be organized, that were designed to spread Dayānanda's novel ideas concerning the vision of the Veda as a 'book' open to all Hindus.[411] During one of such debates, organized in 1877 in Gujarat, he is reported to have exclaimed that: 'the whole town of Gujarat cannot produce a single copy of the *Vedas*. Look at the Christians! They are translating the Bible into all languages and they are available for two annas each!'[412]

---

410 According to C.A. Bayly, print, as such, did not affect information revolution in 19th century India because it met with competition from the long-established networks of the indigenous tradition of written and oral communication channels. Print, however, 'speeded up the velocity and range of communication among the existing communities of knowledge' [Bayly 1996: 243].

411 There exists rich scholarship on Dayānanda's ideas. For major trends and bibliography, see, for instance, Llewellyn 1994. On Dayānanda's idea of the opening of the Veda and his being regarded as 'the Luther of India,' see Llewellyn 1994: 244.

412 Jordens 1960: 166. Cf. also comments on this passage in Stark 2007: 23. Dayānanda could not be aware of the global network of Protestant missionary economy behind the cheap printing.

Soon after this event, the first volumes of Dayānanda's *Ṛgvedādibhāṣya-bhūmikā* appeared in print in 1877, in Benares, pinted by Lazarus Press, and would continue to be completed there in 1888, with two volumes printed by the Bombay Nirṇaya Sagara Press. An anecdote, not without meaning in the context of this study, has it that the first person to show Dayānanda a copy of the *Ṛgveda* was a Christian missionary.[413]

More or less at the same moment, on the Western coast, parallel developments brought the results of an altogether different shape, while deriving their concepts of the printed Veda from radically different suppositions. The same Bombay based Nirṇaya Sagara Press, which had published the last two volumes of Dayānanda's *Ṛgvedādibhāṣyādibhūmikā*, engaged in several publication projects focused on seeing the Veda through print. One of them, unprecedented in its scope and broadness of vision—but never to be completed—had been given an adequate title in Sanskrit and English as *Vedārthayatna*, or *An Attempt to Interpret the Vedas.*[414] Contrary to the concept behind the Dayānanda's work, the editor of this mammoth enterprise showed text-critical ambitions and competence as well as his own idea of 'opening' the Veda to a wider public through a [philologically sound] translation into both Marathi and English.[415]

With minor exceptions, indigenous commercial printing in Bombay and Maharashtra developed late, only sometime after 1835. Save for the expanding journalism, its evolution took different trajectory to that of Calcutta or Madras. Nirṇaya Sagara started operation towards 1863 and Venkateśwara Steam Press towards 1871.[416] The founder of the former earned his necessary

---

413 Jordens 1960: 40.

414 Whether consciously or not, the editorial concept of this mammoth project resembled closely the much modest pioneering project of the missionary John Stevenson's 1837 edition of the beginning part of the *Ṛgvedasaṃhitā* with its original Sanskrit accompanied by a double rendering into English and Marathi.

415 The full title reads: *Vedârthayatna or An Attempt to Interpret the Vedas. Marâṭhī and English Translations, together with a Sanskrit Paraphrase of the Ṛgvedasaṃhitâ with the Original Saṃhitâ and Pada Texts and Notes in Mârathî,* Vol. III, Bombay: Nirṇaya Sagara Press 1880. The whole, but never to be completed project appeared in print between 1876–1882, edited by Shankar Pandurang Pandit, only volumes 1–4, and 5, parts 1–9 appeared in Bombay, first from Indu-Prakash Press, later from Nirṇaya Sāgar Press.

416 See Mukul 2015:11. The founders of this press, the two Bajaj brothers Khemraj and Gangaviṣṇu Kriṣnadas took to printing in 1871 "from a single room in the Moti Bazar area of Bombay." Soon they moved to a new location in Khetwadi and launched the Sri Venkateshwara Steam Press. Their first Sanskrit titles included *Hanuman Caliśa* and *Viṣṇu-sahasranāma.* In the "next few years the press printed 2,800 titles, almost the entire pantheon of texts on religion, spiritualism, philosophy, culture and history". Later the press

experience in the earlier presses operated in Bombay—the American Mission Press (1821), Ganpat Krishnaji (probably 1835), and Induprakash. The two latter ones had made their way through the competitive market partly by accepting commissions from government agencies or taking part in projects subsidized by one of the agencies of the British government. Thus, Induprakash printed several titles of the Bombay Sanskrit Series for the Government Central Book Depot,[417] one of whose editors was the legendary Pandit Pandurang Shankar, involved in the ambitious but discontinued project of *Vedārthayatna*. Other names include Gopala Narayan & Co. Press or Bharatabhūṣaṇa Press of Pune. Almost each and every one of these early printing-publishing enterprises deserves a monograph of its own. Their histories and remaining copies of their prints show also various concepts and strategies of representing in print the Vedic texts to the attention of their respective audiences.

---

divided in two cooperating presses. Though the bulk of their publications was made by purāṇas and other more popular Hindu religious and texts, the Vedas features prominently in their advertisings and catalogues. Later the brothers associated with the ideas of Sanatana Dharma and earned for themselves a name of community heroes among their compatriots. As such they feature in community biographic literature of a somewhat panegiric type. Agrasenputra 1928: 82–83. According to Agrasenaputra, the Marwari (Mārvāḍī) founder, Seth Khemraj, 'rescued thousands of manuscripts, written on palm leaves! from total extinction and gave them life. Today, the number of such books, which might otherwise have shared the fate of similar gems of religious literature, runs into something like five thousand. ... Seth Khemrajji's brother, the late Seth Ganga Bishenji, started his own press at Kalyan, a suburb of Bombay. This press, too, soon prospered and brought out hundreds of religious books ... Within a short time, the Venkateshwar Press had become a place of pilgrimage for the famous Pandits of the land.'

417 For instance, *Vikramorvaśiyam* of 1879.

IV. The Printed Veda

These men, and I know it as a fact, know the whole Rig-Veda by heart, just as their ancestors did, three or four thousand years ago; ...and though they now have a printed text, they do not learn their sacred lore from them.

F. Max Müller 1878: 156

Ever since the very first attempt by Baron Sainte-Croix and his *Ezour Vedam*, nearly all following projects to publish the Veda in print were fraught with emotion and tension. The act of publishing the Veda suggested a disclosure but what actually was, or was imagined to be, disclosed could differ widely, depending on who published it. The gesture of publishing either the allegedly lost or sacred or philologically-mastered Veda entailed articulating a concept of what the Veda actually was. The introduction to Müller's imperial-cum-philological Veda ran for dozens of pages, growing in number in succeeding volumes and the second edition. Other editors of the *Ṛgveda* felt less self-orientated but more inclined to include the printing of the Veda into the network of relationships of early communal, regional, or national symbolism.

All through the late 18th and 19th centuries, with their discovery of mechanized printing, the marginal niche of the printed Veda filled up slowly and with different ideas in mind of those who ventured to publish in print either the imagined or the lost, philological, or imperial Veda—the truly oral or national Veda. In each of these cases, the same thing might look quite different, while reflecting different presuppositions and distinct expectations of variously targeted audiences putting print to different conceptual uses. Only some analogies concerning the profound changes effected by print since the 16th century, to the understanding of what the Bible was when it domesticated itself in the minds of the nineteenth-century-reader as exclusively 'the Book', can be—with due caution—resorted to, when trying to assess the changes in how the nature of the Veda was understood with the appearance of early Indian editions of Vedic texts.[418]

IV.1. The lost and the imagined Veda

I remember Baron Bunsen telling me how his chief object in arranging to go to India with his pupil, Mr. Astor, was to see whether there really was such a book in existence

F. Max Müller, *Auld Lang Syne* II[419]

A lost book of scripture happens to form one of the important *topoi* in Sanskrit narratives belonging to various religious traditions. The practice of identifying an untraceable quotation from the Veda as coming from the 'lost [part of the] Veda' had been even argued for within the exegetical tradition of the Mīmāṃsā school. Thus Śabara (probably 5th century AD) is said to have quoted nearly two thousand passages from various Vedic texts, out of which more than two hundred could not be identified and

---

418 Cf. the illuminating, even though somewhat vague, remarks voiced by M. McLuhan in 1962: 'When the "higher critics" began to explain the nature of manuscript culture to the Bible-reading public in the later nineteenth century, it seemed to many educated people that the Bible was finished. But these people had lived mainly with the illusions of the Bible produced by print technology. The scriptures had had none of that uniform and homogeneous character during the centuries before Gutenberg' [McLuhan 1962: 135].

419 Müller 1899: 170. Müller got in touch with Baron Christian von Bunsen, a German anglophile and a historian, while on his trip to England to consult the East India Company archives in 1846 [Stocking 1991: 57]. Bunsen proved to be instrumental for his contacts in Oxford. Müller speculates what could incite Bunsen to plan such a trip with such a bold, if not bizarre, objective in mind as seeing 'whether there really was such a book [as the Veda] in existence.' According to Müller, Baron Bunsen 'might have known that it was in existence as a real book' [Stocking 1991: 170] by 'consulting *Lettres édifiantes*,' an edited corpus of Jesuit missionary epistolary writings and reports sent, among others, from India, and published in 34 volumes between 1702 and 1776. Some of these letters contain early descriptions of the contents and structure of the Veda [see Letter of 1733 by Calmette in *Lettres Edifiantes* 1819: VII, 506] as well as refer [Pons, *Letter of Nov. 23*, 1740 to *père du* Halde] to '*les vedam ... en arabe*' in the Bibliothèque du Roi in Paris [*Lettres édifiantes*, Vol. VIII, p. 43]. Cf. Sinner 1793: xxvii which quotes this description while doubting the Veda in Arabic being stored in Bibliothèque du Roi: '*Il seroit beaucoup plus utile que quelque Sa vant versé dans la Langue Arabe nous donnât la Traduction des quatre Bets ou Bedas, s'il sft vrai qu'ils soient dans la Bibliothèque du Roi. Je dirai en son lieu ce qu'on doit entendre par ces quatre Bedas.*' What Pons actually reffered to was the Telugu script of the copies of the Veda sent to Paris by Calmette. See Sweetman 2019: 798.

were supposed to be quotations from texts lost to us.[420] According to one modern study, the topos of the lost Veda had become one of the important strategies deployed by authors of the medieval class of *Purāṇic* texts in substantiating their claims for basing their works on the authority of the (lost) Veda.[421] The relative frequency of this topos came to be seen against the background of the allegedly dominating concept of time, as withering or degenerating within the frame of succeeding cycles of eons (*kalpas* and *yugas*) as experienced by the universe and humankind.[422] Furthermore, in cosmological narratives, developing from the last centuries BC, among others, in *the Mahābhārata*, and, over the first millennium, in *Purāṇic* texts, the Veda happens to be pictured as gradually receding from attention, either neglected or given birth to in the waters of the universal deluge and needs to be rescued. In other versions, the Veda, or a part of it, had been lost for good, as a result either of a cosmic catastrophe or of a degeneration of time or due to the negligence of the men supposed to guard it. A simplified picture of this doctrine might have stimulated notions of a more general decline of brahmanic tradition, which reportedly no longer cared enough to keep the Veda alive, resulting allegedly in its being altogether or partly lost. This concept seems to have met with the ready-made expectations of the first Europeans who happened to hear of the Veda. For the tradesmen, evangelists, and early scholars, the Veda remained the lost or concealed 'book' in need of recovery. It was 'known to exist and people began to write about it, long before it had been seen or handled by any European.'[423]

In that way, long before it had actually been seen by Europeans, the Veda had lived a life of an 'absent text'[424] in the imaginations of Europeans, fed by hearsay, half-truths and, sometimes, mystification.[425] All of them merged with whatever the nineteenth Indian editors knew and believed

---

420 GONDA 1975: 53.

421 For a survey of examples of Smṛti texts claiming to be based on the authority of the Veda (*Śruti*), see SMITH 1989: 24–25.

422 A classic study on *dharma* and time remains LINGAT 1973. See also GONZÁLEZ-REIMANN 2009.

423 MÜLLER 1899: 169.

424 FIGUEIRA 1994: 201. On Veda in Bīrūnī and Roberto Nobili, see Halbfass 1988: 26 and 42. On the word Veda in early missionary writings, see B. Tiliander 1974.

425 Cf. MÜLLER 1899: 169—'If all books have their fates, the oldest book of the world, the Veda, has certainly had the most extraordinary fate. It was known to exist and people began to write about it, long before it had been seen or handled by any European.'

about the indigenous concepts of what the Veda actually was. Their decisions must have been determined by this complex history.

Early modern descriptions of the Veda began circulating in Europe at least since the publication in 1651 of a book by the Dutch chaplain Abraham Rogers (Rogerius)[426] and another by Philippus Baldaeus in 1671.[427] Rogers portrayed the Veda as 'a book of laws containing all the beliefs and ceremonies of the Brahmins.'[428] His book formed a paradigm for understanding Hindu religions and conceptualizing the Veda for almost two centuries and, even as late as 1898, A.C. Burnell held it to be 'still perhaps the most complete account of South Indian Hinduism.'[429] According to the account offered by Philip Baldeus:

> ...the Brahmans nowadays have no more than three Books of the Vedam, the fourth which treated of God being lost. For the fifth of these Books treated of God,

---

[426] Rogerius 1915 (1651). The 1651 Dutch edition printed in Amsterdam was subsequently translated into German in 1663 and into French in 1670. For the confusion with the Latin version (original?) titled *Gentilismus Reseratus*, printed in Leiden in 1651, see the editorial Introduction by W. Caland in Rogerius 1915: 27–'In his book "The Dutch Reformed Church in the Dutch East Indies" p. 164, footnote, Troostenburg de Bruijn mentions that Rogerius's work with the title 'Gentilismus reseratus' was submitted to the Synod (Church meeting) held in Leiden and was published posthumously in Leiden in 1651 in quarto, by the scholar of Law A(ndreas) W(issowatius), who also had prepared the Dutch translation (Amsterdam 1651). This report, that our book had originally been composed in Latin, is found in many other publications. However, no trace of the Latin version has been found yet.' (I thank Herman Tieken for translating this fragment from original Dutch of Caland). For the origin of the confusion about the non-existent Latin 'original', see also Neill 2004: 419.

[427] Baldeus 1703 (1671). A brief description is given in Chapter XII.

[428] Killingley 2008. Rogers may have borrowed from the earlier Diogo do Couto's *Decada Quinta da historia da India* (1612). On the Agostinho de Azevedo's account of the Veda and its relation to works by Couto and Lucena (1600), see Sweetman 2019: 785. Azevedo's work remained unpublished until 1960. The idea of the Veda as the 'book(s) of law' can be seen in de Nobili who was the first European to have direct access to some of Vedic texts. Nobili's works came out only long after his death, but an account by Jesuit Jacome Fenicio on Brahma's cut-off head and one Veda being lost (Fenicio mentioned also the story of Viṣṇu as Mātsyāvātara recovering the 'law' stolen by the golden-eyed demon Hiraṇyākṣa) probably got to print in Baldeus (1672) and Manuel de Faria e Sousa (1675). See, Sweetman 2019:791. The idea of the Veda as book(s) of law finds a distant echo on the dedication page of Max Müller's 1849 first edition of the *Ṛgvedasaṃhitā* (see below Chapter IV.5). On early Jesuit views on the Veda, see Zupanov 1999.

[429] See Neill 2004: 419 who identifies the source as *Indian Antiquary* Vol. VIII, p. 98. For a general appraisal of Rogerius' work and its translations, see Sweetman 2003: 89. Cf. Müller's comments on the unnoticed testimony of Calmette ('What is extraordinary is that the announcement of Father Calmette's discovery of the Veda passed off almost unheeded in Europe') and Pons ('[Pons'] communications also excited no curiosity except among a few members of the French Institute') [Müller 1891: 45].

> and of the Origin and Beginning of the Universe. The second, of those who have the Government and Management thereof. The third, of Morality and true Virtue. The fourth of the Ceremonials in their Temples, and Sacrifices. These four Books of the Fedam are by them call'd Roggo Vedam, Jadura Vedam, Santa Vedam, and Tarawana Vedam, and by the Malabars, Icca, Icciya, Saman, and Adaravan. The loss of this firft Part is highly lamented by the Brahmans.[430]

F. Bernier, who travelled to North India in 1656–68, left an interesting account, in which he claims to have been shown some of the Vedas in Benares. In his account, Bernier describes the Vedas (*les beths* in French original) as being apparently composed of extremely numerous different texts and rarely to be seen at the same time. [431] The passage suggests that the event of his lucky occasion to see some of them may have taken place in the famous library of the Benares polymath Kavīndra Sārasvati.[432] By chance, we know quite a bit about the character of the collection mentioned by Bernier. According to a preserved list of manuscript books that might have once made its body, the library of Kāvindra must have been a well-organized collection with books arranged according to a thematic principle. Vedic texts indeed make up a substantial part of the list, and no wonder their number must have impressed Bernier.[433] In the same breath, Bernier makes it clear for his readers how lucky he was to have seen such rare books, whereas his powerful Moghul patron had failed to acquire one:

> ...they are so scarce that my Agah [Danischand Khān]] notwithstanding all his diligence has not succeeded in purchasing a copy. The *Gentiles* indeed conceal

[430] This brief description of the Veda is given in Chapter XII [Baldeus 1703: 891]. For a probable unacknowledged use by Baldeus of earlier Jesuit sources (some of them coming from the Jesuit library in Cochin burnt by the Dutch in 1663), see Baretto Xavier Zupanov: 235–236.

[431] '*...ces beths sont fort gros, di moins s ices sont ceux qu'on memontra à Benares : ils sont meme très rare ...*' [Bernier 1830: 135].

[432] Bernier's account suggests that he saw the library himself: '... the books of their religion, which are of unquestionable antiquity, being all written in Sanskrit. It has also its authors on philosophy, works on medicine written in verse, and many other kinds of books, with which a large hall at Benares is entirely filled' [Bernier 1891: 335].

[433] According to the List, the Vedic texts were represented in a fairly good number both as far as primary *samhitas* as well as ritual manuals are concerned. See *Kāvindrācāryasūcipatram* 1921: 1–3 and 7–9. On the organizing principle of this collection, see Galewicz 2011a.

them with much care, lest they should fall into the hands of the *Mahomet Ans*, and be burn, as frequently has happened.[434]

From the first intelligence by Jesuit missionaries, the Veda(s) had been considered a 'lost text' until first their fragments and later the Polier collection had reached Europe. The eventual identification of the actual body of Vedic texts took a long way to go for the Europeans. The best-known instance of the misidentified Veda is the so called 'Ezour Veda', which made its impact on enlightened thinkers like Voltaire towards the end of 18th century.[435] A list of books sent in 1732 by French Jesuit missionaries from Pondicherry, south from Madras, to the Bibliothèque du Roi in Paris contains the entry: 'Trois livres du Ezour Vedam.'[436] It seems that only one of the three eventually reached France but not directly the library of the king. The three, however, were actually seen in 1816, sometime after the abandonment of the French Jesuit mission, by a British East India Company's employee and a self-taught orientalist, Francis Whyte Ellis (1777–1819).[437] Ellis mentions having seen in the same place not only three but four 'books', bearing titles suggesting a set of four Vedas.[438] In fact, what Ellis had found and meticulously described were eight separate manuscripts: some containing more than one text; some unfinished with blank areas or whole pages left; some bilingual (Sanskrit and French) and intending to present original Sanskrit with French rendering facing it on the opposite page; some in French only. All were in Roman script and all had been provided with titles suggesting a Vedic text.[439] It is not clear what sort of

434 Bernier 1891: 335–36. For the 'Agah' identification with Danischand, see Gode 1969a: 24, fn. 2.

435 See Killingley 2008; Rocher 1984; Figueira 1994; Castets 1935 and Ellis 1822.

436 Omont 1902: 1189 quoted by and commented upon in Killingley 2008.

437 Ellis 1822: 2.

438 Ellis recounts how he came across 'the original' of the text that had been published in 1788 in Paris. He found it among other manuscripts in Pondicherry, remaining 'in the possession of Catholic Missionaries.' The manuscripts—as he continues—were 'understood to have originally belonged to the society of Jesus.' Except for the aforementioned *Ezour Vedam*, in the same location there were also '...imitations of the other three Vedas; each of these are in Sanserif in the Roman character, and in French, these languages being written on the opposite pages of the manuscripts, to give them the appearance of originals with translations annexed' [Ellis 1822: 4].

439 For a description of the eight manuscripts, see Ellis 1822: 19–30. For a more recent evaluation, see Killingley 2008. Ellis' description of the manuscripts suggests either an unfinished project of a bigger scale, or an intention on the part of the author(s) to suggest such a line. The volumes described by Ellis are said by him to have been bound in leather

relationship he actually had in mind, while referring to the manuscripts he saw as 'original' with respect to the one published in France in 1788.[440] The 1788 edition bears testimony to how the manuscript had reached the editor via Voltaire, an already respected figure, who ascertained that the manuscript was a French translation of 'the original', allegedly composed by an old Brahmin in Sri Rangam (?).[441] The 1788 edition presents the *Ezour Vedam* as a translation from '*sancretam*' and identifies its translator quite precisely by providing his name, place and circumstances: a high priest (*grand-prêtre*) of the temple of Cheringham (Śrirangam?), conversant with French and known to the French India Company.[442] Apparently, the three other 'Vedas' of the conseinment never reached France. What Ellis saw

or parchment, which indicates lack of imagination on the part of the author or patron whose intention had been (if it were the case) that the volumes reach the hands of Brahmins. As is a common knowledge, the very idea of touching leather must have been repulsive for the latter.

440 Ellis refers to the French edition of 1788 [Sainte-Croix 1788], which he had seen before his Pondicherry find and which he presumed 'must have been originally composed in one of the Indian dialects' [Ellis 1822: 4]. Ellis remains silent about important evidence by French Jesuits, Calmette and Pons, whose letters had been published among others in *Lettres édifiantes et curieuses* (orig. published in 1704-1776).

441 The story of how the manuscript found its way from Mr. Barthelemy (a member of Pondicherry Council), through a Mr Modave, into Voltaire's hands and was later presented to Bibliothèque du Roi in 1761 can be seen in the preface by the editor to the 1788 edition [Sainte-Croix 1788: viii–x]. The first to undermine the authenticity of the *Ezour-Vedam* as either a 'lost veda' or a 'commentary upon the Veda' was Sonnerat, who already in 1782 (four years after the publication Ezour-Vedam by Sainte-Croix), had written about the 'pretended translation of *Ezour Vedam* deposited in the Library of the King of France (a prétendue traduction de *l'Ezour-Védam*, qu'on trouve a la Bibliothèque du Roi)' [Sonnerat 1782: I, 11] and 'Il faut bien se garder de mettre au nombre des livres canoniques indiens l'Ezourvédam, dont nous avons la prétendue traduction à la Bibliothèque du Roi, et qui a été imprimée en 1778. Ce n'est bien certainement pas l'un des quatre Védams, quoiqu'il en porte le nom; mais plutôt un livre de controverse écrit à Masulipatam par un Missionnaire' [Sonnerat 1782: II, 41–42]. Cf. Castets 1935. Cf. also Rocher 1984: 13 who must have used another edition of the same as he provides reference to this as I.7 and I.215 respectively. A later 1819 edition of Sonnerat's work appears not to contain this passage. Sonnerat himself happened to be later attacked for his opinions by Anquetil--Duperron in 1802, who, in turn, came to be criticized several times for his view. A range of later authors' comments on the nature of *EzourVedam*. For bibliography, see Rocher 1984; Killingley 2008. The debate seems to go on—see http://base-agon.paris-sorbonne.fr/querelles/controverse-de-l-ezour-vedam [accessed on 15 Nov 2017]. Curiously enough, Sonnerat himself uses the same appellation, i.e. *l'Ezour Védam* when apparently referring to Yajur Veda. See Sonnerat 1872: II, 31.

442 '*...grand-prêtre ou archi-bramc de la pagode de Cheringham, vieillard respecté par fa vertu incorruptible.*
Il savait le français, & rendit de grands services à la compagnie des Indes' [Sainte-Croix 1788: ix].

and described as 'imitations of the Vedas' must have had a physical shape of a codex since, as he writes, 'each of these are in Sanserif in the Roman character, and in French, these languages being written on the opposite pages of the manuscripts, to give them the appearance of originals with translations annexed.'[443]

An analysis of the material shape, as well as the orthography, had led Ellis to conclude that the 1788 French publication was made on the basis of a transcript from the Pondicherry original, and also that the 'original' must have been made either in Bengal or by a Bengali hand. The category of 'imitation', used by Ellis with reference to the whole bulk of Pondicherry manuscripts discovered by him, appears to rather adequately convey the type of textuality whose overall message, as it stands out from the excerpts included in Ellis report, was to refute basic tenets of Brahmanical knowledge, while skilfully using the frame of a literary genre familiar to Brahmin intellectuals in general. As far as the authorship of the 'original' texts of the Pondicherry manuscripts is concerned, Ellis came to the rather cautious conclusion that these might have been composed by Roberto Nobili, while, at the same time, not being intended by him as a forgery.[444] Thus, what Ellis suggested was a radical differentiation between the authorship of retouched refutations, probably written by de Nobili in Tmil, and a thorough re-composition of the former in a frame of a Sanskrit genre with a French translation added.[445] In general, however, the whole should be, in Ellis eyes, judged as a forgery and, as a 'Jesuitical forgery', it should be clearly differentiated from the 'genuine' Veda, out of which some little portions were beginning to appear in print in India. In translation, of course. Ellis identifies two such translations, one of the *Iśopaniṣad*, attached to Carey's Sanskrit Grammar (1806), another one of *Iśa* and *Kenopaniṣad*, published by Ram Mohan Roy in Calcutta (1816 and 1819).[446] He, however, does not inform his readers from where he is taking

443 Sainte-Croix 1788: 4.

444 'I am inclined to attribute to him [Nobili] the composition only, not the forgery, of the Pseudo-Vedas' [Ellis 1822: 31].

445 Ellis 1822: 32.

446 Ellis 1822: 36–37. For Ram Mohan Roy's early translation of these and two other *upaniṣads*, see Ghose 1901. Early printed translations from Vedic texts include Duperron's *Oupknekhat* (1801-2), and a number of instances from India: an Atharvaveda hymn translated by William Jones for 1789 *Asiatick Researches*, substantial fragments translated by Colebrooke and published in *Asiatick Researches* 1798, and especially in 1804-5. The *Iśavasya upanishad* published by Carey in 1806 included also a translation. Early translations by Colebrooke

his own (still imperfect, we must add) knowledge about the genuine Veda, though he may have been familiar with the influential Colebrooke's publication on the Vedas of 1806.[447] While identifying the grave differences between the falsified Vedas of Pondicherry and the real ones, he proves, however, to be still under the influence of the powerful myth of the 'lost Veda'; while reflecting upon the meaning of the category of *upa-veda*, he cannot but say that 'the *Upa Vedas* properly so called are now lost.'[448]

As for the very name of *Ezour Vedam*, it was noticed by Ellis and confirmed more recently by Dermot Killingley,[449] that there were other spellings of this title, which, when analyzed together, suggest an intended reference to *Yajur Veda*. The text named *Ezour Veda*, however, has nothing in common with any part of the *Yajurveda* in any version. It has a form of a dialogue in a Purānic style between Vyāsa and Sumantu, in which the former narrates a sort of Purānic cosmology but is then opposed and ridiculed by Sumantu, who, in a reversal of roles, becomes the teacher of Vyāsa and instructs the latter. Sumantu's teaching betrays missionary sources, albeit not of the mainstream Catholic kind.[450] According to Killingley,[451] we should rather see it as a 'presentation of natural religion' and, as such, an example of an approach developed by Jesuits. However, the career of the 'imagined Veda' starts with early accounts by Francis Xavier (1543) whose

in Asiatick Researches vols V, VII and VIII (1805) include *Gayatri Mantra* (RS. 3.64), RS 7.43, 10.125 and 129, fragments of *Aitareya Brahmana* and *Aranyaka, Yajurveda Vajasaneyi Samhita , Brhadaranyaka Upanisad, Taittiriya Samhita, Taittiriya Upanisad, Chandogya Upanisad.* Colebrooke mentions his sources as manuscripts collected in Benares by Robert Chambers and William Jones, Colonel Polier's collection, General Martin's transcript and his own acquisitions (Colebrooke 1808: 428, 469).

447 Except for mentioning very generally in his conclusion the authority of William Jones and Colebrooke's preface to the *Institutes of Manu* and Dissertations on the *Religious Ceremonies and Sacred Writings of the Hindus*. Several passages of his argument, and especially that concerned with Vedic metre, suggest that he must have had some experience with Vedic texts written down (on the other hand his remarks on the way of accent markings suggest the opposite), which he somehow proves by quoting from a manuscript of a selection of *Ṛgvedic* stanzas at the end of his argument [Ellis 1822: 50].

448 Ellis 1822:43. Other instances of 'false Veda' include M.R. Gargam and J-F. Pons' purchasing false Vedas around 1731, father Calmette's false Atharvaveda and Tranquebar Protestant Missionaries' account of allegedly found translation of Yajurveda of 1737. See Sweetman 2019.

449 Killingley 2008.

450 For a summary and evaluation of Sumantu's doctrine, see Killingley 2008. Ellis suspects in the doctrine an affinity with deism and suggests the teaching might have a destabilizing effect and become socially subversive. See Ellis 1882: 35.

451 Killingley 2008.

views find echoes in reports of later Jesuit and other missionaries, and even the testimony including direct exposure to some Vedic texts by Roberto de Nobili (1577–1656) with his peculiar vision of the way to win Indian souls for Christianity did not change much. Nobili's writings emphasized the idea of one 'lost Veda' for practical use but remained long unpublished.'[452]

While trying to assess the process of losing or forgetting the Veda in India, some European authors, even as late as 1975, have argued that:

> In the 19th century many prominent Indians, among whom for instance Vivekananda (1862–1902), knew so little of the contents of the Veda that they mixed them up with beliefs of Buddhist and Hindu origin. Or, calling Vedas what really belongs to the Upaniṣads, they combined, like Gandhi, ancient lore with tenets of other provenance.'[453]

IV.2. The recovered and the philological Veda

> *What in all the world can that Veda be to which this misguided man has devoted the whole of his life?*
>
> Max Müller, *Auld Lang Syne* II[454]

The rise of philology as the queen of the human sciences among other disciplines aspiring to the new order of organizing research universities in Germany—after the early experiments of Pietists in Halle in 1735 AD and the new seminars in Gottingen and Berlin that followed in 1776—coincided with the discovery by Sir William Jones, a Judge in High Court of Calcutta, of the affinity between Sanskrit, Latin, and Greek, and consequently with the rise of the concept of the so-called family of Indo-European (or Indo--German) languages. This led to the crystallization of classical Indology, which, in its early phase, remained close to Indo-European studies (and *Indogermnistik*), that saw Sanskrit as an indispensable link to the lost past, when the hypothetical speakers of the reconstructed languages allegedly lived together as Indo-Europeans.

---

452 See HALBFASS 1989: 42, ŽUPANOV: 1999: 26, 76, 90 and SHULMAN 1984: 25.

453 GONDA 1975: 53.

454 MÜLLER 1899: 167.

The first Europeans began to learn Sanskrit in the late 16th century. The Jesuit Missionary, Roberto de Nobili, is believed to have mastered Sanskrit to a surprising degree. Nobili can also be said to have had his part in triguering, even if unwittingly, the European quest for the supposedly lost Veda.[455] In spite of him and those few like him who expressed any interest in indigenous writing, we do not hear much of early initiatives or anything like regular projects of collecting written artefacts containing native Indian religion, knowledge, or literature.[456] After Bartholomeus Ziegenbalgs's pioneering passion for collecting Indic manuscripts around 1709–1712, the earliest systematic attempt at collecting Indic manuscripts by Europeans came from the French. On the initiative of the King of France and his passion for collecting 'objects', the French missionaries to Carnataka deployed a scheme for research, which started around 1720. The main object of this research was 'the Vedas', and the air of excitement accompanying the search resembled somewhat that shared by Ziegenbalg, who tended to believe that Indic manuscripts—in his case rather Tamil *Śaiva* works—could contain (and reveal) hidden truths.

Between 1729 and 1735, a treasure trove of as many as 287 volumes of handwritten copies of palm-leaf manuscripts of Indic works, made on order in Tamil Nadu, under the supervision of Paris librarians to the king and the French Companie d'Extreme Orient, had been sent overseas to Paris. They came to constitute the earliest Indian collection of the Bibliothèque Nationale (Bibliothèque du Roi). Jean François Pons, another Jesuit scholar passionately interested in Indian intellectual heritage (especially Sanskrit grammar), had the bulk of the 168 books shipped from the French enclave in Chandernagore (West Bengal) to Paris in 1732. The shipment was said to contain:

> 31 books on philology (which was largely his preoccupation and certainly a Jesuit specialty), 22 mythical and philosophical poems, 25 purāṇas, 8 books on

---

455 For a bit different context of understanding of this quest, see Baretto Xavier and Županov 2015: 231. See also Županov 1999: 74, 90, 116 and Shulman 1984: 25.

456 However, the historical role of Catholic missionaries in this respect is underestimated. For an account of the barbarous destruction of the legendary Jesuit library in Cochin by the Dutch in 1663, see Tavernier 1680: 75 commented in Baretto Xavier and Županov 2015: 235. For the early account of the Veda by Agostinho de Azevedo, see Sweetman 2019. Later evidence includes *Lettres édifiantes*,' an edited corpus of Jesuit missionary epistolary writings and reports sent, among others, from India, and published in 34 volumes between 1702 and 1776. Some contain early descriptions of of the Veda [see Letter of 1733 by Calmette in *Lettres Edifiantes* 1819: VII, 506.

> astronomy and astrology, 9 books on poetry, 25 books on laws customs and worship of the gods, 29 books on *nyāya darśaṇam* and 9 on the other *darśaṇam*.[457]

We fail to see much of the Vedic material proper among the collections shipped to France, despite the initial desire expressed by French Jesuit missions to acquire them.[458] While we may suspect that copies of Vedic texts might have been difficult to obtain (and this motif recurs in a good number of reports from missionaries and travellers), for the reason that they would remain predominantly in the possession of their Brahmin users and custodians, and the latter might find it ritually polluting either to deal with Jesuits (or other Europeans of unidentified social status and ritual purity), or their middle men in person, or let their (the Brahmins') personal copies be touched by them. At the time of the early collecting projects of Europeans across India, though not in anything like even distribution, there existed both institutional and private collections of handwritten volumes, and some must have contained Vedic texts as well—which is corroborated by the list of titles in the possession of the seventeenth century polymath of Benares by the name of Kavīndra Ācārya Sarasvatī. The library of the latter was probably seen, or heard of, by the French traveler, François Bernier, around 1665 (?).[459]

In Europe, the Veda had been declared to be a 'lost book' until around 1760, when M. Modave, *un officieur superiere* of the French East India Company,[460] on returning from French Pondicherry on the Coromandel Coast, brought with him to Paris two copies of what was allegedly a French translation of an unidentified Sanskrit text, under the enigmatic title of *Ezour Vedam*. Monsieur Modave deposited one copy at The Bibliothèque du Roi and made a gift of the other to Voltaire, who enthusiastically took it to be a translation from a lost Veda, and the text circulated as such in literary salons of Paris.[461] As we have seen above, after the initial excitement, it

457 Raina 2007: 39. On description of the Veda by Calmette, see *Lettres Édifiantes Et Curieuses* vol. 8, 1819: 1–4.

458 See Raina 2007: 39 and Colas 2012.

459 See Bernier 1830: 135 and Bernier 1891: 335 and fn. 424 above. Also Intro to *Kāvīndrācaryasūcīpatram* ed. by P.K. Gode. For a discussion, see Gode 1940 and 1945. Cf. Galewicz 2011a.

460 Castets 1935.

461 NB, a manuscript of *Ezour Vedam*, deposited in Bibliothèque Nationale de Paris, under the number of MF 34649 continues to this day to be identified under the entry of 'Zozur Bedo', with an accompanying description declaring that it is a '*traduction française du*

soon proved to contain a text that apparently was nothing like the much-searched-for Veda, which thus resumed its status as the 'lost book.' This time not for long.

After an initial confusion in identifying original Vedic texts among the alleged finds and fraudulent or mistaken finds like that of the famous Ezour Vedam,[462] it is believed that one of the first substantial sets of Vedic texts reached British Museum through a gift of a Colonel Polier. In 1789, Polier presented the British Museum with–as it is narrated some time later in 1817 by Crawford–'A complete copy of the Vedas, in eleven volumes in folio, in the Devanagary character, and Sanskrit language, was presented to the British Museum by the late Colonel Polier...'[463] In another narrative of this historical event, Colonel Polier's gift is presented as 'a complete copy of the Vedas,'[464] an expression suggesting a finalizing character of the gesture of depositing 'the whole of the original knowledge of the colonized people' in the Museum space of the Empire.[465] The circumstances of this extraordinary gift involve the person of Sir Joseph Banks, in whose hands Polier actually deposited his find, and can be reconstructed from his letter of 1789 to Banks, then the administrator of the British Museum, published later by H.H. Wilson in the *Asiatic Journal and Monthly Register* for 1819.[466]

Yadjour Veda, 4e livre des Védas.' It is tagged (indexed) as '*Védas. Yadjour Veda, traduction'* (Online Catalogue of Bibliothèque Nationale de France).

462 See Figueira 1994 and Rocher 1984.

463 Craufurd 1817: 186 which continues: '... [Colonel Polier], who is several times mentioned in the Asiatic Researches, and in Rannell's Memoir of a Map of Hindustan. Colonel Polier had resided a number of years in India, first in the military service of the English, afterwards at Delhy in that of the Emperor Shaw Allum, and during his stay in that country, had bestowed much pains in acquiring a knowledge of the learning and religion of the Hindus.' For the circumstances and dating of the acquisition of Polier's manuscript by British Museum, see also Chambers 2007: 93. For a biography of the extraordinary personality of Col. Polier, see Polier and Polier 1809; Wilson 1819; Colas and Richard 1984 and Jasanoff 2005.

464 This wording of the letter, which must have been addressed originally in English to J. Banks and reproduced by Wilson had most probably been rendered into English by him from Mme Polier's French translation in the preface to her *Mythologie des Indous* [Polier and Polier 1809] '*les Baids ou Veds, livre sacrés des Indous.*' Cf. also Colas and Richard 1984: 101. Collection Polier (Fonds Polier) in Bibliothèque Nationale features one Vedic MS identified as the, *Vājasaneyisaṃhitā* [Colas and Richard 1984: 107]. The original letter, dated 20 May 1789, has been deposited alongside the gift in British Museum and, in 1902, it remained bound to the first of the eleven volumes forming the Polier's gift (catalogued as Add. 5346) [Bendall 1902: 2].

465 See Wilson 1819: 360.

466 Wilson 1819: 360. The date of Polier's letter to Banks, given here as May 1789, suggests that the letter as well as the gift had already been sent from Switzerland, after Polier had

The 'complete copy' translates into eleven volumes,[467] 'probably the first collection of Vedic works ever made by a European.' The interesting idea of 'completeness', with respect to the Veda, suggests the long-cherished expectations on the part of the Europeans regarding the 'lost Veda', in terms of a complete 'book,' that was to resemble perhaps that of the Bible, or a complete 'set' of the four Vedas (cf. *livres des vedam* of Pons).

During his service to the Nawab of Audh, Antoine Polier, a Swiss engineer who had had an initial career in the British East India Company, became one of the most successful collector of Indic manuscripts.[468] His

---

returned to Europe in 1788 with a heavy load of manuscripts and other object of curiosity and value.

467 Nos 5346–5356 in the Catalogue of Sanskrit Manuscripts in the British Museum 1902 [Bendall 1902: 1 fn. 1]. According to the assessment of Colas & Richard, the volumes contained '*nombreux brâhmana, textes relatifs à la Rgsamhitâ, au Sâmaveda, à l'Atharvaveda, Vâjasaneyisamhitâ, plusieurs Grhyasûtra et Śrautasutra, Chândogyopanisad...*' [Colas and Richard 1984: 105]. Among those Bendall's catalogue enumerates, of the major Vedic texts, the *Ṛgveda saṃhitā* (Add. 5351) in the shape of a 'European book' of 385 folios dated to 1781 [Bendall 1902: 2], *Aitareya Brāhmaṇa* (Add. 5353), *Aitareya Āraṇyaka* (Add. 5352d), *Āśvalāyana Śrautasūtra* (Add. 5252a) and *Āśvalāyana Gṛhyasūtra* (Add. 5352b), *Atharvavedasaṃhitā* (Add. 5354–5355), *Gopatha Brāhmaṇa* (Add. 5354–5355ab), a set of *Sāmaveda* major texts (Add. 5347a–h): *Sāma-veda Chandas* (or *Purva-)ārcika, saṃhitāpāṭha, Sama-veda Purvārcika, padapāṭha, Tāṇdya-Brāhmaṇa,* three *Brahmanas* of the *Samaveda*: (1) *Devatādhyāya-*, (2) *Vaṃśa-*, (3) *Saṃhitopanishad-Brāhmaṇa.* another set of *Sāmaveda* major texts (Add. 5356a–g): *Sāmaveda Grāma-geya-gāna, Ṣaḍviṃśa Brāhmaṇa, Sāmavidhāna Brāhmaṇa, Ārṣeya Brāhmaṇa, Chandogya Upaniṣad,* etc., *Vājasaneya Saṃhitā* (Add. 5350cd), *Śatapathabrāhmaṇa* (Add. 5348, 5349a–j), *Kātyāyana Śrautasūtra* (Add. 5350). Thus, the *Black Yajurveda* tradition appears almost absent from this 'complete copy' of the Veda, which perhaps reflects the contemporaneous situation in the Pratāpa Singh's territory. We may perhaps say that Polier's 'complete Veda' represents, to some extent, the Vedic tradition prevailing in and around Jaipur in the second part of 18th century. It is interesting to note that the eleven original volumes must have been composed according to a different logic than that of the British Museum catalogue, as can be seen in their numbering.

468 On Polier's early collecting career, see Jasanoff 2005: 82 'Antoine Polier was probably the most vigorous manuscript collector; others included Nathaniel Middleton, ... John Wombwell ... and Richard Johnson,... Johnson collected about as avidly as Polier, and his collection, preserved almost intact today in the British Library, attests to the range—and sheer beauty—of items circulating in the Lucknow art market.' Polier came from a Protestant Swiss family, and his uncle was a collaborator of *the Ecyclopédie.* He was rich enough to entertain a full life of a collector and an early orientalist. According to Jasanoff 2005: 85—'Polier had been studying Hindu texts with the aid of his pandit (teacher) Ram Chand and did eventually commission a book on Hinduism. (Ram Chand was Sikh, not Hindu, but he "had two Brahmins always attached to his suite, whom he consulted on difficult points.") Polier also contributed to Europe's "Oriental Renaissance" by sending the first full copy of the Sanskrit Vedas ... back to Europe.' Polier was on good terms with William Jones and Warren Hastings and was voted a member of the Asiatic Society of Bengal two weeks after its founding in 1784. Apart from being an early Orientalist studying Sanskrit manuscripts, Polier was a successful Mughal nobleman of Lucknow. He led his

Vedic collection luckily ended up with the British Museum—others did not. Soon after his murder in 1795, a new market for Indian manuscripts emerged in London. As Jasanoff notes, 'At Christie's, not a single collection of 'Oriental' manuscripts was sold between the firm's founding in 1766 and 1800. In the first decade of the nineteenth century alone, however, the house sold three major collections of Indian manuscripts.'[469] Striking a melancholy note, Jasanoff concludes:

> After his death his Sanskrit manuscripts would end up staying mostly on the Continent, while his Persian and Arabic manuscripts went to the libraries of Eton and King's College, Cambridge, to be studied by future generations of Indian civil servants. Once divided, and along religious and linguistic lines in particular, the collection that Polier had formed—united by the social environment of Asaf's Lucknow—was forever lost.[470]

As was the case of most of the manuscripts shipped by the French Jesuits to Paris earlier, between 1729 and 1735, Polier's 'complete copy of the Vedas' was also a set of transcripts made to order. That means, they were not inscribed objects that had been for some time in actual circulation or use, but newly produced artefacts commissioned to be made to order.[471] In the case of Polier, the copies were prepared on the orders of Raja Partāp Sengh (Pratap Singh) of Jaipur, and the process of their copying must have taken roughly a year, between 1781 and 1783.[472] The transcripts had been prepared from manuscripts in the possession of Pandit families in the king's entourage, probably by professional scribes who were paid by the 'stanza' under the condition stated by the *Rāja*, that the books should never be bound in any kind of leather but only in silk or velvet.[473] The Brahmins entrusted with the work

easy-going life in Lucknow in Persian style. As Jasanoff [2005: 85] notices: 'His Persian name, given to him by Emperor Shah Alam, was Arsalan-i Jang (Lion of Battle). His *jagir* (revenue-producing land grant) was near Aligarh.' For Polier's life biography, see the introduction to his cousin's Polier 1809.

469 Jasanoff 2005: 138.

470 Jasanoff 2005: 139.

471 The copies were made under an arrangement which looks commercial in nature: the copying was payed '...at a certain rate per every hundred Ashtolc' (probably confused with *anustubh*, or stanza) [Bendall 1902: 1 fn. 1].

472 MS No 5351 in the possession of British Museum is dated to Vikrama Saṃvat 1883 (A.D. 1781). See Bendall 1902: 1.

473 Polier and Polier 1809, I: XIX; Wilson 1819: 470; Bendall 1902: 1 fn. 1; Colas and Richard 1984: 103.

of copying needed several months to complete it, as can be inferred from Polier's own narrative of the event.[474] Being made to order by a European, the copies may not have represented all features to be found in personal handwritten copies of manuscript Vedic texts produced for self-study (*svārtham*), or for the study of others (*parārtham*), or with the intention of a gift (*dāna*).[475] What we know from Polier's letter is that the copy reached him as an unbound and unnumbered bundle (or probably set of bundles) of loose folios. He had them thoroughly scrutinized and ordered in volumes with titles in Persian letters affixed to each volume and section as well as pages numbered by a well-known learned Brahmin, called Raja Ananderam.[476]

IV.2.1. *Les Maîtres de la philologie védique*

In his remarkable essay of 1928, Louis Renou wrote that Vedic philology as such has been made by a few extraordinary personalities (*Quelques hommes remarquables ont fait la philologie védique*[477]). It was them and their passions—notes Renou—rather than methods and tendencies, which had left their stamp on the development of the Vedic studies of the period. For Renou, they were the Masters (*Les Maitres*) of the Vedic philology. And, in 1928, he already believed that, in the times of Burnouf's seminar, it was clear what made a Master in Vedic philology: *sur le domaine du Veda comme ailleurs on reconnaît la marque du maître: largeur de vues dans la conception, rigueur minutieuse dans l'exécution.*[478]

While we may probably still agree with what makes a rigorous study rigorous, it may not be clear what makes a profound and a great concept of philological study. Renou admits that, for his reconstruction attempted by his essay, he used not only the texts proper of Bergaine, Rosen, Roth, Pischel, Max Müller, Oldenberg, and Geldner, but prefaces, prologues and conclusions to their works, where—he believed—they had left the formulations of their academic beliefs.[479] Each and every *maître* had a concept of the Veda which, according to Renou, had to be retrieved and articulated: '*resterait à définir la conception que Roth se faisait du Veda dans la mesure où sa philologie en*

474 Wilson 1819: 470.

475 For a survey of scribal practices concerned with types of motivation for copying the Vedic texts, see Galewicz 2011b.

476 Wilson 1819: 470.

477 Renou 1928: 1.

478 Renou 1928: 2.

479 '*les professions de foi qu'ils ont données dans leur prefaces, ... etc.*' [Renou 1928 : 1]

a subi l'influencer.'[480] For Roth and others this concept had something to do with their understanding of the native philology in the person of Sāyaṇa: '*Ce n'est pas à dire qu'il faille avec Oldenberg rejeter absolument l'autorité de Sāyaṇa*'—says Renou—'*là où il n'est à la merci ni d'une étymologie préconçue ni d'un usage de son temps, il a pu puiser à quelque source authentique.*'[481]

This mixed attitude towards Sāyaṇa as a native philologist, no doubt reflects a basic problem for most of the European masters of Vedic philology, a problem of identifying one's own suppositions and points of reference *vis-à-vis* the question concerning the source of authority. In his essay, Louis Renou appears to conceptualize the history of the knowledge discipline, and he must have been aware in 1928 that he himself had been continuing and 'prolonging'—not re-copying—this current marked by the Masters, but in his own new way. For Renou, there was no case comparable among the *Maitres* to that of the German Rudolf Roth.[482] In India of the period, however, it was rather Max Müller's grand edition of the *Ṛgveda* that went by as the master European editorial accomplishment. Its second edition appeared in 1890–92 thanks to the generosity of a native Indian prince. This, however, did not deter indigenous Indian editing enterprises focused on the *Ṛgveda* which appeared mostly, but not exclusively, in Bombay on a more competitively economic calculation, much different initial impulse and in answer to the needs of differently constituted consumers. Müller himself, who has never ventured to India, also came to be seen there as a distant German professor of (Vedic) Sanskrit, among other German Sanskrit scholars, who, even if actually employed by the British in India (like Kielhorn and Bühler) could at least be imagined as embodying the disinterested ideal of Vedic study—very much resembling the model of scholarship developed long ago among Sanskrit *paṇḍitas*, and formulated in a passage that must have been well-circulated among traditional Vedic scholars:

> *brāhmaṇena niṣkāraṇo dharmaṃ ṣaḍaṅgo vedo 'dhyeyo jñeyaś ceti tadvidhiḥ* |
> 'A Brahmin should study and understand the Veda along with its six aṅgas as his disinterested duty.'[483]

---

480 Renou 1928: 5.

481 Renou 1928: 2.

482 '*...il fallait se borner à ne savoir du Veda que ce qu'en savait Sayaṇa ou il fallait qu'un homme de génie vînt renouveler ces études : ce fut l'oeuvre de Roth*' [Renou 1928: 5].

483 *brâhmana niṣkāraṇo dharmaṃ ṣaḍaṅgo vedo 'dhyeyo jñeyaś ceti tadvidhiḥ*—Sāyaṇa in his introduction to *Ṛksaṃhitā* [RSBh (M) I: 15, 32–33] quoting the Yājñavalkyasmṛti. Cf. Galewicz 2010a: 237.

IV.3. The imperial Veda

After initial negligence the quest for the lost Veda soon came within the fold of a broader, education and information policy of the British empire in India even before the Crown officially took over the power from the Company in 1858. A number of institutions and individuals in the three Presidencies proved to join the quest in their own specific ways and not without the air of competition. After all, the Veda, long considered to be the 'knowledge par excellence' could not but become a prime object of imperial claims for possession, ordering and control.

> British knowledge of Indians was not a self-sealed system. It arose as much from natural inquisitiveness and the desire to comprehend the world as it was, as from a simple aim of domination... [T]hat knowledge was as much an embarrassment as an advantage to its British rulers. For Indians were increasingly producing their own knowledge from reworked fragments of their own tradition melded with western ideas and conveyed through western artefacts.[484]

IV.3.1. The 'Report on the Vedas'

The tidings of the East India Company's governments and institutions' policy in promoting Sanskrit literature through editing and publishing its original texts in print proved to be rather unlucky for the Veda in the early periods of print revolution. At first, there was the failed attempt of the Indian Gujarati enthusiast Bhimjee Parekh who attempted in 1674–75 to convince the English authorities to technically support his financial readiness to put the 'Brahmanee writings' to print in Surat and Bombay.[485] Later on the policy makers of the three presidencies must have been influenced by the widely commented 1805 pioneering study on the Vedas by H.T. Colebrooke, who expressed his scepticism for the immediate projects furthering the study of the Veda. Furthermore, due to internal tensions in decision making in drawing plans for subsidized publishing projects for Sanskrit literature in the first decades of the nineteenth century, the

[484] Bayly 1996: 371–372.

[485] His name appears in the sources also as Bhimjee Parekh or Bhimgee Parakh. For the circumstances of this eventually discontinued roject, see Priolkar 1958: 30–33.

Veda remained outside the scope of interest of such institutions as Fort William College, whose committee adopted a publishing project for Sanskrit literature, which resulted in sixteen Sanskrit works printed at the Bābu Sanskrit Printing Press during 1807–15. Also the joint project of Fort William College and Serampore Mission Press opted for bringing into print rather more popular religious Sanskrit works, such as the *Rāmāyaṇa*, which partly appeared through Serampore press between 1806 and 1810, till it was discontinued because of the suspended financial support on the part of the College. While Europe saw its first attempt at the philological editing of the *Ṛgvedasaṃhitā*, in the shape of the unaccented text and Latin translation of several hymns published as *Rig-vedae Specimen*, by Friedrich Rosen in London in 1830, the American Mission Press of Bombay published in 1833 a lithographed edition of a substantial part of the first book of the *Ṛgvedasaṃhitā*, prepared by the Rev. John Stevenson. Stevenson was a Scottish missionary working independently in Maharashtra on an integral edition of the *Ṛgveda*. His edition contained the initial part of the *Ṛksaṃhitā* in unaccented Devanagari,[486] matched with a gloss in Sanskrit, a Marathi rendering and an English translation. With news and roumors of more Vedic projects by others, it was high time that the Company showed its agency and gave its voice in the race for the recovering and opening the Veda to the public. It was the Asiatic Society of Bengal, that eventually adopted, through a decision of the Secretaries of its Committee of Papers in 1847, a programme for publishing the Veda on accepting the so-called 'Report on the Vedas' prepared by Eduard Röer.[487] Röer was successively elected to the post of the editor of the new series.[488] His 'Report

[486] For an unspecified reason, the opening verse that precedes and introduces the text of the *Ṛksaṃhitā* after the title line features the famous Sāvitrī stanza along with proper Vedic accents marked on it. See STEVENSON 1833: 2.

[487] The circumstances of the official and government-stimulated adoption of the 'Vedic project' by the Asiatic Society in 1847 have been communicated in the Society's 'Proceedings' printed in the *Journal of Asiatic Society* 16 (5)1847: 496 and 505–518 under the title of 'Report on the Vedas'.

[488] 'Proceeding of the Asiatic Society of Bengal for the year 1947' in *Journal of Asiatic Society* 16 (5)1847: 496. The communication of the adoption of the project upon the Report on the Vedas compiled by Röer includes an interesting and telling formulation designed to secure the Society Committee's control over the outcome of the printing project, that is over the form of the 'printed Veda': 'The Committee propose that the report be adopted—the publication of the Vedas forthwith commenced, on the responsibility of the Oriental Section—that Dr. Röer be appointed Editor, subject to the condition of his submitting proofs of the work, both text and commentary, to the Oriental Section, without whose "imprimatur" no portion should be finally sent to press' (Ibid.: 496).

on the Vedas' was published in the *Journal of the Asiatic Society* in the same year of 1847 along with a string of successive documents illustrating the growing process leading to the concluding decision. As we can read in the introductory section, the project became feasible thanks to a grant by the Directors of the Company: 'The expense of the undertaking is to be defrayed from the grant of 500 Rs. per mensem, allowed to the Society by the Hon'ble Court of Directors, for the promotion of Oriental literature.'[489] The report shows that the initial decision had been taken by the Court of Directors a year earlier, in 1846, and communicated to the Bengal Government in due official letter form. In response to this decision, taken in London, the acting authorities of the Asiatic Society issued a document stating the initial frame for the project of editing the Vedas in print:

> In deference to the expressed wishes of the Honourable the Court of Directors, reiterated in Mr. Secretary Bushby's letter, dated the 21st November, 1846, the Asiatic Society are desirous of taking immediate measures for the publication of the Vedas, with a commentary, the expense to the defrayed from the grant from Government of 500 Rs. per mensem for 'Oriental Publications.[490]

In his report, E. Röer indicates two 'essential difficulties' that awaited the project: the securing of the complete collection of the Vedic texts and the understanding of their language. With reference to the latter, he drew a survey of the ongoing work on the editing and understanding of the language of the Vedas, indicating the pioneering work of Rosen on the *Ṛgveda* and Stevenson on the *Sāmaveda* (failing, however, to acknowledge the earlier edition by the same of the *Ṛgveda*).[491] For some reason, he did not mention either the work that had already commenced by F. Max Müller, nor that of H.H. Wilson, neither of whom had yet been published but must have been well underway. Neither did he mention the indigenous *pothī*-shaped Indian edition of *Śukla Yajurveda Vājasaneyī Saṃhitā* by

489 Röer 1847: 505.

490 Röer 1847: 506.

491 Röer either did not have complete knowledge or opted for not fully acknowledging Rev. Stevenson's pioneering work. His report contains among else a letter of 1847 to the Committee by Radhakant who admits to be informed in another letter by H.H. Wilson writing from London that '... the first book of the Sanhita of the Rig Veda has already been published with an English translation, by a gentleman at Bombay. The same letter names Stevenson in the context of his translation of *Sāmaveda* but fails to connect the same to the early Bombay edition of the *Ṛgvedasaṃhitā* [Röer 1847: 515].

Sāmaśrami Satyavrata, printed in Calcutta in 1844 at Satya Press. As for the second 'essential difficulty', he acknowledged the lack of complete texts available in Calcutta and proposed either locating and acquiring copies in Benares and Deccan or applying for the 'complete' copy, believed to have been deposited in London by Col. Polier. The last remark seems highly suggestive of the specific nature of the project and its historical context: even by the mid-nineteenth century the Veda was still seen as a text to be recovered and, paradoxically, it was the centre of the empire, rather than its Indian periphery, where India's proud heritage of the Veda in the form of its 'complete copy' was believed to be actually and tangibly located.[492] It is interesting to note, that the Report does not indicate other copies of various Vedic texts already present in other locations in Europe, such as Berlin or Paris, and that it highlights the possibility of understanding the Vedic language without the assistance of the local native scholars.[493] Testifying to the ongoing spirit of competition animating pioneering projects of putting Veda in print, the Report includes a letter whose author reveals news received by him from London that '... the emperor of Russia had agreed to pay the expense of printing a complete edition of the Rig Veda with the commentary of Sayana Acharya...'[494] At the same time, however, Röer still voices the long cherished idea among the early Orientalists, namely, that any attempt to tackle with the Veda should somehow take into consideration and secure the assistance of the 'native' paṇḍita-scholars, and that the true *paṇḍitas* are to be found exclusively in Benares. Accordingly, he advises the Committee, without indicating any *paṇḍita* by name, to secure such assistance and make the Benares traditional scholars part of the project.[495] The 'Report on the Vedas', as it was published in 1847, comprised of yet a few important studies documenting a research that had been done before the project was announced. One of them was a survey of Vedic manuscripts prepared by Muir. The survey assessed relative chances of securing a 'complete' copy of any of the Veda to be published within

---

492 Röer 1847: 509.

493 This specific underscore should probably be understood against the long established belief in the hermeneutic nature of the Vedic language (and knowledge) as well as the exclusive access to it by the traditional Brahmin scholars that the Committee apparently took ambition to counter in its conviction that a team of British imperial scholars (both European and new Indian intellectuals) trained and armed with modern philological tools were alone ready to bring the Veda within the frame of the imperial control.

494 Röer 1847: 515.

495 Röer 1847: 508.

the project and it shows how limited the knowledge on the actual access to the written copies of Vedic texts was among the scholars of the Asiatic Society of Bengal in mid-1800s.[496]

The implemented project brought its first fruits in the form of *The First Two Lectures of the Sanhita of the Rig Veda with the Commentary of the Madhvacharya and an English Translation of the Text*, published in Calcutta by the Asiatic Society of Bengal and printed by J. Thomas at the Baptist Mission Press. Hower, further works on the *Ṛgveda* came to be suspended in the face of the publication of the first volume of the set of five volumes of the *Ṛgvedasamhitā*, patronized directly by the Court of Directors of the Company and edited by F. Max Müller in London in 1849. The project initiated by Röer continued well into the second part of the nineteenth century, with several volumes of other Vedic texts, edited by eminent scholars and making up an essential part of the important series named *Biblioteca Indica*. All of them represented the empire's claim to control over both the 'properly edited' intellectual heritage of India as well as on the philological instruments believed necessary to appropriately represent this heritage. All volumes featured, until the dissolution of the Company in 1857, a title page indicating the double support of the 'Honorary Court of Directors of the East India Company and the Superintendence of the Asiatic Society of Bengal,' and only the second part of the same, in volumes published after the 1858. One of the first volumes to appear in the new series was *Taittirīya Āraṇyaka of the Black Yajurveda*, edited by Rajendra Lal and printed in the Baptist Mission Press in 1859. With the new series of the *Biblioteca Indica*, the editors and printers slowly changed, with new Indian scholars and indigenous printing enterprises gradually having a stronger involvement in the project (among others the Ganeśa Press of Calcutta).

IV.3.2. Max Müller and his patrons[497]

It may seem that as a type of a perfect cabinet scholar, who had never put his foot on Indian soil, F. Max Müller does not fit into the picture focused mainly on Indian indigenous and colonial printed editions of the Veda. But since his *opus magnum* became entangled in the dense web of argument

[496] See, J. Muir, 'Statement of the Portions of the Vedas and their Commentaries which exist at Benares communicated by J. Muir, 1846' [Röer 1847: 518].

[497] A part of this section appeared before in an earlier version in Galewicz 2016.

and communication with indigenous publishers and editors over the concept of representing the Veda in print, it very much belongs to both the colonial and the colonized worlds. Bayly's concept of the 'dual economy of knowledge'[498] lends itself perfectly to the task of making sense of the two different cultures of representation, as concerns the history of preparing printed editions of Vedic texts in colonial India.

Just like other printed genres, all editions of the Vedic texts carried, along with their typographic concepts and sometimes also explicit introductions by the editors, also their own ideas of what the Veda is or should be. The better known European, and sometimes indeed imperial, editions of the Veda were not exception to this rule, as they soon became famous and almost iconic in their genre. The two Müller's editions of the *Ṛgvedasamhitā* (RS), with Sāyaṇa's commentary, prove rather instructive in that matter. The first volume of his *editio princeps* appeared in 1849 and the first volume of the 2nd edition of the same saw the light of the day in 1890. The roughly forty years that passed in between mark, not only the profound change in historical circumstances that took place over that time, but also Müller's concept of how to (re)present the object of his *opus magnum* to his prospective readers as well as to his patrons. An important change of the concept behind the enterprise of Müller can be seen in the altered subtitle of the second edition of his RS.[499] It seems that what Müller wanted his patrons and/or readers to keep in mind, while attempting to use his RS, changed over time and along with altered socio-political situation. What Müller might himself have thought the *Ṛgveda* to have been was an altogether different question and his answers also changed over time.[500]

As a gargantuan project, the first edition, referred to later as 'editio princeps', was a project that editorially spanned over a quarter of a century, appearing in six bulky volumes in quarto between 1849 and 1874. The

---

498 'What emerged was a dual economy of knowledge: an "advanced" sector, which used western forms of representation and communication subsisting within an attenuated but still massive hinterland employing older styles of information and debate' [Bayly 1996: 372].

499 See Müller 1890 II: title page.

500 As late as 1899, he still appears to be perplexed by the seemingly simple question of what the *Ṛgveda* actually was. One of the answers given was functional: 'The hymns of the Rig-Veda were meant to be recited at sacrifices, and this is no doubt the explanation of their careful preservation during many centuries, by means of a strictly regulated oral tradition' [Müller 1899: 168]. Apparently, he was not fully aware that only some hymns of the *Ṛgveda* had been actually 'recited at sacrifices', at least in the *śrauta* Vedic sacrificial system that came down to us.

appearances of the title pages of successive volumes mirror the history of the empire, which is visible in the outlay, having changed between volume 3 (1856) and volume 4 (1862).[501] In place of 'The Honourable the East India Company', which practically ceased to hold power over India after 1858 (though it was only completely dissolved in 1874, the year of the last volume of Müller's first edition came out) in volumes one to three, now in volumes four through six there was 'Her Majesty's Secretary of State for India in Council'. The second edition brought one more important change. Its title page now featured also a name of an altogether different patron: a somewhat puzzling 'The Maharajah of Vijayanagara.'[502] The enigmatic ruler of the then only legendary empire of Vijayanagara should probably have been identified with the name featuring on the dedication page of the same edition and qualified with 'faithful subject and obedient servant' to Queen Victoria. The name reads 'Pasupati Ananda Gajapati Raj', who should be identified as Pushapati Ananda Gajapati Raju, the Maharajah of Vizhianagaram, an enlightened ruler of a small but ambitious principality in coastal Andhra, who, by his liberal gesture, had saved the endangered second edition of Müller.[503] Besides, the font and diacritics had also changed with the new publisher, and Müller himself apparently did not need to indicate his academic status by his name any more. Furthermore, typographically, the dedication page had changed a lot; in place of a number of names of the Company's acting directors, we can see the name of Queen Victoria, the Empress of India, inscribed in a huge and truly imperial gothic font.

A probably most telling difference can be seen in the formula of dedication, indicating an altered concept of the object of dedication itself. While

---

501 See title pages of Müller 1856 and 1862. The major change reflects the taking over of rule in India by the British Crown and the resulting disappearance of the respectable East India Company from the title page of volume 4 [Müller 1862: title page].

502 See Müller 1890: title page.

503 It was sometime later, in 1899, when Müller fully acknowledged the generosity of Paśupati Gajapati Raju: 'The Maharajah paid to the Press not less than £4,000. I found out afterwards that this Indian nobleman was by no means a student, an antiquarian, or a theologian; but, on the contrary, a man of the world, very fond of racing and hunting. ... When in one of my last letters I asked him what had induced him to spend so large a sum on the Rig-Veda, he replied that India wanted its Bible, and he added, "It may benefit me hereafter." ... I ought to add that his liberality did not stop at paying the expenses of the work, but that he placed a large number of copies at my disposal, which was more than I expected or deserved. Are there many Maharajahs or Zemindars in Europe who would have spent so large a sum on a new edition of the Bible...?' [Müller 1899: 159–160].

the first edition features Max Müller, dedicating the *Ṛgvedasaṃhitā*, as 'This Original Record of the Early Institutions of the Natives of India', the second one actually shows two people—Müller as the editor and Pashupati Raju as a liberal native royal patron—both dedicating apparently the same thing (i.e. the *Ṛgveda*), but now as, 'The Earliest Record of the Religious Institutions of the Natives of India'. This change reflected, perhaps, the concept of the imperial overlordship of Queen Victoria, the Empress of India, to whom Müller chose or felt obliged to dedicate his second edition. Thus, the second edition apparently sought to draw from a double imperial heritage—that of Vijayanagara and that of the British Empire—and the general typography of the title and dedication pages lends itself perfectly to rich speculation on the relationship between empire, knowledge and the power of print. Both editions include also a Sanskrit title page. This too betrays the altered shape and careful hand of the editor. For some reason, the wording of Müller's Sanskrit name had been re-conceptualised (or linguistically corrected)—instead of *Bhaṭṭamokṣamūlara* in the first edition, the second reads *Mokṣamūlarabhaṭṭa*. Likewise, the Sanskrit version of the place of publishing changed from *Ukṣataraṇa*, as a Sanskrit name for Oxford in the first edition, to that of *Gotīrtha* in the second edition.

All in all, the typography of the altered second edition title pages seems to betray much more tension behind the publishing of this voluminous work that, in the changed historical circumstances, had to face competition of both print capitalism and rival ideologies of publishing. The tension reflected the double image of British rule: the colonial power bent over the necessities of effective administration, that included mastering the knowledge of the ruled and a defender of the idea of open and free access to modern media inventions like that of print.[504] In one of his lectures delivered in Edinburgh and published in 1892, Müller makes a confession concerning the circumstances of the beginning of his life's work on the critical edition of the *Ṛgvedasaṃhitā* suggesting it was a kind of historical necessity:

> ...Professor Wilson, in the name of the East India Company, had sent invitations to the most learned Pandits in India, asking them whether they would undertake

[504] A juxtaposition of the two editions perhaps exemplifies, in a sense limited to the intellectual history of India, the words of H. Innis, that 'the effects of printing on nationalism have been conspicuous in common-law countries. "Success of a representative system of government has been materially influenced by the invention of printing", but its limitations have again been largely a result of printing' [Innis 1986: 167].

> an edition of the Rig-veda in India... [T]he Pandits of India [sic!] declined ... for the simple reason that the study of Vedic literature had ... been entirely neglected in India...[505]

The statement seems to express one of the basic tenets of the 19th century philology, tinted with a spirit of a still very much post-Romantic positivism. If not for the preserved correspondence with an Indian editor (see below), it might seem that Müller remained either unaware or unwilling to accept that, in his time, the power of print appealed to some Indian publishers and pandit editors as well. Thus sounds another of his preserved statements (*Lectures on the Origin of Religions* 1878), in which he mentions 'a printed text' of the *Ṛgvedasamhitā*, that Indians eventually possessed in addition to their memory-based transmission, apparently meaning his own first edition and neglecting other—most conspicuously in this context—Indian versions that had started to appear before his second edition was ready for print.[506]

IV.4. The printed Veda for *paṇḍitas* and pundits

The Veda slowly entered the world of print as a textual corpus of limited access and elite character. Patronage rather than print-capitalism was apparently still necessary for any of the Vedic text to be published in print. The early Orientalists among the East India Company administration did not necessarily favour the Veda as the primary object of their interests. The often-utilitarian drive behind the Company's institutions' interest in native knowledge left the Veda on the margins of early publishing projects backed by the Company government institutions. Even H. Colebrooke concluded his now legendary essay on the Vedas with a remark putting in doubt any reward accruing to a further study of the Veda.[507] A somewhat controversial wording of C. Bayly addresses some of the patronage on the part of the British government over Sanskrit scholarship as 'parasitical'.[508]

505 Müller 1892: 20.

506 'These men ... know the whole Rig-Veda by heart, just as their ancestors did, three or four thousand years ago; and though they have MSS., and though they now have a printed text [he probably refers to his own?], they do not learn their sacred lore from them' [Müller 1878: 156].

507 See Colebrooke 1805b; Rocher and Rocher 2012.

508 Bayly 1996: 294.

One instance of such patronage would be the founding of the Banaras Sanskrit College by Jonathan Duncan in 1782. This otherwise remarkable institution had been patronized with a view to supplying native Sanskrit expertise for colonial legal practice. According to Bayly, 'the pandits were highly suspicious of the College, and averse to allowing polluted barbarians "a view of the Shastra", itself a sacred act.'[509] There was also another problem of categories. European scholars wanted to recover the historical genealogy of Sanskrit and the principles of transformative grammar. The pandits, by contrast, 'wished to record all possible variations of grammar in context: to print out, as it were, a full text of the sacred sounds. To Europeans this seemed mere obscurantism.'[510] The ideologies beḥind the new Indian intellectuals' increasing insistence on securing the imperial government patronage for the revival of Sanskrit and those behind the interest for the same on the part of the changing British officials used to differ much. In the words of the same C. Bayly the two could be contrasted in the following way:

> Even in the early nineteenth century, Sanskrit was still regarded by many elite Britons and Indians as the lingua franca of the Hindu intelligentsia ... Like Latin in Europe, it would provide a vehicle for the diffusion of new ideas through native literary societies... Sanskrit was still used as a written language by pandits and teachers who ... [T]he first generation of cultural nationalists argued that Government should actively patronize Sanskrit, as even the Muslim rulers, 'though tyrants,' had done. ... British motives in investigating the Sanskrit canon were mixed. Greed for valuable documents was one incentive.[511]

Also the new pundits who adopted themselves effectively to the new urban job market and information order tended to see the ideology of patronizing Sanskrit culture (and their own role within the frame) in a transformed way differing much from what could be indicated with reference to more traditional *paṇḍitas*, especially those claiming the exclusive link to the Veda and its textual heritage. Both groups had to confront and reshape their attitudes towards the modernity and new language and discourse hierarchy formed by the emerging empire with

509 Bayly 1996: 294.

510 Bayly 1996: 294.

511 Bayly 1996: 293.

its 'useful knowledge' on the one hand and 'pure' and disengaged knowledge of the new university type offered by philology and its cognate ever more specialized discilines.[512]

IV.5. The Veda printed by Indians in India

With this whole book the total Rigveda is reappearing.
V. Ghaisasa, preface to the *Ṛgveda Daśagrantha*

In the second half of the 19th century, print must have retained its association with the colonial form of knowledge and its sinuous relationship to power, while, at the same time, inevitably becoming more and more tempting, by its new potential, to those who remained concerned with indigenous knowledge systems (*śāstras*). Newly set up universities and colleges partly absorbed those systems, in an attempt to reconstitute the colonizer's hold on the knowledge of the colonized.[513] The ideologies and preconceptions directly or indirectly voiced in early printed editions of the Veda seem to have been coupled with particular strategies *vis-à-vis* the rival enterprises or totally silent about them. Thus, in his own editions, Müller does not mention indigenous enterprises and vice versa, and it happens that even much more modern Indian editions keep their silence with regard to predecessors whose works they could or perhaps should have taken into account.

While any general picture of the early Indian attempts at printing Vedic texts would be difficult to reconstruct, we may safely presume that some of such attempts must have stemmed from the air of progressivism usually associated with print and its public appeal. On the other hand we should probably not dismiss the the new nostalgia for retrieving the supposedly glorious Vedic past for the newly forming public space of the cities. Such a tone can be seen even in the sources to the earliest known and eventually failed attempt to publish in print the treasures of Brahmanical learning by Bhimjee Parekh of Surat of 1674–5. Other attempts must also have been

---

512 For a comporative view of the emerging worlds of new Indian pandits and new European, especially German, philologists of the 19th century, see McNeely and Wolverton 2008: 188–191.

513 See Cohn 1996: 16.

connected to the regional and local reconfigurations of power and authority opening to the potentials of print publishing the textual realms realms that used to remain under exclusive hold—as the Veda did—of different regional groups claiming brahmanical status. While complementing, and for some time competing with, the manuscript culture(s) of the subcontinent, the new print publishing enterprises must have answered to the needs as well as stimulated and supported new developments in the regionally specific political, educational or religious transformations. Due to the discontinuos and uneven reconfiguration of the new social order, triggered by the huge political changes in the second half of the 17th through eighteenth centuries—such as the rising and decline of Maratha empire and the early phase of territorial expansion of the British competing with the Portuguese and the French—such early attempts can only be made sense of against these specific regional backgrounds.

A case apart and one that precedes anything that we know to have affected indigenous Indian attempts to publish the Veda in print from around mid-19th century is the above mentioned project embarked upon by Bhimjee Parekh, 'an enterprising Kapol Bania of Gujerat',[514] who resolved to set up a printing press as early as around 1670 and made initial attempts at printing towards 1674.[515] Incidentally, 1674 was the year that saw the coronation ceremony of Śivaji Bhonsle and a new turn in the rising power of confederate Marathas, who soon developed a transregional imperial structure of political power with a rapidly growing transregional network of vivid communication with a new type of *élan vital*, which may appear today to have been ready for adapting to the new medium of print.[516] But it did not, even if to some region-bound historians it could have done or almost did. According to some of the latter, Bhimjee acquired his printing press from none other than Śivaji himself and needed only knowledge in the person of an experienced typesetter to operate it.[517] The idea is said to have crystalized already around 1670. Due letters were exchanged across the ocean between Surat and London. It took roughly six months' time to reach the addressee in London, and another six for an answer to come,

---

[514] K.M. Munshi in *Proceedings of the fifth All India Library Conference held in Bombay, Bombay 1942*, quoted in Priolkar 1958: 29.

[515] Priolkar 1958: 30; *English Records on Shivaji* 1931: 187; Ogborn 2007: 199.

[516] For the development of the transregional information network in Maratha empire, see O'Hanlon 2010; Glushkova 2016.

[517] *English Records on Shivaji* 1931: 187, also quoted in Priolkar 1958: 30.

together with the time to process the request in the Metropole. All that amounted to over four years, and an answer dated 1674 AD must have arrived in Surat towards 1675. London found the idea promising, albeit, for a rather different reason than the original one and set other goals to reach. The initial idea of Bhimjee was 'to have some of the Ancient Brahminy Writings in Print...', which makes an exceptional case for a printer being interested in publishing Sanskrit cultural heritage, probably including the Vedas. And the Surat agent recommending Bhim's request to London added that: 'it's not improbable that this curiosity of his may tend to a common good, and by the industry of some searching spirits produce discovery out of those or other ancient manuscript of these parties which may be useful or at least grateful to posterity... '[518] In one of the letters sent in answer from London in 1675, the aim of the future press to be set up by Bhimjee (with his own expenses) was, however, outlined along a rather different lines: 'We should gladly heare that Bingees design about the printing do take effect, that it may be a means to propogate our religion whereby soules may be gayned as well as Estates.'[519]

The printing press actually arrived in Bombay Island between 1674 and 1675. But neither the printer sent with it nor another one dispatched by East India Company could cope with Bhimji's idea of casting types of 'Banian characters.'[520] It seems that sending an experienced founder in answer to Bhimjee request of 1676, promised in a letter from the Company Directors of 1677, never materialized.[521] There is indirect evidence suggesting that an English press could have been in operation in Bombay sometime between 1678 and 1723, but this probably catered exclusively to the immediate administrative needs of the Company offices.[522] Thus, Bhimjee's vision had to wait for almost another two hundred years and more favourable circumstances in which, however, printing 'Ancient Braminy writings' came to be animated by a different set of preconceptions and expectations. It took place in the period that some scholars tended to label as being marked by an 'information revolution' and drew on an already rich experience with print in climatic and social conditions of subcontinental India, including

518 *English Records on Shivaji* 1931: 327, quoted in Priolkar 1958: 30.

519 Quoted in Priolkar 1958: 31.

520 Priolkar 1958: 31.

521 Priolkar 1958: 32.

522 Part of it includes correspondence showing that the printer sent for Bhimjee was eventually dispatched for the island of Bombay. See Priolkar 1958: 33.

missionary and government printing establishments, as well as the Company's changed policy with regard to print as an important medium in producing and archiving information while building the empire. These experiences proved to have stimulated effects that capitalized on, spilled over, transcended, and many times contradicted the intentions of the policy makers.[523] The overall nature of this process was described by C.A. Bayly:

> Drawing on earlier traditions of learning, debate and the presentation of knowledge, however, Indians soon reacted to this information revolution in ways which instantly subverted its originators' intentions. Their strength was that, increasingly, they could operate in both of the overlapping domains of the colonial information order.[524]

According to the same author, the new information order created an environment in which the medium of print was used with different intentions, seeking to mobilize new social powers, and also to different effects by various actors on the scene. The indigenous printer-publishers found themselves often on both sides, while effectively harnessing the potencies of previous information channels and social expectations with the new technologies and possibilities of appeal. 'They could engage the colonial authorities and the expatriates in their own arenas of publicity through their own media. At the same time they could draw on the huge resources of affective and patrimonial knowledge within their own societies.'[525]

As the colophons to a number of extant manuscript of Vedic texts suggest, the hand-written (*hastalikhita*) copies, most often prepared in a rather limited number, often used to be addressed to specific users, sometimes indicated by family relations (sons, grandsons, brothers, nephews) or even proper names.[526] All the same, we probably cannot say that a process of circulation, if initiated by such copies at all, amounted to publishing in any sense of the word, since such copies were neither addressed to a wider public nor were they meant to circulate freely or be prescribed to be read

[523] Cf. a generalized formulation on this matter offered by Harold Innis in Innis 1986: 167 (quoted above fn. 297).
[524] Bayly 1996: 373.
[525] Bayly 1996: 373.
[526] For a brief survey of reasons for preparing handwritten copies of the Vedic texts, see Galewicz 2011b.

or recited publicly;[527] the more so, that a good number of them appear to have been prepared for reasons other than reading. They used to be produced with probably an altogether different intention than that of being publicly available on either commercial, political, religious or any other grounds. On the other hand, it seems that printing, i.e. *mudrita* copying, which must have included editing and producing a number of similar looking copies, would a bold gesture of opening the Veda to a wider circle of users, if not some kind of public (what sort of public space for readership could be imagined for the 19th India in general, or for any of its regions in particular, is another question). The latter must have been imagined by the editors in a way related to the specific status of the Veda, the limited accessibility of its language, and a claim for exclusivity of access on the part of its customary custodians.[528] Some of the early printing ventures by Indian publishers focused on (editions of) the Veda would indicate their intended users to be either students in new education systems or traditional or *paṇḍitas*.[529]

After a long period of a rather unsuccessful competing with regional manuscript cultures, print slowly gained momentum in India, first as a response to the 'media revolution' triggered largely by the activities of the Baptist Mission Press in Serampore, and later in relation to the reconstitution of the colonial power by means of a new hold on education and knowledge control. The process of spreading new print culture long remained rather fragmentary and limited, varying in degree in different parts of the subcontinent. Bengal took the early lead, with the exceptionally busy Baptist Missionary Press, started by the visionary William Carey, towards 1800, in Serampore. It soon came to constitute a precedent to be followed by later regional publishing enterprises. By 1857, the year of the great Mutiny, Calcutta emerged as the most active centre for the sprawling medium of print. During that year, as many as forty-six presses worked in

527 Cf. remarks by Kielhorn on the Sanskrit part of the *Catalogue of Native Publications* 1867: 'There never has been, at least for the two thousand years, an Indian public' [Kielhorn 1867: 13].

528 Introductory chapters to early Indian printed editions contain interesting hints at how their editors constructed their intended readers and users.

529 The striking difference in the form and layout between editions intended for the two groups can be seen in such instances as Bombay *Vedārthayatna* of 1876 and Peterson's edition of Ṛgvedic hymns on one hand and Calcutta 1847 edition of *Yajurveda* or Bombay Gurjara and Nirnaya Sagara editions of *Ṛksaṃhitā* and minor Vedic texts of 1900 on the other.

Calcutta and 'the publishing industry was booming', with 322 new titles having appeared that very year just in Bengali.[530] On the opposite coast, in Bombay, things appeared to be a bit less spectacular in terms of numbers and pace of growth but several Indian printing houses had emerged towards the middle of the 19th century, after the precedence of the printing press set up by American Baptist Mission there in 1816.[531]

The process intensified, especially with a new demand on textbooks after a new education policy adopted by the British government in 1857.[532] Due to the newly realized need of the now British colonial state to reorganize and redefine itself in face of the new circumstances, the Indian Civil Service initiated monitoring the quickly developing native publishing industry. One of the results of this policy that—luckily for book historians—survived are annual catalogues of native publications for each of the presidencies as well as reports offering lists, titles, classifications, and description in principle of every new title to appear.[533] The authors of the catalogues happenned, from time to time, to be well known Indologists, since it took practical language skills to effectively publish more and more numerous titles appearing from native publishers. A quick look into the first two catalogues for the Bombay Presidency, covering the period up to 1867, shows a rapidly growing number not only of Marathi, but also of Sanskrit titles. But among the latter, no Vedic text can be seen.

While numerous religious, *śāstric* and other works in Sanskrit co-exist with vernacular works in the making of the new public print culture, the Veda remain outside of its fold. Both the first and the second catalogue feature no Vedic text proper known to be printed within the Bombay Presidency up to 1867. In the opinion of Kielhorn, who accounts for the disappointing fact that... 'there are no Vedic works at all contained in this catalogue',[534] since there was no 'native printer' that would venture to publish a serious Sanskrit work in the situation where there was hardly any reading public to address, a situation in which there was no prospective groups of readers—even among the native scholars—who, in

---

530 See Darnton 2002: 242 which quotes an estimation from a report by James Long (Long 1855).

531 For a different dating of this press foundation, see *Memorial Papers* 1882.

532 Priolkar 1958.

533 For a general review of these catalogues and their ideology, see Darnton 2002. The cataloguing project had it spredecessor in Bengal in the ingenuous works by rev. James Long (Long 1855).

534 Kielhorn 1867: 15.

his view, preferred more traditional way of studying, which would have made any enterprise at printing such a book a rather considerable loss to the publisher.[535]

This situation must have changed with the later half of the century, when Indian editions of Vedic texts eventually begin slowly to appear. Till that time, the Veda remained as intellectual property held within a very limited number of hands. It was being transmitted in two, most probably strongly interconnected, streams of memory reproduction systems, on one hand, and regional manuscript cultures, on the other—both in their respective regional inflections. In the prevailing orthodox ideology of transmission, the Veda required shelter and protection from corruption and improper use by the ignorant. The allegory of the *vedavṛkṣa* or the 'Tree of the Veda' features—in contrast with the allegory of the printing press mentioned above—the living organism of a tree standing upright and bearing leaves of *dharma* practices thanks to its roots represented as human beings who embody the textualized traditions of the four Vedas. It seems that such popular representations went with the time-honoured belief in the crippling mistakes awaiting those who opted for studying the Veda through reading or a grave sin threatening those who ventured to live by proliferation of the Veda through writing it down. They would hardly allow any room for publishing the Veda in print or circulating written copies in place of such transmission.[536] The printing and publishing of the Veda in early modern India must have been for the reasons indicated above a gesture of considerable courage on the one hand and an act of imagination with respect to the prospective users of its copies with rather weak chances for commercial success on the other. This accounts probably for the fact that the earliest printing initiatives known from Indian subcontinent did not include Vedic texts.[537] We can imagine that this courage must have needed an ideology for the new medium to absorb the Veda and the backing of an institutional authority. It must have required a new conceptual

[535] KIELHORN 1867: 14.

[536] On orthodox beliefs guarding the Veda against writing, see MÜLLER 1891. See also GALEWICZ 2011b.

[537] This fact may sound natural and logical in the light of theories like McLuhan's for whom the new medium of print emerged along with and for the medium of vernacular languages. See MCLUHAN 1995 (1964): 7. On the same level another 'old' idea of McLuhan seems still to promise some interpretive potential for the historians of book and media studies: '...the "message" of medium or technology is the change of scale or pace or pattern that it introduces into human affairs' [MCLUHAN 1995 (1964): 8].

justification in relation to the exigencies of the culture of memory and personal written copies produced often in order to be handed over in an act of humble donation rather than a commercial venture.

IV.5.1. The polluting ink

The complex of beliefs and attitudes of suspicion that put in an uneasy relationship the Veda and the writing, no doubt influenced the early attempts to circulate printed copies of the Veda and shaped the expectations of their prospective users. Thisprobably accounts for the fact that the earliest printing initiatives known from the Indian subcontinent did not include Vedic texts. We can imagine that such courage must have needed an ideology for the new medium to absorb the Veda and a backing from an institutional authority. This, in turn, must have required a new conceptual justification in relation to the exigencies of the culture of memory and personal written copies often produced in order to be handed over in an act of humble donation rather than a commercial offer.

We must remember that a relatively strong opposition towards print, even from the circles of new 'intelligentsia',[538] otherwise open to technical novelties from Europe, made itself felt in big cities across the subcontinent, on the basis of a suspicion that the ink used in the process of printing allegedly contained animal fat–a substance considered highly impure. Like other objects in daily use of orthodox Hindu families, written copies of Vedic texts were also subject to scrutiny concerning the identity of the scribe, as well as the provenience of paper and ink, which was rather difficult in the case of print, coming from a distant and unknown printing workshop, that is, from a highly insecure source. Objectionable ingredients were feared to defile both the text and the reader by physical contact. Evidence to this effect, gathered by Priolkar, tended to picture even the modernizing part of the regional learned *paṇḍitas* to prefer hand written texts in their textual practices to the printed ones.[539] Perhaps, this is what additionally accounts

---

538 Priolkar 1958.

539 Cf. Priolkar 1958. Priolkar remarks that 'Many orthodox Hindus felt that printing of holy texts by the use of such ink would result in defiling them' and that among else after the first printing of Tukārām's *Gāthās* by Ganapat Krishnaji press in Bombay 'the members of the Vārakarī sect ... would not be persuaded to use the printed edition of the *Gāthās* until they could be assured that the ink used in their printing contained no objectionable ingredients' or that 'the plan of bringing out an edition of Pāṇiṇi's *Aṣṭādhyāyi* with its Marathi translation had to be given up, as ... printing of its sacred text would cause

for the absence of Vedic texts among early native publications deplored by Kielhorn in 1867.[540] On the other hand, suspicion towards European books, actually experienced or rumoured to be bound in leather—a highly polluting substance—may have eventually led to a preference towards the emerging local Indian printers, whose printing process could be more effectively controlled.[541]

Such fear of pollution was nothing new. It no doubt supplied a major organizing principle in manuscript cultures across the subcontinent, which can be seen in the well-rooted tendencies for the ritualization of the processes of copying the scriptures in many religious traditions.[542] The same may also account for a good number of extant manuscripts of Vedic texts bearing traces of self-copying by the Brahmins themselves.[543] Furthermore, while judging the presence or absence of data in the official British administration reports investigating the 'native' publishing market, we must remember that the regulations introduced by the British government, with respect to compulsory registration of every new title by native printers, especially those corrected by the Printing and Publishing Act of 1867, could actually have prevented a number of them from registering, since the costs of such registration could have made them opt out of the official circulation and distribute their titles in the grey zone outside the officially registered channels. This eventually resulted in new libraries often failing to acquire such unregistered books.[544] All that suggests that early attempts to print the Veda must have represented an act of interference with rather unpredictable and potentially dangerous powers, if not controlled. To a lesser degree, that remained the case later on, in those socio-linguistic areas where a more traditional ideology of transmitting Vedic texts either continued in some form (through communities laying claim to such continuity or reconstituted itself in a new shape, through kinds of variously-motivated revivalism. When printed in various scripts and circulated, the Veda at large entered a variety of social functions, one

popular resentment' [Priolkar 1958: 128–129]. For an interesting parallel of distrust towards print and printers in early modern England, see Johns 1998: Intro.

540 'There are no Vedic works at all contained in this catalogue. We proceed therefore at once to the Post-Vedic Literature' [Kielhorn 1867: 15].

541 Cf. evidence on missionaries circulating books in binding made of leather.

542 For evidence and detailed descriptions of ritualized copying of scriptures within early Śaiva and Vaiṣṇava communities, see Simini 2016.

543 See Galewicz 2011b.

544 See Darnton 2002 and Kielhorn 1867.

of them being that of interplay with the memory-based system of transmission. Even if this interplay happened, it was not to easily admitted, as in the case of a part of the Kerala Nampūtiri community associated with Trichur Brahmasvam Maṭham *pāṭhaśālā* (Figure 1), a school of Ṛgvedic recitation claiming, in highly successful rhetoric, to be a continuation of a supposedly pure variety of memory transmission, with no reference to either written or printed text.[545]

A regional edition-cum-translation in Malayalam script of the *saṃhitā* of the *Ṛgveda* tends to reflect not only the pronunciation peculiarities related to the mother tongue of the regional Nampūtiri Ṛgvedic virtuoso reciters represented by *Malayāḷam* script, but also a regional variety of the traditional memorization technique. The basic unit of this edition remains that of one *varga* (group of stanzas—a unit established mechanically for the purpose of memorization), which is retained even in translation, contrary to the universally accepted rule of a *ṛc*/*sūkta* (stanza/hymn) as the basic unit of meaning. Perhaps, this specific case calls for more sustained attention towards other regional scripts within a wider cultural context. An early case of interest comes from Calcutta, where the new policy of Charles Metcalfe, initiated in 1835, had opened wider opportunities for private and indigenous printing enterprises and allegedly guaranteed the circulation of free press and publications.[546] No wonder that perhaps one of the first Vedic texts to appear in print from an Indian publishing house, and perhaps one of the first Indian 'Vedic prints'—the *Śuklayajurvedah Vājasaneyisaṃhitā* with commentaries—came from Satya Press in Calcutta in 1844 (Figure 12). Its very appearance seems to corroborate McLuhan's once famous thesis that the new medium of print tended at first to communicate as its message the older medium of manuscript.

---

545 In the actual practice of re-memorization overseen by elder masters, the teachers of the school happen to refer to a printed edition of *Ṛksaṃhitā* in Malayāḷam script, *Ṛksaṃhitā*, the copies of which are kept at hand in case a teacher's memory falters. See Galewicz 2011c. For other cases, see Larios 2017.

546 See Priolkar 1958: 127. According to Priolkar 'the day ... September 15, 1835, was celebrated with great enthusiasm by the European and Indian citizens of Calcutta, who also raised contributions to build "Metcalfe Hall" on the banks of the Hooghly in honour of its author.' Incidentally, the same year saw T.B. Macaulay's infamous 'Minute on Indian Education' (1835), that eventually put an end to the East India Company's funding of *pāthśālās* and madrasas while favouring English medium government schools.

IV.5.2. Whose is the printed Veda?

It seems quite natural that the appearance of the printed Veda in the land where it had always been meant to be chanted and heard must have required an effort towards a new re-imagination of its very concept or at least a newly re-constituted presentation. What actually was to be printed? Which Veda? In which form? New Indian editors of the early printed editions of Vedic texts must have cherished many different ideas about the socio-religious meaning of their respective decisions of putting the Veda to print. In this respect, it may be of interest to comment briefly on ideological presuppositions of selected early and also more contemporary Indian editors and publishers, with respect to publishing the Vedic canonical texts in general and that of the *Ṛksaṃhitā* in particular—both those directly voiced in introductory passages as well as those indirectly visible in various formulas of beginning and closure, and the features of their typography.

While looking through titles of 19th century Indian editions of *Ṛgvedasamhitā*, it is rather difficult to miss the impression that two mutually exclusive channels of circulation emerged, which were often silent on each other's activities. The first and the better known to written history, for obvious reasons, is that connected to European philology and the newly emerging Indian universities. An example here is the *Vedārthayatna or an Attempt to Interpret the Vedas*, published in Bombay between 1876 and 1882 (to be commented on below), and P. Peterson's *Hymns of the Rigveda* from 1888, also published in Bombay by the Government Central Book Depot and specifically dedicated by Peterson 'for the use of Bombay University B.A. students.'[547] The *Riksangraha, or A University Selection of Vedic hymns with the commentary of Sâyaṇâchârya*, edited, with notes, by V.G. Bijâpûrkar, Bombay 1895, also falls into this category, as do a score of modern editions from the early 20th century, including a notable example of the national project of the critical edition of the *Ṛigvedasaṃhitā* with commentaries, in 1933-42, authorized by the, by Poona Vaidika Saṃśodhana Maṇḍala.[548]

---

547 PETERSON 1888: 1.

548 All these cases, however, should be treated with due caution, since the intended, or 'assumed' public, as the target of a printing project can, by no means, be taken as equivalent of the actual 'audience' or readers. Cf. still valid remarks in this respect in EISENSTEIN 1979: 64.

An altogether different type of readers/users must have been addressed by an earlier two separate editions published by Tookaram Tatya, heading the Theosophical Society Publication Trust in the eighties of the 19th century. In 1887, 'the Rig Veda without Bhashya' appeared and a year later, in 1888, the better known edition, including Sāyaṇa's commentary: *Rig-Veda Samhita in eight ashtakas (parts) with pada patha & Sayanacharya's Bhasyha* ed. by Rājārām Bodas and Shiwarām Gore, Bombay: Tukaram Tatya, Ganpat Krishnaji Press, Śaka 1810 (= A.D. 1888).

A point that might be of some interest here is that, contrary to his words quoted above, Müller knew of his Indian rivals and actually tried to discourage Tookaram Tatya from bringing out this edition by sending emotionally charged letters to the editor of the *Theosophist*, however, with no result.[549] Luckily, we know that at least the former, basic edition, was conceived specifically to be addressed to pandits, as admitted by the then Theosophical Society President in the 1888 issue of the *Theosophist*. In his address to the subscribers and readers, he was proud to announce that the edition of the *Rig-Veda* by Tookaram Tatya had almost sold a thousand copies at 'a very low price of RS 5 each, to bring it within the means of our pandits.'[550] The same passage announces continuation with budget editions of Sāyaṇa's *bhāṣya*.[551] I failed in my search to find any information concerning a commercial success of the latter edition with Sāyāṇa's commentary, but we may expect that Müller's edition might have faced rather hard times, when compared pricewise with Indian ones (in his Introduction to his second edition of RS Müller mentions £15 as the value of each set of his five volume edition of the *Ṛgveda Saṃhitā*[552]). To compare this with the commercial endeavour of the Theosophical Society Publication Fund, the academic edition of the *Hymns from the Rigveda edited with Sayana's commentary* of 1888 by Peterson came out in 500 copies. Some of the Indian editions were

---

549 In a letter to the editor of the *Lucifer*, Müller writes that 'to print the same text twice would have been a woeful extravagance.' *Lucifer* Sept. 1888–Feb. 1889, p. 255 and proposes that Tookaram print the Upanishads and their commentaries instead. In the same letter to the editor of the London based *Lucifer*, he tried, in a statement infused with an almost imperial air, to influence the Theosophical Publication Fund to focus its printing activity exclusively on the Upanishads: '...if the Theosophical Society means to do any real good, it must take its stand on the Upanishads, and on nothing else.'

550 Max Müller, 'Presidential address' in *The Theosophist*, Oct. 1887—March 1888, p. xiii.

551 It is difficult to establish whether these somewhat idealistic plans for making Sāyaṇa's learned commentary available in cheap format mass print editions ever materialized.

552 Müller 1890 I, Preface: ii.

distributed in London, as were English books in Indian cities. For instance, the Bombay edition of *Vedārthayatna* was distributed by Trubner and Co, at the price of 3 s. 6d per volume, which must have been more than a moderate one in comparison to European editions.[553]

The success of the 1887 Tookaram Tatya's edition is quite interesting as it raises questions as to who might have been the prospective buyers of his *Rig-Veda*. It had an unusual shape of a double *pothī* bound at a longer side to be leafed vertically. Visually, it brought a manuscript-like print on a double-sized surface and could appeal to a traditional eye.[554] What sort of 'pandits' did the Theosophical Society's president have in mind? The bulky and codex-shaped 1888 edition (containing commentary) apparently targeted new urban elites that started to rapidly form themselves in Bombay, and to a different degree in Pune and a few other Maharashtrian cities, after the final collapse of Maratha networks of administration and intellectual patronage. It is not sure what we could sensibly imagine the use of the printed Veda outside new university circles to be. Did the printed Veda easily substitute for manuscript copies in their social roles? If so, should we assume that the personal aspect of handwritten copies of the Veda could be replaced with the neat and legible look of the same copies of the printed text? The print basically presupposes an altogether different situation, with numerous copies produced by unknown hands and addressed to unspecified (or undisclosed) users.[555]

While trying to make out a picture of a possible use that the new printed editions could be put to by those buyers who claimed their social status as Brahmins and had remained active in the Vedic practice or religious service of one sort or another, perhaps, of some help, might prove the ideas of those scholars who resolved to account for the coexistence of the oral and the written/printed registers in other, sometimes radically different, textual traditions. According to one such study, 'once they both exist, orality and literacy are never independent of each other.'[556] Mutual

---

553 See Advertisement List in *Journal of the Royal Asiatic Society*, Vol. IX, Part I, October 1876, p. 51. Compare in the same List: '*The Hymns of the Rig-Veda In the Samhita And Pada Text*, without the commentary of the Sayana, edited by Prof. Max Müller. In 2 vols. 8vo. paper, pp. 1704. £3 3s.' or '*The Sacred Hymns Of The Brahmans*. Translated and explained by F. Max Müller ... Vol. I. Hymns To The Maruts, Or The Storm-Gods. 8vo. pp. clii. and 264. cloth. 1869. 12s. 6d' (ibid.: 48).

554 See Tātya 1887.

555 See Galewicz 2011c.

556 Swiderski 1988: 122.

interplay between orality and literacy, in the case of the literary tradition of Vedic Sanskrit, is no doubt a specific, if not a unique, one. The unprecedented focus on aural in the ideology and rhetoric of the Vedic textual transmission makes it a radical case to look at, while trying to understand the relationship between the two.[557]

Nevertheless, I believe that Swiderski's formulation may also hold true for the literary culture of Vedic Sanskrit (if one may borrow a useful formula by Sheldon Pollock against his own choice to exclude Veda from the realm of literature).[558] Be that as it may, the early attempts to put the Veda to print and circulate its copies would not have been possible at all, if not for a steady change of a more general social context and a reconfiguration of the whole cultural matrix in a regional perspective. In the case of Bombay Presidency, the process of change and reconfiguration must have been initiated with the fall of the Peshwa, the sudden decline of the Maratha rulers' patronage for the literate elite, and especially with the new policy adopted by the British after the Great Mutiny.

The office of the Public Instruction for the Bombay Presidency was created in 1857. One of the first decisions taken by the Director was the establishment of a network of book depots destined, in the first place, for intensifying primary education through Marathi vernacular in the new schooling system, introduced and organized with what is often believed to be the colonial idea of knowing and controlling the subjects of the empire more efficiently. The network of 334 sale points, expanded in 1862 to 540 government book stores, constituted the necessary basic infrastructure for the rise of the distribution channels and the market for printed books in general. For the task of printing Marathi education textbooks, the Government is said to have had at its disposal, before 1857, only its two operating presses, and the ensuing demand for printing triggered the rise of indigenous printing establishments, that must have sprouted up especially after adopting the policy of outsourcing Government prints with local printers.[559] One of these early Indian printing enterprises which took orders from the government to print Marathi textbooks was Induprakash, the same one that had ventured, in 1876, to print the first volume of the huge editorial

557 A new look along with a promising new terminology concerning the 'rhetoric' of Vedic transmission is offered in Gerety 2016.

558 See Pollock 2003.

559 For a general picture, see McDonald 1968: 600.

and publishing project named *Vedārthayatna or an Attempt to Understand the Veda*, which ran for several years but eventually discontinued and remained never to be completed.[560]

A number of Indian editions of the *Ṛgvedasaṃhitā* adopted, in one way or another, the Western academic ideology of print and publishing and followed the path of basic rules behind the idea of a text critical editions set, in the case of the *Ṛksaṃhitā*, predominantly by the work of Müller, and some did it very well. The aforementioned represents an early and ambitious instance of projects, including translation to vernaculars, and it was noticed in Europe, among others, by Kaegi in 1880.[561] Unfortunately, it was discontinued after volume five came out. The somewhat enigmatic *Vedārthayatna* started to appear in Bombay in 1876, two years after Müller completed his own *editio princeps*.[562] It included not only the Devanagari text of the *Samhitā* and *Pada-pāṭha*, with selections from *bhāṣya*, but also offered a translation into Marathi, as well as a rendition into English that withstood the criticism by contemporary European scholars.[563] The successive volumes of the *Vedārthayatna* were first printed jointly with Induprakash Press, but later taken over by Nirnaya Sagara Press. The latter, now already legendary Indian printing and publishing house, was started and developed by Sheth Javaji Dadaji, a visionary man who, among others, developed his own high quality movable types.[564] They soon became known for not only editorially reliable, but also for its aesthetically acknowledged print, and later on became famous, among others, for the Sanskrit source-text editing series, like that of *Kāvya-mālā*.

---

560 All succeeding volumes, were published by the Nirnaya Sagara Press.

561 Kaegi 1886, 108. A remark (from this English version of Kaegi's original German work of 1880) concerning *Vedārthayatna* is perhaps of interest: 'The publisher, Shankar Pandurang Pandit, beside the complete Sanhita- and Pada- text (Note 77), gives three translations, in Sanskrit, in Mahrathi, and in English (imgraji).'

562 The appearance of the first parts of *Vedārthayatna* was noticed not only in London (*Journal of Royal Asiatic Society* 1876), but even in the American academic press. *The Notre Dame Scholastic* of Dec. 23, 1876 remarks: 'Under the title of Vedarthayatna, or an attempt to Interpret the Vedas, an edition of the "Rig-Veda" has been commenced at Bombay, which for correctness and usefulness deserves high commendation. The anonymous editor, evidently a Maratha Brahmin, has dedicated his work to all his Aryan brothers and sisters' (*Notre Dame Scholastic*, Vol. X, No. 16, 1867, pp. 246–247).

563 In a letter from Pune, reprinted in an addendum to the edition, F. Kielhorn remarks that '...the English translation appears to have been prepared with great care ...' [*Vedārthayatna*, Addendum, p. 5].

564 For his biography as well as early history of Nirṇaya Sagar, see Kulkarni 1967.

Another group, however, is made up of those editions whose authors chose to base their claim to prestige and authority not necessarily on the grounds of text-criticism as developed in 19th century Europe. And, for the main purpose of this short study, it is this group that is of more interest than the other. Both groups show how the concept of the Veda and the idea of the most proper way of presenting it in print changed over time, space, and socio-historical circumstances. Specimens of the second group can still be found today in the form of a semi-pirated reprints, available in independent small bookstalls across India and outside the new big distribution chains and proving the living demand for such publications in the modern, globalized Indian state. One of the more aesthetically appealing editions of this group—with its water-coloured shades of the block printed vignette—remains the *Ṛksaṃhitā*, edited by Janardana Mahādeva Gurjara, in 1900 in Bombay. It retains all the typographic features of the *pothī* type paper manuscript.[565]

A case apart is that made by the publication known as the *Bhagvān Ved*, or the *Bhagavān Vedaḥ*. This gargantuan-sized book of 15' × 40', weighing 22 kg, was published in 1970 after long preparations and much publicity among religious and pandit circles. Its compilation was credited to Svāmigaṅgeśvarānanda. The editorial board, headed by Narhari Baijapurkar, included a choice of acknowledged traditional pandits and daśagranthis, and the publishers stressed that all of them knew all the Vedic mantras by heart. The *Bhagvān Veda* comprised of four *saṃhitās*, one for each of the Veda. This gigantic mega-book of the Veda was chosen to be printed in Kashi, and a special printing-cum-editing house was established for this purpose. Thus, all the elements of the process of editing-printing-publishing were under control. As one of the pamphlets (accessible via Internet) announced:

---

565 I use the term *pothī* here mostly in its regional Maharashtrian context, connoted by the Marathi noun *pothī* = 'book, manuscript' [of a specific oblong shape]. The term has been used in contemporary scholarship also in a trans-regional meaning, referring to a particular type and shape of paper manuscript, predominant mostly in pre- and early modern periods in northern and central regions of Indian subcontinent. For recent examples of its use, see, for instance, Formigatti 2016: 85 ('The *pothī* format of South Asian origin is used to print canonical texts …'); Formigatti 2016: 88 referring to early instances of *pothī* xylographic prints from Silk Road areas; Formigatti 2016: 98 referring to a comparison of main features of manuscript and *pothī* lithographs: '…basically there are no differences between the two: they are both *pothīs*, the writing space is delimited only by double marginal frame lines, and for the segmentation of the text the same set of symbols and strategies are used.'

> Numerous *Ved-Paathis* (readers who could read the Vedas) co-operated with Guruji and helped Him and as a result the treatise *Bhagwan Ved* could be published without any mistakes and shortcomings... Special paper was sourced from J.K. Mills so that the pages last for at least a hundred years. There was no use of animal fat in the paper.[566]

An interesting formulation in the same pamphlet proves to be rather suggestive as far as the concept of such a material object representing the Veda is concerned. It reads: 'The cover has BHAGWAN VED written in bold gold letters by which the adorned book form becomes *Vigraaha swaroop*.' Thus, the once memory-retained treasure-text has acquired an aura of a sacred object, well on the way to become the centre of the cult of the book.[567] Another instance of this group is the compilation named the *Ṛgvedadaśagrantha*.[568] A substantial part of it is made up of a compendium of related texts, named *Sasvāhākāraprayoganirṇayā Samantrakośā ca Ṛk-saṃhitā*. It was published twice under this title by the Nirṇaya Sāgara Press (both edited by V.L. Panśikar) in 1910 and 1930. Most of the texts making up the compendium had earlier appeared separately. From the same publisher.

IV.5.2.1. The Sasvāhākāraprayoganirṇāyā Samantrakośā ca Ṛksaṃhitā of 1910 and 1930

The case selected here for an illustration of how the prestige and power of the printed Veda could be conceptualized is made by two different editorial initiatives focused on publishing the *Ṛgvedasaṃhitā*. Both come from Maharashtra and remain closely related through an ideology of a regional variety of the supposedly complete and genuine tradition of the *Ṛgveda*. In fact, the second one includes a version of the first, as a part of its more complex structure. The former, with a pretty long and informative title:

---

566 See http://gurugangeshwaranandjimaharaj.org/vedasdetail.aspx?id=111 [accessed on 6 June 2012].

567 I happened to have noticed in 2005 something of this aura visible in the way the Bhagvān Ved was actually handled by members of a respected Ṛgvedic brāhmaṇa family from Gokarna, otherwise very much active in disseminating the Veda in more traditional ways. While the gigantic Bhagvan Ved was kept locked in a prestigious place, within the Guru--kula paṭhaśālā, in one of the respected local Ṛgvedī families of Gokarna, the members of the family actually used for their daily practice and teaching quite a different printed 'Vedic textbook' named the *Ṛgvedadaśagrantha*.

568 Edited by Vinayaka Ghaisasa and published in Pune, at the Ghaisasa Veda Pathaśala in 1986.

Sasvāhākāraprayoganirṇāyā Samantrakośā ca *Ṛksaṃhitā* (from now on SRS), was edited by Wāsudev Laxman Paṇśīkar, one of the famous editors associated with the legendary Nirṇaya Sāgara Press.[569] It was initially published in Bombay by Tukaram Javaji, the then proprietor of the Nirṇaya Sagara Press, in 1910. This edition was later substantially improved, and markedly re-configured, while appearing as a second edition, under the same title, in 1930. The 1910 edition of SRS is rather hard to be in libraries today, while the 1930 improved and rearranged edition can sporadically be found.[570] Both editions of SRS feature a graphically enhanced formula of officially declaring the aim of the editor, thus resembling the otherwise known conventional formulas of intention (*saṃkalpa*). It is directed to 'those who know [the Veda]' and is named *Vidvadabhyarthanam* ('A request to experts'?). This somewhat puzzling name may, in my opinion, refer to the closing formula at the end of the section, initiated at the bottom part of the same folio 1a, and named *Vedaprāstāvika* (Introduction to the Veda). The formula which ends the *Vedaprāstāvika* testifies again to the direct link between the editorial concept behind this type of print publication and that prevailing in the old world of hand-written editions. After having declared the most sincere effort towards eliminating errors, the editor admits, nevertheless the inevitability of mistakes and formally requests those who may detect them to show their kind understanding and rectify them:

> *pramāṇasiddhāntaviruddham atra yat kiṃcanābhūn matimāndyadoṣāt. mātsaryam utsārya tadāryacittāḥ prasādam ādhāya viśodhayantu.*
> 'if by a mistake caused by slow mind something contrary to the established truth might crept in here, let the noble-minded hide away their dissatisfaction and showing their favour correct [whatever mistakes need to be corrected].'

It would be difficult to miss the tenor of this statement, however conventional it may be. Through adopting such a formula from the manuscript culture, the editor subscribes to the need of acknowledging the superiority

---

[569] The name of this now legendary editor of multiple Sanskrit source texts appears in several different forms. The Sanskritized version to be seen in Sanskrit introductions, after-words and colophons usually reads Vāsudeva Lakṣmaṇa Paṇaśīkara. A number of editions that use English title pages prefer the English version, Wāsudev Laxman Śāstrī Paṇśīkar. For the whole list of the varieties of his name in different editions, see Library of Congress Catalogue.

[570] For instance, in the former Kern Institute Library in Leiden (now University Library) or Vaidika Saṃśodhana Library in Pune (where it remained, unfortunately, uncatalogued when I last saw copies of it in 2011).

of the text, perfected in the memory of a virtuoso Vedic expert, over that of print. The printed Veda still appears to need the active cooperation of experienced learned men (*vidvans*) in order to secure for itself the right for claiming to represent the perfected true Veda. At the same time, what comes directly after the closing formula of apology and request to the Vedic experts, however, betrays a recognition of a text-critical need for convincingly indicating sources for the prepared edition. V.L. Panshikar (Paṇaśīkar) identifies four such manuscript sources for his editorship, giving the names of their owners and hints at their location. The same strategy also probably accounts for the bottom line of folio 3a identifying an authoritative Vedic expert who took part in editorial process of preparing the copy for print. Here, the name is Kṛṣṇa Bhaṭ(ṭ)aji Gore. The disclosure of sources and information given, as well as typographic layout and critical apparatus, appear to highlight a convincing claim for an independent text-critical convention to that of the European philology.

The two lines of text inscribed within the vignette at the top of *Vedaprāstāvika*, folio 1a, seem quite informative: the line to the left indicates the editor's main reference texts (*Ṛgvedakalpadruma* and *Śaunakādidrupuṣpāṇi*), that the editor apparently considered important to mention, as those that had been thoroughly consulted by him during the editing process. They probably must have guided him when compiling the sequence of minor but technically important texts to accompany the *Saṃhitā*. The line to the right features a figuratively worded idea behind the concept of the whole project of publication: *rksaṃhitāḍhyām parikalpyāmālām samarpaye vaidikakaṇṭhadeśe.*[571] The following aforementioned *Vedaprāstāvika* has likewise been fitted with a sort of *saṃkalpa*, or a declaration of intention, concerning the editor's idea of introducing the *homa* and other rituals related to the *Ṛksaṃhitā* (*ṛksaṃhitāyā homādeḥ kurve prāstāvikaṃ*).

All these framing devices suggest that the SRS recycles a rather interesting idea of publishing, through a printed edition, an allegedly living oral tradition of transmission held to be the true source of authority and prestige. The editorial *Prastāvika* by Panshikar, consists of three sections

571 The mention of the *kaṇṭhastha deśa* in the upper right corner of the vignette sounds a bit puzzling and probably suggests Maharashtra as the land where the true knowledge of the Veda (i.e. that which 'rests in the throat' [ready to be sounded] and not only in the book) is to be found. Incidentally a parallel idea can be seen in *Devī Bhagavata Purāṇa* I.5.7 (*same deśe śubhe sthāne kṛtvā padmāsanam vibhuḥ avalambya dhunaḥ sajyaṃ kaṇṭhadeśe dharāsthitaṃ*).

highlighted typographically by the bold Devanagari font of the initial clause. In its general tenor, and especially in its first section, the *Prastāvika* draws heavily from Sāyaṇa's Introductions to *bhāṣyas* of *Ṛksaṃhitā* and *Taittirīyasaṃhitā*, both in convention as well as in matter; in the second, from the later, well-known authority of Gāgābhaṭṭa; in the third, from the work titled *Ṛgvedakalpadruma*.[572] Following the example of classic commentators, Panshikar offers a definition of Vedic textuality as such, and continues in the quasi-scholastic way of proving the validity of the Veda by the old, time-honoured way of defining the 'fourfold connection' (*anubandha catuṣṭaya*).[573] In his opinion, the four elements are: *viṣaya* = *alaukikopāya*, *prayojana* = *tadboddha*, *ādhikārī* = *tadboddhārthī*, *sambandha* = *tenasahopakāryopakāraka*-bhāva. The authoritative Veda is declared at the beginning to be the 'otherworldly (*alaukika*) means of reaching the goals which cannot be reached through any other means'—this definition of the Veda is taken from Sāyaṇa.[574] The 1930 SRS edition repeats the text almost verbatim, with a few minor alterations. However, the 1930 edition differs radically from its 1910 predecessor in the number and layout of its minor texts on ritual procedure. The 1986 RDG reprints this very same *prastāvika*, while preceding it with as many as three prefaces of its own.

All in all, the text of the *Veda-prastāvika* appears to proclaim a specific concept behind publishing of the *Ṛgveda* in this rather unusual textual configuration in particular, and behind printing the Veda in general. It appears as markedly different either from the general concept behind printing the catechism by Jesuit missionaries, or printing the vernacular Bible by missionary Protestant Pietists, different from fixing the Veda in print by romantic philologists, or a totalizing attempt at recovering the Veda's meaning in three modern languages of the Bombay's *Vedārthayatna*. The concept is also markedly different from the one behind the act of the national re-appropriating of the Veda through the *Vedasaṃśodhikamaṇḍala* critical edition of 1933-42.

---

572 For the content, authorship and dating of this still little known late treatise, see Galewicz 2014, 2016.

573 For a discussion on this commentarial strategy, see Galewicz 2010a.

574 This definition is thus worded in Sāyaṇa: *iṣṭaprāptyaniṣṭaparihārayor alaukikaṃ upāyaṃ yo grantho vedayati sa vedaḥ*: 'The book which makes known other-worldly means of attaining what is desired and avoiding of what is not desired is known [by the name of] the Veda.' Cf. a version of the same in the KSBhBh [VBhBhS: 109, 28–29]: *kaṇvasaṃbandhiśākhāyā vedatvaṃ cālaukikapuruṣārthopāyavedanahetutvād avagantavyam*. Sāyaṇa offered several distinct definitions of the Veda. For a short survey of them, see Galewicz 2010a: 132, 177–180.

IV.5.2.2. The Ṛgvedadaśagrantha of 1986

The second of the two publishing initiatives focused on the *Ṛgvedasaṃhitā*, that I signalled above is relatively recent and was edited by Vinayaka Ghaisasa, the head of an influential centre for Vedic education in suburban Pune, in 1986. It was published by Ghaisasa Patha Śala, under the title of *Ṛgvedadaśagrantha* (RDG) or The *Decalogy of the Ṛgveda* (not to be confused with the ten *maṇḍalas* in the inner division of the *Ṛgvedasaṃhitā*). Before entering into the concept of the *Ṛgveda* propagated by the former and the latter it is perhaps worthwhile to draw attention to the form of relationship between the two compendia. Both bear the form of a *pothī* book, apparently seeking the recognition enjoyed by the previous medium in the form of a manuscript copy, featuring certain well-recognizable characteristics of its typography and layout. The larger 1986 RDG appears to incorporate the SRS as one of its ten 'books', however, in the latter's 1930 re-edited shape.[575] This incorporation, however, is nowhere admitted directly by the editors of RDG. Yet, indirect hints to a relationship, albeit conceptualized in terms of continuation of tradition rather than inter-textual borrowing, can be seen both in English and Marathi prefaces to RDG, where an alledged gap of more than seventy years is suggested to have elapsed between the two with no *Ṛgvedasaṃhitā* available in print in the meantime. This time span seems to suggest a relationship with the first edition of the SRS printed in 1910, while, in fact, it is the second edition which has been incorporated by Vinayaka Ghaisasa into his 1986 RDG. In fact, the 1986 RDG seems to incorporate, in a directly reprinted shape, not just the 1930 SRS, but a whole series of earlier Nirṇaya Sāgara Press editions of various primary as well as secondary technical texts on ritual procedure related to the *Ṛgveda*. Adopting the name of RDG, the compendium claims to represent a particular regional concept of a 'complete' (*sampūrṇa*) tradition of the *Ṛgveda*.[576] At least, this is what inevitably follows from the wording of the preface (*Puraskāra*).[577]

575 I leave a discussion of quite interesting consequences of this to another occasion. Suffice to mention here, that the 1930 edition of SRS comprises of a short text of a presumably Tantric character, which cannot be seen in the first 1910 edition of SRS. My earlier findings concerning this problem can be seen in Galewicz 2012, 2014.

576 See *Puraskāra* Sanskrit preface to RDG discussed below. The alternate, and much shorter, English preface to the same volume speaks of a 'total *Ṛgveda*' (sic!).

577 To my best knowledge there is no earlier printed edition of the whole corpus entitled *Ṛgvedadaśagrantha* as it is presented in the 1986 Ghaisasa edition in spite of the latter's

IV.5.2.3. The Sanskrit introduction to RDG

Out of the three different introductions to the RDG supplied by the editors (one English, one Marathi and one Sanskrit), the Sanskrit *Puraskāra* no doubt addresses an audience versed in the Vedic lore. Operating with well-established Sanskrit concepts of learning and perfecting the Veda, it targets the world of the *paṇḍitas* and Vedic teachers. In an interesting turn of speech, it takes the task of publishing in print the *Ṛgvedadaśagrantha* as an act of *tapas*, or concentrated religious exertion, on the part of the editors—an act consisting of an extension of the unbroken chain of teaching and learning (*akhaṇḍādhyāyanādhyāpanātmaka*). It seems generally to argue for the superiority of this very printed edition of the *Ṛgveda*, among others, on the grounds of this edition's supposedly close links to the living knowledge of the Veda (*vedavidyā*), represented arguably by the editor(s) of the very volume. This allegedly superior knowledge is said, in the same preface, to be 'residing in the throat [ready to be voiced]' (*kaṇṭhasthā*), and to be 'fixed in the mind' (*buddhisthā*) and is contrasted with an admittedly altogether different knowledge of the Veda, that is merely bookish (*pustakasthā*), and thus unable fully to represent the specific textuality of the Veda, nor to account for the total experience of the Veda.[578]

And yet, after all, it is a printed book which has been embarked on by the same editors praised by the *Puraskāra*. The print edition apparently aims at spreading a particular type of knowledge of the Veda (*vedavidyā*). The very act of publishing through print happens to be conceptualized in an interesting way by the author of the *Puraskāra* preface. It is praised as a religiously meritorious and morally edifying action; this consists in the opening of the treasure of the presumably most respected oral tradition of the locally acknowledged succession of legitimized teachers with their *paramparā*. The act of publishing is next imagined as a gift offering, a long-known motif of *vidyādāna*.[579] Here, it is imagined as a ceremonial donating of such a treasure in order for it to be shared 'nationwide' by all India [whether this necessarily meant an egalitarian turn in handling of the Veda by Brahmin circles involved in the edition is another question].

---

editor's hints to such in his introduction as well as in personal communication to the present author.

578 On the more general consequences of these concepts, see, for instance, Pollock 2006: 82.

579 For a systematic survey of early Sanskrit sources of *vidyādana*, see Simini 2016.

The following wording of the *Puraskāra* suggests a bit more of the peculiar concept of putting 'oral tradition' to print:

> this knowledge of the Veda is not like a knowledge that remains in the book, despised by the knowledge abiding in intellect or knowledge of the throat [memorized in order to be voiced]; through its relationship to every possible thing it makes known far and wide the greatness of all the Vedic teachers and makes all of them indebted to itself. Such a self-ruled receptacle of knowledge cannot be secured with only the printing itself... Even if by viewing the printed book a voicing of syllables and sounds can be affected, still many a saṃskāra-perfections to be realized through [oral] study will remain void causing ignorance in the matter of *udatta* and other accents and making impossible any attempt to shed light on the Veda.[580]

Thus, the close link between script and performance appears here to be extended over the world of print, with a clear signal that even the best printed Veda needs to be filled and completed during performance, with the help of human knowledge that transcends and escapes inscription through inking, either hand-written or printed. While taking such a declaration at its face value, we must keep in mind that, at the same time, when judged on text-critical grounds, this very edition proves to be a reprint, albeit now under one heading, of a sequence of earlier Indian printed editions, prepared in Nirṇaya Sagara Press by V.L. Paṇśīkar. This sequence had been presented as embodying a somewhat enigmatic idea of the *ṛgvediyāḥ daśagranthāḥ* or the Decalogue (Ten Books) of the *Ṛgveda* (rephrased in the 1986 RDG in the compound form of the *Ṛgvedadaśagrantha*), an idea ascribed to the ancient grammarian(?) Vyāḍi.[581]

The 1986 *Ṛgvedadaśagrantha*, published by Vinayaka Ghaisāsa, appears to represent an interesting and complex editorial enterprise, aiming at retaining links with a local concept of the canon of the *Ṛgveda* and the knowledge system associated with it. As such, it arouses several questions as concerns its very idea as well as the circumstances of its inception. At

[580] *pustakasthavidyāvan neyaṃ vedavidyā apraśastā buddhisthatayā, kanthasthatayā ca sarvāpekṣayā sarveṣāṃ vedācāryānāṃ mahattvam ākhyāpayantī sarvān etān uttamarṇī karoti etādṛśaṃ svāyattaṃ vidyādhāraṇaṃ na kevalaṃ mudraṇena siddhyayati mudritagranthāvalokanena kevalam akṣaravācanasaṃbhave 'pi vedādhyayanasaṃskāraśūnyaiḥ, tatratyodāttādisvarajñānam˙ tatprakaśanaṃ ca kartum aśakyam eva* ... (RDG: *Puraskāra*).

[581] More on the concept of the ten books of the *Ṛgveda*, see Galewicz 2012.

closer look, the compound *daśagrantha* must have initially been rather a concept than a name of any specific and recognized set of texts, although, as such, it was probably used in the above-mentioned publication. The very name *Ṛgvedadaśagrantha* (RDG) as the title of a publication, refers to a compendium of *brahmanic* texts which, to my best knowledge, as a whole have not yet become the objects of academic study. From a point which I elaborate upon elsewhere,[582] the RDG can be seen as a sort of textual eco-system, in which a number of practical manuals of secondary character had been arranged with scriptural Vedic texts proper, in answer to the need for adaptation to the process of changing religious ideas and practices of the region. It represents an idea of a closed knowledge system, socially constructed with a view, apparently, to systematize and order a specific variety of religious practices to which *Ṛgvedic* texts used to be put to, in the changing socio-historical realities of the region. As its name suggests, the RDG refers to an idea of a sequence of 'ten books' of the *Ṛgveda*, which might be taken to correspond roughly to the notion of a Vedic *śākhā*.

In his *Lectures on the Origin on the Origin and Growth of Religion*, published in 1878, F. Max Müller happens to mention the concept of *daśagrantha*, while quoting a letter from one of his informants in Pune which says that 'a student of a Rig-veda-śākhā ... if sharp and assiduous, takes out eight years to learn the Dasagranthas, the ten books, which consist of (1) The Saṃhitā of the hymns, (2) the Brāhmaṇa ... (3) the Āraṇyaka, the forest book, (4) the Grihya-sūtras, (5–10) the six Angas...'[583]

The term *daśagrantha* does not seem to have attracted much attention from either modern scholars or Indian lexicographers. However, the modern *Bhāratīya Saṃskṛtikośa*[584] explains *daśagrantha* by enumerating the ten 'books' as: *saṃhitā, brāhmaṇa, padakrama, āraṇyaka, śikṣā, chanda, jyotiṣa, nighaṇṭu, nirukta* and *aṣṭādhyāyī*. The same entry indicates that it is a concept of some antiquity; it refers to Vyāḍi, who is said to have stressed the importance of a regular study (*adhyāyana*) of the *daśagrantha*, made of the following 'books': *saṃhitā, brāhmaṇa, āraṇyaka, śikṣā, kalpa, aṣṭādhyāyī, nighaṇṭu, nirukta, chanda, jyotiṣa.*[585] The editor of *the kośa* does not elaborate on the

582 Galewicz 2012.

583 Müller 1878: 161 and 380. Note the plural form of *Ṛgvedadaśagranthas*.

584 *Bhāratīya Saṃskṛtikośa* by Pt Bhattadevaśāstri Jośi, Part IV, p. 307.

585 The grammarian Vyāḍi seems to have been first mentioned by Kātyāyana. Patañjali [MBh 1.2.64.9] discusses Vyāḍi versus Vājapyāyana on the question of the meaning of words while elaborating on PāSū 1.2.64. According to Matilal 1990: 386 '...Vyāḍi held that

difference in the component *granthas*. On closer look, the Ghaisasa's RDG contains yet another list of ten books which proves to be neither identical with the *kośa's*, nor with the Vyāḍi's, namely: the *(Ṛk)saṃhitā, (Aitareya) brāhmaṇa, (Aitareya) āraṇyaka, (Āśvalāyanīya) gṛhyasūtra, Śikṣā, Jyotiṣa, Chanda, Nighaṇṭu & Nirukta, (Āśvalāyanasya) Śrautasūtra, Āṣṭādhyāyī (sūtrapātha).*

As we can easily see, each of the lists mentioned above (Vyāḍi, Müller, Joshi, Varadarajan, RDG) has been constructed of different elements and the concept seems to have been adaptive enough to accommodate alternate versions of components. Being rather flexible and to a certain degree open, it might prove a useful vehicle for various ideas or an integrative force in those situations where boundaries needed to be crossed.[586] As a concept deriving from the world of transmission through manuscript aided memory, aural experience and performance, it met a rather striking embodiment in the medium of print, aiming at both retaining the aura of the authority of the oral and handwritten as well as acquiring the new power of the print.

IV.5.3. The codex and the *pothī*

It has been argued that a general rule for the evolution of print culture anywhere is that the initial phase of the new print order continues, for some time, to contain certain features peculiar to the manuscript order

---

words primarily refer to *dravya* (substance or individual essence) whereas Vājapyāyana ... held that words refer to universal concepts.' See also Hiriyanna 1938: 261 ff. According to H. Nakamura, a *Saṃgraha* of Vyāḍi might have been composed around 300 BC [Nakamura 1983: 436], but Ganeri takes Vyāḍi to be active around 400 BC [Ganeri 1995: 410]. From a certain perspective, Vyāḍi's lost *Saṃmgraha* seems to represent an early *vaiyākaraṇa* tradition which makes possible formulations like this: '*The Mahābhāṣya* is a commentary on both the *Aṣṭādhyāyī* and the *Vārttika* on the basis of the *Saṃgraha*. The *Saṃgraha* is lost ... But all the linguistic and philosophical speculations of Vyāḍi are the foundation for *Pāṇinian* literature. The *Vākyapadīya* is a concise account of the *Saṃgraha*' [Murti 1997: 20]. Probably quite another and much later Vyāḍi is held to have composed one of the basic works on *vedavikṛtis*. See Abhyankar and Devasthali 1978.

586 According to one of my informants, a *Śuklayajurvedin* by family, the concept of *daśagrantha* should be understood rather as referring to four vedas and six *śāstras* (*darśanas*?) (personal information by Dr. Manjul). According to another opinion (Dr. B. Pataskar, personal communication 2008), there have been two basic versions of *daśagrantha*, both representing the minimum syllabus for 'understanding' the Veda: version I: *Mantra (Saṃhitā), Brāhmaṇa, pada-pāṭha, krama-pāṭha* + six *vedāṅgas*; version II: *Saṃhitā, Brāhmaṇa, Āraṇyaka + Upaniṣad, Pada-pāṭha* + six *vedāṅgas*. In this scheme it is during the (four) *anadhyāya* days when the six *vedāṅgas* are supposed to be studied by a student during his Veda studies, aided in that by his elder colleagues, 'sequentially, one by one'.

that preceded it.[587] This, however, does not entail that these features and the transition process looked similar everywhere and that each and every text followed this rule. For the simple reason of the distinctly different materiality of Indic manuscripts, the features transferred to early print cultures were also different, not only in comparison to the major print cultures of Europe, but also among regions across the Indian subcontinent. This also used to differ in reference to the type of the text that the manuscript represented and the type of readers they intended to address. In many cases, it was religious texts printed with the devotees in mind that tended to resemble the form of the manuscripts. While, for the early modern era, the major divide among those regional manuscript cultures would be that between the northern, using predominantly paper, and the southern, preferring processed palm leaves, the other characteristic was that of shape. The general shape being rather oblong with palm leaves more elongated than paper ones; both stood in stark contrast to the major European form of the codex. The Maharashtra variety of the paper manuscript shape (of several formats), which is important for this study, was especially that known by the name *pothī*.

IV.5.3.1. The evidence of the Nirṇaya Sāgara edition of the *Ṛgvedamantrasaṃhitā*

The puzzle of the source of the initial idea of RDG finds a plausible solution in another compendium circulated in the printed *pothī* form in Maharashtra and incidentally also edited by the unwary V.L. Paṇśīkar. The SRS, reprinted later as the core of the compendium named RDG, seems to stand in a series of printed editions of Vedic texts that started to appear in Mumbai after the establishment of Nirṇaya Sāgara in 1867. While Sanskrit works in Indian scripts begin to appear in print in other regions and centres, notably Calcutta and Benares, earlier than in Mumbai, the early Maharashtrian Sanskrit, and especially Vedic prints, feature a number of traits specific to the region. Copies of these early Vedic prints are, in general, very poorly represented in modern libraries. However, in a few cases their later and contemporary reprints, newly available on the market in the old *pothī* form, can be consulted with a view to reconstructing their editorial histories.

---

587 See, among others, Pettegree 2005: 129.

Especially interesting in the present context appears to be a recent (2009) reprint of an earlier Nirṇaya Sāgara edition of the *Ṛgvedamantras-aṃhitā* (edited once again by the same untiring V.L. Paṇśīkar). This features an introduction (*prastāvana*), that appears to refer to a history of his editing nothing other than the ten books (*daśagranthāḥ*) of the Ṛgveda. In this introduction, Paṇśīkar enumerates his previous editions as comprising of: *śikṣacatuṣṭayam, vedaṣaḍaṅgāni, ṛgvedasaṃhitā saparibhāṣāsarvānukramā saṃhitāpārāyaṇahoma (= svāhākara) ..., ṛksaṃhitāpadapāṭhaḥ (= padāni), aitareyopaniṣadaḥ (araṇāni) ca mudritāni santi iti aitareyabrāhmaṇam api sāṅgaṃ bhāṣyapāṭhaiḥ saṃvadya saṃśodhitam asti.* Concluding the list, he states: 'Thus the ten books along with their auxiliaries are completed so that one who needs it may consult them together or one by one according to his preferences' (*evaṃ sāṅgā daśagranthāpy atra saṃpūrṇā ekasamayāvacchedena pṛthag vā grāhakāṇāṃ yathābhilaṣitaṃ labdhum arhā eva*).

The plural form of *daśagranthā(ḥ)* in this preface suggests a series of publications completing the ten books of the Ṛgveda, in contradistinction to the 1986 Ghaisasa edition, which reads on its title page: *Ṛgvedadaśagrantha-prāraṃbhaḥ*—suggesting a fixed compendium. A list of ten *granthas*, given in the preface to the *Ṛgvedamantrasaṃhitā* (RS, *Padāni, Aitareyopaniṣadaḥ, Aitareyabrāhmaṇam*, six *vedāṅgas*), proves, however, to be somewhat different than that given in the 1986 Ghaisasa edition of RDG (RS, AB, AĀ, AśvGS, six *vedāṅgas*), standing against a generally shared opinion among the interviewed contemporary traditional Vedic experts of Pune, that the 1986 edition was an exact reprint of an earlier (1910?) edition of the same by Nirṇaya Sāgara Press.[588]

Most of the minor texts that have been incorporated, along with the *Saṃhitā*, into the SRS—and subsequently accommodated within RDG—are short practical manuals, concerned with the ritual handling of the *Ṛgvedic*

[588] The same Preface features a formulation that betrays a spirit of careful editorial enterprise otherwise visible in most editions prepared by Paṇśīkar: *prārthayāmaś ca 'gacchataḥkhalana' nyāyena saṃskaraṇāvasare dṛgdoṣādibhir atra skhalitaṃ kṣamāśīlaiḥ śodhanīyam anugrāhyāśca tādṛśasthalanidarśanena vayaṃ yenopakṛtena bhūyo 'ṅkanāvasare sāhāyyaṃ syād iti* ('We wish that by the force of the '*gacchataḥ nyāya*' all that has been spoiled be improved/refined by the patient knowledgeable men and that we be furthered by way of their pointing of locations and by such a help even more assistance may be rendered in the auspicious moment of stamping [of the pages?]'). An idea of a close sequence of *granthas* can also be seen in a para-textual frame to another publication edited by Paṇśīkar: *imāni pustakāni prācinapustakaiḥ vaidikapāṭhakrameṇa saṃvādya vaidikadvārā ca saṃśodhya tatra śrautasūtram kenāpyamudritaṃ ca mudrayitvā 'dhyetṛvargasaulabhyāyāsmābhir mudritāni mūlyaṃ* 1 (*Śikṣādivedaṣaḍaṅga*, ed. V.L. Paṇśīkar, Mumbai 1915).

mantras. Most of them could probably be best classed as *Vedalakṣaṇa* literature and subscribed under the labels of: *prayoga*, *paddhati*, *nirṇaya*, *vicāra* or *vidhāna*. These mostly deal with classificatory and technical aspects of the practical application of *pārāyaṇa*, or ceremonial recitation of the *Ṛksaṃhitā*, *japa*, or muttered recitation of mantras, and *homa*, or burnt oblations accompanied by such recitation.[589] While focused mostly on identification and classification of *devatās*, *ṛṣis*, *chandas* and *homas*, they showed relatively close affinity to the better known *Ṛgvidhāna*, which they frequently referred to or quoted from and which they actually spatially preceded within the compendium. They drew, however, also from other, later sources, of *purāṇic* provenance.[590]

The type of textual environment constituted by the RDG points to some specific, perhaps regional, tradition of ritual practice that, in one way or another, must have engaged the 'ten books' of the *Ṛgveda*. These regional ritual and textual practices translated into a sort of sub-genre of print culture, represented by a group of works repeating the same oblong shape and typography and edited to the same standard, resulting from the editing hand of Vasudeva Lakṣman Panśikar, and his affiliation to the Nirṇaya Sāgara Press. The extensive publishing project appears to have aimed at a total representation in print of the textual and performance tradition of leading Maharashtra Āśvalāyana Ṛigvedi group of Brahmins and, beside the above-mentioned compendium of RDG, also comprised of editions of more specific manuals focused on domestic rituals, like the *Ṛgveda Brahmakarmasamuccaya* and *Prayogaratna* of Nārāyana Bhāṭṭa.[591]

---

[589] Identification of these ancillary literature is not an easy task since Indological scholarship in general tended to neglect these minor works concerned with aspects of *svādhyāya*. See general remarks of Parameśwara Aithal [1991: 15]: 'The position of the printed editions of the *Vedalakṣaṇa* texts is no better. There is a great deal of confusion regarding the authorship, exact titles, and even the extent of the texts.' Some of the minor works included in the RDG and SRS can be identified with manuscript sources listed in Aithal 1991.

[590] *Kālikapurāṇa*. Others include *Paraśurāmasmṛti*, *Ṛgvedakalpadruma* (probably a late, 19th century work by Keśava Maṭe), *Rudrakalpadruma*, *Parāśarasmṛti*, Gāgabhaṭṭa's works, as well as Nārāyaṇa Baṭṭa's *Prayogaratna* (alias *Nārāyaṇabhāṭṭi*) being a compendium of technical manuals concerned with domestic rites said to be preferred by the majority of Mahārāṣtra and Konkan littoral Āśvalāyana Ṛgvedī Brahmin groups [see Bhandarkar 1874: 138].

[591] Cf. Bhandarkar 1874: 133.

IV.5.3.2. The RDG's success story as predicted in its Sanskrit preface

It has often been stressed that the medium of print worked hand-in-hand with that of a standardized vernacular, which it allegedly would help to shape, while feeding on its capacities of the big numbers represented by potential readership. And yet the first print to appear in Europe was in Latin, and Sanskrit printed matter has been visualized as being potentially appealing too—although perhaps not in the same degree of number and not in the same way as could be offered by the vernacular. The idea of fixity and stability, so often associated with print and its promise, does not seem to offer much for the textuality of the Veda - itself the paragon of stability and fixity.

The case of RDG shows that even the most orthodox religious canons remained models rather than actual practice, and regional and local scholarly, as well as religious. Communities struggled for control over either the message (*vedārtha*), ritual use (*vedaprayoga*), or just a typographical/communication form, which might give locally some advantage over other groups (knowing more Vedic mantras than rivals, controlling the proper way of implementing Vedic mantras in religious practice, could give advantage in the market for religious services). This reason might have, among others, contributed to the emergence of a rich and culturally divergent environment for the contest in the control over the Vedic textual heritage, expressed by historically, socially and religiously differentiated groups, claiming brahminhood through establishing connections to the Veda in many interesting ways yet to be investigated. The idea represented by the RDG must have once been a product of such an environment. A short survey[592] and a field study showed that the compendium of RDG has remained in circulation and use among *brāhmaṇa* communities of Maharashtra and Konkan littoral, while being rather unknown to Brahmin groups in other regions of India.[593] The results of the survey also suggested a regional tradition of a community of Daśagranthis—the users of the compendium in the proper sense—those

592 A field study performed by the present author over the years 2003–2010 showed that copies of RDG have been prefered for teaching in most of the Vedic education centres (*vedapāṭhaśālās*) of the region.

593 With some rather telling exceptions like that of the *Sīta-Rāma pāṭhaśālā* in Trivandrum, where the introduction of RDG was (at the moment surveyed by the present author between 2002–2006) apparently linked to the trans-regional activity of the Somayaji Nana Kale group of Barśi that provided teachers for the *Ṛgveda* classes.

who were believed to be actually toiling themselves with the regular study of the Ten Books of the *Ṛgveda.*

In its cleverly prepared printed form referring to a living tradition, the RDG made a relatively successful claim to represent the key to mastering the knowledge of the Veda (*vedavidyā*) in its Ṛgvedic variety. It made the case for a successful representation of a textual eco-system developed regionally and, to a varying degree, accepted for use in the form of a quasi-canonical compendium, by the regional Vedic education centres or *pāṭhaśālās*. In this textual eco-system, a number of short practical manuals of secondary degree had been arranged with scriptural Vedic texts proper, with a view to apparently systematize and order a wide variety of religious practices, to which Ṛgvedic texts used to be placed in the changing socio-historical realities of the region. A field study among its users showed that to deconstruct it made no sense whatsoever to any of the interviewed parties.[594]

The editor of the apparently successful publishing initiative of the RDG felt it necessary to support its credibility with a preface in Sanskrit, written not by a *Vaidika*, but by a person with authority of a religious and charismatic kind, represented by the titles of the undersigned author—Vedamūrti Kṛpākāṅṣī Kavīśvarakulajanur Dattatreya Śarmā. By this very act, the authority of the printed Veda aspires to a peculiar composite nature; the wide-reaching print remains to be backed with the typographic shape of a *hastalikhita pothī* book and the personal authority of a living embodiment (*Vedamūrti*) of the oral Veda. The logic of these associations permeates the words of the Sanskrit *Puraskāra* to RDG:[595]

---

594 An attempt at finding an insider's answer to the question concerning the source of the idea of constructing the compendium of RDG proved impracticable, since the very idea of RDG must have taken strong roots among practitioners of whatever has survived and what has been recently revived of the Ṛgvedic tradition among Brahmin communities of Maharashtra.

595 *iti nirdhārya śrīghaisāsaguruvaryaiḥ puṇyapattane 'smin matprabandhena vedabhavanaṃ nirmāya taddvārā kanthasthā buddhisthā ceyaṃ praśastatamā vedavidyāparaṃ parā saṃcālayitum abhilaṣyate / tad idam teṣām abhīpsitaṃ viśvopakārakaṃ pavitratamaṃ kāryaṃ viśvasaṃrakṣakasya śāstrayoneḥ paramakṛpayā dharmaśraddhālūnāṃ sajjanānāṃ ātmīyatāprakaṭanena ca niṣpratyūhaṃ saṃpadyataṃ, samedhatāṃca vedādhyayanādhyāpana-paraṃ paradvārā viśuddhā dharmabuddhiḥ rāṣṭrahitakāriṇī ityeva sarvāntaryāmiṇaḥ sarvadhīprerakasya parameśvarasya caraṇakamalayoḥ saṃtatam anunāthāmahe kāmayāmahe ca vedācāryaghaisāsaguruvaryāṇāṃ dīrghāyurārogyavedaparaṃparāsaṃrakṣaputrachātrādy abhivṛddhiṃ ca sarvakalyāṇanidānabhūtam iti.*

> Now, having determined that [the mere bookish knowledge cannot represent the complete *Ṛgveda*], the noble Gurus of the Ghaisāsa family desire to circulate with the help of this great collection, and by means of the house of the Veda which has been erected in the city of Puṇyapattana, this most praised tradition of Vedic knowledge which is the one [fixed] in the mind and [ready to be voiced] in the throat. Let this very act of theirs, sprouting from the all-protecting Womb of Śāstras, most desired, of highest refining power, and a remedy to all, become smoothly successful through the paramount grace of those true humans who remain attached to the Law and Faith as well as with the help of its own enlightening power. Let us pray incessantly to the feet-lotuses of the Supreme Lord—the Inner Traveller—who is the promoter of all pious visions that this pure idea of the rightful minds, most beneficial to the land, ever prosper through the uninterrupted tradition of learning and teaching.

All through this Preface, as well as in the other two, the Marathi and the English versions, both independent and by no means just linguistic versions of the same, the printing of the Veda, considered as a community treasure, appears most problematic. And this remains so, in spite of the scores of other editions available on the market (this is, by principle, not acknowledged by the editors of the RDG). According to the logic of the rhetoric of the tradition that the authors of the prefaces to the RDG claim to embody , this very publishing initiative was imagined to be an act of opening the local Brahmin community's textual treasure to the world around. In this logic, the RDG is held to represent an altogether different quality in comparison to all other published 'books' of the Veda, which had been 'just printed' while remaining incomplete images of the complex *vedavidyā*. We should not fail to notice how this peculiar logic revives the idea of *phalaśruti* – a traditional strategy of securing success for a text to be circulated in manuscript or performance form. Adapted to fit the context of print capitalismin the regional variety, the formulation aims to secure success in terms of wide circulation within the network of Vedic education centres of Wetern Maharashtra. Apparently, the editors of the RDG chose to understand 'the grammar of print' in their own way and for their own purposes. An essential part of this 'understanding' may be emphasized: both the SRS and the RDG seem to combine, in an interesting way, a specific ideology of publishing oral tradition with a text-critical attitude. The latter one is clearly visible in the formulas of closure, which identify both learned pandits who reviewed the pre-printed materials, as well as manuscript sources for its preparation. The printing histories of the SRS and RDG suggest that 'the uniformity and continuity of the new visual print culture' (spelled out by McLuhan [1995: 14]) happens not only to accommodate, but also to creatively conserve certain formal and ideological concepts quite peculiar to regional varieties of previous media of memory and manuscript culture. It makes any understanding of the former rather difficult or misleading without appreciating peculiarities of the latter. As one of the leading editors of Nirṇaya Sāgara Press, V.L. Panshikar probably can be counted among those who not only understood, but also actively used 'the grammar of print' (McLuhan's sense) while, at the same time, actively playing with the grammar of script within the territory of the then new medium of print.

V. Towards social history of print cultures in colonial India

Increasing volume of recent scholarship focused on regionally differentiated print cultures, especially Bengal, Maharashtra, and South India, tends to belie the simplistic subsuming of all the diverse phenomena of the rise of print in India towards the mid-1800s under one label.[596] A good number of printing enterprises of the earlier stage of these developments remained hybrid in terms of social composition, resting on collaboration between foreign missionaries, Company administration officers, and Indians of a variety of social provenance. Such was the case of the Company's printing press in Calcutta at the very beginning and later on when its operation was handed over to a local printer. Furthermore, the Serampore Press of William Carey, which started around 1800, soon, after its first heroic years, entered a complex relationship of service and commission work, at first for the Bengal Government, Fort William College, and later other institutions, such as the Calcutta Bible Society. In Bombay, the American Mission Society came to accept orders from outside towards 1830 and trained indigenous printers, who later began to establish their own enterprises. Many of the early government and missionary printing enterprises benefitted from the collaboration of the local craftsmen, who brought within their respective orbits of operation their experiences, knowledge, and patterns of work, often inherited from the regional manuscript cultures they were brought up in. This collaborative spirit resulted not only in recreating European patterns of print production and consumption, but also gave rise

---

596 See, for instace, Gupta 2010, 2012, 2013, 2016, Orsini 2016, Simini 2016, Venkatachalapathy 2012, Ebeling 2010, Ogborn 2007, Stark 2007, Wujastyk 2012 and 2014, Trivedi 2008, Shaw 2007, Shaw and Randall 2014, Ghosh 2008, Hall 2016, Colier and Connolly 2016, Raman 2012, Killingley 2008, Green 2010, Formigatti 2016,

to a number of innovative forms and practices, that continued and creatively reappropriated regional traditions of writing and reading, specific to particular spaces, communities, religious traditions, and literary genres.[597]

V.1. Printing revolution and social change

Several studies that appeared in the last two decades bring often contradictory images of the allegedly 'revolutionary' change brought to South Asia by print and its growing use in the middle of the 19th century. Furthermore, the picture of the relationship between the cultural order of the former medium of the manuscript and the new one of print happens to look different, depending on the region under investigation. In one study, S. Ebeling[598] argues for the Tamil case that:

> ...in the pre-modern period Tamil manuscripts were a deeply personal medium unlike the 'publicly' circulating book, which was a saleable commodity. Since for centuries the ultimate goal of scholarly activity was to know a text by heart and be able to explicate and elaborate on every aspect of it, a manuscript served mainly as an aide-mémoire, or as a kind of textbook for teaching young pulavar apprentices. Of course, manuscripts were copied and re-copied, and teachers often dictated texts to students so that several copies could be made simultaneously, but these copies then belonged to the individual student or teacher, and they would not generally be lent to anyone.[599]

The growing presence of print towards the midle of 19th century, with its ideas and new forms of circulating printed matter, challenged the practices referred to above with graded success and in a variety of ways and degrees, from missionaries distributing free copies of tracts and (usually parts of) scripture to prospective converts, through textbooks for new educational use, low price almanacs and other 'bazaar' printed material, to diversely

---

597 These phenomena have been differently conceptualized in recent scholarship. See for instance, Hall 2016: 91 – '...supposedly peripheral settings were sites of locally initiated creativity, inclusive of modifications of existing textual communities ... [In] early colonial India ... the collaborative character of publishing provided opportunity for indigenous populations and their pre-existing communal literary expressions to shape an emerging print culture in a manner that belies simplistic formulations of Orientalism.'

598 Ebeling 2009.

599 Ebeling 2009: 238. See also Sweetman 2012: 29.

priced literary and religious works in the vernacular, and religious as well as śāstric works in Sanskrit. Each and every one of them strove to address the expectations as well as develop new reading practices among their readers audiences. Within these developments, the early initiatives aiming at putting the Veda to print stand out conspicuously as marginal on one hand and specific on the other, due to the unusual character of the Vedic textuality. Held to be elitarian, if not hermetic, guarded as exclusive possession of one social class, believed to be purposely hidden from open access, the Veda appears to have been resisting the very idea of 'publishing'.

While the textual history and the very concept of the Veda seem to contradict the idea of social change, a redefined idea of the Veda—in the hands of Dayananda Saraswati—was articulated in print as an instrument of a new cultural, social, and national project of change. This, however, remains beyond the scope of the present study. In the new transforming social matrix of later colonial India with its many regional anti-Brahmin movements and growing competition for status in face of coming modernity, the printed Veda also happened to assist regionally reconstituted Brahmin communities to assert their new place in the new social configurations of contested rights, duties, and privileges. In the new situation, the old class claim for exclusive possession had to be redefined as regional group claim for status in new terms specific to print culture.

We may safely presume, that an appearance of a religious text like the Veda in print would not inevitably trigger the onset of widespread reading practices. It would be also naive to take for granted that publishing the *Ṛgvedasaṃhitā* or any other major Vedic texts in the socio-historical context of nineteenth century India should be tantamount to the opening of the hitherto concealed and guarded sacred text to a wide reading public , and thus to directly benefitting all through the miraculous effect of print. Sanskrit religious texts entered the domain of print with different preconceptions and aims, which, in many instances, revealed imaginative and original concepts of textuality and reading. Their editors and publishers had in no mere way to invent their new audiences. In the case of the Veda in general, and more specifically the *Ṛgveda*, the reading practices were to be associated with print and to be constructed with respect to the potential power offered by print in relation to parallel reading practices, continuing the centuries old customs accompanying the production, circulation, and consumption of sacred texts in the symbiotic relationship between the oral and the written. It is revealing to see how initiatives for printing the *Ṛgveda* remained influenced by the social, political, and economic circumstances of specific regional print cultures, while influencing them at the same time.[600] The prefaces, introductions, colophons, and other paratextual devices that appear to have been used for the forging of a new type of readership open us to the concepts of reading and other uses of religious texts, that perpetuated, modified, or transformed and opened to change, the old prevailing concepts in shaping print cultures, at times quite different from those naturally associated with print and print capitalism. All reveal the search for new ways of constituting and/or affecting reading constituencies with instruments and potencies of print and its alleged civilizational mission. In this process of change and transformation, the newly emerging cultures of print and communities of reading remained anxious with reference to their access to effective reading practices. They often sustained or strengthened their focus on proper protocols and procedures of reading, which became textualized along with the texts proper.

Towards the mid-19th century, the fast growing print industry gradually transformed heavily patronized enterprises into commercial entities which, eventually, though not without problems, started to forge their own reading practices more specifically suited to the character of the print medium and its newly shaped relationship of differently constituted reading constituencies. The latter remained shaped as much by purchasing capacity as by religion, status and gender. Even so, in the fifties, as shown by a recent study, the price of most of the printed books made it still a rather luxurious commodity, and this situation began to change only around the 1860s.[601] During this process, the new print cultures retained, appropriated, adopted, or transformed many textual practices that came from the order of manuscript as well as oral and memory cultures of reading. Through their mediation, the printed book adopted new meanings and functions, not

600 Relatively little attention to reading practices in relation to printing Sanskrit religious texts on the part of contemporary scholarship has been slowly compensated by recent studies. See, for instance, Bhatia 2016, which, while being concerned with cultural consequences of the projects of publishing in print of the *Bhāgavata Purāṇa*, brings important general insight, especially remarks on p. 111: '...merely appearance of a sacred text in print does not suggest an immediate, widespread diffusion of reading practices. Religious readership ... falls within certain kinds of disciplinary regimes, access to which is carefully regulated. Post-print, religious reading is still a matter of active and gradual constitution.'

601 See Stark 2007: Introduction and p. 69 showing that, as late as 1849, half the titles offered by a printer-publisher in Benares were Sanskrit books and their print run also features as the highest among the listed titles in Hindi, Urdu and Persian.

always necessarily those imagined or expected by the early entrepreneurs. While those processes have become the object of sustained scholarship with reference to the vernacular book, almost no attention has been given to the change and the nature of transformation, that print brought to the reading practices and use of the Sanskrit book.

V.2. Publishing Indian religions in print

Any survey of titles offered by early Indian printers-publishers will show that no mere part of them were religious texts. Especially popular religious works in vernaculars as well as Sanskrit used to dominate the title lists of many an Indian publisher in later half of the 1800s. Attempts at putting some of them to print mark also the earlier period. The circumstances and motifs of their publishing in print do not necessarily resemble those that accompanied missionary or Orientalists initiatives from early 19th century. Extant copy of the *Bhagavadgīta* attests to its printing in Miraj, Western Maharashtra, in 1805 in wooden block technology, as the result of an earlier unfinished project by Nana Farnevis.[602] A motif for publishing in print of this—probably the most widely known classic of Sanskrit religious literature of North India was nothing other than the well-known (and attested from early medieval *dāna*) custom of ceremonial offering as gifts to men of knowledge (teachers, preceptors, holy men) of beautifully handwritten copies of *Bhagavadgīta* (as well as other religious texts), and such a custom 'was at that time much in vogue.'[603] Thus, an old religious tradition of *vidyā-dāna* (offering of knowledge), forming, very much, part and parcel of both Śaiva and Vaiṣnava groups from at least the early second millennium, proved to be a vehicle for the new use of the new medium of print.[604] Not only the basic concepts, but also more general material features of the previous manuscript media and its performance component found its articulation in the new use of print, as far as it concerned the production and circulation of religious texts and ideas. As noticed by C. Bayly:

---

602 Priolkar 1958: 34.

603 Priolkar 1958: 34.

604 On the origin, history and actual practices of the cultural institution of 'the gift of knowledge' (*vidyādāna*), see Simini 2016.

> the key categories of manuscript material which had been common before the printing press passed directly into print media. Apart from school-books which disseminated western scientific and moral ideas ..., the most common types of early printed book in north India remained strikingly similar to the types of manuscripts which had circulated before the supposed print 'revolution'.[605]

We can see this in the instances from Maharashtra commented above, that such features of early print as the substratum material, oblong shape of the page, overall typography conventions, formulaic strategies of beginning and end, long and informative colophons—as well as reading practices of the printed editions of regionally conceptualized Vedic compendia—reiterated forms and modalities of the manuscript culture, while claiming to remain true representations of the genuine oral tradition. From the perspective adopted by Bayly, such regional print cultures could be seen as disappointing:

> All these types of works had antecedents in the tracts produced and disseminated previously by the armies of bazaar and household scribes. This continuity was a disappointment to those contemporaries who wished to believe that 'print capitalism' would create a revolution in sensibility.[606]

However, a closer look reveals that they happen to feature many, if not all, of the necessary text-critical discipline that, at times, stands the critical eye of a modern philologist, while offering alternative modes of editorial discipline. Among else they often feature description of manuscripts that where consulted for the edition along with the indication of their owners and the provenance of the latter. In contradistinction to the philologists' bias for the description of the material aspects of the manuscripts, rather the status of the persons of the owners was highlighted as apparently adding authority to the texts in their possession.

The actual rationale behind a decision to publish, or to support publishing in print of a particular Indian religious work, could differ widely. And in most cases we are left to guess this from hints left in the printed text itself. In some instances, it could refer or relate to the exemplary instance of the Bible, since the missionary ideology of print established itself as

605 Bayly 1996: 243.

606 Bayly 1996: 243.

a point of reference—that was the case of the second edition of Max Müller's *Rig-veda-Saṁhitā*. With the initial financial shortcomings overcome, it eventually came out in 1890–1892, only thanks to the patronage of an Indian prince from the far south. The generosity of Paśupati Gajapati Raju was fully acknowledged by Müller only later, in 1899.[607] When asked by Müller for the reasons of his liberal gesture towards the project of printing the *Ṛgveda*, the Rajah 'replied that India wanted its Bible, and he added that "it may benefit him hereafter."'[608]

Among the initiatives believed to be the earliest instances of putting religious works was the 1818 *Khardeh Avesta*, the Parsi Scriptures in Gujarati with commentary published by Fardunji Marzban. Still earlier, in 1814, he is said to have published the first Hindu *pañcāng* calendar in Gujarati (six years before the first Bengali calendar appeared). Other early Initiatives for publishing in print popular religious texts that remained in oral circulation include Ganpat Krishnaji who started to publish popular Sanskrit and Prakrit ślokas focused on *Bhagavadgīta* in his newspaper *Jñāncandrodaya* around 1840.[609]

Some of the locally established and regionally expanding printer-publisher apparently specialized in Sanskrit religious texts. This is the case of the famous Veṅkateśvara Steam Press of Bombay started around 1871 by two Bajaj brothers, Khemraj and Gaṅgāviṣṇu. The brothers, extremely active on the apparently growing market of publishing in print of the well-known religious texts in Sanskrit must have facing also a growing competition. Especially from the more experienced Nirṇaya Sāgara Press, that was quickly developing its expertise in printing Sanskrit religious texts, including Vedic. The brothers tried to work out an ideology for their engagement in the printed Sanskrit world. In the concluding part of one of their publications (*Mādhyandina Mantra Saṃhitā*) they included a sort of advertising-declaration to their readers which must have served also the practical function of advertising their networks of distribution based on subscription sale through postal orders.[610] The advertising features a comprehensive list of titles of major Vedic texts, from *Ṛgvedasaṃhitā*, through ritual manuals that apparently had been either already published

607 'The Maharajah paid to the Press not less than £4,000' [Müller 1899: 159].

608 Müller 1899: 160.

609 Naregal 2001: 183–5.

610 *Mādhyandinīyamantrasaṃhitā*, Veṅkateśwara Steam Press 1929: penultimate folio: *atrāsmakām mudrānalāye ṛgvedādi.*

by Venkateśwara Steam Press or ready for publishing in print on subscription. Apart from the Vedic texts, however, the bulk of the Veṅkateśwara Steam Press publications apparently constituted more popular Sanskrit religious classics, such as various *purāṇas*, Pañcarātra *saṃhitās*, *mahātmyas* and an array of other texts of popular Hinduism. In the later phase of their operation the two brothers parted with Gangāviṣṇu establishing his own Lākṣmiveṅkateśwara Steam Press, while Khemraj remained with the name Śrī Veṅkateśwara Steam Press, Mumbai.

While, on average, we may agree with Bayly that 'printing obviously gave as much of a boost to palmistry and necromancy as it did to astronomy/astrology,' this statement only confirms print's role as a medium of communication, understood as being based on, and working from—to use an expression domesticated within a current of media communication studies—the 'abyss of non-meaning.' Nevertheless, the regional print cultures remain to be studied, as far as their original and creative ways of appropriating the powers of print for their own functions and aims are concerned.[611]

V.2.1. Printing and appropriation of the past

As seen above, Sanskrit proved to be far from the first language to appear in print in India, as were the scripts in which Sanskrit works used to be most often written. With the early and rare—though important—instances of xylographic prints, found in the Silk Road area, and dated to early centuries CE, the first Sanskrit texts in Indic scripts do not appear in print until the early 19th century.[612] After the initial steps taken by the Baptist Mission Press in Serampore, the early pattern for Sanskrit texts published in print seems to have been set by the Fort William College Press, operated at the time by Bābū Rām, which managed to publish—between 1807 and 1815—as many as sixteen Sanskrit works, selected under recommendation of Henry Th. Colebrooke.[613] This early pattern included the imitation of the oblong shape of the paper manuscripts along with several paratextual features characteristic for the manuscript culture of North India, such as no binding, the absence of title pages, versified introductory formulas, and

611 Bayly 1996: 250.

612 On the evidence of, nature, and dating of xylographic prints of Sanskrit texts, see Formigatti 2016.

613 For a general survey of Colebrooke's involvement in promoting the publishing of Sanskrit works in print, see Rocher and Rocher 2012: 72–75. See also Formigatti 2016: 104.

extensive formulaic colophons. Most of these features would be reproduced by the successive indigenous Indian printing in Bengal and also influence the other two new centres of print–Bombay and Madras. In spite of the quintessential role of H. Colebrooke–whose essays set the path for future Vedic studies and the understanding of the nature of the Veda and its textuality–the earliest Calcutta phase of printing did not include Vedic texts. One of the reasons for this development–at least as far as it concerned government publishing–might have been the ambivalent attitude of Colebroke himself towards the sense of studying the Veda.[614] Others comprised a lack of–or difficult access to–reliable manuscripts, technical problems with typographical representation of the language of Vedic texts, not to mention the hermetic nature of the Vedic variety of Sanskrit itself.

Print began to bed in regionally at a much-variegated pace and in profoundly distinct ways. Also the government regulations concerning printing press prior to 1835 did not have the same shape and effect in the three Presidencies with Madras government said not to have its press law at all before that date.[615] In general, however, it seems that in the other two Presedencies Indians were not banned from owning or operaring the printing press but rather restricted by a system of licencing. The licence system affexted as much any English who intended to run a press, and the law at first intended to control rather English owners of independent journals in Calcutta and Bombay. The early Indian printers-publishers tried to cater to the needs of several different reader communities and, in consequence, adopted different policies towards the religious and cultural heritage of their respective regional and linguistic traditions. Apart from the government patronized initiatives of imperial knowledge production, of an educational or legal character, religious texts in Sanskrit paved their way to the world of print mostly, though not exclusively, through initiatives of Brahmin printer-publishers as well as religious and social activists, who saw print and its appeal as a new way of mobilizing their constituencies. It was, however, with publishers coming from the social strata of much lower status that proved to be most vigorour publishers and printers of Sanskrit and Vedic texts. Among them Kriṣṇadas Gaṇpat Ji, Javaji Dada

[614] The foundational early study for understanding the historical nature, inner architecture as well as type of textuality of the Vedic corpus proved to be H. Colebrooke's essays 'On the Védas or Sacred Writings of the Hindus' published in *Asiatick Researches* in 1805 [Colebrooke 1805b].

[615] See Blacburn 2006: 80.

Ji and Khemraj and GāṅgaViṣṇu Bajaj showed that one did not have to be a Brahmin to seriously engage with publishing Sanskrit and the Vedic texts. They, however, needed major assistance in the form of the expertize of mostly Brahmin editors, like Vāsudeva Lakṣman Pāṇśīkar who edited numerous Sanskrit (including Vedic) works for Nirṇāya Sāgara press in the late 1800s and early 1900s.[616] The same printers-publishers ventured also into the emerging market for the printed 'text-book' Veda that opened with the new education policy of Bombay government and the foundation of government Sanskrit Colleges and Universities. This instance too can be seen as a new opening in the race for the hold on the Indian cultural heritage as well as the claim on the part of the new reading elites for the control over the cultural memory of the ancient Vedic past through the implementation of modern academic tools of philology and history.[617]

In Bengal, one of the earlier initiatives for bringing out printed editions of Sanskrit religious text was that of printing the *Bhāgavata Purāṇa*. It was one of the more popular *purāṇas* among the Vaiṣṇavas of Bengal who, at the time, followed a few distinct traditions, that shared some common fundamental texts, among which *Bhāgavata Purāṇa*, or *Śrī Bhāgavatam*, was one of–if not the–most influential. It was Bhabānīcaran Bandyopādhyāy, a Brahmin from Burdvan, whose efforts brought to print one of the earliest edition of this *purāṇa*, in 1830. This was printed on so-called cotton paper in a tedious process that took as long as three full years. It attempted to sell at an exorbitant price of RS 40 for ordinary buyers and RS 32 for subscribers.[618] The editions 'tried to simulate the outward appearance of a manuscript', and this strategy proved to be attractive to a number of other

---

616 For a tantalizing numer of edited Sanskrit works by V.L. Paṇśīkar, see Appendix 1: Bombay.

617 For the instances of 'text-book' Veda, see Appendix 1: Bombay. One may not deny the logic of the revealing remarks by Veena Naregal [NAREGAL 2001: 49] when she says that the 'act of specifying the social and spatial boundaries of the [new] "cultivated" elite ... was also simultaneously to assert control over the claims to collective memory, of extending themselves all the way into the ancient past in ways that could now claim the status of "historical" truth' [NAREGAL 2001: 49]. Some of these developments led to rather unexpected effects, like the publication of the History of Vedic literature in Sanskrit (being a partial translation into Sanskrit of an English History of Sanskrit Literature) that came out in Palghat, Kerala from Vadhyar&Sons Press. The Publisher's Foreword to this publication reads: 'Till now the history of Sanskrit Literature was known to Sanskrit Pandits only by name' [Publisher's Forward to *A history of Vedic literature in Sanskrit*, PALGHAT 1928: 3].

618 See BHATIA 2016: 118.

publishers of Sanskrit religious texts. The *Bhāgavata Purāṇa* came to be edited and translated several times by different publishers in the second half of the 19th century. Some of these Bengal publishers also attempted to bring in print editions or translations of Vedic texts. Such was the case of the Bangabasi Press, which, among an array of Sanskrit religious texts, also initiated a translation of the entire four Vedas into Bengali in the last decade of the century.[619] This last initiative seems to have been in line with the general policy of this publisher, to introduce into the emerging literary readership of the modernizing Bengal province, a choice of fundamental religious texts in the new shape of translations into the vernacular, which turned them into a new commodity ready for consumption by the emerging literary public. All those initiatives inevitably situated themselves in specific ways within the shared heritage of the past, either by highlighting the distance between the (allegedly deteriorated) present and the glorious past, or by creating a shortcut through translation, without detail pointing to the time frame. In either case, they represented forms of appropriating the past for the new time and its new challenges.[620]

The act of publishing the Veda in print must have appeared as a bold gesture of appropriation for the present of the glorious past of the Vedic times through a new means of media communication. In the case of texts with such a long history of transmission, this might also include the past of a particularly famous and acknowledged commentary that, in the course of transmission through the ages, became highly authoritative and attached itself to the Vedic text proper. Such was the case of a series of highly authoritative commentaries commissioned in the mid-14th century by the rulers of the Vijayanagara empire and often included in early printed editions of the Vedic *saṃhitās* and *brāhmaṇas* of the 19th century.[621] The very phenomenon, perhaps, should not be seen as anything decisively new and pertaining to the cultural technique of print only. We must remember that the deep-rooted tradition of producing commentaries to religious and scientific works and circulating them in writing could be seen largely in the same way.

---

619 Bhatia 2016: 120.

620 Some of the instances appear to have tacitly taken for granted the magic of print as a powerful means of recreating the canonicity of the Veda. Cf. McLuhan's words on a 'new hypnotic superstition of the book' [McLuhan 1962: 144].

621 See Appendix 1.

Just about the time when the Jesuits were consolidating their early hold on the use of print in the Portuguese possessions of Goa and Kerala, Bhaṭṭoji Dīkṣita, an accomplished grammarian and polymath belonging to a Brahmin community originating from Goa, composed a commentary on the *Ṛgvedasaṃhitā*, which could have been patronized by the Keḷadi kings, the rulers of one of the successor states to the Vijayanagara empire.[622] Titled *Vedabhāṣyasāra*, or the *Essence of the Commentary on the Veda*, the commentary used the generic convention of *sāra*, suggesting the essence or an abridged version of the acknowledged medieval commentary, patronized by the once powerful empire. Not only the title but also elements of its framing formula of beggining (borrowed verbatim from formulas of Vjayanagara period) appear to have operated as a textual strategy for retrieval of the glorious past of the Veda and its imperially sanctioned commentary for its author's contemporaries. Through such a strategy Bhaṭṭoji claimed to have established with his glorious predecessors a communication act in which his own *sāra*-commentary functioned as a necessary medium. Some of the strategies for early publishing the Veda in print seem to bear resemblance to this instance.

As was the case with other Sanskrit texts, the reasons for actual publishing the Veda in print used to differ from case to case, but each of the cases shows how the particular initiative reflected the time and place of its inception and how it took part in shaping the print culture in which it itself was embedded. A number of these enterprises fell within what was generally perceived as a 'reformist' movement, and they often continue to be subsumed in modern academic reflection under this very label. The nationalists and reformists, active in Calcutta and Bombay of the second half of the 19th century, often from upper caste intellectuals and social activists, appropriated the Veda—or rather the idea of the Veda—in ways specific to their own political or social agenda. They put it in the central place in their reinterpretations of what they thought should be acknowledged as Indian original religious tradition. In its allegedly disclosed, or rather redefined image, now represented in print, the Veda was used to to argue either for the Veda's allegedly pristine Hindu beginnings in contrast to colonial reality or—quite to the contrary—for the indigenous Indian roots

622 We know from its colophon that at least one of Bhaṭṭoji's works, the *Tattvakaustubha*, had been patronized by Veṅkatappa Nāyaka, one of the Keḷadi kings, probably around 1600 AD. On Bhaṭṭoji's patrons, see Galewicz 2019.

of demystified modernity. But there were other, less known instances. In a recent study, Shraddha Kumbhojkar shows how the rationale behind the ambitious 1876 *Vedārthayatna*—a gargantuan size edition cum translation of *the Ṛgvedasaṃhitā*—was presented by its initiator and editor Shankar Pandurang in words showing that yet another motif accompanying the initiative of rescuing the 'true' Veda by publishing it in print could be rooted in the idea of modern rationality:

> Shankar Pandurang Pandit was one of the reformers who tried to point out the fallacy of the sacrosanct nature attributed to the Vedas. He noted, 'The Vedic hymns are not composed by sages that were always engaged in penance, and lived in mountain caves, but by poets who were householders, had children and always fought with their enemies riding on horsebacks. We term these poets as Sages and indulge in unprecedented and unfounded imaginations about them. If one of these poets was to resurrect and come in this world, he will be wonderstruck by our prejudices about him.'[623]

The unprecedented and totalizing ambition of this unique project, in the longer run, proved to have fallen victim to its own unrealistic vision, that could not stand the demands of the regional colonial version of print capitalism and, after the first seven volumes appeared, involving the leading indigenous printers of Bombay, it eventually dissipated its initial energy and had to be given up, never to be completed. All in all, in the second half of the 19th century, a decision and act of print publishing of Vedic texts, heavily loaded ideologically as they were, must have been a form of intervention into a new emerging colonial public sphere of social communication. At the same time we can perhaps see in such bald enterprizes an attempt at re-canonization in print, and perhaps also an act of defiance against the colonial machanisms of 'monopolized normative authority over cultural and political spheres.' An act of re-appropriation of one's cultural past and memory.[624]

---

623 Kumbhojkar 2009: 127.

624 For the ideas of imperial control over culture through print, see Naregal 2001: 205.

V.3. Regional print cultures and the Veda

Taking shape slowly towards the middle of the 19th century, regional cultures of print showed an uneven and spatially discontinuous, fragmented development across the Indian subcontinent, while feeding on regional patterns of communication and textual circulation, configurations of power, patronage, and a new economic and political regime. Their development mirrored, answered, and inspired tremendous transformations in the structures of power, statecraft, authority, and communication that the subcontinent was going through, while being gradually absorbed into the globalizing orbit of the emerging British Empire. It marked a general shift of knowledge-production sites and relocation of distribution and text-circulation networks towards new urban centres. In the face of the consolidation of many forms of British hegemony on the subcontinent, a complex interplay evolved between colonial institutions (with their policies towards information, education, religion, and the intellectual heritage of India and their bias for specifically conceived and controlled modalities of circulating information) with diversely conceived and orientated modalities of print use and circulation on the part of missionary and indigenous printing enterprises it came to constitute a newly emerging constellation of media communication, which shaped the Indian part of the British empire. In this process, the emerging regional cultures of print created conditions for, inspired, and accommodated differently configured projects of bringing out authoritative printed editions of Vedic texts in an uneven way, leaving distinct traces of their respective nature on their editorial principles, book format, typographic form, and publishing ideology. While the Company's government activities stimulated editorial projects focused on the Veda in Calcutta, the case of Bombay involved more independent Indian enterprises exploring markets for the printed Vedic texts. At the same time Madras, which had the earliest experiences with print with missionary printing operations well established before 1800 did not develop an early environment for publishing neither Sanskrit nor Vedic texts of any extent comparable to the two former case. This was perhaps due to the regional classic traditions of Tamil that tended to overshadow those of Sanskrit. Among the early books published in print in the Madras at the Government Asylum Press and the Fort St. George College Press (founded 1813) there were no Sanskrit texts at all.[625] Nor did the growing market for printed matter including the operation of numerous pundit printer-publishers in 1830es, felt need for publishing Sanskrit texts which continued up to the times of the beginnings of Madras University and the new missionary printing activities on the Malabar Coast (Basel Mission Press in Mangalore). While benefitting from early and rich printing culture in Tamil and Telugu, in the mid- and later 1800es Madras saw no developments comparable to either that of Calcutta's longstanding considerable patronage for the Sanskrit publishing series of the Asiatic Society of Bengal's Oriental Literary Series or Bombay's Government Book Depot's policy towards publications in Sanskrit, or Bombay indigenous printers' interest in and efforts for building audiences for printing in Sanskrit, including numerous Vedic texts.

Some of those traces continued the earlier and parallel preferences of the regional manuscript cultures and influenced the choice of script, type of text or literary genre. A majority of editions, prepared especially in the north, opted for Devanagari, as did most early modern manuscript 'editions' of this region. In the south, however, things might have looked different; somewhat later, an edition from Kerala in Malayalam script had been produced and preferred to Devanagari by members of the Brahmin communities, among whom memory transmission still persisted in some form or another.[626] Regional preferences may also have had an effect on the form and shape of the book–the *pothī* shape in Maharashtra persisted well into the 20th century–with pirated reprints still in circulation in the second decade of the third millennium (these editions met with some distribution also in other parts of India because of the transregional appeal of Devanagari script, yet in the latter case their shape remained rather foreign to their new users and readers). The choice of typographic format seems to have answered familiar or emerging reading practices or–to use the notion in circulation in a recent current in media studies–distinctly specific cultural techniques of reading. These tendencies might show attempts to reconstitute anew an old communication partner or call to being a new one with the purpose of communicating [the message of] the ancient [treasure of the] Veda to its intended or expected reading constituency. All that took place in the context of the newly formed Indian colonial empire, with

---

625 For a comprehensive survey of the emerging print culture of Madras, see especially Blackburn 2006: 73–116.

626 Nambudiripad 1982.

its diverging, sometimes complementing, sometimes conflicting interests in its own past, and highly contested expectations for the future, in the unknown, transformed post-colonial realities.

More or less distant echoes of European concepts of philologically established Vedic texts can be traced—with varied degrees of success—across Indian editions, starting around the mid-19th century. These gained momentum towards the last two decades and spilled over into the first decades of the 20th century, with monumental national projects like the Poona Vaidika Samśodhana Maṇḍala edition or the gargantuan Vedic translation project of the Calcutta Indian Research Institute, initiated in the forties of the twentieth century. An interesting voice from the milieu of the Indian trained philologists, trying to evaluate a dimension of Indian work done on the field of translating the Veda into Indian regional vernaculars, can be seen in Dandekar, 1942, a year when the WWII raged with not yet not yet known outcome, and the destiny of the new independent Indian state still in the balance. In the opinion by Dandekar formulated at this moment a decisive change in approach among Indian writers could be sensed:

> The Vedas were formerly studied, or rather learnt, mainly as scriptures. The present attitude is that of a historian, who regards the Vedic texts not merely as sacred books but also as valuable sources of the cultural history of ancient India. The spirit of acceptance has given place to the spirit of inquiry. Among the translations in Indian languages, a reference may be made to the Telugu translation of the Vedas by K. C. Ran (Bellary, 1913–15), the Kanarese translation of RV by T.R.S. Venkata-Krishnayya (Bangalore, 1913–15), the Bengalee translation of the four Vedas by D. Lahiri (Howrah, 1919), the Hindi translation of AV by K. Trivedi (Allahabad, 1912–21), the Malyalam translation of RV by P.K. Nambyadiri (Quilon, 1925), and the two Marathi translations of RV, one by Chitravshastri (Poona, 1928) and the other by Patwardhan (Poona, 1942). Of course, in each case the translation is influenced by the view taken by the translator regarding the origin and the nature of the Veda. A complete translation in English of the Vedic samhitas ... is still a desideratum.[627]

Dandekar concluded his 1942 report by indicating that the exemplary Vedic translation project, initiated by the Calcutta Indian Research

[627] Dandekar 1942: 30–31.

Institute, through the process of opening the Veda to the—at least theoretically wide-reading vernacular public—once began, had entered a process of never-ending progress, in which translation from Vedic Sanskrit to the regional languages of modern India became not only a vehicle and medium of transferring the Vedic past to the modern present, but also of unquestionable value in itself. It is rather difficult to measure the impact of the emerging new urban intelligentsia and its urban reading practices on the growth in publishing Sanskrit and Vedic texts. While some of the printed editions of the Veda from late 19th and early 20th centuries were definitely meant for new literate audience, others sought audiences among traditional users whom they targeted by making the print resemble mamuscripts in shape, format and reading practices they implied. Slowly, the printed Veda entered the new public sphere. It may not necessarily be true that the print might 'reinforce the authority of traditional brahmanical texts by making them more generally available.'[628] But the printed Veda might indeed embody the need by the new intelligentsia to contest the 'authority of the traditional brahmanical elite to interpret the shastric and religious texts...'[629]

V.4. Towards a new understanding of reading cultures

This brief concluding paragraph attempts to embrace the concept of 'cultural techniques,' one that has been proposed anew in recent studies as a substitute for that of media, in order to allow for and inspire a new understanding of the working of media communication in cultures and civilizations. The concept emerged earlier in German media studies and gained momentum in the last decade, through its adoption into the Anglo-American tradition of media and communication studies.[630] From this perspective, the technical modalities of specific practices of reading acquire a cultural agency, since in a given historical culture it is not entirely optional how one reads a book. Neither are the options universal, as books always varied widely in concept, material form, modalities of use and social status across cultural milieus. So did manuscript cultures, print cultures as well

628 Naregal 2001: 226.
629 Naregal 2001: 226.
630 See, among else, Siegert 2015, Vismann 2013, Young 2017.

as cultures of reading and communities of readers whose practices would shape, reproduce and modify these cultures.

Complex, uneven, and fragmentary as it was during the nineteenth century Indian subcontinent, the medium of print—as elsewhere, though not necessarily through exactly the same modalities – proved not just to be a carrier of meanings or a 'passive carrier of content' but an 'ontological shifter.'[631] The nature of this shift, however, is not easy to be assessed, since it was necessarily made up of diverse, only partly overlapping—sometimes heterogenous and—meaning-producing practices. We may cautiously say that, as far as the immediate object of this study is concerned, in a general effect, it translated the power of exclusive possession into the new power of control through [selective] inclusion. It largely—though not entirely—took the Veda from the hands of those who possessed it—through class privilege—either by memory or through guarded scripted copies, and transferred it into the new spaces of use in search of new power, new reading constituencies, along with new reading practices. It is of utmost interest to highlight different modalities of this transfer as hidden, or implicit, in the differently conceived of medium of print. The whole spectrum of these varied concepts behind print media will become more visible by indicating its extremes: one would be the use of imperial print as a medium for the monumental uncovering, taking over, and transferring the lost, confused, misconceived, and misunderstood Veda from the plethora of rare, partial, fast deteriorating, handmade copies, with their fragmentary nature, endangered status, and casual storage, into the hands of philology and the empire, with a view to enabling posterity to communicate with the Veda of the past, through its perfected and transparent form, that will not suffer from any kind of communication noise any more.[632] With no intermediary of either a contiguous personal copy or faltering human agency needed any more. To some, this looked like a miracle and the utmost triumph of reason and science, that the Veda could be reconstituted as a transparent and linear textual document, ordered on civilized principles, without the assistance of its hitherto self-made custodians—the Brahmin *paṇḍitas.* In cases from the other end of the spectrum (the SRS 1910 and 1930 and

[631] For the contemporary media studies context and provenance of the terms, see Peters 2015: 25, Siegert 2015.

[632] For this idea of media communication and cultural techniques as conceptual frame for new understanding of historical cultural transfer through printed edition, see Siegert 2015: 33–37.

Ghaisasa RDG 1986), the print with its new cultural technique of reading was imagined to accommodate an equally radical transfer or translation from the medium of memory performance, directly to the print reading performance. Along with the latter, a new conceptualization was offered for the prospective consumers to be convinced. Publishing the Veda in print might also become a political intervention into the public sphere in order to either reinforce, question or contest the brahmanical exclusive hegemony over the right of interpretation of the Vedic traditional scriptural texts.[633] The new spaces of circulation, reading, and use of printed matter proved to be constituted with either old or new kind of users. The early Bombay editors of Stevenson's *Ṛgveda*, early Calcutta publishers of *Śukla Yajurveda*, and late nineteenth century Bombay editors and printers, happened to issue the same Vedic text in entirely different shapes and formats, thus not only targeting diverse expectations of the already known users and practices, but also differentiating, or creating, the new spaces of circulation that remained separate or overlapped with the former. In some cases, one and the same printer-publisher could offer for circulation the same Vedic compendium, as was the case with the *Ṛgvedasaṃhitā*, in codex format for the use of new universities and colleges and the oblong *pothī* format for the use of more traditional Brahmin households, *paṇḍitas* and Vedic recitation schools. Others imagined for the Veda the so-called public space (William Carey dreamed of publishing the Veda for '*publico bono*') or a new kind of reader, the 'Hindu youth'—in the expression of J. Stevenson—who could for themselves see, after the Veda has been exposed to them, and, by comparison, find out the superiority of the Christian truth.

From that time on—in theory at least—anyone could become an actor to populate one of the new spaces of circulation, access to the Veda was believed to have been opened, at least to those who could afford a copy and knew how to read it and make sense of it. At the same time, however, the new elites produced by the new medium of print soon came to seek control over the circulation of the copies in a variety of new inventive ways, and with a view to a new form of empowerment promised by the print and its cultural regimes. Translation into regional vernaculars, that had grown by the end of the nineteenth century and culminated in the late colonial period along with the rise of diverse regional forms of nationalistic movements before WWII, remained just one among an array of these ways.

---

[633] For a discussion on this topic, see Naregal 2017: 257.

Others included control over resources through the systematic collection of manuscripts to be stored in institutionally controlled libraries and represented in an ordered way through printed descriptive catalogues, that organized the indigenous knowledge of colonial subjects according to rational principles. Incidentally, the Veda assumed prominent position in the imperial cataloguing project. Along with these developments, the rise of English medium education with universities and colleges that marked the mid-nineteenth century in all the three Presidencies, and late Provinces, brought the emergence of the modern reading communities and an inevitable re-establishment of literary and scriptural canons through education programs. They involved the Veda not only in print but in a new configuration of the university text-book.[634] Though rather short-lived and sensitive to political trends, the new market for the 'text-book Veda' in the Bombay Province in late 1800es and early 1900es contributed in no mere way to the ongoing process of re-distribution of the sites of textual production, networks of circulation, as well as to redefinition of 'prevailing aesthetic and intellectual norms' and 'meanings of literacy and cultivation.'[635]

With the passage of time, more and more of these organizing principles were seen to have taken over from the pre-print traditional knowledge systems themselves, while more and more new custodians of the Veda showed their mission as serving other goals. The long anxiety accompanying the race for the retrieval and control over the ancient Veda, through the modernity of print media, in the emerging and consolidating colonial empire, culminated, by the late colonial era, in a considerable body of knowledge, which no longer represented exclusively the domain of the empire. The newly formed modern Indian state inherited this anxiety and gave it new shapes, while claiming once again for itself the civilized mission of opening the Veda as part of the greater whole of pan-Indian textual heritage to the global public space of reading, through the medium of digital archive. Once again, the project of opening the heritage of the past through institutionally controlled transfer into new media for new readers, inevitably created new forms of control and closure specific to the new digital world.

---

634 For the numerous instances of the indegenous printer-publishers answer to the emerging market for the college and University oriented 'text-book Veda', see Appendix 1.

635 For an attempt at a conceptualization of these processes, see Naregal 2017: 19.

Abbreviations

ĀpGS: Āpastamba Gṛhya Sūtra
AVS: Atharvaveda Saṃhitā
BU: Bṛhadāraṇyaka Upaniṣad
ChU: Chandogya Upaniṣad
KK: Kṛtya Kalpataru
RDG: Ṛgveda Daśa Grantha
RS: Ṛksaṃhitā = Ṛgvedasaṃhitā
RSBhBh: Ṛksaṃhitā Bhāṣya Bhumikā
RSBh (M): Ṛksaṃhitā Bhāṣya (Müller's edition)
RVidh: Ṛgvidhāna
SALNAQ: South Asia Library Notes & Queries
SRS: Sasvāhākaraprayoganirṇayā samantrakośā ca ṛksaṃhitā
TS: Taittirīyasaṃhitā
YājSm: Yājñavalkya Smṛti

References

Abhyankar, K.V. and G.V. Devasthali, eds., 1978, *Vedavikṛtilakṣaṇa-Saṃgraha*, Poona: Bhandarkar Oriental Research Institute.

A Memoir for the Serampore Tranlations for 1813..., 1815, Kettering: J.G. Fuller.

Baldeus, Ph., 1703 (1671), *A true and exact description of the most celebrated East-India coasts of Malabar and Coromandel* (tr. from Dutch, originally published in 1671), London: Annsham and John Churchill.

Belvalkar, S.K., 1916, 'Foreward' to *Descriptive Catalogue of the Government Collections of Manuscripts Deposited at the Deccan College, Poona*, compiled by the Assistant to the Professor of Sanskrit, Deccan College, Poona, Vol. I, Part I, Bombay: The Government of Bombay, pp. xi–xxxix.

Bernier, F., 1891, *Travels in the Moghul Empire A.D. 1656–1668*, translated by A. Constable, edited by V.A. Smith, Westminster: A. Constable & Co.

Bernier, F., 1830, *Les Voyages de François Bernier ... contenants la descriptions des états du Grand Mogol...*, Vol. I, Paris.

Bhagavat, R.R., 1899, 'Three Interesting Vedic Hymns', *Journal of the Bombay Branch of the Royal Asiatic Society*, 20: 234–56.

Bhandarkar, K.G., 1874, 'The Veda in India', *Indian Antiquary*, Vol. III, pp. 123–135.

Bhandarkar, S.R., 1903, 'On the Search of Sanskrit MSS in the Bombay Circle', *JASB*, Vol. 21, pp. 58–66.

Bijâpûrkar, V.G., ed., 1895, *Ṛiksangraha, or A university selection of vedic hymns; with the commentary of Sâyaṇâchârya*, Bombay.

Bodas, Râjârâm Shâstri and Gore, Shiwarâm, Shâstri, eds., 1888–1890, *Rig-Veda. With Pada pátha and Sáyaná-cháryás Bháshya*, Bomaby.

Bolts, W., 1772, *Considerations on India Affairs respecting the Present State of Bengal and its Dependencies*, London: J. Almon.

Buchanan, F., 1807, *A Journey From Madras Through The Countries Of Mysore, Canara, And Malabar*, Vol. II, London: T. Cadell and W. Davies.

Buchanan, C., 1811, *Christian Researches in Asia: with Notices on the Translation of the Scriptures into the Oriental Languages*, Boston: S.T. Armstrong.

Burnell, A.C., ed., 1873, *The Vaṃśabrāhmaṇa*, (Texte imprimé): being the eighth Brāhmaṇa of the Sāma Veda, together with the commentary of Sāyaṇa, a preface, and index of words, Mangalore: Basel Mission Press.

Bühler, G., 1868, 'Report of: Tour to Southern Maratha Country in search of Sanskrit manuscripts', *Zeitschrift der Deutschen Morgenländischen Gesellschaft*, 22, pp. 315–325.

Bühler, G., 1871, *A catalogue of Sanskrit manuscripts contained in the private libraries of Gujarat, Kathiavad, Kachchh, Sindh, and Khandes*, Bombay.

Bühler, G., 1880, *Report on the search for Sanskrit manuscripts in the Bombay Circle, i.e, Rajputana, the Central Agency, Central India, Berar and the Bombay Presidency, during the year 1879–1880*, Bombay.

Burnell, A.C., 1880, *A Classified Index to the Sanskrit Mss. in the Palace at Tanjore*, London: Trübner.

Carey, W., 1792, *An Enquiry Into The Obligations Of Christians, To Use Means For The Conversion of the Heathens*, Leicester: Ann Ireland.

Carey, W. 1806, *A Grammar of the Sungskrit Language*, Serampore: Mission Press.

Carey, W. and J. Marshman, 1806, *The Ramayuna of Valmeeki in the original Sungskrit with a prose translation and explanatory notes*, Vol. I, Serampore: [Mission Press].

Cassiano, da Macerata, 1771, *Alphabetum Brammhanicum sev Indostanum Universitatis Kasi*, Romae: Typis Sac. Congregationis de Propag. Fide.

Colebrooke, H.T., 1805a, *A grammar of the Sanskrit language*, Calcutta: Company's Press.

Colebrooke, H.T, 1805b, 'On the Vedas or Sacred Writings of the Hindus', *Asiatic Researches* 8: 369–476; (repr. in Colebrooke 1837, 1: 9–113).

Craufurd, Q., 1817, *Researches concerning the Law, Theology, Learning and Commerce, etc. of Ancient and Modern India*, Vol. I, London: Cadell and Davies.

Cunha, J.G. da, 1900, *The origin of Bombay*, Bombay: Royal Asiatic Society's Library.

Dayānanda Sarasvati, 1877-78, *Ṛgvedādibhāṣyabhūmikā*, in *Ṛgvedabhāṣyam*, edited by Yudhiṣṭhir Mīmāṃsak, Āryasamāja-Śatābdi-Saṃskaraṇam, Bahalgarh (Sonipat): Ram Lal Kapoor Trust.

Der Königl. Dänischen Missionarien aus Ost-Indien eingesandter Ausführlichen Berichten, Von dem Werck ihres Amts unter den Heyden, Teil 1–9 (Continuation 1–108) [= *Hallesche Berichte*], Halle: Waisenhaus, 1710–1772.

Downing, J., ed., 1715, *A Brief Account Of The Measures Taken In Denmark, For The Conversion of the Heathen in the East-Indies: And Of The College or Incorporated Society, erected by the King of Denmark for the Propagation of the Gospel* ... (tr. from the High Dutch), London: J. Downing.

Duperron, Anquetil, [Abraham-Hyacynth], 1801–1802, Oupnek'hat (id est Secretum Tegendum),vols 1–2, Argentoratum (Strassbourg)-Paris: Fratres Levrault.

Dutt, N., Manmatha, ed., 1906, *The Rig-Veda Samhita*, Calcutta: Society for the Resuscitation of Indian Literature.

Dutta, Ramesh, Chandra, ed., *Rigbed Sanghita*, 1885, Vol. 1–7, Kolkata.

Edwardes, S.M., 1902, *The Rise of Bombay (Reprinted from the Census of India vol. X 1901)*, Bombay: Times of India Press.

Ellis, F., 1822, 'Account of a Discovery of a modern imitation of the Vedas, with Remarks on the Genuine Works*', *Asiatick Researches*, 14, Calcutta: Filip Pereira, Hindoostani Press, pp. 1–59.

English Records on Shivaji (1659–1682), 1931, Poona: Shiva Charitra Karyalaya.

Fenger, J.F.J., 1863, *History of the Tranquebar Mission: Worked out from the original papers*, Tranquebar: Evangelical Lutheran Missionary Press.

Friend of India (Monthly series), 1824, Vol. VII, Serampore: Mission Press.

Gazeteer of the Bombay Presidency, Vol. XIII, Part I, *Poona*, 1885, Bombay: Government Central Press.

Germann, W., ed., 1867, *Bartholomeus Ziegenbalg's Genealogie der Malabarische Götter*, Madras: Christian Knowledge Society's Press.

Ghose, J.Ch., 1901, *The Engish Works of Raja Rammohun Roy*, Calcutta: Srikanta Roy.

Gildemeister, J., 1847, *Bibliotecae Sanscritae sive Recensus Librorum Sanskritorum...*, Londini: Williams & Norgate.

Gough A., 1878, *Papers Related to the Collection and Preservation of the Records of Ancient Sanskrit Literature in India*, Calcutta: Office of Superintendent of Government Printing 1878.

Gurjara, Janārdana, Mahādeva, ed., 1900, *Ṛksaṃhitā*, Bombay: Nirṇaya Sāgara.

Halhed, B.L., 1778, *A Grammar of the Bengal Language*, Hoogly in Bengal.

Halhed, B.L., 1781 (1776), *A Code of Gentoo Laws or Ordinations of the Pundits from a Persian Translation made from the original written in the Shanscrit language*, London

Henriques, H., 1967 (1586), *Flos Sanctorumm, eṉaṟ Aṭiyār Varalāṟu*, edited by S. Rajamanickam, Tuticorin: Tamil Ilakkiyak Kalakam.

Jacobi, Ch., 1912 (1792), *Some notes on Books and Printing*, London: The Chiswick Press.

Jones, William, 1788, "On the Orthography of Asiatic Words in Roman Letters," *Asiatick Researches* vol. 1 (1788), pp. 1-56.

Jones, William, 1788, "On the Literature of the Hindus" in *Asiatick Researches* vol. I.

Jośi, Bhattadevaśāstri, Pt., ed., *Bhāratīya Saṃskṛtikośa*, Part IV, Pune.

Imperial Gazeteer of India, Vol. VIII: *Behampore to Bombay*, 1908, London: Clarendon Press.

Kaegi, A., 1886, *The Rigveda: the Oldest Literature of the Indians*, translated by R. Arrowsmith, Boston–New York: Ginn and Company (originally published in 1880).

Kaye, J.W., 1854, *The Life and correspondence of Charles, Lord Metcalfe*, Vol. II, London.

Kielhorn, F., 1867, 'Remarks on the Sanskrit Portions of the Catalogue', in *Catalogue of Native Publications in the Bombay Presidency up to 31 Dec. 1864*, 2nd ed., edited by A. Grant, Bombay: Education Society Press, pp. 13–25.

Kṛṣṇācārya, T.A., ed., 1902, *Ṛk-saṃhitā-pada-pāṭhaḥ (padāni)*, Muṃbayyām: Nirṇaya-sāgara Press.

[*Kṛtyakalpataru*:] *Kṛtyakalpataru of Bhaṭṭa Lakṣmīdhara*, 1941, Vol. V, Dānakāṇḍa, edited by K.V. Rangaswami Aiyengar, Baroda: Oriental Institute.

Lettres édifiantes et curieuses, écrites des missions étrangères. nouvelle édition, mémoires des indes, 1819, vol. 8, Lyon: J. Vernarel (second edition).

Lettres édifiantes et curieuses, écrites des missions étrangères, 1819, edited by Y.M.M.T. de Querbeuf, T. 7, Lyon: Vernarel et al.

LONG, James, 1855, 'Returns Relating to the ative Printing Presses and Publications in Bengal' in *Selections from the Recods of the Bengal Government* No 22, Calcutta: Thos. Jones, pp. 83–119.

Mādhyandina Mantra Saṃhita, 1929, Bombay: Veṅkateśwara Steam Press.

MALABARI, Phiroze, B.M., 1910, *Bombay in the Making*, London: Fisher Unwin.

MARSHMAN, J.C., 1859, *The Life and Times of Carey, Marshman, and Ward: Embracing the History of the Serampore Mission*, 2 vols., London: Longman, Brown, Green, Longmans, and Roberts.

MENON, P.Sh., 1878, *A History of Travancore*, Madras: Higginbotham and Co.

Memorial Papers 1882, *Memorial Papers of the American Marathi Mission 1813–1881*, Bombay: Education Society's Press, Byculla.

METZGER, G.J., tr., 1869, *Genealogy of the South Indian Gods ... by Bartholomeus Ziegenbalg*, Madras: Higginbotham & Co.

Missionary Register for the M DCCCXXV, 1825, London: L.B. Seeley & Son.

Missionary Register for the M DCCCXXXIII, 1833, London: L.B. Seeley & Son.

MITCHELL, J.M., 1899, *In Western India: Recollections of My Early Missionary Life*, Edinburgh: David Douglas.

MITRA, Rājendralāla, ed., 1876, *Aitareya Áranyaka*, with the commentary of Sāyaṇa Āchārya, Calcutta: Asiatic Society of Bengal.

MITRA, Rājendralāla, ed., 1859–1862, *Taittirīyabrāhmaṇam*, Fasciculus III–XXII (Texte imprimé) of the Black Yajurveda, with the commentary of Sāyanācārya, Calcutta.

MÜLLER, F.M., 1878, *Lectures on the Origin and Growth of Religion as Illustrated by the Religions of India*, London: Longman, Green, and Co.

MÜLLER, F.M., 1882, *Lectures on the Origin and Growth of Religion*, London: Longmans, Green and Co (a facsimile reprint of 2005 by Adamans Media) [Lecture III: 'The Ancient Literature of India. So far as it supplies materials for the study of the origin of religion', pp. 132–172].

MÜLLER, F.M., 1891, *The Physical Religion: The Gifford Lectures*, London: Longmans, Green & Co.

MÜLLER, F.M., 1892, *Natural Religion: The Gifford Lectures delivered before the University of Glasgow in 1888*, London: Longman, Green and Co.

MÜLLER, F.M., 1899, *Auld Lang Syne Second Series: My Indian Friends*, London–Bombay: Longmans, Green, And Co.

MÜLLER, (F.)M., ed., 1849–1874, *Rig-Veda-Sanhita, The Sacred Hymns of the Brahmans, together with the Commentary of Sayanacharya*, 6 vols., London: W.H. Allen & Co.

MÜLLER, F.M., ed., 1890–1892, *Rig-Veda-Samhitâ, the Sacred Hymns of the Brâhmans, together with the Commentary of Sâyanâkârya*, 2nd ed., 4 vols., London: Henry Frowde.

MÜLLER, M.F., 1983, *Rig-Veda-Samhitā, the Sacred Hymns of the Brāhmans, together with the Commentary of Sāyanāchārya*, 5 vols., Varanasi: Motilal Banarsidas (originally printed in 1890–1892).

NAGAM AIYA, V., 1906, *The Travancore State Manual*, 3 vols., Trivandrum: Travancore Government Press.

NAMBUDIRIPAD, O.M.C. Narayanan, ed., 1982, *Ṛgvedam Bhaṣa Bhaṣyam (Deviprasādam)*, Vol. I, Trichur: Vadakke Madham Brahmaswom.

OMONT, H.A., 1902, *Missions archéologiques françaises en Orient aux XVIIe et XVIIIe siècles*, Documents publiés par Henri Omont, Paris: Imprimerie nationale.

PAṆAŚĪKARA, V.L, ed., 1910, *Sasvāhākaraprayoganirṇayā samantrakośāca ṛksaṃhitā*, Bombay: Tukaram Javaji.

PAṆŚĪKAR, ŚĀSTRĪ, V.L., ed., 1930, *Sasvāhākaraprayoganirṇayā samantrakośā ca ṛksaṃhitā*, Mumbai: Nirṇaya Sāgara Press.

PETERSON, P., 1888, *Hymns from the Rigveda edited with Sayana's commentary, notes and a translation*, Bombay: Government Central Book Depot.

PHILIPPS, J.T., tr., 1718, *Thirty Four Conferences between Danish Missionaries and the Malabarian Bramans (or heathen Priests) in the East Indies*, London: Saint Paul's Church Yard.

POLIER, M.É. DE and A.-L.-H. DE POLIER 1809, *Mythologie des Indous* [Texte imprimé], travaillée par Mme la Chnesse de Polier, sur des manuscrits authentiques apportés de l'Inde, par feu Mr. le Colonel de Polier, membre de la Société asiatique de Calcutta..., Roudolfstadt and Paris: F. Schoell.

Prayogaratnam by Nārāyaṇa Bhaṭṭa, edited by Vāsudeva Lakṣmaṇa Śarmā Paṇaśīkara, Bombay: Nirṇaya Sāgara Press, 1915.

Ṛgvedadaśagrantha, 1986, ed. Vinayaka Ghaisasa, Pune.

Ṛgvedakalpadruma, MS N191, Cat. No 45, in the Catalogue of MSS in the Manuscript Library of Chatrapati Shahuji Maharaj University, Kolhapur.

Ṛgvedamantrasaṃhitā (*yajñikaprayogānukrāma*), pothī, Śake 1826 (= A.D. 1904), edited by Janārdana Mahādeva Gurjara, Rāmavāḍī, Mumbai.

Ṛgvedamantrasaṃhitā, 1910, edited by Janardana Mahādeva Gurjara, Mumbai.

Ṛgvedamantrasaṃhitā, 2009, edited by V.L. Panshikar, Mumbai: Nirṇaya Sāgar (reprint of an earlier edition probably from the beginning of the 20th century).

Rig-Veda Samhita in eight ashtakas (parts) with pada patha & Sayanacharya's Bhasyha, Śaka 1810 (= A.D. 1888), edited by Maha-mahopadhyaya Rajaram Shastri Bodas & Shiwaram Shastri Gore, Bombay: Tukaram Tatya, Ganpat Krishnaji Press.

ROEBUCK, Th., 1819, *The Annals of the College of Fort William*, Calcutta: Philip Pereira, Hindostanee Press.

RÖER, H., 1847, 'Report on the Vedas', 1847, *Journal of the Asiatic Society of Bengal* XVI, part I, pp. 505–18.

RÖER, E., 1848, *The First Two Lectures of the Sanhita of the Rig Veda with the Commentary of the Madhvacharya and an English Translation of the Text*, Calcutta: Asiatic Society of Bengal, printed by J. Thomas at the Baptist Mission Press.

ROGERIUS, A., 1915 (1651), *De Open-Deure Tot Het Verborgen Heydendom*, edited by W. Caland, 'S-Gravenhage: Martinus Nijhoff.

ROGERS, A., 1663, *Offne Thür zu dem verborgenen Heydenthum* (tr. from Dutch original of 1651), Nurnberg: Johan Andreas Endters.

ROSEN, F., ed., 1830, *Rig-Vedae Specimen*, London: Impensis Joannis Taylor, printed by J.L. Cox.

ROSEN, F., 1838, *Rigveda Sanhita. Liber Primus, Sanscritè et Latinè*, London: Printed for the Oriental Translation Fund of Great Britain and Ireland, W. Allen & Co.

SAINTE-CROIX, Guillaume Emmanuel Joseph Guilhem de Clermont Lodève, baron de, 1788, *L'Ezour-Vedam Ou Ancien Commentaire Du Vedam Contenant l'exposition des opinions religieuses et philosophiques des Indiens. Traduit du Samscretan par un Brame*, Revu & publié avec des observations préliminaires, des notes & des éclaircissemens, 2 vols., Yverdon: De Felice. 'Sacred Literature of the Hindus', 1844 [no author mentioned], *The North British Review*, Vol. I, No 1, pp. 366–97.

SASTRY ANANTA KRISHNA, L., ed., 1921, *Kavīndrācāryasūcipatram, Kavindracharya List*, Baroda: Central Library.

SHARMA, Śrīpad, ed., 1940, *Ṛgveda saṃhitā. Mahārāṣṭrīyānekavaidikānam sahāyyena vividha prācīnalikhita pustaka-pāṭhānusāreṇa ca*, Aundh: Bhārat mudraṇālya mudrayitvā svādhyāyamandala dvārā prakāśita.

SONTAKE, N.S. et al, eds., *Ṛgvedasaṃhitā with the Commentary of Sāyaṇācārya*, 1933–42, Poona: Vaidika Saṃśodhana Maṇḍala.

SHASTRI, P.P.S. AND SHASTRI, K.L.V., 1927, *A History of Vedic Literature in Sanskrit* (translation of Chapters I–IX of MacDonell's *History of Sanskrit Literature*), Kalpati-Palghat: Subraahmanya Vadhyar, printed at St. Johseph Industrial School, Trichinopoly and K.E.P. Works, Palghat.

SHIVANATHA AHITAGNI and SHANKARDATTA SHASTRI, eds., 1904–, *Ṛgvedasaṃhitā* (*vaidika jivan vyākhyāyutā*), Lahore: Panjab Ekanomikal Yantralay (9 vols.).

SINNER, J.R., 1793, *La religion des Bramins de l'Indostan: sur le purgatoire et la metempsychose*, Bern: Société Typographique.

SMITH, G., 1902 (1884), *The life of William Carey, shoe-maker & missionary*, London: J.M. Dent; New York: E.P. Dutton.

SONNERAT, P., 1782, *Voyage aux Indes Orientale et la Chine 1774–81*, 2 vols., Paris: Sonnerat, Froulé, Nyon, Barrois.

STEVENSON, J., 1833, *Trividyā Trigunātmikā = The Threefold Knowledge* (Sukta 1–35 of the first mandal of the Ṛgveda, with Sanskrit notes), Bombay: American Mission Press.

STEVENSON, J., 1842, *Translation of the Sanhitá of the Sámaveda*, London: Printed for the Oriental Fund of Great Britain and Irland, Allec & Co.

STEVENSON, J., 1843a (1833), *Principles of Murathee Grammar*, Bombay: Collete & Co., American Mission Press, (originally published Calcutta 1833).

STEVENSON, J., 1843b, ed., *Sanhitá of the Sáma-Veda*, From mss. prepared for the press by the Rev. J. Stevenson and printed under the supervision of H.H. Wilson, London: For the Society for the publication of oriental texts.

SVĀMIGAṄEŚVARĀNANDA, 1970, *Bhagavān Vedaḥ / sampādakah. Svāmigaṅgeśvarānanda Udāsīnaḥ*, Bambāi: Udāsīnasadgurugaṅgeśvarajanakalyāṇanyāsaḥ.

Śabdakalpadruma, 1961, Vol. IV, Delhi: Motilal Banarsidas.

ŚASTRI, Ganapati, T., ed., 1923, *Âśvalâyanagrihyasûtra*, Trivandrum: Government Press.

Śuklayajurvedaḥ Vājasaneyisaṃhitā Mādhyandinīśākhā (*with Mahīdharadīpa*), 1844, Kolkatta: Satya Press.

Tātya, Tukārāma, ed., 1887, *Ṛgvedasaṃhitā* [without Bhashya, Theosophical Society Fund], Mumbai: Gaṇapatakṛṣṇājī Mudrālaya.

Tavernier, J.B., 1680, *A Collection of Several Relations and Treatises*, London: at the Angel in St Paul's Churchyard.

The Oriental Christian Spectator, Vol. IV (1833) and Vol. CLIV (1854), Bombay: American Missionary Press.

The Theosophist, 1888, Vol. X, No. 110 and 1889, No. 112 (January).

Trisandhā = Bhattatiripatu, K.P.C. Anujanan & Viṣṇu Bhaṭṭatirippāṭu, eds., 1988, *Trisandhāparipāṭī of Kunnattūr Paṭiññāṟēṭattu Kṛṣṇan Bhaṭṭatirippāṭṭu with a Vivaraṇa of Kaliyattu Parameśvarabhārati Svāmiyāl*, Kunnaṃkuḷam: Pañcāṅgaṃ Press.

Upadhyaya, P. Baladeva, ed., 1958, *Vedabhāṣyabhūmikāsaṅgrahaḥ* [VBhBhS], Varanasi: Caukhambā Saṃskṛta Sīrīja Āphisa (originally published in 1934).

Vedârthayatna or an Attempt to Interpret the Vedas. A Marâṭhî and English translation of the Rig Veda, with the Original Saṃhitâ and Pada Texts in Sanskrit, 1876–1882, edited by Shankar Pandurang Pandit, Vol. 1–4, 5, parts 1–9, Bombay: Indu-Prakash Press / Nirṇaya Sāgar Press.

Vithal, Shamarav, ed., 1889, *Viśvaguṇādarśacampū mahākavi śrīveṅkatādhvariviracitā śrīmanmadhurasubbāśāstriṇā viracitayā bhāvadarpaṇākhyāyā ṭīkayā saṇāthīkṛtā*, Bombay: Karnataka Press.

Vishva Bandhu, ed., 1965, *Ṛgveda with the Padapāṭha and the Available Portions of the Bhāṣya-s by Skandasvāmin and Udgītha, the Vyākhyā by Veṅkaṭa-Mādhva and Mudgala's Vṛtti Based on Sāyaṅabhāṣya*, Part I, Hoshiarpur.

Wilkins, Ch., 1808, *A Grammar of the Sanskrĭta language*, London: W. Bulmer.

Wilson, H.H., 1819, 'Biographic notice on Colonel Polier', *The Asiatic Asiatic Journal and Monthly Register for British India and its Dependencies*, Vol. 7, No. 41, pp. 465–471 and 569–571.

Winternitz, M., 1897, *Mantrapatha or the Prayer Book of the Āpastambins (Anecdota Oxonienisia, Aryan Series* VIII), Oxford: Clarendon Press.

Catalogues

Aufrecht, T.H., 1962, *Catalogus Catalogorum. An Alphabetical Register of Sanskrit Works and Authors*, Pt. I–III, Wiesbaden: Steiner (originally published 1891–1896).

Bendall, C., ed., 1902, *Catalogue of the Sanskrit manuscripts in the British Museum*, British Museum, Dept. of Oriental Printed Books and Manuscripts, London: [Gilbert and Rivington].

Biswas S.C. and M.K. Prajapati, eds., 1998, *Bibliographic Survey of Indian Manuscript Catalogues*, Delhi: Eastern Book Linkers.

Burnell, A.C., 1880, *A Classified Index to the Sanskrit Mss. in the Palace at Tanjore*, London: Trübner.

Catalogue of Native Publications in the Bombay Presidency up to 31 Dec. 1864, 1867, 2nd ed., Bombay: Education Society Press.

Catalogue of Native Publications in the Bombay Presidency from 1st Jan. 1865 to 30 June 1867, 1869, prepared by J.B. Peile, Bombay: Education Society Press.

Catalogue of the India Office Library: Sanskrit Books, 1953, edited by P. Natha and J.B. Chaudhuri, 1953, London: Her Majesty's Stationary Office.

Catalogus Catalogorum. An Alphabetical Register of Sanskrit Works and Authors, edited by T. Aufrecht, 1891, Leipzig: Brockhaus.

DANDEKAR, R.N., 1946, *Vedic Bibliography*, Vol. I, Bombay: Karnatak Publishing House.

[C INDIA OFFICE 1887:] *Catalogue of the Sanskrit Manuscripts in the Library of the India Office*, Part I: Vedic Manuscripts, edited by J. Eggeling, London.

[DC MADRAS 1901:] *Descriptive Catalogue of the Sanskrit Manuscripts of the Government Oriental Manuscript Library, Madras*, 1901, Vol. I, Part 1, edited by M. Seshagiri Sastri, Madras.

[DC MADRAS 1904:] *A Descriptive Catalogue of the Sanskrit Manuscripts in the Government Oriental Manuscripts Library, Madras*, 1904, Vol. I, part 2–3, edited by M. Shagiri Sastri, M. Rangacharya & Rao Bahadur, Madras Government Press.

[DC TANJORE 1928:] *A Descriptive Catalogue of the Sanskrit Manuscripts in the Tanjore Mahārāja Serfoji's Sarasvatī Mahāl Library, Tanjore*, 1928, Vol. I–II, edited by P.P.S. Sastri, Srirangam: Vani Vilas Press.

[DC POONA 1916:] *Descriptive Catalogue of the Government Collections of Manuscripts Deposited at the Deccan College, Poona*, 1916, Vol. I, part I, compiled by N.D. Banhatti et al., Bombay: Government Central Press.

[DC ADYAR 1908:] *Descriptive Catalogue of Sanskrit Manuscripts in the Adyar Library*, 1908, Vol. I – *Upaniṣads*, edited by O. Schrader, Mylapore–Georgetown.

[DC ADYAR 1947:] *Descriptive Catalogue of Sanskrit Manuscripts in the Adyar Library*, 1947, Vol. VI – *Grammar, Prosody, Lexicography*, edited by P. Krishnamacharya, Madras.

FOSTER, W., 1919, *A Guide to the India Office Records 1600–1858*, London: Eyre and Spottiswoode.

New Catalogus Catalogorum, 1937–2012, Vol. I–XIX, Madras.

Secondary Sources

AGRASENPUTRA, R., 1928, *The Marwari Leaders of India*, Calcutta: Lajpatrai.

AITHAL, Parameswara K., 1991, *Veda-Lakṣaṇa: Vedic Ancillary Literature: A Descriptive Bibligraphy*, Stuttgart: Steiner.

AIYENGAR, Rangaswami K.V., ed., 1941, 'Introduction' to *Kṛtyakalpataru of Bhaṭṭa Lakṣmīdhara*, Vol. V, *Dānakāṇda*, Baroda: Oriental Institute.

ALI, Daud, 2013, 'The Image of the Scribe in Early Medieval Sources', in: *Irreverent History: Essays for M.G.S. Narayanan*, edited by D. Davis and K. Veluthat, Delhi: Primus Books.

ANDERSON, B., 1991, *Imagined Communities: Reflections on the Origin and Spread of Nationalism*, revised edition, New York: Verso (originally published in 1983).

Ballantyne, T., 2007, 'What Difference Does Colonialism Make: Reassessing Print and Social Change in the Age of Global Imperialism', in: *Agent of Change: Print Culture Studies after Elizabeth L. Eisenstein*, edited by S.A. Baron, E.N. Lindquist, and E.F. Shevlin, Amherst: University of Massachusetts Press, pp. 342–353.

Bauman, Z., 1987, *Legislators and Interpreters: On Modernity, Post-Modernity and Intellectuals*, Cambridge: Polity Press.

Baretto Xavier, A., Županov, I.G., 2015, *Catholic Orientalism: Portuguese Empire: Indian Knowledge (16th–18th Centuries)*, Delhi: Oxford University Press.

Bayly, C.A., 1996, *Empire and Information: Intelligence Gathering and Social Communication in India, 1780–1870*, Cambridge: Cambridge University Press.

Bellenoit, H.J., 2017, *The Formation of the Colonial State in India: Scribes, Paper and Taxes, 1760–1860*, London and New York: Routledge.

Bhabha, H.K., 1987, 'Signs Taken for Wonders: Questions of Ambivalence and Authority under a Tree outside Delhi, May 1817', *Critical Inquiry*, Vol. 12, No. 1 ('"Race," Writing, and Difference'), pp. 144–165.

Bhatia, V., 2016, 'Six Blind Men and the Elephant', in *Founts of Knowledge: Book History in India*, edited by A. Gupta and S. Chakravorty, New Delhi: Orient Black Swan.

Blackburn, S., 2006 (2003), *Print, Folklore and Nationalism in Colonial South India*, Delhi: Permanent Black.

Blackburn, S., 1988, *Singing of Birth and Death Texts in Performance*, Philadelphia: University of Pennsylvania Press.

Bolter, J.D. and R. Grusin, 1999, *Remediation: Understanding New Media*, Cambridge, MA: MIT Press.

Bowen, H.V., 2006, *The Business Of Empire: The East India Company And Imperial Britain, 1756–1833*, New York: Cambridge University Press.

Bowker, G. and S.L. Star, 1999, *Sorting Things Out: Classification and Its Consequences*, Cambridge, MA: MIT Press.

Boyarin, J., ed., 1993, *The Ethnography of Reading*, Berkeley: University of California Press [electronic text at http://ark.cdlib.org/ark:/13030/ft009nb089/, accessed on 25 August 2018].

Bronkhorst, J., 2002, 'Literacy and Rationality in Ancient India', *Asiatische Studien / Études Asiatiques*, Vol. 56, No. 4, pp. 797–831.

Bronkhorst, J., 2011, *Buddhism in the Shadow of Brahmanism*, Leide-Bostone, Brill.

Carruthers, M., 2008 (1990), *The Book of Memory: A Study of Memory in Medieval Culture*, Cambridge: Cambridge University Press.

Castets, J., 1935, *L'ezour védam de voltaire et les pseudo-védams de Pondichéry*, Pondichéry: Imprimerie Moderne.

Cavallo, G., 2001, 'Lire, écrire et mémoriser les Saintes Ecritures', in: *Des Alexandries II. Les metamorphoses du lecteur*, edited by C. Jacob, Paris: Bibliothèque Nationale, pp. 87–102.

Certeau de, M., 1990 (1980), *L'invention du quotidien. 1. Arts de faire*, Paris: Gallimard.

Certeau de, M., 1975, *L'écriture de l'histoire*, Paris: Gallimard.

CHAKRAVARTY, A., 2017, 'Catholic Missionary Texts', in: *Early Modern Emotions: An introduction*, edited by S. Broomhall, New York: Routledge, pp. 118–120.

CHAMBERS, N., 2007, *Joseph Banks and the British Museum: The World of Collecting, 1770–1830*, London: Pickering & Chatto.

CHARTIER, R., 1989, 'General Introduction: Print Culture', in: *Culture of Print: Power and the Uses of Print in Early Modern Europe*, edited by R. Chartier, translated by L.G. Cochrane, Cambridge: Polity Press, pp. 1–10.

CHARTIER, R., 2003 (1985), *Pratiques de la lecture*, Paris: Payot.

CHARTIER, R., 2004, 'The Text Between the Voice and the Book', in: *Voice Text Hypertext: Emerging Practices in Textual Studies*, edited by R. Mondiano et al., Seattle and London: University of Washington Press, pp. 54–71.

CHATTERJEE, R., 2006, *Empires of the Mind: A History of the Oxford University Press in India Under the Raj*, New Delhi: Oxford University Press.

CIOTTI, G. and M. FRANCESCHINI, 2016, 'Certain Times in Uncertain Places: A Study on Scribal Colophons of Manuscripts Written in Tamil and Tamilian Grantha Scripts', in: *Tracing Manuscripts in Time and Space Through Paratexts*, edited by G. Ciotti and H. Lin, Berlin and Boston: De Gruyter, pp. 59–130.

COHN, B.S., 1996, *Colonialism and Its Forms of Knowledge: The British in India*, Princeton: Princeton University Press.

COLAS, G., 1999, 'The Criticism and Transmission of Texts in Classical India', *Diogenes*, Vol. 47, Issue 186, pp. 30–43.

COLAS, G., 2001, 'Critique et transmission des textes dans la littérature sanskrite', in: *Des Alexandries I. Du livre au texte*, edited by L. Giard and Ch. Jacob, Paris: Bibliothèque nationale de France, pp. 309–328.

COLAS, G., 2012, 'A Cultural Encounter in the Early 18th Century: The Collection of South Indian Manuscripts by the French Jesuit Fathers of the Carnatic Mission', in: *Aspects of Manuscript Culture in South India*, edited by S. Rath, Leiden and Boston: Brill, pp. 69–80.

COLAS, G. and F. RICHARD, 1984, 'Le fonds Polier à la Bibliothèque nationale', *Bulletin de l'Ecole française d'Extrême-Orient*, Vol. 73, No. 1, pp. 99–123.

COLIER, P. and J.R. CONNOLLY, 2016, 'Print Culture Histories Beyond the Metropolies: An Introduction', in: *Print Culture Histories Beyond the Metropolies*, edited by J.R. Connolly et al., Toronto, Buffalo and London: University of Toronto Press, pp. 3–25.

CONNOLLY, J.R. et al., eds., 2016, *Print Culture Histories Beyond the Metropolis*, Toronto, Buffalo and London: University of Toronto Press.

COPLAND, J., 2006, 'Christianity as an Arm of Empire: The Ambiguous Case of India under the Company, c. 1813–1858', *The Historical Journal*, Vol. 49, No. 4, pp. 1025–1054.

COTTON, E., 1949, *East Indiamen: The East India Company's Maritime Service*, London: Batchworth Press.

DAGENAIS, J., 1994, *The Ethics of Reading in Manuscript Culture: Glossing the Libro de Buen Amor*, Princeton: Princeton University Press.

DANDEKAR, R.N., ed., 1942, *Progress of Indic Studies 1917–1942*, Poona: Bori.

Dandekar, R.N., 1961, *Vedic Bibliography*, Vol. 2, Poona: University of Poona.

Dane, J.A., 2003, *The Myth of Print Culture Essays on Evidence, Textuality, and Bibliographical Method*, Toronto: University of Toronto Press.

Darnton, R., 2007, '"What Is the History of Books?' Revisited', *Modern Intellectual History*, Vol. 4, No. 3, pp. 495–508.

Darnton, R., 2001, 'Literary Surveillance in the British Raj: The Contradictions of Liberal Imperialism', *Book History*, Vol. 4, pp. 133–176.

Darnton, R., 2002, 'Book Production in British India', *Book History*, Vol. 5, pp. 239–262.

Darnton, R., 2005, 'Discourse and Diffusion', *Contributions to the History of Concepts*, Vol. 1, No. 1, pp. 21–28.

Dash, S., 2007, *New Lights on Manuscriptology: A Collection of Articles of Prof. K.V. Sharma*, Chennai: Sree Sarada Education Society Research Centre (especially 'Propagation of Written Literature in Indian Tradition', pp. 80–94, originally printed in *Adyar Library Bulletin* 1991 Vol. 55, pp. 15–31).

Deshpande, M., 1990, 'The Changing Concept of the Veda: From Speech-Acts to Magical Sounds', *Adyar Library Bulletin*, Vol. 54, pp. 1–40.

Deshpande, M., 2001, 'Pandit and Professor: Transformations in the 19th Century Maharashtra', in: *The Pandit: Traditional Scholarship in India*, edited by A. Michaels, Delhi: Manohar, pp. 119–153.

Deshpande, M., 2011, 'From Orality to Writing: Transmission and Interpretation of Pāṇini's Aṣṭādhyāyī', in: *Veda-Vedanga and Avesta Between Orality and Writing*, edited by J. Rotaru and J.E.M. Houben, Bucharest: Biblioteca Metropolitană Bucuresti, pp. 57–100.

Diehl, K.S., 1968, 'Bengali Types and Their Founders', *The Journal of Asian Studies*, Vol. 27, No. 2 (Feb.), pp. 335–338.

Diehl, K.S., 1981, 'Cover [article for]', *The Journal of Library History (1974–1987)*, Vol. 16, No. 1, Libraries & Culture I (Winter), pp. 4–7.

Ebeling, S., 2010, *Colonzing the Realm of Words: Transformations in Nineteenth Century Tamil Literature*, Albany: State University of New York Press.

Ebeling, S., 2009, 'The College of Fort St George and the Transformation of Tamil Philology During the Nineteenth Century', in: *The Madras School of Orientalism: Producing Knowledge in Colonial South India*, edited by Th.R. Trautmann, New Delhi: Oxford University Press, pp. 233–262.

Eisenstein, E.L., 1979, *The Printing Press as an Agent of Change: Communications and Cultural Transformations in Early-Modern Europe*, Cambridge: Cambridge University Press.

Eisenstein, E.L., 2005 (1986), *Printing Revolution in Early Modern Europe*, new edition, Cambridge: Cambridge University Press.

Eisenstein, E.L., 2011, *Divine Art, Infernal Machine: The Reception of Printing in the West from First Impressions to the Sense of an Ending*, Philadelphia and Oxford: University of Pennsylvania Press.

Febvre, L. and H.-J. Martin, 1976, *The Coming of the Book: The Impact of Printing, 1450–1800*, London: Verso (originally published in French in 1956).

Figueira, D., 1994, 'The Authority of an Absent Text: The Veda, Upangas, Upavedas and Upnekhata in European Thought', in: *Authority, Anxiety, and Canon: Essays in Vedic Interpretation*, edited by L. Patton, Albany: State University of New York Press, pp. 201–233.

Fihl, E. and A.R. Venkatachalapathy, eds., 2014, *Beyond Tranquebar: Grappling Across Cultural Borders in South India*, Delhi: Orient Blackswan.

Finkelstein, D. and A. McCleery, 2013 (2005), *An Introduction to Book History*, 2nd ed., London and New York: Routledge.

Fischer, S.R., 2004, *A History of Reading*, London: Reaktion Books.

Fleming, B. and R. Mann, eds., 2014, 'Introduction' to *Material Culture and Asian Religions: Text, Image, Object*, edited by B. Fleming and R. Mann, London: Rutledge.

Formigatti, C., 2016, 'A Forgotten Chapter in South Asian Book History? A Bird's Eye View of Sanskrit Print Culture', in: *Tibetan Printing: Comparison, Continuities, and Change*, edited by H. Diemberger, F.-K. Ehrhard, and P. Kornicki, Leiden and Boston: Brill.

Fraser, R. and Hammond, M., eds., 2008, *Books Without Borders*, Vol. 2: *Perspectives from South Asia*, New York: Palgrave Macmillan.

Frykenberg, R.E., 1965, 'Elite Groups in a South Indian District: 1788–1858', *The Journal of Asian Studies*, Vol. 24, No. 2, pp. 261–281.

Galewicz, C., 2003, 'A Keen Eye on Details: Reviving Ritual Perfection in Trichur Somayaga 2003', *Bulletin d'études indiennes*, Vol. 21, No. 1, pp. 239–253.

Galewicz, C., 2004, 'Kaṭavallūr Ānyōnyam: A Competition in Vedic Chanting?', in: *The Vedas: Texts, Languag & Ritual*, edited by A. Griffiths and J.E.M. Houben, Groningen: Egbert Forsten, pp. 361–383.

Galewicz, C., 2005a, 'L'Anyōnyam: Un rituel de récitation des textes sacrés au Kerala', *Annales. Histoire, Sciences Sociales*, 60e Année, No. 3, pp. 551–571.

Galewicz, C., 2005b, 'Why Should the Flower of Dharma be Invisible? Sāyaṇa's Vision of the Unity of the Veda', in: *Boundaries, Dynamics and Construction of Traditions in South Asia*, edited by F. Squarcini, Firenze: Firenze University Press, pp. 325–360.

Galewicz, C. and Sudyka, L. 2005, 'If you know one thousand ślokas, you are half a poet: on the aksara-śloka traditions of Kerala' (with L. Sudyka), in *Cracow Indological Studies*, Vol. VII, 2005, pp. 295–315.

Galewicz, C., 2006, 'Fourteen Strongholds of Knowledge: On Scholarly Commentaries, Authority and Power in XIV century India', in: *Texts of Power: The Power of the Text*, edited by C. Galewicz, Kraków: Homini.

Galewicz, C., 2010a, *A Commentator in Service of the Empire: Sāyaṇa and the Royal Project of Commenting on the Whole of the Veda*, Wien: DeNobili.

Galewicz, C., 2010b, 'Inscribing Scripture Through Ritual: On the Ritual Cycle of Trisandha', in: *Grammars and Morphologies of Ritual Practices in Asia*, edited by A. Michaels and A. Mishra, Wiessbaden: Harassowitz, pp. 117–140.

Galewicz, C., 2011a, 'All the Books You Need to Understand the World Around You: Knowledge Classifications in the Yāmalāṣṭakatantra and the Library of Kāvīndrācārya

Sarasvatī', in: *Text Divisions & Classifications of Knowledge in Literary and Epistemic Cultures of Pre-Modern India*, edited by C. Galewicz, Kraków: Institute of Oriental Philology, Jagiellonian University, pp. 127–164.

Galewicz, C., 2011b, 'Let Siva's Favour be Alike with Scribes and with Reciters: Motifs for Copying or not Copying the Veda', in: *Veda-Vedanga and Avesta Between Orality and Writing*, edited by J. Rotaru and J.E.M. Houben, Bucharest: Biblioteca Metropolitană Bucuresti, pp. 113–146.

Galewicz, C., 2011c, 'La mémoire et l'oubli. La mémorisation du Ṛgveda chez les Nambudiris du Kérala', in: *Les mains de l'intellect, Lieux de Savoir* II, edited by C. Jacob, Paris: Éditions Albin Michel, pp. 681–703.

Galewicz, C., 2012, 'Texts and Communities: The Manuscripts of the Lost Yāmalāṣṭakatantra', in: *Aspects in Manuscript Culture in South India*, edited by S. Rath, Leiden: Brill, pp. 81–107.

Galewicz, C., 2014, 'A Socio-textual Ecology of the Ṛgvedadaśagrantha', in: *Rethinking Western Inida: The Changing Contexts of Culture, Society and Religion*, edited by D. Deak and J. Jaspers, Delhi: Orient Blackswan, pp. 48–71.

Galewicz, C., 2016, 'The Power of the Printed Veda', in: *Vedic Śākhas: Past, Present, Future*, edited by J.E.M. Houben, J. Rotaru, and M. Witzel, Cambridge: Harvard University Press, pp. 359–390.

Galewicz, C. 2019, 'The Rājapur Manuscript of Bhaṭṭoji's *Vedabhāṣyasāra*', in: S. d'Intino, S. Pollock (eds.), *L'espace du sens. Approches de la philologie indienne.* Paris, Collège de France – De Boccard (forthcoming), pp. 95–126.

Gandz, S., 1939, 'The Dawn of Literature: [Prolegomena to a History of Unwritten Literature]', *Osiris*, Vol. 7, pp. 261–522.

Ganeri, J., 1995, 'Vyāḍi and the Realist Theory of Meaning', *Journal of Indian Philosophy*, Vol. 23, pp. 403–428.

Gaur, A., 1967, 'Bartholomäus Ziegenbalg's "Verzeichnis der Malabarischen Bücher"', *The Journal of the Royal Asiatic Society of Great Britain and Ireland*, No. ¾, pp. 63–95.

Gensichen, H.-W., 1967, 'Abominable Heathenism: A Rediscovered Tract by Bartholomeus Ziegenbalg', *Indian Church History Review*, Vol. 6, No. 1, pp. 29–40.

Gerety, F.M.M., 2016, 'Survivals & Revivals: The Transmission of Jaiminīya Sāmaveda in Modern South India', in: *Vedic Śākhas: Past, Present, Future*, edited by J.E.M. Houben, J. Rotaru and M. Witzel, Cambridge: Harvard University Press, pp. 633–644.

Ghosh, A., 2003, 'An Uncertain "Coming of the Book": Early Print Cultures in Colonial India', *Book History*, Vol. 6, pp. 23–55.

Ghosh, A., 2008, 'The Many Worlds of the Vernacular Book: Performance, Literacy and Print in Colonial Bengal', in: *Books Without Borders*, Vol. 2: *Perspectives from South Asia*, edited by R. Fraser and M. Hammond, New York: Palgrave Macmillan, pp. 34–57.

Glushkova, I., 2016, 'Looking Around the Institution of *Tīrtha-Yātrā* in the Context of Maratha Expansion', in: *Narratives, Routes and Intersections in Pre-Modern Asia*, edited by R. Seshan, Routledge India, pp. 167–206.

Gode, P.K., 1940, 'Bernier and Kavīndrācārya Sarasvatī at the Mughal Court', in *Annals of S.V. Oriental Institute (Tirupati)*, Vol. 1, pp. 1–16.

GODE, P.K., 1945, 'Some Evidence About the Location of the Manuscript Library of Kavīndrācārya Sarasvatī at Benares in A.D. 1665', in Jagadvijayachandas of Kavindracharya, edited by C. Kunhan Raja, Bikaner: Anup Sanskrit Library, pp. xlvii–lvii.

GODE, P.K., 1946, 'An Interesting Anecdote About Kavīndrācārya Sarasvatī Recorded by Bernier in His Letter from Delhi Dated the 1st July 1663', *Journal of the Kalinga Historical Research Society*, Vol. 1, pp. 183–185.

GODE, P.K., 1969a, 'The Regional History of Indian Paper Industry (The paper manufacture at Behar and Arwal in A. D. 1811–1812 as described by Francis Buchanan)', in: P.K. Gode, *Studies in Indian Cutural History*, Vol. 3, Pune: BORI, pp. 23–30.

GODE, P.K., 1969b, 'Studies in the Regional History of Indian Paper Industry (The paper manufacture at Harihar on the bank of the Tungabhadra in A. D. 1790 as described by Capt. Edward Moor)', in: P.K. Gode, *Studies in Indian Cutural History*, Vol. 3, Pune: BORI, pp. 18–22.

GONDA, J., 1975, *A History of Vedic Literature*, Wiesbaden: Harrassowitz.

GONZÁLEZ-REIMANN, L., 2009, 'Cosmic Cycles, Cosmology, and Cosmography', in: *Brill's Encyclopedia of Hinduism*, edited by K.A. Jacobsen, H. Basu, A. Malinar, and V. Narayanan, http://dx.doi.org/10.1163/2212-5019_beh_COM_1020020 [accessed on 3 November 2017].

GOODY, J., 1986, *The Logic of Writing and the Organization of Society*, Cambridge: Cambridge University Press.

GOUGH, A.E., 1878, *Papers Relating to the Collection and Preservation of the Records of Ancient Sanskrit Literature of India*, Calcutta: Office of Super-intendent of Government Printing.

GOVINDAN Namboodiri, V., 2002, *Śrauta Sacrifices in Kerala*, Calicut: Calicut University.

GRAY, J.E.B., 1959, 'An Analysis of Nambudiri Ṛgvedic Recitation and the Nature of the Vedic Accent', *Bulletin of the School of Oriental and African Studies*, Vol. 22, No. 1, pp. 499–530.

GREEN, N., 2010, 'The Uses of Books in a Late Mughal Takiyya: Persianate Knowledge Between Person and Paper', *Modern Asian Studies*, Vol. 44, No. 2, pp. 241–265.

GUPTA, A., 2010, 'The History of the Book in the Indian Subcontinent', in: *Oxford Companion to the Book*, edited by M. Suarez and H. Woudhuysen, Oxford: Oxford University Press.

GUPTA, A., 2012, 'Book History in India', *Histoire et civilisation du livre – Revue internationale*, Vol. 8, pp. 147–160.

GUPTA, A., 2013, 'The History of the Book in the Indian Subcontinent", in: *The Book: A Global History*, edited by M. Suarez and H.R. Woudhuysen, Oxford: Oxford University Press, pp. 553–572 (originally published in: *Oxford Companion to the Book*, edited by M. Souarez and H. Woudhuysen, Oxford: Oxford University Press 2010).

GUPTA, A., 2016, 'What Happened Under a Tree Outside Delhi, May 1817', in: *Printing Areas: Book History in India*, edited by A. Gupta and S. Chakravorty, Delhi: Permanent Black.

HABERMAS, J., 1991, *The Structural Transformation of the Public Sphere*, Cambridge, MA: The MIT Press (originally published in German in 1962).

HALBFASS, W., 1988, *India and Europe: An Essay in Understanding* (Engl. tr.), Albany: State University of New York Press.

HALL, K.R., 2016, 'The Eighteenth- and Early Nineteenth-century Evolution of Indian Print Culture and Knowledge Networks in Calcutta and Madras', in: *Print Culture Histories Beyond the Metropolis*, edited by J. Connolly et al., Toronto: University of Toronto Press.

HARIDAS, V.V., ed., *Appattu aṭizuṭe ātmakatha*, Kottayam: NBS 2018

HATCHER, B.A. and F.G.E. Ross, 2001, 'How the Giriśa Vidyāratna Press Acquired Its Fonts: A Supplement to the Work of Fiona G.E. Ross', *Journal of the American Oriental Society*, Vol. 121, No. 4, pp. 637–639.

O'HANLON, R., 2012, 'Speaking from Śiva's Temple', in: *Religious Cultures in Early Modern India: New Perspecives*, edited by R. O'Hanlon and D. Washbrook, London and New York: Routledge. pp. 121–145.

O'HANLON, R., 2010, 'Letters Home: Banaras Pandits and the Maratha Regions in Early Modern India', *Modern Asian Studies*, Vol. 44, No. 2, pp. 201–240.

O'HANLON, R. and CH. MINKOWSKI, 2008, 'What Makes People Who They Are? Pandit Networks and the Problem of Livelihoods in Early Modern Western India', *Indian Economic & Social History Review*, Vol. 45, pp. 381–416.

HAYNES, D.E., 1987, 'The Politics of Gift Giving in a Western Indian City', *The Journal of Asian Studies*, Vol. 46, No. 2, pp. 339–360.

HEESTERMAN, J., 1985, *The Inner Conflict of Tradition: Essays in Indian Ritual, Kingship, and Society*, Chicago: University of Chicago Press.

HIRIYANNA, M., 1938, 'Vyāḍī and Vājapyāyana', *Indian Historical Quarterly* (Calcutta), Vol. 14, pp. 61–67.

HOUBEN, J.E.M. and S. RATH, 2012, 'Manuscript Culture and Its Impact in India: Contours and Parameters', in: *Aspects of Manuscript Culture in South India*, edited by S. Rath, Leiden: Brill, pp. 1–53.

http:/nrs.harvard.edu/urn-3:HUL.Inst.Repos:2641801 [accessed on 30 Oct 2010].

HOWARD, W., 1986, *Veda Recitation in Vārāṇasī*, Varanasi: Motilal Banarsidas.

HUDSON, D.D., 1992, 'Arumuga Navalar and the Hindu Renaissance Among the Tamils', in: *Religious Controversy in British India: Dialogues in South Asian Languages*, edited by K.W. Jones, Albany: State University of New York Press, pp. 27–51.

HUDSON, D.D., 1993, 'The First Protestant Mission to India: Its Social and Religious Developments', *Sociological Bulletin*, Vol. 42, No. ½, pp. 37–63.

INNIS, H., 1986 (1950), *Empire and Communications*, edited by D. Godfrey, Toronto: Press Porcépic.

INSLEY, J., 1995, 'Making Mountains out of Molehills? George Everest and Henry Barrow, 1830–39', *Indian Journal of History of Science*, Vol. 30. No. 1, pp. 47–55.

D'Intino, S., 2008, 'Meaningful Mantras: The Introductory Portion of the Ṛgvedabhāṣya by Skandasvāmin', in: *Śāstrārambha: Inquiries into the Preamble in Sanskrit*, edited by W. Slaje, Wiesbaden: Harrassowitz Verlag, pp. 149–170.

D'Intino, S., 2016, 'Les Écoles védiques et la pratique de l'exégèse. Le cas de Skandasvāmin', in: *The Vedic Śākhās: Past, Present and Future*, edited by J. Houben, J. Rotaru, and M. Witzel (Harvard Oriental Series: Opera Minora 9), Cambridge, MA: Department of South Asian Studies, Harvard University, pp. 341–358.

Irschick, E.F., 1994, *Dialogue and History: Constructing South India, 1795–1895*, Berkeley: University of California Press.

Israel, H., 2010, 'Protestant Translations of the Bible in Indian Languages', *Religion Compass*, Vol. 4, No. 2, pp. 86–98.

Jacob, Ch., 2001, 'Réunir', in *Des Alexandries I. Du Livre au texte*, edited by L. Giard and Ch. Jacob, Paris: Bibliothèque nationale de France.

Jacob, Ch., 2007, 'Introduction' to *Lieux de savoir*, Vol. 1: *Espaces et communautés*, edited by Ch. Jacob, Paris: Albin Michel.

Jacob, Ch., ed., 2011, *Lieux de savoir*, Vol. 2: *Les mains de l'intellect*, Paris: Albin Michel.

Jacob, Ch., 2014, *Qu'est-ce qu'un lieu de savoir ?*, Marseille: Open Edition Press.

Jasanoff, M., 2005, *Edge of Empire: Lives, Culture, and Conquest in the East, 1750–1850*, New York: Vintage Books.

Jeyaraj, D., tr., 2005, *Genealogy of the South Indian Deities: An English Translation of Bartholomäus Ziegenbalg's Original German Manuscript with a Textual Analysis and Glossary*, New York: Routledge.

Jeyaraj, D. and Young, F.R., eds., 2013, *Hindu-Christian Epistolary Self-Disclosures: 'Malabarian Correspondence' Between German Pietist Missionaries and South Indian Hindus (1712–1714)*, Wiesbaden: Harrassowitz Verlag.

Johns, A., 1998, *The Nature of the Book: Print and Knowledge in the Making*, Chicago: University of Chicago Press.

Jordens, J.T.F., 1960, *Dayānanda Sarasvatī: His Life and Ideas*, Delhi: Oxford University Press.

Kane, P., 1941, *History of Dharmaśāstra*, Vol. II, Poona: Bhandarkar Research Institute.

Khan, S.M., 1962, 'The Early History of Bengali Printing', *The Library Quarterly: Information, Community, Policy*, Vol. 32, No. 1, pp. 51–61.

Killingley, D., 2008, 'Ezour-Védam: Europe's Illusory First Glimpse of the Veda', *Religions of South Asia*, Vol. 2, No. 1, pp. 23–43.

Killingley, D., 2012, 'Svādhyāya: An Ancient Way of Using the Veda', *Religions of South Asia*, Vol. 8, No. 1, pp. 109–30.

Kinra, R., 2015, *Writing Self, Writing Empire: Chandar Bhan Brahman and the Cultural World of the Indo-Persian State Secretary*, Oakland: University of California Press (doi:http://dx.doi.org/10.1525/luminos.3).

Krämer, S. and H. Bredekamp, 2013, 'Culture, Technology, Cultural Techniques – Moving Beyond Text', *Theory, Culture & Society*, Vol. 30, No. 6, pp. 20–29.

Kubicek, R., 1999, 'British Expansion, Empire, and Technological Change', in *The Oxford History of the British Empire: The Nineteenth Century*, edited by A. Porter, Oxford and New York: Oxford University Press, pp. 247–269.

Kulkarni, P.B. 1967, *Nirṇayasāgaracī akṣar-sādhanā. Śeṭh Jāvajī Dādājī hyāṃceṃ caritr* (in Marathi), Nirṇaya Sagar Press.

Kumbhojkar, Sh., 2009, 'Denial of Centrality of Vedic Texts: Alternative Route to a Subaltern Utopia', in *19th Century Maharashtra: A Reassessment*, edited by S. Kumbhojkar, New Castle: Cambridge Scholars Publishing, pp. 99–112.

Kunhan Raja, C., 1936, 'The Chronology of the Vedabhāṣyakāras', *Journal of Oriental Research*, Vol. 10, pp. 256–268.

Lach, D.F., ed., 1977, *Asia in the Making of Europe*, Vol. 2: *A Century of Wonder*, Book II: *The Literary Arts*, Chicago: University of Chicago Press.

Larios, B., 2017, *Embodying the Vedas Traditional Vedic Schools of Contemporary Maharashtra*, Warsaw and Berlin: De Gruyter Open Ltd.

Liebau, H., 2017, *Cultural Encounters in India: The Local Co-workers of Tranquebar Mission, 18th to 19th Centuries*, London: Routledge.

Lingat, R., 1973, *The Classical Law of India*, Berkeley: Center for South and Southeast Asia Studies.

Llevellyn, J.E., 1994, 'From Interpretation to Reform: Dayānand's Reading of the Vedas', in *Authority, Anxiety, and Canon*, edited by L.L. Patton, Albany: State University of New York Press, pp. 235–252.

Losty, J., 1982, *The Art of the Book in India*, London: The British Library.

Mahadevan, T.P. and F. Staal, 2003, 'The Turning Point in a Living Tradition', *Electronic Journal of Vedic Studies*, Vol. 10, Issue 1, Part A.

Malamoud, Ch., 1977, *Le Svādhyāya. Récitation personelle du Veda*, Paris: Institut de civilisation indienne.

Marchand, S.L., 2009, *German Orientalism in the Age of Empire: Religion, Race, and Scholarship*, Cambridge: Cambridge University Press.

Matilal, B.K., 1990, *Logic, Language and Reality: Indian Philosophy and Contemporary Issues*, New Delhi: Motilal Banarsidas.

Mauss, M., 1924, 'Essai sur le don. Forme et raison de l'échange dans les sociétés primitives', *L'Année Sociologique*, seconde série, 1923–24.

McDonald, E.E., 1968, 'The Modernizing of Communication: Vernacular Publishing in Nineteenth Century Maharashtra', *Asian Survey* (University of California, Berkeley, Institute of International Studies), Vol. 8, No. 7 (*Modernization in South Asian Studies: Essays in a Changing Field*), pp. 589–560.

McKenzie, D.F., 2004 (1999), *Bibliography and Sociology of Texts*, Cambridge: Cambridge University Press.

McLuhan, M., 1962, *The Gutenbberg Galaxy: The Making of Typographic Man*, Toronto: University of Toronto Press.

McLuhan, M., 1995 (1964), *Understanding Media: The Extensions of Man*, Cambridge, MA: MIT Press.

McNeely, I.F. and L. Wolverton, 2009, *Reinventing Knowledge: From Alexandria to Internet*, New York and London: W.W. Norton & Company.

Michaels, A., 1997, "Gift and Return Gift. Greeting and Return Greeting in India...", *Numen*, 44 (3), pp. 242–269.

Michaels, A., 2005, 'Saṃkalpa: The Beginnings of a Ritual', in: *Words and Deeds: Hindu and Buddhist Rituals in South Asia*, edited by J. Gengnagel, U. Hüsken, and S. Raman, Wiesbaden: Harrassowitz Verlag, pp. 45–64.

Minkowski, Ch., 2010, 'Sanskrit Scientific Libraries and Their Uses: Examples and Problems of the Early Modern Period', in: *Looking at It from Asia: The Processes that Shaped the Sources of History of Science* (Boston Studies in the Philosophy of Science, Vol. 265), edited by F. Bretelle-Establet, Dordrecht: Springer, pp. 81–114.

Minkowski, Ch., 2008, 'Why Should We Read the Maṅgala Verses?', in: *Śāstrārambha: Inquiries into the Preamble in Sanskrit*, edited by W. Slaje, Wiesbaden: Harrassowitz Verlag, pp. 1–24.

Minkowski, Ch., 2005, 'What Makes a Work "Traditional"? On the Success of Nīlakaṇṭha's Mahābhārata Commentary', in: *Boundaries, Dynamics and Construction of Traditions in South Asia*, edited by F. Squarcini, Firenze: Firenze University Press, 2005, pp. 225–252.

Minkowski, Ch., 2002, 'Nīlakaṇṭha Caturdhara and the Genre of Mantrarahasya-prakāśikā', *forthcoming*, available at http://www.columbia.edu/itc/mealac/pollock/sks/ papers/minkowski_nilakantha.pdf [accessed on 14 July 2010].

Modak, B.R., 1995, *Sāyaṇa*, Delhi: Sahitya Academy.

Molendijk, A.L., 2016, *Friedrich Max Müller and the Sacred Books of the East*, Oxford: Oxford University Press.

More, P.J.B., 2004, *Muslim Identity, Print Culture, and the Dravidian Factor in Tamil Nadu*, New Delhi: Orient Longman.

Mukhopadhyaya, S. 2010. 'The Rigvedasamhita: Editions and Translations – a Bibliographic Survey', *Namami*, Vol. 20, pp. 4–8.

Murti, M.S., 1997, *Bhartṛhari, the Grammarian*, New Delhi: Sahitya Akademi.

Mukul, A., 2015, *Gita Press and the Making of Hindu India*, Noida: Harper Collins

Nair, S.P., 2005, 'Native Collecting and Natural Knowledge (1798–1832): Raja Serfoji II of Tanjore as a "Centre of Calculation"', *Journal of the Royal Asiatic Society*, Third Series, Vol. 15, No. 3, pp. 279–302.

Nair, S.P., 2011, '"...Of Real Use to the People": The Tanjore Printing Press and the Spread of Useful Knowledge', *The Indian Economic and Social History Review*, Vol. 48, No. 4, pp. 497–529.

Nakamura, H., 1983, *History of Early Vedānta Philosophy*, Part II, Delhi: Motilal Banarsidas.

Naregal, V., 2017 (2001), *Language Politics, Elites, and the Public Sphere*, New Delhi: Permanent Black.

Naregal, V., 2004, 'Vernacular Culture and Political Formation in Western India', in: *Printing Areas: Book History in India*, edited by A. Gupta and S. Chakravorty, Delhi: Permanent Black, pp. 169–196.

Neill, S., 2002 (1985), *A History of Christianity in India: 1707–1858*, Cambridge: Cambridge University Press.

Neill, S., 2004 (1984), *A History of Christianity in India: The Beginnings to AD 1707*, Cambridge: Cambridge University Press.

Ogborn, M., 2007, *Indian Ink: Script and Print in the Making of the English East India Company*, Chicago: University of Chicago Press.

Orsini, F., 2002, *The Hindi Public Sphere, 1920–1940: Language and Literature in the Age of Nationalism*, New Delhi: Oxford University Press.

Orsini, F., 2009, *Pleasure and Print: Popular Literature and Entertaining Fictions in Colonial North India*, New Delhi: Permanent Black.

Orsini, F., 2016, 'Journals, Publishing, and the Literary System', in: *The History of the Book in South Asia*, edited by F. Orsini, Farnham: Ashgate, pp. (originally published in F. Orsini, *The Hindi Public Sphere 1920–1940*, Oxford: Oxford University Press 2002, pp. 51–80).

Otis, A., 2018, *Hicky's Bengal Gazette: The Untold Story of India's First Newspaper*, Chennai: Tranquebar Press.

Parry, J., 1986, 'The Gift, Indian Gift, and "the Indian Gift"', *Man*, New Series, Vol. 21, No. 3, pp. 453–73.

Patton, L., 1996, *Myth as Argument: The Bṛhaddevatā as Canonical Commentary*, Berlin: de Gruyter.

Patton, L., 1997, 'Making the Canon Commonplace: Ṛgvidhāna as Commentarial Practice', *The Journal of Religion*, Vol. 77, No. 1, pp. 1–19.

Peters, J.D., 2015, *The Marvelous Clouds: Towards a Philosophy of Elemental Media*, Chicago: University of Chicago Press.

Pettegree, A., 2004, 'The Reformation and the Book: A Reconsideration', *The Historical Journal*, Vol. 47, No. 4, pp. 785–808.

Pettegree, A., 2005, *Reformation and the Culture of Persuasion*, Cambridge and New York: Cambridge University Press.

Pinto, R., 2007, *Between Empires: Print and Politics in Goa*, New Delhi and Oxford: Oxford University Press.

Pisharoti, K.R., 1928, 'Religion and Philosophy in Kerala', *The Indian Historical Quarterly*, Vol. 4, pp. 702–719.

Pollock, S., 2003, 'Introduction' to *Literary Cultures in History: Reconstructions from South Asia*, edited by S. Pollock, Berkeley: University of California Press.

Pollock, S., 2005, 'The Revelation of Tradition: śruti, smṛti and the Sanskrit Discourse of Power', in *Boundaries, Dynamics and Construction of Traditions in South Asia*, edited by F. Squarcini, Firenze: Firenze University Press, pp. 41–61.

Pollock, S., 2006, *The Language of Gods in the World of Men: Sanskrit, Culture and Power in Premodern India*, Berkeley: University of California Press.

Pollock, S., 2007, 'Literary Culture and Manuscript Culture in Precolonial India', *Literary Cultures and the Material Book*, edited by S. Eliot et al., London: British Library, pp. 77–94.

POLLOCK, S., B. ELMAN, and K. CHANG, eds., 2015, *World Philology*, Cambridge, MA: Harvard University Press.

POMIAN, K., 1999, *Sur l'histoire*, Paris: Gallimard.

PORTER, A., ed., 1999, *The Oxford History of the British Empire: The Nineteenth Century*, Oxford and New York: Oxford University Press.

PRICE, L., 2009, 'From the History of a Book to a "History of the Book"', *Representations*, Vol. 108, No. 1, pp. 120–138, http://nrs.harvard.edu/urn-3:HUL.InstRepos:2641801 [accessed on 29 Nov 2017].

PRIOLKAR, A.K., 1958, *The Printing Press in India: Its Beginnings and Early Development, Being a Quatercentenary Commemoration Study of the Advent of Printing in India in 1556*, Bombay: Marathi Samshodhana Mandala.

RAINA, DH., 2007, 'Jesuit Collections of Indian Scientific Manuscripts: Ideologies and Interpretations', *Indian Journal of History of Science*, Vol. 42, Vol. 1, pp. 31–45.

RAMAN, BH., 2012, *Document Raj: Writing and Scribes in Early Colonial South India*, Bangalore: Orient Blackswan.

RENOU, L., 1928, *Les Maitres de la Philologie Védique*, Paris: Librairie Orientaliste Paul Geuthner.

RENOU, L., 1931, *Bibliographie Vedique*, Paris: Adrien Maisonneuve.

ROBERTS, J., 1971, 'The Movement of Elites in Western India under Early British Rule', *The Historical Journal*, Vol. 14, No. 2, pp. 241–262.

ROCHER, L., 1984, *Ezourvedam: A French Veda of the Eighteenth Century*, Amsterdam: John Benjamins Publishing.

ROCHER, L., 2012, 'The Historical Foundations of Ancient Indian Law' (translated from the Dutch by S. de Backer), in: L. Rocher, *Studies in Hindu Law and Dharmaśāstra*, edited by D.R. Davis Jr., London, New York, and Delhi: Anthem Press, pp. 59–81.

ROCHER, R. and L. ROCHER, 2012, *The Making of Western Indology: Henry Thomas Colebrooke and the East India Company*, Abingdon: Oxon nad New York: Routledge

RUBIÉS, J.-P., 2001 (2000), *Travel and Ethnology in the Renaissance South India Through European Eyes, 1250–1625*, Cambridge: Cambridge University Press.

SAENGER, P., 1997, *Space Between Words: The Origins of Silent Reading*, Stanford: Stanford University Press.

SATYA SHRAVA, 1977, *A Comprehensive History of Vedic Literature*, Vol. 3, New Delhi: Pranava Prakasha.

SCHARFE, H., 2002, *Education in Ancient India*, Leiden: Brill.

SEBASTIAN, M., 2015, 'Localised Cosmopolitanism and Globalised Faith: Echoes of "Native" Voices in Eighteenth- and Nineteenth-Century Missionary Documents", in: *European Missions in Contact Zones*, edited by J. Becker, Göttingen: Vandenhoeck & Ruprecht.

SENGUPTA, I. and D. ALI, 2011, *Knowledge Production, Pedagogy, and Institutions in Colonial India*, New York: Palgrave Macmillan.

SEVERSON, T., 2009, 'European Arrival and the Colonial Period', in *Cultural History of Reading*, edited by G. Watling, Westport, CT and London: Greenwood Press, pp. 443–463.

Shaw, G., 1977, 'Printing in Mangalore and Tellicherry by the Basel Mission', *Libri*, Vol. 27, No. 2, pp. 154–164.

Shaw, G., 1981, *Printing in Calcutta to 1800*, London: The Bibliographical Society.

Shaw, G., 1993a, 'The Copenhagen Copy of Henriques' Flos Sanctorum', *Fund og Forskning*, Bind 32, pp. 39–50.

Shaw, G., 1993b, 'Lithography v. Letter-Press in India. Part I: Lithography in Bombay', *South Asia Library Notes & Queries* (CONSALD), No. 29, online version: http://www.consald.org/sites/default/files/SALNAQ/Issue_29/29_1993_01_Lithography1.pdf [accessed on 2 Oct 2017].

Shaw, G., 1994, 'Lithography v. Letter-Press in India. Part II: Lithography and the Vernacular Book', *South Asia Library Notes & Queries* (CONSALD), No. 30, online version: http://www.consald.org/sites/default/files/SALNAQ/Issue_30/30_199495_01_Lithography2.pdf [accessed on 2 Oct 2017].

Shaw, G.W., 2007, 'South Asia', in: *A Companion to the History of the Book* (Blackwell Companions to Literature & Culture), edited by S. Eliot and J. Rose, Oxford: Blackwell Publishing, pp. 126–137.

Shaw, G., 2010, 'First English Book in India' (literary review), *The Hindu*, 28 May, http://www.thehindu.com/books/literary-review/First-English-book-in-India/article14342427.ece [accessed on 15 Oct 2017].

Shaw, G. and J. Randall, 2014, *From Conversion to Subversion: 250 Years of the Printed Book in India*, Rye: John Randall (Books of Asia).

Shep, S.J., 2010, 'Cultures of Print: Materiality, Memory, and the Rituals of Transmission', *Journal of New Zealand Literature*, No. 28, Part 2, Special Issue: *Cultures of Print in Colonial New Zealand*, pp. 183–210.

Shulman, D., 1984, "The Enemy within: Ideas and Dissent in South Indian Hinduism," in S.N.Eisenstadt, K.Reuven, D. Shulman, eds., *Orthodoxy, Heterodoxy and Dissent in India*, Berlin: Mouton, pp. 11-57.

Shulman, D., 2007, *Spring, Heat, Rains: A South Indian Diary*, Chicago: University of Chicago Press.

Siegert, B., 2015, *Cultural Techniques: Grids, Filters, Doors, and Other Articulations of the Real*, translated by G. Wynthrop-Young, New York: Fordham University Press.

Simini, F. de, 2016, *Of Gods and Books: Ritual and Knowledge Transmission in the Manuscript Cultures of Premodern India*, Berlin and Boston: DeGruyter.

Skinner, Q., 2005, 'On Intellectual History and the History of Books', *Contributions to the History of Concepts*, Vol. 1, No. 1, pp. 29–36.

Slaje, W., ed., 2008, *Śāstrārambha: Inquiries into the Preamble in Sanskrit*, Wiesbaden: Harrassowitz Verlag.

Smith, B.K., 1989, *Reflections on Resemblance, Ritual, and Religion*, New York nad Oxford: Oxford University Press.

Squarcini, F., ed., 2005, *Boundaries, Dynamics and Construction of Traditions in South Asia*, Firenze: Firenze University Press.

Staal, J.F., 1961, *Nambudiri Veda Recitation*, The Hague: Mouton & Co.

STAAL, F., 1983, *Agni: The Vedic Ritual of the Fire Altar*, 2 vols., Berkeley: University of California Press.

STAAL, F., 2008, *Discovering the Vedas: Origins, Mantras, Rituals, Insights*, Delhi: Penguin Books India.

STARK, U., 2007, *An Empire of Books: The Naval Kishore Press and the Diffusion of the Printed Word in Colonial India*, Ranikhet: Permanent Black.

STOCKING, G.W., 1991, *Victorian Anthropology*, New York: Free Press.

SWEETMAN, W., 2003, *Mapping Hinduism: 'Hinduism' and the Study of Indian Religions, 1600–1776*, Wiesbaden: Harrassowitz.

SWEETMAN, W. (with R. ILLAKKUVAN), 2012, *Bibliotheca Malabarica: Batholomeus Ziegenbalg's Tamil Library*, Pondichery: EFEO & IFP.

SWEETMAN, W., 2014, 'Retracing Bartholomaeus Ziegenbalg's Path', in: *Beyond Tranquebar: Grappling Across Cultural Borders in South India*, edited by E. Fiel and A.R. Venkatachalapathy, Delhi: Orient Blackswan, pp. 304–21.

SWEETMAN, W., 2004, The Prehistory of orientalism *New Zeland Journal of Asiatic Studies* 6(2): 12–38.

SWEETMAN, W., 2015, 'Empire and Mission: Protestant Beginnings in India and the "pious clause"', *Social Sciences and Missions*, Vol. 28, pp. 11–31.

SWEETMAN, W., 2019, 'The Absent Vedas', Journal of the American Oriental Society 139.4 (2019), pp. 781-803.

SWIDERSKI, R., 1988, 'Oral Text: A South Indian Instance", *Oral Tradition*, Vol. 3, No. 1–2, pp. 122–37.

TIEKEN, H., 2006, 'The Role of the So-called Aśoka Inscriptions in the Attempt to Date the Buddha', *Rivista di Studi Sudasiatici*, I, 2006, pp. 69–88.

Tiliander, B., 1974, *Christian and Hindu Terminology*. Uppsala.

TORRI, M., 1991, 'Trapped Inside the Colonial Order: The Hindu Bankers of Surat and Their Business World During the Second Half of the Eighteenth Century', *Modern Asian Studies*, Vol. 25, No. 2, pp. 367–401.

TOUATI, H., 2003, *L'armoire à sagesse. Bibliothèques et collections en Islam*, Paris: Aubier.

TRAUTMANN, T.R., 2009, 'Introduction' to *The Madras School of Orientalism: Producing Knowledge in Colonial South India*, edited by T.R. Trautmann, New Delhi: Oxford University Press.

TRIVEDI, H., 2008, 'The "Book" in India: Orality, Manu-Script, Print (Post)Colonialism', in: *Books Without Borders*, Vol. 2: *Perspectives from South Asia*, edited by R. Fraser and M. Hammond, New York: Palgrave Macmillan.

ÜÇERLER, A., J., 2013, "Missionary Printing," In: M.F. Suarez and H.R. Woudhuysen, eds., *The Book: A Global History*, Oxford: Oxford Univ. Press, pp. 107-15.

VARADARAJAN, L., 1979, 'Oral Testimony as Historical Source Material for Traditional and Modern India', *Economic and Political Weekly*, Vol. 14, No. 24, pp. 1009–14.

VENKATACHALAPATHY, A.R., 2009, '"Written on Leaves in the Malabarian Manner" Print and the Cultural Encounter in Eighteenth Century Tranquebar', *Review of Development & Change*, Vol. 14, No. 1 & 2, pp. 131–46.

VENKATACHALAPATHY, A.R., 2012, *The Province of the Book: Scholars, Scribes and Scribblers in Colonial Tamil Nadu*, Ranikhet: Permanent Black.

VIELLE, CH., T. VAN HAL, and J.-C. MULLER, 2013, *Grammatica Grandonica: The Sanskrit Grammar of Johann Ernst Hanxleden s.j. (1681–1732), introduced and edited, with a photographical reproduction of the original manuscript*, Universitätsverlag Potsdam.

VIELLE, Ch., (forthcoming), 'Devotional Christianity and pre-Indology in early 18th century Kerala: Johann Ernst Hanxleden s.j., alias Arnos Padiri, scholar and poet', in: *Dimensions of the Christian Encounter with the Religions of India: Aims, Possibilities, Ramifications*, edited by K. Preisendanz and J. Buss, Vienne: De Nobili Research Library, Publications of the De Nobili Research.

VISHWANATH, K.T., 2007, 'Daśagranthi Tradition of Vedic Chanting', in: *Veda Society: Modernity*, edited by C.M. Neelakandhan and K.A. Ravindran, Kunnamkulam: Panchangam Press, pp. 74–82.

VISMANN, C., 2013, 'Cultural Techniques and Sovereignty', *Theory, Culture & Society*, Vol. 30, No. 6, pp. 83–93.

VISMANN, C., 2008, *Files. Law and Media Technology*, fr. G. Winthrop-Young, Stanford: Stanford University Press.

WEISS, R.S., 2016, 'Religion and the Emergence of Print in Colonial India: Arumuga Navalar's Publishing Project', *The Indian Economic and Social History Review*, Vol. 53, No. 4, pp. 473–500.

WICKI, J., 1965, 'Father Henrique Henriques S. I. (1520–1600): An Exemplary Missionary of India', *Indian Ecclesiastical Studies*, Vol. 4, pp. 142–50.

WITZEL, M. 1997, 'The Development of the Vedic Canon and Its Schools: The Social and Political Milieu', in *Inside the Texts, Beyond the Texts: New Approaches to the Study of the Vedas*, edited by M. Witzel, Cambridge, MA: Harvard University, pp. 257–345.

WITZEL, M., 2003, 'Veda and Upanishads', in *A Blackwell Companion to Hinduism*, edited by G. Flood, London: Blackwell, pp. 68–101.

WITZEL, M. 2011, 'Gandhāra and the Formation of the Vedic and Zoroastrian Canons', in: *Veda-Vedāṅga et Avesta entre oralité et écriture. Travaux de symposium international: Le livre. La Roumanie. L'Europe. Etudes euro- et afro-asiatiques*, edited by J. Houben and J. Rotaru, Bucharest: Biblioteca Bucurestilor, pp. 490–532.

WOOD, A.E., 1985, *Knowledge Before Printing and After*, Delhi: Oxford University Press.

WUJASTYK, D., 2012, 'Rāmasubrahmaṇya's Manuscripts: Intellectual Networks in the Kāveri Delta', in: *Aspects of Manuscript Culture in South India*, edited by S. Rath, Leiden and Boston: Brill, pp. 235–52.

WUJASTYK, D., 2014, 'Indian Manuscripts', in *Manuscript Cultures: Mapping the Field*, edited by J.B. Quenzer et al., Berlin and Boston: De Gruyter, pp. 159–82.

YOUNG, L.C., 2017, *List Cultures: Knowledge and Poetics from Mesopotamia to BuzzFeed*, Amsterdam: Amsterdam University Press.

ZVELEBIL, K.V., 1974, *Tamil Literature*, Wiesbaden: Otto Harrassowitz.

Zysk, K.G. 2012, 'The Use of Manuscript Catalogues as Sources of Regional Intellectual History in India's Early Modern period', in: *Aspects of Manuscript Culture in South India*, edited by S. Rath, Leiden and Boston: Brill, pp. 253–93.

Županov, I.G., 1999, *Disputed Mission: Jesuit Experiments and Brahmanical Knowledge in Seventeenth-century India*, Oxford: Oxford University Press.

Županov, I.G., 2012. '"I Am a Great Sinner": Jesuit Missionary Dialogues in Southern India (Sixteenth Century)', *Journal of the Economic and Social History of the Orient*, Vol. 55, pp. 415–46.

APPENDIX. Early Indian printed editions of Vedic texts in regional distribution [with a specific focus on Ṛgveda-related texts]

Region	Year	Title	Editor	Publisher/printer
Bombay Presidency (Province)	1833	Trividyā Trigunātmikā = *The Threefold Knowledge* (Sukta 1–35 of mandala I of the Ṛgveda, with Sanskrit notes and Marathi translation)	John Stevenson	Bombay: American Mission Press [*pothī* format, lithographed]
	1863	Aitareya Brāhmaṇa	M. Haug	Bombay: Government Book Dept., printed at Education Society Press, Byculla
	1867–1869	Ṛksaṃhitā, with Sāyaṇabhāṣya	Rājārāma Śāstrī and Śivarāma Śāstrī	Mumbai
	1868	Aitareya Āraṇyakam with Sāyaṇa's Commentary	Bābāśāstrī Phadake	Pune: Ānanadāśrama
	1876–1882	Vedārthayatna or an Attempt to Interpret the Vedas. A Marathi and English translation of the Rig Veda, with the Original Saṃhitā and Pada Texts in Sanskrit, vol. 1–4,5, parts 1–9	Shankar Pandurang Pandit	Bombay: Indu-Prakash Press / Nirṇaya Sagar Press
	1880	The portion of the Rigveda. Appointed for the B.A. Examinations of 1881 and 1882. In the Sanhita and Pada texts	Krishnāji Bāpu· Mande	Pune: Shivaji Press
	1881	Sayana's bhasya. On the Rigveda portion for the B.A. Examinations	Krishnarao Bapu Mande	Pune: Shivaji Press
	1882	Ṛgvedīya-cchandaḥ-prabhṛti--saṃgraha	Gaṇeśa Ṣạman Āṭhalye	Poona: Jagadtecchu Press
	1884	Ṛgvedī-Brahmakarma		Bombai: Native Opinion Press
	1885	Hymns from the Rig-veda. Appointed for the first B.A. course. Part 1 (The Mantra Text)		Poona: Dhyāna Prakāś Press
	1887	Ṛig-Veda Samhita without Bhashya	Tukārām Tātyā	Bombay: Tookaram Tatya for the Bombay Theosophical Publication Fundation, Gaṇapati Kṛṣṇajī Press

Region	Year	Title	Editor	Publisher/printer
Bombay Presidency (Province)	1888–1890	Rig-Veda Samhita with Pada-Pāṭha and Sāyaṇacharaya's Bhāshya	Rājārām Shāstri Bodas and Shivarām Shāstri Gore	Bombay: Tukārām Tātyā for the Bombay Theosophical Publication Fund, Ganapat Krishnaji Press
	1888	Hymns from the Rigveda edited with Sayana's commentary, notes and a translation	P. Peterson	Bombay: Government Central Book Depot
	1889	Gaṇeśātharvaśīrṣam Sābhāṣyam	Vāmanaśāstrī Isalāmapurakar	Pune: Ānāndāśrama
	1889	Bṛhadāraṇyakopaṇiṣat Sāṭīkabhāṣyopetā	Vāmanaśāstrī Isalāmapurakar	Pune: Ānandāśrama
	1890	Handbook to the Study of the Ṛgveda	P. Peterson	Bombay: Government Central Book Depot
	1891	Bṛhadāraṇyakopaniṣat Śankara Bhāṣyām and Ānandagiri Ṭīka	K.S. Agase	Pune: Ānandāśrama
	1892	Handbook to the Study of the Ṛgveda, part II: The Seventh Mandala of the Ṛgveda	P. Peterson	Bombay: Government Central Book Depot
	1892–93	Brahadaranyakopnishad Bhashya Vartikam 3vols	K.S. Agase	Pune: Ānandāśrama
	1895	Upanishadam Samucchayah (32 Upanishads)	H.N. Apte	Pune: Ānandāśrama
	1895	Ṛiksangraha, or A university selection of Vedic hymns; with the commentary of *Sâyaṇâchârya*	ed. with notes by V.G. Bijâpûrkar	Bombay
	1895	Atharvavedasaṃhitā Sāyaṇācāryaviracitena bhāṣyeṇa sahitā	Pāṇḍurangasūnu Śaṅkar	Mumbai: Nirṇaya Sāgara
	1895–1898	Atharvaveda Saṃhitā with the Commentary by Sāyaṇācārya	Śankara Pāṇduranga	published in *Pandita* 1895–98
	1895	E,iksangraha, or a University selection of Vedic Hymns with the com. of Sāyanācharya	Vishnu Govind Bijāpkūmar	Bombay: Nirṇaya Sāgar Press
	1896	Aitareya Brahmanam with Sayanabhashya	Kasinathsastri Agase	Pune: Ānadāśrama
	1897	Āśvalāyana Gṛhya Kārikā	V.L. Paṇaśīkar	Mumbai: Nirṇaya Sāgara
	1898	Taittiriya Brahmanam with Sayanabhashya	Narayanasastri Godbole	Pune: Ānandāśrama
	1898	Taittirīyāraṇyakam Sāyaṇācaryaviracitabhāṣyasametam	Bābāśāstrī Phāṭke	Punyapattana (Pune): Ānandāśrama

Region	Year	Title	Editor	Publisher/printer
Bombay Presidency (Province)	1898	Aitareyaranyakam with Sayanabhashya	Babasastri Phadke	Pune: Ānandāśrama
	1899	Ṛgvedīya Brahmakarmasamuccaya	V.L. Paṇśīkar	Mumbay: Nirṇaya Sāgara
	1899	A second selection of hymns from the Rigveda, edited with *Sāyana's commentary*	P. Peterson	Education Society's Press
	1900	Ṛksaṃhitā, Śaka 1822 (= A.D. 1900), ed., Bombay	Janārdana Mahādeva Gurjara	Mumbai, Janārdana Mahādeva Gurjara Nirṇaya Sāgara, [*pothī* format]
	1902	Ṛk-saṃhitā-pada-pāṭhaḥ (padāni).	T.A. Kṛṣṇācārya	Muṃbayyām: Nirṇaya-sāgara Press
	1904 (1826)	Ṛgvedī Mantrasaṃhitā	Gajānana Cintāmana Śāstrī	Mumbai: Ganapat Kṛṣṇājī Press [pothī format]
	1904 (1826)	Ṛgvedamantrasaṃhitā (yajñikaprayogānukrāma)	Janārdana Mahādeva Gurjara, Rāmavāḍī,	Mumbai [*pothī* format]
	1907	Satyashada Śrauta Sūtra with commentaries of Gopinātha and Mahādeva		Pune: Ānandāśrama
	1909	Āśvalāyana Gṛhya Sūtra	Bhavāni Śankara Śarma	Bombay
	1910	Ṛgvedamantrasaṃhitā	Janardana Mahādeva Gurjara	Mumbai: Nirṇaya Sāgara [*pothī* format]
	1910	The Thirty Eight Upanishads		Mumbai: Khemraj Shrikrishnadas, Venkateśwara Steam Press
	1910	Isha to Taittiriya Upanishads with Visishtadvaita Commentaries	HN Apte	Pune: Ānandāśrama
	1910	Chandogyopanishad with Ramanujabhashya	Ganeshsastri Gokhale	Pune: Ānandāśrama
	1910	Sasvāhākaraprayoganirṇayā samantrakośāca ṛksaṃhitā	V.L. Paṇaśīkara	Bombay: Tukaram Javaji, Nirṇaya Sāgara [*pothī* format]
	1910	Ṛgvedīya-nitya-viddhi		Poona: Bharata Bhushana Press
	1911	Utsarjanopākaraṇaprayoga	V.L. Paṇaśīkara	Bombay: Tukaram Javaji [*pothī* format]

Region	Year	Title	Editor	Publisher/printer
Bombay Presidency (Province)	1911	Bṛhadaranyakopanishad with Prakasika by Rangaramanuja	S.S. Venegavkar	Pune: Anadaśrama
	1911	Aitareya Brāhmaṇa	V.L. Paṇaśīkara	Bombay: Tukaram Javaji
	1911	Sankhayana Brahmanam	Vajhesankar Chaya Gulabrao	Pune: Anadaśrama
	1911	Ṛk-saṃhitā [Ṛg-vidhāna-sahitā] Mahārāṣtra-tātparyopetaVedārtha-prakāśa-sametā	Kaśinatha Vāmana Lele	Wai: Śrī Kṛṣṇa Press
	1911	Ṛg-veda-saṃhitā. Mula rcā, pada-pāṭha, [...], ŚriVidyāraṇya -bhāṣya āṇi bhāṣyācā [Marāthi]	Kaśinatha Vāmana Lele	Wai: Śrī Kṛṣṇa Press
	1912	Śukla Yajurveda-Saṃhitā (Śrimad Vājasaneyi-Mādhyandina) with the Mantra-Bhāṣā of Uvatācārya and Veda-dīpa-bhāṣya of Mahīdharake	V.L. Paṇśikar	Bombay: Tukārām Jāvajī, Nirṇaya Sāgara Press
	1912	Vajasaneyi Sri Sukla Yajuevedasamhita		Bombay: Venkateswara Steam Press
	1915	Śikṣādivedaṣaḍaṅga	V.L. Pāṇśkar	Mumbai: Nirṇaya Sāgar Press [*pothī* format]
	1915	Prayogaratnam = Nārāyaṇabhāṭṭī	V.L. Pāṇśīkar	Mumbay: Tukarama Javaji, Nirṇaya Sāgara Press [*pothī* format]
	1916	Nṛsiṃhiyasya Prayogapārijātasya ṣaḍaśasaṃskārakaṇḍam pākasaṃsthākaṇḍa samkṣepaśca	V.L. Pāṇśīkar	Mumbai: Tūkarāma Jāvajī, Nirṇaya Sāgara Press [*pothī* format]
	1916	Ṛk-stabakaḥ (Boquet [*sic*] of Hymns from the Rgveda). With intro, translation and notes	Krishnarao M. Joglekar	Bombai: Nirṇaya Sāgara Press
	1916	Ṛgveda-bhāṣya by Tulāsi Svāmin		Meerut: Swāmi Press
	1917	Āśvalāyana Śrauta Sūtra with Vivṛtti by Nārāyaṇa Ganeśa Gokhale		Pune: Ānandāśrama
	1917	Pāraskara Gṛhya Sūtra		Mumbai
	1920	Ṛgveda, prathamo 'ṣṭakaḥ	R.V. Paṭavardhana, A.B. Kolhaṭakara, D.A. Tulajapurakara	Mumbai: Śrutibodha Mudrā-Maṇḍire

Region	Year	Title	Editor	Publisher/printer
Bombay Presidency (Province)	1921	Agnihotra-candrikā		Pune: Ānandāśrama
	1921–1926	Niruktam with Durgacharya's Vritti	V.K. Rajawade	Pune: Ānadāśrama
	1922	Śāṅkhayana Āraṇyakam	Sridhar Sastri Pathak	Pune: Ānadāśrama
	1925	Aitareya Brāhamaṇa	V.L. Paṇśikar	Bombay: Nirṇaya Sāgara Press
	1925	Nighaṇṭu		Pune: Ānandāśrama
	1925	Upaniṣādām Samuchchaya		Pune: Ānandāśrama
	1926	Ṛgvedī-sārtha-deva-pūja-prayoga		Poona: Kālikā Press
	1927	Svetasvatara Upanishad with Sankara Bhashya and three Commenataries	V.G. Apte	Pune: Ānandāśrama
	1927	Chandaśāstra by Pingala	V.L. Paṇśīkar	Bombay: Pāndurang Jāvajī, Nirṇaya Sāgar Press
	1928	Śruti-bodha (Uttara-khaṇḍ). Ṛg-vedacem Marathibhāṣā antara. Maṇḍala 8–9. [Part of a monthly magazine containing text and translation of the Vedas]	Rāmacaṃdra Vināyaka Paṭavardhana	Bombay: Śrīlākṣmīnārāyaṇa Press
	1929	ŚuklaYajurveda-Saṃhitā (Śrimad Vājasaneyi Mādhyandina) with the Mantra-Bhāṣā of Uvatācārya and Veda-dīpa-bhāṣya of Mahīdhara	V.L. Paṇśīkar (second edition)	Bombay: Pāndurang Jāvajī, Nirṇaya Sāgar Press
	1929	Mādhyandina Mantra Saṃhitā	Gangāviṣṇu Śrīkṛṣṇadāsa [publisher]	Mumbai-Kalyana: Lakshmi-Venkateswara Steam Press [*pothī* format]
	1930	Sasvāhākaraprayoganirṇayā samantrakośāca ṛksaṃhitā	V.L. Paṇaśīkara	Mumbai: Nirṇaya Sāgara [*pothī* format]
	1933–1951	Ṛgvedasaṃhitā with the commentary of Sāyaṇācārya, 5 vols	N.S. Sontake, C.G. Kaśikar	Pune: Vaidikasaṃśodhana Maṇḍala
	1934	Hiraṇyakeśīya Mantrasaṃhitā	L. Gokhale	Mumbai: Pandurang Javaji, Nirṇaya Sāgara [*pothī* format]
	1940	KṛṣṇaYajurvedīya Taittirīya-saṃhitā		Pune: Ānandāśrama

Region	Year	Title	Editor	Publisher/printer
Calcutta and Bengal Presidency/Province	1816	Translation of Ishopanishad, one of the chapters of the Yajurveda acc. to the comm. of Shankar-Āchārya	Rammohun Roy	Calcutta: Philip Pereira, Hindoostanee Press
	1816	Translation of the Cena Upanishad, one of the chapters of the Sāmaveda acc. to the Gloss. of Shancarāchārya	Rammohun Roy	Calcutta: Philip Pereira, Hindoostanee Press
	1817	Translation of the Muṇḍaka Upanishad, one of the chapters of the Atharvaveda acc. to the Gloss. of Shancarāchārya	Rammohun Roy	Calcutta: Philip Pereira, Hindoostanee Press
	1817	Translation of the Katha Upanishad, one of the chapters of the Yajurveda acc. to the Gloss. of Shancarāchārya	Rammohun Roy	Calcutta: Philip Pereira, Hindoostanee Press
	1838	Bṛhadaraṇyakopaniṣad	E. Röer	Calcutta: J. Thomas at the Baptist Mission Press
	1844	Śuklayajurvedaḥ Vājasaneyisaṃhitā Mādhyandinīśākhā (with Mahīdharadīpa)		Kolkatta: Satya Press
	1848	The First Two lectures of the Ṛgveda with the Commentary of Madhavacharya	E. Röer	Calcutta: J. Thomas at the Baptist Mission Press
	1849	The Brhad Aranyaka Upanishad with the Commentary of Sankara Acharyaand the Gloss of Ananda Giri	E. Röer	Calcutta: J. Thomas, Baptist Mission Press
	1850	Īśa, Kena, Praśa, Muṇḍaka, Māṇḍukya Upaniṣads with the Commentary of Śaṅkara and the Gloss of Anandagiri	E. Röer	Calcutta: J. Thomas, Baptist Mission Press
	1850	Chandogyopanishad with the Commentary of Sankara Acharya and the Gloss of Ananda Giri	E. Röer	Calcutta: J. Thomas, Baptist Mission Press
	1859–1862	The Taittirīya Brāhmaṇa with the Comment of Sāyaṇācārya	Rajendra Mitra Lāl	Calcutta: R.C. Lewis at Missionary Press
	1860–1866	The Samhitā of Black Yajur Veda with the Commentary of Mādhava Āchārya, vol. I–II	E. Röer & E.B. Cowell	Calcutta: Asiatic Society, printed at Baptist Mission Press
	1861	Kauṣītakī Brāhmaṇa-Upaniṣad with the Commentary of Śankarānanda	E.B. Cowell	Calcutta
	1861	Śāṅkhāyana Āraṇyaka	E.B. Cowell	Calcutta

Region	Year	Title	Editor	Publisher/printer
Calcutta and Bengal Presidency/Province	1862	Chandogyopaniṣad	Rajendralāla Mitra	Calcutta: Asiatic Society, printed at Baptist Missionary Press
	1866	Aśvalayana Gṛhya Sūtra, fasc. 1	Rama Nārāyaṇa Vidyaratna	Calcutta: Asiatic Society, Biblioteca Indica, C.B. Lewis in Baptist Mission Press
	1872–1884	The Sanhitá of the Black Yajur Veda: with the commentary of Mádhava Áchárya. Vols III–V	Maheśa Candra Nyāyaratna	Calcutta: Asiatic Society, Biblioteca Indica: Baptist Mission Press
	1872	Taittirīyāraṇyakam Sāyaṇācarya-bhāṣyaviracita	Rājendralāla Mitra	Calcutta: Asiatic Society, Biblioteca Indica: Baptist Mission Press
	1872	Lāṭyāyana Śrauta Sūtra	Ānandacandra Ved ānta Vāgīśa	Calcutta
	1872	Gopatha Brāhmaṇa	Rajendralal Mitra	Calcutta
	1873	Īśa, Kena, Praśa, Muṇḍaka, Māṇḍukya Upaniṣads with the Commentary of Śaṅkara	Jibananda Vidyasagara	Calcutta: Sucharu Press
	1874–1878	Sāmaveda Saṃhitā with the Commentary of Sāyaṇācārya	Satyavrata Śarmā Sāmaśramī	Calcutta: Asiatic Society, Ganesh Press
	1874	Āśvalāyana Śrauta Sūtra	Vidyāratna	Calcutta
	1875	Rig-veda sanhitā, first and second adhyayas of the first ashtaka, with notes and explanations	Rev. K.M. Banerjea	Calcutta: Thaker Spinak
	1876	Aitareya Āranyaka, with the commentary of Sāyaṇa Āchārya	Rājendralāla Mitra	Calcutta: Asiatic Society of Bengal
	1877	Rgveda-bhāṣya-ṭīkā by Rāmānātha Ghoṣa Sāraswati	Ramanath Saraswatee	Calcutta: Prākrita Press
	1878	Rigveda sanhita. The first four adhyayas of the first ashtaka. With a Sanskrit commentary, a Bengalee translation	Ramanatha Saraswatee	Calcutta: Prākrita Press
	1878	Daivata Brahmana and Shadbigsha Brahmana of the Samaveda with the Commentary of Sayanacharya	Jibananda Vidyasagara	Calcutta: Saraswati Press
	1879	Yajurvediya Katha Upanishad		Calcutta : Samvad Gyan Ratnakar Press

Region	Year	Title	Editor	Publisher/printer
Calcutta and Bengal Presidency/Province	1881	Daivata Brāhmaṇa and Ṣaḍvimśa Brāhmaṇa	Jivānanda Vidyāsāgara	Calcutta
	1882–1902	Āpastamba Śrauta Sūtra	R. Garbe	Calcutta
	1882	Nighantu with the commentary of devarāja Yajvā,	Satyavrata Samaśrami	Calcutta
	1884	Ṛgveda-saṃhitā	Rāmeś Candra Dutta	Calcutta: Stanhope Press
	1884	Ṛgvedī-Sandhya Prayoga		Calcutta: Girīśa Vidyāratna Press
	1885	Ṛgvedī-Brahmakarma		Gopāla-Nārāyaṇa & Co Pess
	1885	Rigbed Sanghita, vol. 1–7	Ramesh Chandra Dutta	Kolkata
	1887	Ṛg-veda-saṃhitā. Sāyaṇācārya-kṛta-bhāṣyanuyāyi	Prasannakumara Vidyaratna	Calcutta: Veda Press
	1888	Śāṅkhāyana Śrauta Sūtra	A. Hillebrandt	Calcutta
	1891	Aranyasamhita of Samaveda with the Commentary of Sayanacharya	Jibananda Vidyasagara	Calcutta: Saraswati Press
	1891	Atharvavdasya Gopathabrāhmaṇam	Jibananda Vidyasagara	Kalīkata: Nārāyaṇayantre
	1892	Atharvanopaniṣadaḥ with Nārāyaṇabhātta's Dīpika	Jivananda Vidyāsāgara Bhātta	Kalikātānagaryām: Nārāyanayantre
	1892	Ārṣānukramaṇī	Rajendra Mitra Lāl	Calcutta
	1892	Sāmaveda with the Commentary of Sāyanācārya	Jivānanda Vidyāsāgara	Calcutta
	1894	Baudhāyana Śrautasūtra belonging to Taittirīya Saṃhitā	W. Caland	Calcutta: Asiatic Society, Baptist Mission Press
	1895	Iśopaniṣad	Aghoranāthadatta	Kalīkātā: Rākhāla Candṭrabhāṭṭācārya
	1899	The Saṃhitā of the Black Yajurveda with the Commentary of Mādhvācārya, vol. VI	Maheśa Candra Nyāyaratna	Calcutta: Asiatic Society of Bengal, Baptist Mission Press
	1903–11	Śatapatha Brāhmaṇa (Mādhyandina) with the Commentary of Sāyaṇācārya	Satyavrata Samaśrami	Calcutta
	1904	Baudhāyana Śrauta Sūtra	W. Caland	Calcutta
	1906–1908	The Rig-Veda Samhita, text with Sāyaṇa's Commentary and a Literal Prose English Translation	Manmatha, Nath, Dutt	Calcutta: Society for the Resuscitation of Indian Literature, Elysium Press

Region	Year	Title	Editor	Publisher/printer
Calcutta and Bengal Presidency/Province	1906	Aitareya Ālocanam	Satyavrata Sāmaśtami	Calcutta
	1907–11	The Śatapatha Brāhmaṇa of the White Yajurveda	Satyavrata Samashrami	Asiatic Society of Bengal, Printed in Satya Press
	1908	Ṛg-veda-saṃhitā Utka-la-bhāṣā-Saṃskrta-ṭīkā-sameta	Śri Rāma Śaṅka-ra Rāya	Cuttack: Engine Press
	1913	Baudhāyana Śulba Sūtra	W. Caland	Calcutta
	1916	Rigveda Hymns, with the Commentary of Sayana		Calcutta: Baptist Mission Press
	1916	Ṛgveda-saṃhitā (mula, Sāyaṇa-bhāṣya o [Vāṅga-bhāṣā-] anuvāda saha...	Surendranātha Gosvāmi	Calcutta: Suhrit Press
	1917	Ṛg-veda-saṃhitā	Umeśacandra Vidyāratna	Calcutta: Vidyodaya Press
	1919	Ṛgveda-saṃhitā, Sāyaṇabhāsya	Durgādā-sa-Lāhiḍī Śarmā	Howrah: Prithivira-ja Itihāsa Press
	1926	Gobhila Gṛhya Sūtra	Cintamāni and Bhāṭṭācārya	Calcutta
	1931	Pañcaviṃśa Brāhmaṇa	W. Caland	Asiatic Society of Bengal, Baptist Mission Press
Lahore & Central Provinces	1903	Hymns from the Rigveda [Ṛg-sūkta-saṃgraha], edited with Sayana's commentary	Hirananda Mu-laraja Shastri	Lahore: Mafid-i-ām Press
	1906–1915	Ṛgvedasaṃhitā (vaidika jivan vyākhyāyutā), 9 vols.	SHIVANATHA AHITAGNI and SHANKARDAT-TA SHASTRI	Lahore : Panjab Eka-nomikal Yantralay
	1916	Index to Ṛgvedasaṃhitā (vaidika jivan vyākhyāyutā)		Dehradun: Gaḍhāvāli Press
	1917	Ṛg-mantra-vyākhyā arthāt ... Dayānanda viracita Ṛg-veda bhāṣya	Dayānanda Sāraswati	Lahore: Model Press
	1918	Svādhyāya-kusumañjali. [A collection of hymns from the Ṛg-veda with Hindi translation]		Lahore: Bombay Machine Press
	1921	Jaiminīya Upaniṣad Brāhmaṇa	Rāmadeva	Lahore
	1923	Ātharvan Pātiśākhya	Viśvabandhu	Lahore: Punjab University
	1925	Kāṭhaka Gṛhyasūtra	Caland	Lahore
	1925	Udgīthācāryapraṇītam Ṛg-Veda bhaṣyam		Lahore: D.A.V. College

Region	Year	Title	Editor	Publisher/printer
Lahore & Central Provinces	1928	Ṛg-Atharva-sūkta-saṃgraha	Lakṣaṇapālena Śāstriṇā...	Lahore: Bombay Machine Press
	1926	Śatapatha Brāhmaṇa in Kānvīya recension	W. Caland	Lahore
	1926	Vedic Kośa	Hansa Rāja	Lahore
	1905	Īśāvāsyam vājasanejīsaṃhito-paniṣad kī bhāṣā ṭīkā	Vaikuṇṭha Nāthajī	Lakhnau: Naval Kiśor
Delhii and Unite D Provinces	1906	Aitareyopaniṣad bhāṣāṭīkasametaḥ		Lakhnau: Navala Kishor
	1907	Muṇḍakoaniṣad bhāṣāṭīkasahita, hindi translation		Lakhnau: Navala Kishor
Benares	1908	Kātyāyana Śrautasūtra with the Commentary of kārkācārya	Madanamohan Pāthaka	Benares: Chawkhamba Sanskrit Book Depot, Vidyā-Vilas Press
	1883	Uvaṭa's Comm to Yajyrveda Prātiśākhya		Banaras
	1889–1893	Śīkṣā Saṃgraha, A collection of Śikshás by Yájñavalkya and others, with commentaries on some of them	Yugala Kiśora Vyāsa	Benares: Benares Sanskrit Series, Benares Press
	1894–1903	Ṛg-veda-prātiśākhya by Śaunaka, with the commentary of Uvvata	Yugala Kiśora Vyāsa	Benares: Benares Sanskrit Series, Vidyā-vilāsa Press
	1911	Śaunaka's Prātiśākhya of the Ṛgveda with the Commentary of Uvata	Nityānanda Śarmā	Benares: Chawkhamba Sanskrit Series
	1915	Āhnika Prakāśa by Viramitrodaya		Benares: Chawkhamba Sanskrit Series
	1915–16	Rg-veda-saṃhitā. Sāyaṇācāryā-kṛ-ta-Upodghāta-prakaraṇam [Khaṇḍas 1 and 2.]		Benares: Mahālakṣmī Press
	1917–23	Ṛgvedabhāṣya by Āryamuni		Benares: George Press, Candra Prabhā Press, Hita-cintaka Press
	1922	Pūpa Sūtra (Sāma Prātiśākhya)		Benares: Chawkhamba Sanskrit Series
	1926	Pāraskara Gṛhya Sūtra	Gopala Śastri Nene	Benares
	1926	Śatapatha Brāhmaṇa (Kānva)	W. Caland	Moti Lal Baridas
	1928	Āpastamba-Gṛhya-sūtra with Ānakula commentary by Haradatta Miśra		Benares: Chawkhamba Sanskrit Series

Region	Year	Title	Editor	Publisher/printer
Madras Presidency/Province	1873	The Vaṃśabrāhmaṇa, being the eighth Brāhmaṇa of the Sāma Veda, ed. together with the commentary of Sāyaṇa, a preface, and index of words	A.C. Burnell	Mangalore: Basel Mission Press
	1912	Nārada Parivrājakopaniṣad	Otto Shraeder	Madras: Adyar Library
	1876	Ārṣeya Brāhmṇa	A.C. Burnell	Mangalore: Basel Mission Press
	1876	Ṛg-vedokta-madhva-saṃdhya-vandana [Telugu char.]		Madras: Vartamāna Taraṅginī Press
	1877	Saṃhitopaniṣad Brāhmaṇa	A.C. Burnell	Mangalore: Basel Mission Press
	1878	Jaiminīya Ārṣeya Brāhaṇa	A.C. Burnell	Mangalore: Basel Mission Press
	1904	Ṛgvedī-Vaiṣṇava-Sandhyā-van-dana		Mangalore: Dhar-ma-prakāśa Press
	1906	Ṛgveda-vyākhyā by Raghunatha		Kumbhakonam: Gopāla-Vilāsa Press
	1912	Ṛg-vedāhnikam		Kumbakonam: Standard Press
	1913	Ṛg-vedāhnikam		Madras: Sāstra-Sam-jīvini Press
	1915	Rigvidhanam of Maharishi Sownaka		Śrirangam: Vāni-Vilāsam Press
	1917	Ṛgveda-abdika-prayoga		Masulipatanam: Āryānanda Press
	1924	ṛgvedī+Vaiṣṇava+Sandhya-van-dana		Udipi: Śrīkṛṣṇa Press
	1930	Taittirīya Prātiśākhya	Rama Śarma Vidyabhushana	Madras
Travancore	1923	Âśvalâyanagrihyasûtra	T. Ganapati Śastri	Trivandrum: Gov-ernment Press
	1929	The Ṛksaṃhitā with the Bhāṣya of Skandasvāmin and Dīpikā of Venkatamādhavārya	Sāmbaśiva Śāstrī	Trivandrum: Superintendent of Government Press
	1942	Aitareya Brāhmaṇa with the Vṛttisukhapradā of Ṣaḍguruśiṣya	R. Anantakṛṣṇa Śāstri	Trivandrum: Uni-versity of Travan-core Sansktir Series, Printed at Bhaskara Press
	1940	Agniveśyagrihyasuta	Varma, Ravi, L.A.	Trivandrum: Bhas-kara Press

Region	Year	Title	Editor	Publisher/printer
Mysore	1922	Baudhāyana Gṛhya Sūtra	Shama Śāstrī	Mysore
	1881	The Kena Upanishad with a Commentary by Sankarācārya	Satchidananda Saraswati	Holenarshipur: Adhyatma Prakasha Karyalaya (Mysore)
	1910	Ṛgveda-saṃhitāyāḥ mantrāṇām varṇānukrama-sūcī		Ajmer: Vaidika Press
	1926	Rig-Veda Saṃhitā		Ajmer: Vaidika Yantrālaya
	1930	Ṛg-veda-saṃhitā [Hindī-] bhāṣa-bhāṣya ... Bhāṣya-kāra Śrī paṇḍita Jayadevajī Śarmā		Ajmer: Omkara Press

General index

Anderson, B. 135, 267
Aufrecht, T.H. 167, 265–66
American Mission Press (of Bombay) 62, 108, 137–142, 175, 195, 209, 237, 262, 264, 265, 283,
Arumuga Navalar 123, 133, 273, 281
Asiatic Society of Bengal 154, 159–60, 190, 195–96, 198, 198, 251, 262

Bābūrām(a) Bābū Rām's Sanskrit Press 158, 160, 195
Baldeus, Ph. 31, 180–81, 259
Baptist(s) 113, 134, 138, 198, 208–9, 244
Baptist Mission Press (of Calcutta) 138, 198, 263, 288–291, 303
Baptist Missionary Press (Serampore), see Serampore Mission Press
Baretto Xavier, A. 105, 181, 187, 267
Basel Mission 143–45, 251, 260, 279, 293
Bayly, C.A. 135, 147, 162, 170, 172, 173, 194, 199, 202, 203, 207, 241, 242, 244, 267
Bendall, C. 68, 189–91
Bengali 104, 148–49, 156–57, 172, 184, 209, 243, 247, 261, 269, 274
Bernier, F. 181–82, 188, 259, 272
Bhandarkar, R.G. 37, 53, 58, 231, 259
Bhatia, V. 240, 246, 247, 267
Bhaṭṭoji Dīkṣita 97, 248
Bhim(jee) Parekh/Bhimgee Parakh 153, 194, 204–206
Biblioteca Indica 198, 289
Blackburn, S. 15, 105–9, 114, 124–25, 128, 133–34, 152, 251, 267
Bolts, W. 148, 149, 151, 153, 259
book(s)
  as cultural object(s) 8, 13, 14–16, 18, 27–29, 58, 61, 88–89, 109, 111, 117, 220
  as inscribed objects 191
  as objects of prestige, curiosity 125, 135
  as sacred objects 220
  as wonder objects 106
Bowen, H.V. 150, 169, 267
Bowker, G. 52, 53, 267
Boyle, R. 24, 138
Brahmin/*brāhmaṇa* communities 123, 129, 153, 157, 172–73, 184, 190, 239, 245, 246, 248
  and the Veda(s) 20, 27, 31–33, 37, 38, 52–55, 57–59, 62–64, 69, 78, 83–87, 96, 106, 109, 116, 170, 180, 183, 188, 191–93, 197, 206, 212, 216, 218, 225, 231–34, 239, 246, 251, 254–55
Bronkhorst, J. 34, 59, 61, 63, 267
Buchanan, C. 58, 110, 125–26, 130, 259
Buchanan, F. 150, 259
Burnell, A.C. 180, 260, 266, 293
Bühler, G. 163, 193, 260

canon, canonocity, canonization 18, 20, 34, 53, 68, 92–93, 97–98, 100, 183, 214, 219, 226, 232, 233, 247, 249, 256, 277, 281,
Calcutta Bible Society 237
Carey, W. 113, 126, 134, 137, 156, 160, 184, 208, 237, 255, 260
Castets, J. 182–83, 188, 267

catalogue(s) 22, 57, 70, 72, 84, 128, 130, 161–168, 189, 190, 208, 209, 212, 221, 256, 260, 261, 263, 265, 266,
Cavallo, G. 16, 45, 53, 267
Chartier, R. 12, 13, 14, 16, 69, 268
circulation,
of manuscripts, [printed] texts and knowledge 16, 19, 25, 28–30, 69, 97, 99, 104, 107, 112, 117, 120, 125, 127, 128, 133, 135, 139, 147, 149, 158, 160, 170, 191, 207, 212–214, 232, 234, 239, 241, 243, 250–251, 255–256
civilization 8, 13, 15, 16, 20, 22, 24, 60, 63, 98, 110, 132, 133, 253
civilizing project/mission 23, 24, 133, 136, 166, 172, 240, 254, 256
classification 52, 53, 167, 170, 209, 231, 267, 271
Cohn, B.S. 18, 204, 268
Colas, G. 54, 163, 188–91
Colebrooke H.T. 156, 158, 159, 184–185, 194, 244–245, 260
Colier, P. and Connolly J.R. 25, 237, 268
copies, copying, copyists 7, 16–17, 19, 21, 29, 31, 57–61, 63–64, 67–79, 81–89, 100, 105, 106, 109, 110, 120, 125, 127, 131, 137, 139, 140, 148, 163, 173, 174, 181, 188–193, 197, 208, 212, 222, 224, 241, 254, 255, 271, 279
motives for copying the Veda 67–89
colonial, colonialism 9, 14, 18–26, 30, 58, 64, 70, 103, 113, 143, 147–48, 152, 155, 162, 166, 168, 172, 198–99, 201, 203–4, 207–9, 217, 237–39, 248–52, 255–57, 267–69, 271, 277–81
cultural techniques, 16, 21, 247, 251, 253, 254, 255, 275, 279, 281
culture(s) of print, see print culture(s)

Dandekar, R.N., 22, 252, 266, 269
Darnton, R. 12, 69, 209, 212, 269
Dash, S. 65–67, 87–88, 269
daśagrantha, Daśagranthis 38, 86, 95, 204, 219, 226–28, 230, 232 see *Ṛgveda-daśagrantha*
Dayānanda Sarasvatī 7, 173–74, 239, 274, 275
Deshpande, M. 31, 38–39, 269
Devanagari 62, 108, 139, 141, 156–57, 159–60, 195, 218, 223, 251
dharma 65–67, 78–80, 83, 87–88, 92, 94–96, 175, 179, 193, 210, 233, 270, 274, 278
Diehl, K.S. 138–39, 141, 154, 156
D'Intino, S. 90, 271, 274
Downing, J. 117–18, 260
Duperron, A. 183–84, 260

East India Company (British) 23–26, 113, 121, 128, 134–35, 138–39, 142, 146–47, 150–55, 157–60, 164, 169, 171, 178, 182, 190, 194–96, 198, 200–02, 206–07, 213, 237, 250, 260, 267, 268, 277, 278
East India Company (Danish) 116, 121
East India Company (French) 183, 188
Ebeling, S. 237–38, 269
Eisenstein, E. L. 11–12, 111, 267, 269
Ellis, F.W. 182–85, 261
empire, imperial 13, 18, 23, 25, 27, 34, 52, 55, 84, 89, 95, 97–101, 113, 115, 145–49, 152–53, 165, 168–69, 189, 194, 197–98, 200–2, 205, 207, 217, 247–48, 250–51, 254, 256, 259, 267–68, 270, 273–75, 277–78, 280
ethnographic 9, 37, 169–70
state 143, 145, 168
Ezour Vedam 157, 177, 182–83, 185, 188–89, 264, 267, 274, 278, Fig, 6. See *Zozur Bedo*, Veda: false Veda

Fenger, J.F.J. 119, 125, 261
Figueira, D. 179, 182, 189, 270
Formigatti, C. 16, 18, 112, 156, 219, 237, 244, 270
Fort William College 137, 156, 158–60, 195, 237, 244, 263
Fort St. George College 124, 128, 133, 147, 152, 250, 269

Ganeri, J. 228, 271
Ganpat Krishnaji/Gaṇapat Kṛṣṇaji (Press), Bombay 25, 62, 175, 211, 215, 243, 263, 265, 283, 284, 285
Gaur, A. 116, 130–31, 271

Glushkova, I. 9, 205, 271
Gode, P.K. 122, 127, 182, 188, 272
Gonda, J. 90, 92, 179, 186, 272
Gough, A. 159, 161, 165, 261
Gujarati, early printing in 108, 194, 243
Gupta, A. 15, 19, 135, 237, 267, 272–73
Gurjara, J.M. 62–63, 208, 219, 261, 263, 285

Halbfass, W. 124, 179, 186, 273
Halhed, N.B. 31, 149, 155–58, 261
Hall, K.R. 24, 26, 154–55, 237–38, 273
O'Hanlon, R. 15, 20, 205, 273
Hastings, W. 151, 153–55, 190
Henriques, H. 105–07, 261, 279
Hicky, J. 151, 154, 277
Hudson, D.D. 115, 119–20, 123, 133

imperial/royal project of commenting on the Veda 89, 91–94, 96–98, 100
Indu Prakash Press (Mumbai) 174, 175, 217–18, 265, 283
information 17, 18, 52, 62, 71, 89, 91, 134, 147, 149, 150, 162, 170, 173, 194, 199, 203, 205–07, 250, 267
ink 29, 72, 121–22, 211, 226, 277
Innis, H. 8, 13, 22, 23, 98–101, 109, 126, 147–48, 201, 207, 273

Jacob, C. 9, 16, 164, 166, 267, 268
japa, murmured recitation 43, 50, 86, 231
Jasanoff, M. 154, 189–91, 274
jaṭā [*-pāṭha*] (mode of Vedic recitation) 75, 85
Jesuit(s) 12, 24, 104–110, 114, 125, 129, 145–46, 156, 163, 178, 180–88, 191, 223, 248, 268, 278, 282
Jeyaraj, D. 116, 132, 274
Johns, A. 18, 212, 274
Jones, W. 156, 159, 167, 184–86, 190, 261
Jordens, J.T.F. 173–74, 274

Kaegi, A. 218, 261
Kane, P.V. 61, 274
Kaye, J.W. 145, 151, 261
Kielhorn, F. 163, 193, 208–10, 212, 218, 261
Killingley, D. 48, 180, 182–83, 185, 237, 274
knowledge 17–19, 24, 34–35, 43, 46–47, 52, 54, 56, 58, 62, 65–69, 74–75, 82, 84, 94, 95, 109, 113, 116, 123–24, 129–31, 133, 135, 137, 140, 143, 152, 161–67, 169–71, 173, 184–85, 187, 189, 194, 196–97, 199, 201–2, 204, 205, 207, 208, 222, 225–27, 233–34, 237, 241, 256, 264, 267, 268, 269, 272–74, 276,
  disciplines of, 'strongholds' of 94, 99, 167–8, 193, 270, 271 see *vidyāsthāna*
  production of 56, 167, 170, 245, 250, 278
  transmission, circulation of, see circulation
  gift of, see *vidyādāna*,
koṭṭu (inarticulate Vedic recitation) 47
krama [*-pāṭha*] (mode of Vedic recitation) 37–38, 42–43, 45, 47, 50, 85, 227, 228
Kubicek, R. 149, 150, 275

Larios, B. 31, 33, 213, 275
legitimacy, legitimation 95, 98,
library/-ies 22, 37, 52, 53, 57, 70, 72, 74, 78, 88, 97, 112, 123, 127–28, 130, 157, 162–64, 167, 181–83, 187–88, 190, 191, 205, 212, 221, 229, 256, 257, 260, 263–64, 266, 269, 271–72, 274–76, 278–81, 293
literary, literature 15–19, 22, 37, 53, 57, 65, 71–72, 92, 112, 121, 124, 127–28, 135, 137, 151, 158, 172, 175, 184, 187–88, 194–96, 202, 203, 212, 228, 231, 238–39, 242, 246–48, 251, 256, 260–62, 264, 266, 269, 271–72, 275, 277–79, 282, 290
  cultures 15, 60, 62, 89, 217
Liebau, H. 114–15, 120, 127, 129, 131–32, 275

Mādhava (brother of Sāyaṇa) 85, 91–92, 95–96, 288–89
Mahāvākyavivāraṇa 156
Malamoud, Ch. 48, 59, 275
Malayalam 62, 86, 107, 112, 120, 125, 144–45, 161, 213, 251
mangala [*caraṇa*/*vacana*] (benedictory verses) 76, 276
mantra 32, 39, 41, 52, 54, 62–63, 68, 96, 159, 185, 219–21, 228–32, 243, 257, 262–63, 265, 274, 276, 280, 283, 285–87, 291, 294

manuscript(s) 8, 9, 11, 13, 16-17, 19, 49, 57-58, 60-61, 63-65, 68-75, 77-85, 87-90, 92, 97-101, 107, 112, 114, 120, 123, 127-31, 139, 156, 159-67, 171-72, 175, 181-85, 187-92, 197, 206-7, 212-13, 216, 219, 222, 224, 228-29, 231, 234-35 238, 240-42, 244-46, 256, 259-60, 263, 265-66, 268-69, 271-72, 278-79, 281-82
cultures, 9, 11-12, 17, 19, 23, 58-60, 63, 69, 71-72, 88-89, 99, 112, 114, 120, 123, 127-29, 167, 171, 178, 205, 208, 210, 212, 221, 229, 235, 237, 242, 244, 251, 253, 268-69, 271, 273, 274, 278, 281
Marathi, early printing in 108, 120, 139-42, 174, 195, 209, 211, 217-19, 224-25, 234, 252, 262, 265, 275, 283, 286, 287
Marwari, community of 175, 266
maṭha (monastery) 38, 62, 69, 100, 109, 123, 213, Fig.1
McLuhan, M. 8, 11-13, 30, 98, 103, 178, 210, 213, 235, 247, 275-76
McNeely, I.F. and Wolverton L. 110, 119, 133, 135, 204, 276
media 8, 13, 15-16, 20-21, 27, 31, 34, 44, 60, 95, 98-101, 109-10, 112, 113, 120, 128, 134, 147, 153, 164, 201, 207-8, 210, 235, 240-42, 244, 247, 250-51, 253-54, 256, 267, 276-77, 281
memory 17, 19-22, 24, 27, 29-30, 33-36, 38-50, 52-53, 58-59, 61-63, 69, 71-73, 86, 88, 129, 170, 202, 210, 211, 213, 220, 222, 228, 235, 240, 246, 249, 251, 254-55, 267, 279
memorization 21, 27-29, 31, 36-40, 42-47, 49-50, 52, 54-56, 59, 61, 63, 68, 71, 85-87, 213, 226, Fig. 1
Metcalfe, Ch. 145, 213, 261
Mīmāṃsā (school of Vedic exegesis) 53-56, 67, 95, 178
Minkowski, Ch. 15, 20, 90, 93, 164, 166, 273, 276
missionary/ies 12, 18, 24-26, 62, 103, 105-13, 115-17, 119-27, 129-46, 151-52, 154, 158, 160, 173-74, 178-79, 182, 185-88, 195, 207-8, 212, 223, 237-38, 241-42, 250-51, 260-65, 268, 274, 278, 280-82, 288-89
modernity 18, 24, 132, 146, 156, 166, 168, 172, 203, 211, 239, 247, 249, 256, 267, 275, 281
Muṟajapam (royal ceremony of Vedic recitation) 43, 50, 86
Müller, F. Max 7, 17, 31, 37-38, 58, 61-62, 72, 92-94, 150, 155, 177-80, 186, 192-93, 196, 198-202, 204, 210, 215-16, 218, 227-28, 243, 257, 262, 276, Fig. 8ab, Fig. 9ab

Nair, S.P. 108, 128, 133, 276
Nampūtiri 21, 37-40, 43-50, 52-53, 85-86, 109, 213
Naregal, V. 108, 170, 243, 246, 249, 253, 255-56, 276-77
Naval Kiśor Press, Lakhnau 280, 292
Neill, S. 180,
Nirṇaya Sagara Press 62, 174, 218, 220-24, 226, 229-31, 235, 243, 246, 261, 263, 265, 275, 283-87, Fig. 11, Fig. 13-16
Nobili, de, R. 107, 179-80, 184, 186-87

Ogborn, M. 15, 18-19, 24, 104, 146-47, 149-53, 156-57, 159, 172, 205, 237, 277
oral, orality 11-13, 17, 21, 24, 27, 30, 34-38, 40, 52, 54-55, 57-59, 62-64, 69, 71-73, 76, 86-87, 89, 94, 107, 173, 177, 199, 216-17, 222, 225-26, 228, 233-34, 239-40, 242-43, 269, 271, 280-81
Orsini, F. 15, 19, 237, 277

pada [*-pāṭha*] (mode of Vedic recitation, form of Vedic text) 37-39, 42, 45-46, 50, 72, 76-78, 80-81, 83, 85, 174, 190, 215-16, 218, 227-28, 230, 259, 261, 263, 265, 283-86
palm-leaf (manuscripts on) 57, 98-101, 123, 127-29, 175, 187, 229
pārāyaṇa ('going over' a text, mode of reading) 45, 49, 86-87, 230-31
Paṇśīkar/ Paṇaśīkar/Panshikar, W.L. 63-64, 220-223, 226, 229-31, 235, 246, 263, 284-87, Fig. 13-16
paper 13, 22, 57, 99, 121-22, 126-27, 136, 156, 169, 195, 211, 219-20, 229, 244, 246, 267, 272
Paramahaṃsa 95

Paratext, paratextual 20, 95, 240, 244, 268
Paśupati Gajapati Raju 200-1, 243
pāṭha-śālā, school of Vedic recitation 68, 171, 213, 220, 232-33
patrons, patronage 14, 16, 18-19, 23, 29, 55, 57, 69-70, 72-74, 76-77, 79-80, 83-85, 91, 97, 100, 117, 127, 132, 136, 150, 157-59, 161, 164, 172, 181, 183, 198-203, 216-17, 240, 243, 245, 248, 250-51
Peters, J. 16, 21, 168, 254, 277
Peterson, P. 163, 208, 214-15, 263, 284-85
Pettegree, A. 111-12, 229, 277
phalaśruti 234,
Philipps, J.T. 132-33, 263
Pietist(s) 12, 25, 110, 113, 115, 119-20, 127, 133, 144, 186, 223, 274
Polier, A.-L.-H. 68, 159, 182, 185, 189-92, 197, 263, 265, 268
Pollock, S. 15, 23, 54, 61, 89, 93, 112, 129, 166, 217, 225, 271, 277-78
Pomian, K. 53, 278
Portuguese 104-08, 113-18, 121-22, 145, 205, 248, 267
pothī 7, 62, 139, 160, 196, 216, 219, 224, 228-29, 233, 251, 255, 263, 283, 285-87
print
  culture(s) 7, 11, 12-15, 17-19, 25, 29-31, 60, 103-4, 111-13, 138, 148, 158, 208-09, 228-29, 231, 235, 237-40, 242, 244, 248, 250-51, 253, 267-71, 273, 276, 279
  order of 17, 120, 141, 170, 228
printing press 11, 23, 25-26, 62, 104-05, 107-11, 113-14, 117-18, 121-28, 130-34, 136-48, 150-61, 168, 170-72, 174-75, 195, 197-98, 200, 205-6, 207-11, 213, 215, 217-18, 220-21, 224, 226, 230-31, 235, 237, 242-51
  lithograph 7, 63, 137, 139-44, 171-72, 195, 219, 279, 283
Priolkar, A.K. 15, 23, 105, 108, 114, 139, 142, 151, 154-55, 194, 205-6, 209, 211-13, 241, 278

Raina, Dh. 188, 278
Raman, Bh. 15, 237, 278
Ram Mohan Roy 7, 184, 261, 288
ratha [*-pāṭha*] (mode of Vedic recitation) 85
reading, readers 7-9, 12, 14, 16, 18-19, 21, 23-25, 27, 29, 36, 38-39, 43, 58, 60-63, 65, 73, 76, 80, 86-89, 93-94, 99-100, 103, 106, 117, 119-20, 127, 129-30, 133, 136, 140, 149, 155, 158, 160, 163, 173, 177-78, 181, 184, 199, 207-11, 214-15, 220, 229, 232, 238-43, 245-47, 251, 253-56, 267, 269-70, 275-76, 278-79
  constituencies 9, 240, 251, 254
  cultures of 28, 253-54
  practices 27-28, 58, 87, 119-20, 149, 173, 239-42, 251, 253
  protocols of 29, 43, 48, 53, 57, 58, 86
recitation, modes of, see Veda
Reig Beid (Ṛgveda) 156
Renou, L. 22, 192-93, 278
Ṛgveda, Ṛgvedasaṃhitā, Ṛksaṃhitā (RS) 7, 17, 19, 34-36, 38, 40, 42-43, 45, 48-50, 52, 60-62, 68, 70, 72, 74, 77-79, 82-83, 88, 90-96, 137, 140, 155-56, 174, 177, 180, 190, 193, 195-96, 198-99, 201-2, 204, 213-15, 218, 220, 223-27, 230-34, 239, 243, 248-49, 255, 257, 260-61, 263-65, 271, 283-294
Ṛgvedadaśagrantha (RDG) 38, 68, 86, 95, 204, 220, 224-28, 230, 263, 271, 274, Fig. 17-18
Ṛgvedakalpadruma 222-23, 231
Ṛgvedamantrasaṃhitā 229-30, 63
Ṛgveda Prātiśākhya 85
Ṛgvedasaṃhitābhāṣya of Sāyaṇa (RSBh) 75, 85, 90, 92, 274
  Bhūmikā 57, 90, 92, 95, 174, 265
Rocher, L. 182-83, 189, 202, 244, 278
Rocher, R. and L. Rocher 16, 137, 153, 155-56, 158-60, 182
Röer, E. 138, 195-98, 263, 288, Fig. 10
Rogerius (Rogers), A. 180, 263
Rosen, F. 7, 139, 192, 195-96, 263-64
Roth, R. 145, 192-93
Royal Asiatic Society 137, 216, 218, 259-60
Rubiés, J.-P. 109, 146, 278

saṃhitā [-*pāṭha*] ('continuous' mode of Vedic recitation) 37–40, 42, 46, 50
Sāmaveda, Sāmavedasaṃhitā 35, 80–81, 137, 190, 196, 264, 271, 288–90
Sainte-Croix, G.L.J. 177, 183–84, 264
Sanskrit, early printing in 16, 18, 136, 140, 142, 156, 158–60, 174–75, 195, 206, 208–09, 218, 221, 229, 232, 239–41, 243–48, 250–51, 253
Sanskrit Printing Press 156, 159, 195
Satya Press, Calcutta 197, 213, 264, 288, Fig. 14
Sāyaṇa, Sāyaṇācārya 32, 55–57, 61, 63, 67, 85, 89–97, 139, 193, 197, 199, 214–16, 223, 259–60, 262–65, 270, 276, 283–293, Fig. 4
Scharfe, H. 38, 42–43, 48, 53, 61, 278
scribe(s), scribal, inscribing 16–17, 21, 27–28, 57, 60, 69–73, 81, 91, 99–100, 116, 129, 140, 152, 168, 172, 191–92, 211, 242, 266–68, 270–71, 278, 281
Sebastian, M. 111, 127, 132, 143, 145, 278
Sengupta, I. and Ali D. 167–69, 278
Serampore Mission Press 18, 24, 108, 113, 122–23, 126, 133–36, 138, 156, 160, 195, 208, 237, 244, 259–62
Serfoji II's printing press, Tanjore 108, 127–28, 133, 160, 276
Shaw, G. 15, 17, 106, 139, 141–44, 147, 154, 157, 171–72, 237, 279
Shulman, D. 86, 186–87, 279
Siegert, B. 16, 21, 253–54, 279
Simini, de 15, 65, 71, 82, 212, 225, 237, 241, 279
social practices 16, 27, 71, 89, 111, 167
social status 188, 216, 253
Sonnerat, P. 183, 264
SPCK (Society for Propagation of Christian Knowledge) 104, 121–22, 125, 147, 152–53
Staal, F. 38, 43–44, 46, 85, 275, 280
Stark, U. 15, 18–19, 23, 122, 173, 237, 240, 280
Stevenson, J. 7, 62, 137, 139–41, 174, 195–96, 255, 264, 283
svādhyāya (self-study of the Veda) 48, 61–62, 85, 231, 274–75, 291
svaras (Vedic pitch accents) 31, 52, 69–72, 74, 87, 226
Sweetman, W. 104, 116–17, 123–24, 131, 134, 138, 142, 178, 180, 185, 187, 238, 280
Swiderski, R. 216–17, 280
Syriac 107, 125–26

Taittirīyasaṃhitā (TS) 74, 159. 185, 198, 223, 262, 287, 290
Tamil 17, 105–10, 112–14, 116–26, 128, 130, 133, 153, 163, 187, 238, 250, 268–69, 273, 276, 280–82
Telugu 112, 120, 163, 178, 251–52, 293
Tieken, H. 28, 180, 280
Tookaram Tatya/Tukārāma Tātya 215–16, 263, 265, 283–84
Theosophical Society Publication Fund, 215–16, 265, 283–84
Tranquebar Mission 104, 111–19, 121–27, 129–34, 147, 153, 185, 261, 270, 275, 277, 280–81, Fig. 5
Trisandhā 41, 47–50, 51, 86, 265, 270, Fg. 3, Fig. 19
typography 11, 29, 141, 152, 171, 199–201, 214, 219, 222–24, 231–33, 242, 245, 250–51, 275

upaveda 185

Vājasaneyisaṃhitā 7, 159, 185, 189–190, 196, 213, 264, 286–88, Fig. 12
Varadarajan (grammarian) 226–28, 273
Veda(s)
authority of 31–32, 34, 54, 91, 94, 96–97, 179, 223, 228, 233, 250, 253, 270, 275
authoritative commentary on 63, 67, 85, 91–97, 223, 233, 247
authoritative printed editions of 233, 249–50, 253
canon, canonical, scriptural 18, 20, 34, 53, 68, 92–93, 97–98, 100, 183, 214, 219, 226, 232–33, 247, 249, 256, 270, 275, 277, 281
commented on, commentaries on 21, 31–32, 34–35, 48, 55–56, 61, 63, 68, 74, 89–98, 100, 108, 139, 155–56, 183,

196–99, 213–16, 223, 247–48, 259–60, 262–64, 270, 276–77, 283–294, Fig. 4
definitions of 32, 39, 56, 93, 192, 223, 239
description of 178, 180–81, 187–88
divisions, parts, portions of 39–40, 52, 91, 224, 271
false 185, see *Ezour Vedam*
idea(s), concept(s), vision(s) of 21, 91, 173, 180, 192, 219, 239, 248, 269
imagined 178, 185
imitations of 184
interpretation of 7, 31, 53, 55, 255, 270, 275
kept in secret, guarded, withheld 84, 95, 239, 254
knowledge embodied by
lost, lost part of 20, 44, 54, 68, 124, 177–80, 182–83, 185–91, 194, 254
making money on 7, 61
manuscripts of 17, 57–61, 63–65, 68–90, 97, 99–101, 139, 159, 181–85, 187–92, 205, 207, 210, 212, 216, 219, 221–22, 224, 228–29, 231, 234–35, 242, 245, 251, 259–60, 266–68
mastery over 38, 43, 50, 55, 94, 96, 177, 233
meaning and purpose of, message of (*vedārtha*) 60, 84, 91, 93, 97, 174-75, 208, 214, 216, 218, 223, 232, 249, 265, 283, 286
memorized, memorization of, learning of, see memorization, memory
modes of recitation 38–55
motives for copying 67–89, 208
orality of 12, 17, 21, 27, 30, 34–38, 40, 52, 54–55, 57–59, 62–64, 69, 71–73, 76, 86–87, 89, 94, 173, 177, 199, 216–17, 222, 225–26, 228, 233–34, 239, 242–43, 271, 281
performative competence in 47, 55–56
reading, protocols of reading 8–9, 27–29, 36, 43, 48, 53, 58, 60, 62–63, 80, 86–89, 99, 155, 173, 208–10, 239–42, 246, 251, 253–56
pseudo 184, 267
ritual 33–36, 45, 47–49, 52, 55–56, 62, 64, 68, 71, 85–86, 89, 181, 222–24, 230-32, 243, 270, 280
textuality of 7, 20, 27–28, 31–32, 34–35, 64, 91, 173, 223, 225, 232,239, 245
transmission 20, 22, 27, 30–31, 34, 36–38, 46, 49, 53–64, 67, 86, 98, 202, 210, 212–13, 217, 221, 228, 247, 251, 271
vidhi, injunction to study 61, 94, 193
vidyā, knowledge of the Veda 56, 67–68, 74, 225–26, 233–34
written down 21–22, 29–31, 34, 37, 43, 55, 57–79, 84–89, 92, 99–100, 131, 139–41, 173, 185, 187–88, 192, 198, 207, 210–11, 213, 216, 220–21, 226, 228, 233, 239, 247
vedabhāṣya 80, 85, 97, 248 see *Ṛgvedabhāṣya*
Vedabhāṣyasāra of Bhaṭṭoji 97, 248, 271
Vedamūrti 233
vedāṅga, 'limbs', auxiliary sciences of the V. 66, 97, 141, 228, 230, 269, 271
vedārthaprakāśa, explaining of the meaning of the Veda, see Veda meaning and purpose
Venkatachalapathy, 15, 17, 118, 237, 270, 280–81
Venkateśwara Steam Press 174, 243–44, 262, 285–87
vicāra, investigation, 231
vidyādāna, the gift of knowledge, see *vidyā*
Vidyāraṇya, see Mādhava
vidyāsthāna, 'strongholds of knowledge' 67, see knowledge disciplines
Vijayanagara 52, 55, 84, 91–92, 95, 98–101, 115, 145, 200–1, 247–48
Vismann, C. 16, 168, 253, 281
Vypery Press 124–126, 147

Wilkins, Charles 108, 148–49, 151, 154, 156–57, 265
Wilson, H.H. 164, 189, 191–92, 196, 201, 264–65
Winternitz, M. 63, 265
Wujastyk, D. 16, 99, 112, 127–29, 237, 281
Witzel, M. 21, 33–36, 53, 271, 274, 281

Yajurveda 7, 35, 94, 159, 185, 190, 196, 198, 208, 213, 255, 262, 264, 286–88, 290–91, Fig. 12
Young, L.C. 16, 53, 253, 282

Ziegenbalg, B. 104, 113, 115–24, 126–27, 130–32, 187, 261–62, 271, 274, 280, Fig. 5
Zozur Bedo 188, Fig. 7, see Ezour Vedam, Veda: false Veda
Zysk, K.G. 128, 166, 282

Županov, I.G. 105, 106, 109, 180, 181, 186, 187, 267, 282

Editor
Renata Włodek

Copy editor
Agnieszka Lipińska

Proofreader
Katarzyna Borzęcka

Typographic designer
Hanna Wiechecka

Jagiellonian University Press
Editorial Offices: ul. Michałowskiego 9/2, 31-126 Krakow
Phone: +48 12 663 23 80, Fax: +48 12 663 23 83

CPSIA information can be obtained
at www.ICGtesting.com
Printed in the USA
JSHW011344110523
41580JS00003B/9

9 788323 343912